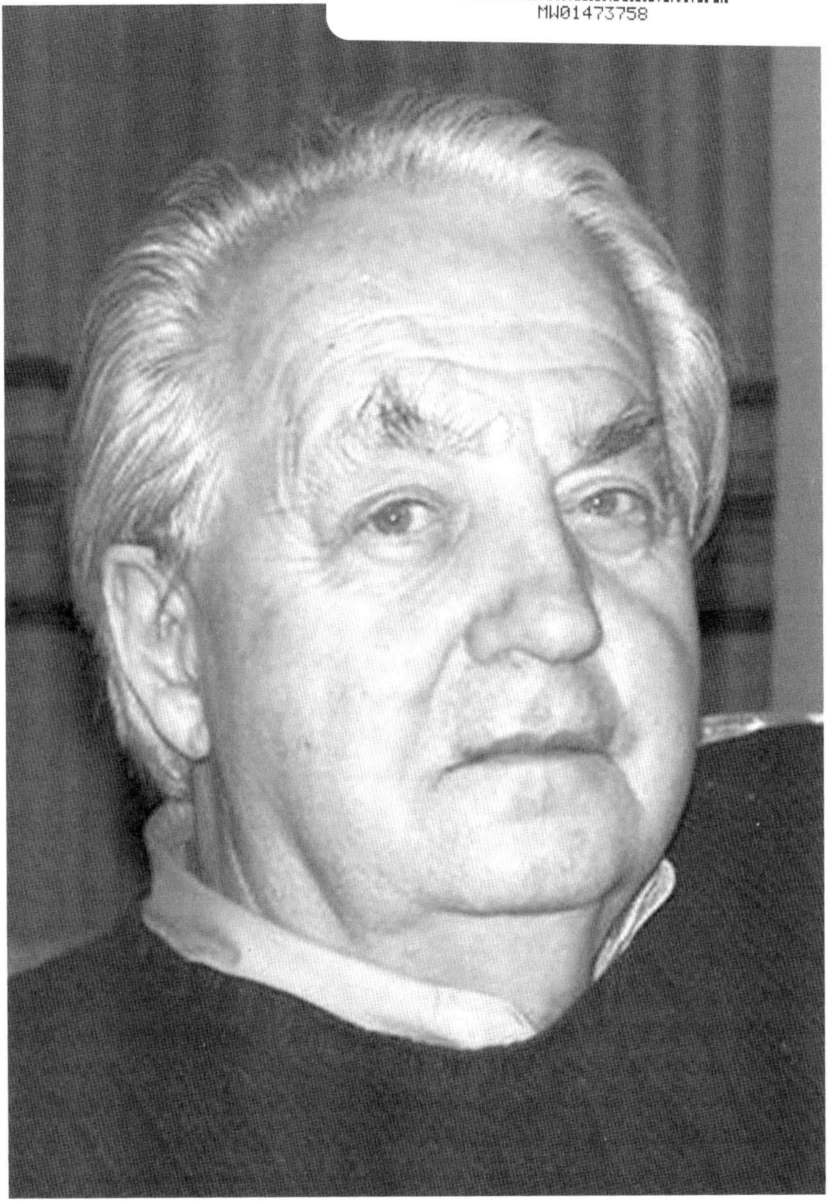

Gilles
Paquet

GOVERNANCE SERIES

Governance is the process of effective coordination whereby an organization or a system guides itself when resources, power, and information are widely distributed. Studying governance means probing the pattern of rights and obligations that underpins organizations and social systems, understanding how they coordinate their parallel activities and maintain their coherence, exploring the sources of dysfunction, and suggesting ways to redesign organizations whose governance is in need of repair.

The series welcomes a range of contributions – from conceptual and theoretical reflections, ethnographic and case studies, and proceedings of conferences and symposia, to works of a very practical nature – that deal with problems or issues on the governance front. The series publishes works both in French and in English.

The Governance Series is part of the publications division of the Centre on Governance and of the Graduate School of Public and International Affairs at the University of Ottawa. This is the 20th volume published in the series. The Centre on Governance and the Graduate School of Public and International Affairs also publish a quarterly electronic journal, www.optimumonline.ca.

Editorial Committee

Caroline Andrew
Linda Cardinal
Monica Gattinger
Luc Juillet
Daniel Lane
Gilles Paquet (Director)

The published titles in the series are listed at the end of this book.

Gilles Paquet

homo hereticus

edited by
Caroline Andrew
Ruth Hubbard
and Jeffrey Roy

University of Ottawa Press
Ottawa

© University of Ottawa Press, 2009

All rights reserved.

The University of Ottawa Press acknowledges with gratitude the support extended to its publishing list by Heritage Canada through its Book Publishing Industry Development Program, by the Canada Council for the Arts, by the Canadian Federation for the Humanities and Social Sciences through its Aid to Scholarly Publications Program, by the Social Sciences and Humanities Research Council, and by the University of Ottawa.

We also gratefully acknowledge INVENIRE whose financial support has contributed to the publication of this book.

CATALOGAGE AVANT PUBLICATION DE BIBLIOTHÈQUE ET ARCHIVES CANADA

Gilles Paquet : homo hereticus / edited by Caroline Andrew, Ruth Hubbard and Jeffrey Roy.

(Governance series, 1487-3052)
Comprend du texte en français.
Comprend des références bibliographiques.

ISBN 978-0-7766-0692-7

1. Paquet, Gilles, 1936-. 2. Spécialistes des sciences sociales--Canada--Biographies.
I. Andrew, Caroline, 1942- II. Roy, Jeffrey III. Hubbard, Ruth, 1942- IV. Titre: Homo hereticus. V. Collection: Governance series (Ottawa, Ont.)

H59.P37 G45 2009   300.92   C2009-901101-8F

Published by the University of Ottawa Press, 2009
542 King Edward Avenue
Ottawa, Ontario K1N 6N5
www.press.uottawa.ca

uOttawa

Democracy is a way of life controlled by a working faith in the possibilities of human nature ... [and] faith in the capacity of human beings for intelligent judgement and action if proper conditions are furnished.

—John Dewey

Hommage au Professeur émérite Gilles Paquet
à l'occasion du 45ᵉ anniversaire de sa carrière universitaire

Table of Contents

Preface   1

Introduction
    Ruth Hubbard   4

SECTION I: THE PERSON

Part One: *The Educator*

Chapter 1
The Al Pacino of Carleton University
    Tony Going   32

Chapter 2
High Noon
    Meyer Burstein   35

Chapter 3
Courtesy of Gilles Paquet
    Pedro Arroja   40

Part Two: *The Colleague*

Chapter 4
Getting to Know Gilles Paquet, an Unexpected Pleasure
    Tom Brzustowski   48

Chapter 5
Fifty Books per Year and Counting
   Wojtek Michalowski   50

Chapter 6
En hommage à Gilles Paquet
   Monique Bégin   53

Part Three: *The Associate*

Chapter 7
Le journaliste et le communicateur
   Pierre Bergeron   60

Chapter 8
Unbundling Paquet
   Robin Higham   70

Part Four: *The Fellow Traveller*

Chapter 9
Notes sur une longue et fructueuse collaboration
   Jean-Pierre Wallot   78

Chapter 10
An Intimate Vignette
   John Meisel   86

SECTION II: THE IMPACT

Part Five: *Repositioning*

Chapter 11
Dean of Graduate Studies and Research,
Carleton University, 1973–1979
   Don McEown and H. Blair Neatby   100

Chapter 12
Gilles Paquet et son rayonment au sein de l'ASDEQ
   Jac-André Boulet   112

Chapter 13
Une passage marquant à la présidence
de la Société royale du Canada
    Bernard Bonin   117

Part Six: *Influencing*

Chapter 14
Paquet and Jacobs: On Sectoral Relations and
a Search for Common Ground
    Jeffrey Roy   128

Chapter 15
Urban Governance *à la* Paquet
    Caroline Andrew   140

Chapter 16
Building Cooperation through Conversation
    Chris Wilson   151

Part Seven: *Engaging*

Chapter 17
Paquet as Ironist and *Agent Provocateur*
    James R. Mitchell   166

Chapter 18
Looking Past the Dots
    Ruth Hubbard   174

Chapter 19
Gilles Paquet and the Federal Public Service
    David Zussman   187

Chapter 20
Letter to the Editor-in-Chief of *Optimum Online*
    McEvoy Galbreath   198

SECTION III: THE ISSUE DOMAINS

Part Eight: *Organizing Ideas and Concepts*

Chapter 21
The New Geo-Governance
    H. George Frederickson   206

Chapter 22
Contribution to Governance Scholarship: Definitions, Debates, and Omissions
    Monica Gattinger   210

Chapter 23
Centralité de la mésoanalyse
    Paul Laurent   224

Chapter 24
Contribution to Civic Governance, Social Learning, and Smart Communities
    David A. Wolfe   233

Chapter 25
D'une industrie automobile à gouvernance centralisée à l'invention d'une chaîne de valeur de distribution de services de mobilité à gouvernance distribuée
    Christian Navarre   247

Chapter 26
Gilles Paquet's Contributions to the Study of Higher Education
    Michael L. Skolnik   269

Part Nine: *Interpretations*

Chapter 27
Six observations sur la croissance québécoise à la manière de Gilles Paquet
    Pierre Fortin   284

Chapter 28
The Dialectics of the Heart: Gilles Paquet on
Moral Contracts and Social Learning
    Ralph Heintzman   300

Chapter 29
Skills: Banal Creativity and Spontaneity
 in a Learning Intensive Society
    Riel Miller   321

Part Ten: *A Tip of the Hat*

Chapter 30
Carbon Pricing as a Wicked Problem
    Thomas J. Courchene   338

Chapter 31
Working Past Age Sixty-Five Will Soon
Get More Respect in Canada
    Leroy O. Stone   360

Conclusion   371

Bio-bibliographie de Gilles Paquet
    L'homme   373
    Sélection des œuvres   374

Contributors   377

Preface

What we are is written on the people we have met and known, touched, loved, hated and passed by. It is the lives of others that testify for or against us, not our own.
—Sir Geoffrey Vickers (from a letter to his son)

We are fortunate to know Gilles Paquet; to us, he continues to be a trusted adviser, an intellectual sparring partner of significant power and a lively conversationalist, as well as a colleague and a friend.

At the same time, Gilles has given so much to so many over a professional career of forty-five years and still counting that we wanted to honour his contributions to a broad and varied range of activities and fields of study. This project is our way of saying thank you to him for ourselves and on behalf of all those who have been touched by his work in some way. When we reflect on what it is about him that holds particular significance for us, it is because of his ideas, his ideals, and how they show themselves in his life.

Through his incisive and persistent argumentation, we find ourselves understanding the reality around us in a fuller and richer way than before. At the same time, Gilles has reassured us at a profound level that, despite sporadic evidence to the contrary, it is worth betting on people's innate desire to learn to serve the public good better themselves and, through their institutions, to make our democracy better.

The burden of office of his professional life—the duties and obligations to serve the public interest—is ever-present for Gilles. Combined with his deep conviction that a freed capacity to think provides a necessary governor for the engine of freedom of action, it manifests as great patience with, and support for, those willing to listen and learn and, at the same time, an occasional need to remind others of their own burden of office.

We admire his wisdom and integrity, his tough-minded keenness of thought and endless curiosity, and his genuine interest in helping people (almost always verbalized in the language of ideas). Gilles is sensitive and open to the breadth and diversity of human experience, and the passion that he brings to his ideas as well as to his work is a demonstration of his personal integrity. He presents powerful and thoughtful reflections on a broad range of topics, often in ways that are intended to provoke reactions (both positive and negative) that incite innovative thinking, while making room for concrete experience and accepting what is possible (albeit sometimes a little reluctantly). Fundamentally, this is a man who cares deeply about the human condition both in terms of the larger questions of how societies steer themselves today and in terms of "day-to-day" and "on-the-ground" realities.

Notwithstanding how easy it was to decide that a festschrift was in order, finding a good way to celebrate what Gilles has accomplished was not, given the breadth and scope of his pursuits as well as his ways of going about them. The disciplines that he employs in grappling with problems and issues are several and are applied in ways that interact to different degrees, in ways that are sometimes invisible to the naked eye. Gilles proceeds by trial and error, and uses frequent writing and publishing as sounding boards. The channels of communication that he employs are numerous, and while he uses great care and precision in choosing and using language, he can and does select from a vast storehouse of French, English, and Latin words, and when he cannot find exactly what he wants he simply invents one or uses an existing word in an unusual way. This means that, like the children's string game cat's cradle, what Gilles produces is almost infinitely variable in scope and substance, usually intricately put together, occasionally unexpected, and, like the game itself, sometimes difficult to achieve.

We have chosen, as a result, to present his work through the eyes of a variegated group of his friends, colleagues, associates, and others whose lives Gilles has touched in important ways. More than thirty have contributed essays to this festschrift celebrating the forty-fifth anniversary of the taking up of his first academic post at Carleton University in 1963.

The introduction, intended to provide some insights into his thinking, traces a path through his professional career from the 1960s to the present, focusing particularly on a few key areas that have not been touched on by the contributors and providing a backdrop for what follows. The participants' essays have been grouped as viewing Gilles through three different lenses: the person, the impact, and the issue domains. The conclusion attempts to tie together the many contributions.

We wish to thank Marie Clausén for her professional assistance in moving this manuscript through production to publication. Our own participation in this project has been a rare and satisfying adventure.

Introduction

Ruth Hubbard

[A] truly scientific attitude . . . is characterized by engagement in open debate, willingness to learn, cooperative striving, respect for the facts, and reverence for continually changing process.
—Gordon L. Ziniewicz on Dewey's practical idealism

During Gilles Paquet's lifetime, the world has changed in profound ways.

In 1936, the year that Gilles was born, the father of modern computer science, Alan Turing, published his famous paper "On Computable Numbers." It would be another ten years before the idea of a computer would move from imagination to electronics. At the beginning of that decade, Canada had no central bank, the federal finance department was "mostly concerned with wharves and post offices" (Granatstein 1998, 48–49), and the Department of External Affairs got its international news from Great Britain. Maurice Duplessis, vilified by many as a leader during "*les années noires*" (a view that has softened recently), was elected premier of Quebec in 1936 and, except for 1939–44, held the job until his death in 1959.

The decades immediately after the Great Depression of the 1930s and World War II gave rise to the welfare state in advanced western democracies as the national state stepped into the everyday lives of ordinary people. During Paquet's formative years, Canada's version blossomed and was to last relatively unchallenged by citizens until the 1980s.

Gilles took up his first academic post at Carleton University in 1963, the year that John F. Kennedy was assassinated and the year before IBM announced its System/360 computer. Canada's welfare state continued to expand, but the second half of his nearly two decades at Carleton saw growing provincial restiveness that ranged from Alberta's Peter Lougheed's soft approach (1971) to the more strident one of Quebec's René Lévesque (1976).

By the time that Gilles moved to the University of Ottawa in 1981, IBM was launching its PC, and Canada's welfare state was slowly starting to crumble under pressure from political, social, technological, and economic developments at home and abroad. The Canadian Constitution was patriated over Quebec's objections (1982), and the 1995 Quebec Referendum over separation came very close to being lost.

Since Gilles "officially" retired in 2002, the pace of change has only increased, bringing new and often "wicked" problems. The decade-long, multi-stakeholder discussion *Crossing Boundaries* that worked to find the common ground in Canada's long transition from an industrial to an information society published its findings in book form in 2007. Web 2.0—shorthand for innovations that include wikis and blogs—was launched in 2004, and Sunnyvale, California, started the first city-wide wireless (wi-fi) network in 2005. Genetically engineered chickens have appeared (2007) as well as the first "human-cow cross" embryo (2008).

It is against this background that a review of Paquet's work reveals a man who has made and continues to make modest but important and positive contributions to academics and practitioners, to Quebeckers, to Canadians, and to people everywhere on many fronts. As a matter of fact, Gilles has turned out to be one of the right people in the right place at the right time to help us make a bit more sense of what has been happening all around. Tracing the evolution of his professional persona helps to show why.

The Formative Years (1936–62)

Gilles Paquet was blessed with a certain degree of luck from the beginning: luck in terms of his formal education; his strongly felt need to use his talents (particularly a formidable intellect, a significant creativity, a deep-rooted contrariness, a passion for reading widely, and an extraordinary ability to communicate) and to embrace difference at a time when this combination of attributes emerged as a key characteristic of the modern world; and his place among a rare generation of academics who, as he told one of us, "had the freedom to take the chance to 'do things differently and allow different perspectives to be given room at the table' that earlier generations (especially, but not only, in Quebec) were denied because they would have lost their jobs."

For example, Gilles is an omnivorous reader, and anyone who has conversed with him somewhat regularly knows that there are some authors to whom he has returned regularly since the 1950s: Jean Paulhan, Jacques Perret, William Saroyan, Henri Thomas, Alexandre Vialatte, and some more recent additions such as Paul Auster, Friedrich Dürrenmatt and Jean Echenoz. This very heterogeneous set of novelists and *conteurs* has in common a sense of the baroque and a delight in wordsmithing. These aspects have had an impact on Gilles. He has never hesitated to coin a phrase or invent a word if and when it became convenient or useful.

He is also among one of the last graduates of Quebec's *cours classique*, with formal training in the arts and social sciences before earning an MA in economics from Laval in 1960, pursuing doctoral studies at Queen's University, and then joining the rapidly expanding Department of Economics at Carleton University in 1963.[1]

While his university training in economics gave Gilles a language that would turn out to be useful throughout his career, his early classical training prepared him well for a wide variety of tasks (Paquet 1978). He also learned that academics were (and should be) deeply immersed in public policy—in helping politicians decide what to do—so that serving the broader society was deeply enmeshed with scholarship.

At the same time and perhaps even more importantly, his choice of human sciences as an area of study (at a time when it was not yet well defined) combined with his pursuit of it at Laval in the 1950s found Gilles studying in a climate that welcomed the overflowing of one field into another (Paquet 1978). As a result, while economists there invited specialization, other voices could be heard loud and clear, and he listened attentively.

It was from this training—when Gilles studied Bachelard and Callois even more carefully than Friedman and Keynes—that, as he recalled more than a decade later, "*j'ai hérité d'un goût pour la 'logique flexible' et d'un intérêt pour les 'cohérences aventureuses' (Callois) et conservé un certain malaise en face de l'intolérance de l'instrumentalisme et du conventionalisme qui dominaient la construction de la science économique. . . . [V]oilà où la souplesse de Bachelard devait s'avérer avenante*" (Paquet 1978, 111).

INTRODUCTION

Gilles would also observe at that time that Bachelard's philosophy was really one of renewing, reorganizing, recommencing, redoing, and restarting by building on the past (Paquet 1978). For Paquet, it was a rationalism turned toward the future with lots of room for imagination as well as searching for coherence that was more and more extensive. All the while, he leaned on Callois's ideas, quoting Callois this way: "*dans l'investigation rigoureuse, le génie consiste presque toujours à emprunter ailleurs une méthode éprouvée ou une hypothèse fertile et à les appliquer là où personne encore n'avait imaginé qu'elles pouvaient l'être*" (Paquet 1978, 112).

This kind of approach Paquet would use over and over almost from the beginning of his academic career. At the same time, as he himself has said, his penchant for crossing boundaries, for *chemins de traverse* ("the art of trespassing," as he calls it), was urged on him "from the very beginning of my own life in my own neighbourhood '*au pied de la Pente Douce*' in Quebec City where it was a way of life" (Paquet 1993, 4).

Paquet also possesses an approach to creativity, problem solving, and decision making that is almost certainly at the high-innovation end of Kirton's method well-researched and widely accepted (normally distributed) personality adaption-innovation continuum (KAI) that measures thinking style—that is, a preferred method of tackling problems. This has shaped not only his own creativity and his actions but also how others see and experience him.

The KAI measure is not about ability (cognitive capacity) and is value free, and while all people can use both styles they also have a preference. Interestingly, significant difference in style tends to create inherent difficulties in communication that can inhibit mutual understanding and collaboration, and require explicit bridging efforts to be effectively overcome.

Adaptors "tend to accept the paradigm within which a problem is embedded" and are at their best " (as Kirton says) in the smooth, efficient operation of an existing system; creatively refining, improving, and extending the thinking that underlies it" (Bast 1999). They "accept rules as an aid to efficiency in problem-solving, placing more emphasis on group consensus and group cohesion" (Sim and Wright 2002). Innovators, on the other hand, "tend to "detach the problem from its cocoon of accepted thought," to step out of the "box" or paradigm. They tend to redefine a problem, produce many ideas, break through what the organization perceives as givens and constraints, provide solutions aimed at doing things differently. . . . [B]ecause . . . [they] are less easily understood and have unpredictable outcomes, and because such break-through change is threatening, innovators are often seen . . . as undisciplined, impractical, irreverent, abrasive and/or insensitive to people" (Bast 1999). Unlike adaptors, "innovators see rules and group conformity as limitations to efficient problem solving and will often break or ignore rules in the pursuit of their ideas" (Sim and Wright 2002).

Paquet describes himself as "*homo hereticus*," someone who is always critical and sometimes controversial, and whose standard advice (which he often employs) is to "scheme virtuously." He has always been deeply committed, nevertheless, to democracy both as a way of life and as how humans ought to relate to one another. Democracy in John Dewey's sense of defining a worthy social life in terms of the degree to which it "makes provision for participation in its good of all of its members on equal terms and which secures flexible readjustment of its institutions through interaction of the different forms of associated life" (1916, 60). And democracy as a way of human interaction like the one described by Learned Hand in his parable of children at play. Lee Bollinger (2005), the president of Columbia University, tells Hand's story this way: at first, they are

> confused about how to organize their games and defer . . . to an older, more experienced peer for direction. But that solution satisfies no one, as each child is unhappy to be bossed about by another, and eventually confusion reigns again—until [as] Hand wrote, "in the end slowly and with infinite disappointment they learn a little; they learn to forbear, to reckon with one another, accept a little where they wanted much, to live and let live, to yield when they must yield; perhaps we may hope, not to take all they can get. But the condition is that they shall be willing at least to listen to one another to the habit of pooling their wishes. Somehow or other they must do this, if play is to go on. . ." (30).

To elaborate, Paquet believes that "communities" are created by what Albert Hirschman calls "a steady diet of conflicts that need to be addressed and that the society learns to manage" (Hirschmann 1995: 243). He points out that it is "both a utopian dream and a fundamental misconception of democracy to hope for an end to conflict . . . [for it would] kill the very dynamics that generates social learning and trust" (Paquet 2008a, 178).

INTRODUCTION

For Paquet, then, conflict is not just inevitable but also necessary for democracies like Canada's to thrive. In fact, he would describe democracy as an ongoing conversation. He sees conflict as an inevitable part of human interaction—his own included. The trick is to find constructive ways to work it through—a view that he assumes ought to be widely shared even if (as he would readily acknowledge) this might be difficult and even painful. As a result, difficulties that arise in human interactions in which *he* is involved that are triggered to a significant degree by real differences in individual preferences for an adaptive as opposed to an innovative style of thinking, would never be understood as such by Paquet (or probably by the others involved). This means that the extent to which his commitment to democracy is seen to be played out in his actions and behaviour vis-à-vis others as well as in his intellectual endeavours, might be given quite different weights by those who interact with him.

For individuals (regardless of profession) whose preferred type of creativity tends toward adaptation and thus places more emphasis on group consensus and cohesion, for example, Paquet would not be seen as paying enough attention to the value of these characteristics in practical problem solving. As a result, when reflecting on his actions and behaviour, they would likely be inclined to reserve judgment on his commitment to democracy as it relates to human interaction. For others, especially those tending toward the innovation end of the continuum, any misalignment between what Paquet believes and how he might behave from time to time is simply part of who he is and not what he stands for.

Regardless, his fundamentally democratic view underpins the person that Gilles is and the burdens of office that he carries as professional scholar, public intellectual, and classical educator (in the sense of paideia). He works at each of these roles with the passion, enthusiasm, and energy that characterize everything he does. These three threads help to explain the contributions that he has made throughout his professional career. Not surprisingly, they have varied in thickness and makeup as his professional life has evolved.

Professional Scholar
As Bollinger (2005) also remarked, the burden of office of the professional scholar is more than simply the search for truth: "the most valued (of all qualities of mind) is that of having the imaginative range and the mental courage to take in, to explore, the full complexity of the subject. To set aside one's pre-existing

beliefs, to hold simultaneously in one's mind multiple angles of seeing things, to actually allow yourself seemingly to believe another view as you consider it—these are the kinds of intellectual qualities that characterize the very best faculty and students" (8). Bollinger went on to explain the kind of intellectual capacities needed by democracies (and enhanced by academic freedom) this way: "we teach ourselves and our students in the academy, a capacity that is useful in the search for truth but has many purposes in life beyond that. . . . [E]ngaging with ideas, as it turns out, is actually a very hard thing to do. The demands it places on our powers of reason, of imagination, of tolerance often seem overwhelming. Yet, robustly engaging with difficult ideas is the basic purpose of academic freedom" (13).

Throughout his professional career, Paquet has displayed this kind of intellectual quality. He has always "robustly engag[ed] with difficult ideas." He expects, stimulates, and enables it in established and aspiring scholars, and throughout his professional life he has devoted considerable time and energy to a number of key professional associations dedicated to honouring and harnessing excellence for the good of humankind (e.g., la Société canadienne de science économique, l'Association des économistes québécois, and the Royal Society of Canada).

At the same time, Paquet is well served by his own predilections. A voracious reader with an enormous range of interests as well as a careful listener, he is a natural integrator of the disparate notions that he encounters, guided by a great deal of intuition and creativity. With good reason, academic colleagues have called him a true "renaissance man."

Public Intellectual

Paquet is also the quintessential public intellectual of the sort described by Ralph Waldo Emerson. Alan Lightman (2000), John Burchard professor of humanities and senior lecturer in physics at MIT, explains Emerson's view this way: the public intellectual "preserves great ideas of the past, communicates them, and creates new ideas. He is the 'world's eye.' And he communicates his ideas to the world, not just to fellow intellectuals . . . [and] not out of obligation to his society, but out of obligation to himself. Public action is part of being . . . the whole person" (1). As a media personality, in print, on radio and television, and in both French and English, Gilles has carried this burden of office well.

He incites citizens and opinion moulders to reflect upon, rethink, and reframe common problems and issues, and to become engaged in addressing them at local, regional, national, and global levels. Paquet is willing to tackle taboo topics and has the courage to say out loud that the emperor has no clothes. This temerity includes pointing out the nature of society's outermost ethical boundaries, the boundaries that define the corridors within which it can operate freely without inevitable decline or self-destruction.

Paquet is someone who has developed a good sense of how to introduce the right idea using the right vehicle at the right time, whether it is in stimulating and/or chairing round tables on contentious topics, leading seminars or designing learning events, acting as consultant, writing or co-writing books and articles, or editing journals. A significant proportion of what he does is designed to engage his audience by provoking and by entertaining at the same time. This dual purpose leads Gilles to pay a great deal of attention to the results, and he has learned how to put himself in the shoes of the audience and to design his interventions accordingly. At the same time, he does this not just as a job but also as a part of who he is.

Classical Educator

Paquet is also an educator in the classical sense of *paideia*, the nurture and growth of persons as individuals and citizens. In this capacity, his goals align with those of John Dewey, described by others as essentially encouraging the imagination of new possibilities from what exists, regardless of an individual's age.

Whether in the classroom or outside the academic sphere entirely, Paquet aims to engage people—to get them to think, perhaps see things a bit differently, or at least never be the same again. He has inspired many and marked even more forever. A lot of people know his name; a good number can remember key messages that he delivered even years later; few who have tripped across him are neutral in their opinion of him. Gilles has an army of fans as well as a contingent of detractors.

What follows is a brief description that divides his career into three parts: his eighteen years at Carleton University, beginning in 1963; the twenty-one years Gilles spent as a faculty member at the University of Ottawa (1981–2001); and the period beginning in mid-2002 to the present. The material deliberately tries to put an emphasis on aspects left essentially untouched elsewhere as well as offer some backdrop to what follows. As a result, it is by no means a systematic treatment of his work or of its key threads.

Early Years (1964–80)

As an aside that will become important later in this introduction, it is worth bearing in mind that the state has held centre stage in advanced western democracies because of what helps to underpin them—a nineteenth-century institutional philosophy that saw the national state as the agent for securing the eighteenth century's individualistic ideal of societal progress (Dewey 1916, 60).

At the time that Paquet's formal career was launched in the 1960s, the kind of collaboration needed in a democratic society such as Canada was presumed to exist naturally—and not unreasonably so. "Governance" (or societal stewardship) was the same as "government" and amounted to elite accommodation behind closed doors. There was no question, therefore, that Paquet would be asked to work on important public policy choices facing governments, and that he would do so willingly and even eagerly. As he would write decades later, "at Carleton, research had to be meaningful, it had to make a difference. My president Davidson Dunton was chairing a Royal Commission, my chairman, Scott Gordon was writing a weekly column in the *Financial Times* and had written a vitriolic pamphlet that led to the Governor of the Bank of Canada being fired" (1993, 272). In fact, it was propitious that for nearly the first decade of Paquet's professional career Dunton—who was comfortable with his imaginative and multidisciplined approaches—was Carleton's president.

Even in those early days, Paquet was slowly broadening the notion of the economy and shifting to social history. Almost from the beginning, it became clear to him that the tools at his disposal were not always useful. Unable to proceed further, he paused to take the time to understand, focusing attention at the mesolevel of issue domains (and later of regions) because the whole was too complex to tackle in one piece. That he was allowed and enabled to do so he later attributed to the decade of the 1960s, when, as he puts it, "it was forbidden to forbid."

During this period of nearly twenty years, Paquet became strongly influenced by a few key ideas: by Dewey's (1935) experimental and socially organized intelligence; by the young Karl Marx of the eighteenth *brumaire* of Louis Napoléon Bonaparte, in which social groups were depicted as designing strategies that could only lead to their own destruction; by Keith Boulding's (1970) methods of integration; by the dynamic conservatism written about by Donald Schön (1971) as well as his ideas about theory/structure and technologies; and by the "social learning" model for policy research of John Friedman and George Abonyi (1976).

In fact, over time, Paquet would push the Friedman-Abonyi concept—that it is only through trying to change something that one can know—much further and make it a kind of leitmotif of his work. His philosophy of action would become both "activism" and "changism" together. He was already groping for a new way of seeing things.

Professional Scholar

As a professional scholar, Paquet made significant contributions during this period. Lent to work on a number of crucial public policy files, he found himself a consulting economist to the Committee on Aging in 1964–65 led by Senator Croll that resulted in the Guaranteed Income Supplement (GIS) that topped up the monthly universal Old Age Security payment for the financially needy. He played a similar role on a review of health care in the province of Quebec led by Claude Castonguay (seen as the father of Quebec's health care system) in 1965–66, assisted the Unemployment Insurance Commission and the federal Department of Manpower in 1968–69 to look into reforms of the Unemployment Insurance system, and worked on science policy, a subject being examined by the Senate committee chaired by Senator Lamontagne.

In 1965–66 and 1966–67, together with Harvey Lithwick, Paquet directed the experimental and multidisciplinary work of a study group dealing with the problems of cities and regions in Canada when the field was anything but crystallized. The idea, later set out in a book that they co-edited (Lithwick and Paquet 1968), was to deal with the convergence of economics and geography, "a middle ground where urban analysis can fruitfully be discussed" (15). This work reframed much of the debate on urban problems of the time, and Routledge now plans to reprint it.

Paquet organized an international conference on the multinational firm and the nation-state in 1969 that broke much new ground and led to a book in 1972 which he edited, and that had a large diffusion. That experience led him to begin to have real doubts about the "usual" ways of understanding what was going on. Interestingly, the acknowledged challenges of usefully tackling the "potential and actual dilemmas that are bound to emerge as a result of the coexistence of the political logic of collective interests of national communities and the economic logic of growth and efficiency" (Paquet 1972, ix) with which the book dealt were probably one of the first signs of the fast-paced, globalized world so familiar to us four decades later.

Paquet was already worrying about the lack of "new network[s] between the population, Parliament and technocrats" (1968, 158). In fact, in 1968 he proposed "a refurbishment of the Senate in order to make it into a Council of Social Values providing a forum for discussion by individuals, groups and technical experts on the goals to be pursued" (155). It was an idea that would reappear two decades later.

His deanship of Graduate Studies from 1973 to 1978 (dealt with by McEown and Neatby in their contribution to this volume) was significant (e.g., doubling the number of students as well as increasing the number and quality of research production) and occurred at a time of dramatic change at Carleton.

On his induction into the Royal Society of Canada in 1976, his long-time mentor Albert Faucher (1978, 107), professor of economic history at Laval, observed that "*Gilles Paquet projette sur les phénomènes humains des vues d'ensemble; son approche est globale*" and referred to his way of finding a unity in divergent roads or seemingly unrelated texts as a dominant methodology (Paquet 1978). Paquet was to become and remain an active member of the society throughout his career.

Public Intellectual

Paquet's work as a public intellectual started almost from the beginning, first as an offshoot of his professional scholarship, and toward the end of this period in the launching of an adventure that would become an ongoing one, using vehicles of more widespread communication.

Near the beginning, building on work stimulated by Faucher that also led to a joint paper in 1966, Paquet began a collaboration with Jean-Pierre Wallot (one of the contributors to this volume) that was to last for forty years. It explored the interface between economics and history, and provided an alternative evolution of Lower Canada at the turn of the nineteenth century that remains in good currency today.

By 1978, at the end of his deanship, his media journey had begun with work as a journalist/interviewer on *Le magazine économique* for Radio-Canada. It was to last for more than a decade and to involve 1,500 interviews. In 1979, Paquet travelled throughout Canada to prepare ten seventy-five-minute radio programs on *La socio-économie canadienne* (aired on Radio-Canada AM), and in 1981 he designed a twenty-five-hour-long economic history of Canada (splicing in the testimonies of over fifty Canadian historians in support of his hypotheses) that was aired on Radio-Canada FM.

Classical Educator

Paquet was a sought-after teacher virtually from the beginning of his career at Carleton. In fact, 1973 saw him being given an award by the Ontario Confederation of University Faculty Associations for excellence in teaching.

In the academic sphere, two of his former students at Carleton, Meyer Burstein and Tony Going, are contributors to this volume. In fact, Going established a scholarship in his honour. Another former student told one of the editors that, even after a quarter of a century, she vividly remembers his undergraduate class on the Economic Development of Canada. She recounted how the students avidly awaited each of his lectures, enthralled and engaged, only beginning to panic after two months of the session when they realized that they had forgotten to take any notes and that final exams were approaching.

Middle Years (1981–2001)

These two decades are "book ended" by Paquet's decision to take up the post of dean of administration at the University of Ottawa and his official retirement, which took place in mid-2002. The move was more than simply changing venues and the formal link to the discipline of economics. It was a manifestation of what Gilles would describe as "becoming a different person," someone who had concluded that the real influence on public policy was not social scientists but ordinary people. The choice to take this road had its roots in the end of the period before, especially in his work co-hosting a regular radio show on the national network of Radio-Canada and the sabbatical that he spent at Carleton's School of Journalism in 1979–80.

Toward the end of that period, his experience in academe had left him with the feeling that the right questions were not being dealt with in the right ways, something that was confirmed by his radio experiences and reinforced as his media work continued in the next one. The role of public intellectual that Paquet had witnessed in the 1950s and 1960s had fallen out of favour. More than that, he had come to agree with Donald Schön's view, which, he later observed, "shows that the model of technical rationality has failed in important ways in the realm of social sciences which have imported uncritically this late 19th century version of medical and engineering schools without realizing the perversions to which it has led" (Paquet 1985, 109). At the same time, Paquet began to see that "the neat process of cascading knowledge from basic disciplines to practitioners does not work" and that an important impediment existed to their advancement in part because of "the little use . . . practitioners could make of academic output and . . . the general irrelevance for the academic community of any work emanating from reflection-in-action" (110).

The result was that Paquet moved to what seemed to be a more issue-oriented and less disciplinary approach in the field of public administration as it was carried out at the University of Ottawa, all the while insisting on maintaining his weekly journalistic role. It was the attempt to find ways to enable and stimulate the University of Ottawa to bridge the gap between scholars and reflective practitioners—for the results as well as for its reputation—that was to become a hallmark of this two-decade-long period. In addition, he was sure that his own intellectual foraging would be more fruitful if he could keep a foot in each camp.

Once ensconced at the university, Paquet tried a variety of routes to encourage the broader perception of types of knowledge and the richer view of methodologies to produce a real change in the social system of knowledge production that he was sure was needed—with at best mixed success—ranging from trying to generate executive development as one facet of this portion of the university's work, to generating more catholic production by colleagues than disciplinary papers alone, to involving practitioners (e.g., the former senior federal cabinet minister Robert de Cotret) in work that was scholarly and relevant, through the Centre on Governance. Paquet invented vehicles such as PRIME (together with John de la Mothe) to carry out multidisciplinary research and later the Centre on Governance.

At the same time, it was also clear to Paquet that he needed a new language to help reframe the public debate. He spent the first years of this period in a kind of intellectual foraging before settling on the words *governance* ("effective coordination when information, power, and resources are widely distributed," in his language) and *social learning*, making them his own toward the end of this period.

In 1988, Paquet returned to the idea of a Council on Social Values that he had first put forward much earlier. This time he described it as "a permanent forum for all groups and individuals in Canada to meet and discuss the nature of the goals and objectives to be pursued and the strategy designed to reach them in light of what are regarded as the main threats and challenges facing Canadian society today" (1988, 46–47).

In fact, while Paquet had known almost from the beginning of his academic career that things were changing in the external world and that he could show signs of this happening, it was not until the 1990s that he developed a more sophisticated understanding of social architecture and was able to capture its essence in two important books: *Épistémologie et économie de la relation*, co-authored with Paul Laurent (Laurent and Paquet 1998), and *Governance through Social Learning* (Paquet 1999). The collaboration that had been assumed to be possible in the 1960s now needed to take place in a world that was rapidly growing more and more complex. It would be toward the end of this period that he would finally find the *manière de voir* for which he had been searching.

Professional Scholar
Paquet continued the work of the professional scholar during this period, earning the Jean Jacques Rousseau Medal for advancement of sciences in 1982 and the University of Ottawa Award for Excellence in Research in 1993. At the same time, consistent with his strong commitment to scholarly excellence, he grew increasingly concerned about the danger of the Royal Society of Canada becoming irrelevant and told its members so (Paquet 2005a). For him, it was crucial for those in government making public policy decisions to have access to the best minds. He saw the pan-Canadian Royal Society as a vehicle that was potentially well placed to play such a role and badly wanted it to position itself well to serve. Unsuccessful in this attempt, he would return to this goal as president in 2003 (a period that is outlined in Bernard Bonin's contribution to this volume).

Paquet explored and wrote about what he saw in the case of energy policy development, including the interesting innovation in stakeholder consultation beginning in late 1987. He was to argue for similar social inquiry in the field of post-secondary education in 1989. By the time of his sabbatical at the IRPP in 1988–89, Paquet was able to consolidate his thinking about advanced socioeconomies and approaches to steering them that seemed to hold some promise, and he returned reassured that he was on the right track. It was a period during which he worked with half a dozen new colleagues in issue domains such as education, entrepreneurship, innovation, intercultural relations, public management, the world of work, and ethics (becoming the first director of the Centre on Governance when it opened its doors in 1997).

By 1994, Paquet was making the point publicly that "we are already living through a revolution which is dispersing power throughout society. The question is not whether it will occur but whether it will evolve in an orderly or disorderly way. That, in turn, will depend on the speed with which the existing governance system is transformed." (Paquet 1994, 5)

A significant contribution that appeared during this period came with the insight about the importance of the kind of knowledge that comes from "all sorts of aspects of making and doing" (Gilles and Paquet 1989, 19) that the authors named "δ knowledge"—including, for example, management and design—to distinguish it from the three types of knowledge "traditionally" institutionalized in places of higher learning (and called α [humanistic], β [scientific], and γ [social scientific] in European university circles). They argued cogently that there are important costs as a result of δ knowledge not being acknowledged as intellectually legitimate and economically useful. The idea of embracing as much variety as possible and acknowledging excellence well beyond the "usual" scholarly constraints would begin to shape his thinking.

Public Intellectual

Paquet's work as public intellectual gathered steam during this period. Gilles tackled tough issues in earnest and often in everyday language that could not be ignored by elites or by working men and women in the street.

His crucial radio work as journalist/interviewer for *Le magazine économique*, which had begun in 1978, lasted for the first nine years of this period as well. In addition, Paquet was co-animator for sixty interviews for the TV program *Aujourd'hui dimanche* in 1990–91 and was involved in 100 *chroniques* between 1991 and 1994 for radio as well as editorials for *Le Droit* between 1992 and 1997. He was a weekly panellist for TV Ontario from 1994, involved in 400 sessions until it went off the air. In 1994, he became editor in chief of the management magazine *Optimum*, which went online from 2000, and he continues in this capacity. With Gilles at its helm, subscriptions have increased from 1,500 to more than 10,000.

This kind of dissemination and influence was not restricted to the popular media. For example, Paquet was able to synthesize the work he had been doing on his IRPP sabbatical and to present it to the 1991 Liberal Party conference in Aylmer (Paquet 1992). In addition throughout this period, his collaboration with Jean-Pierre Wallot examining and reframing the history of Lower Canada continued. Like water slowly dripping on a rock, the view of that era was gradually transforming.

Classical Educator
Paquet's reputation as an excellent teacher—in substance and in style—continued, and Gilles was given an award for teaching and research excellence by the university's Faculty of Administration in 1996–97.

His educational endeavours were not restricted to his university or to the academic sphere. Nevertheless, as a lecturer in economics, Pedro Arroja (a contributor to this volume), besides experiencing academic freedom in their collaborative teaching, was so taken with Paquet's ideas about governance and the approaches of the Centre on Governance that he subsequently created the online review www.governancia.com in Portugal when he returned there.

At the same time, Paquet was recognized by organizations such as the Quebec Association of Economists (ASDEQ) (as you will see among the contributions) for the generosity that he extended over the years not only to the organization but also to the up-and-coming new members and to the profession of economics in general.

In 1992, Gilles began a six-year stint as senior research fellow at the federal school of public administration (the Canadian Centre for Management Development, now called the Canada School of Public Service), during which time he was a regular teacher of executives and middle-level high flyers.

This opportunity epitomizes an important aspect of his role as educator (as well as helping his thinking). For him, it was another chance to polish his ideas and learn from practitioners. For them, it was an opportunity to be engaged and, as a result, to have their eyes opened wider and to confront the assumptions that they did not know they were making.

Later Years (2002–)
The passion, enthusiasm, and energy that Paquet has brought to everything has not diminished now that he has become professor emeritus at what is now the Telfer School of Management. He is also senior research fellow in the Faculty of Social Sciences, with links to the Centre on Governance and the Graduate School

of Public and International Affairs, and he focuses on the areas that particularly interest him.

On reflection, Paquet would argue that, except for his work in the early days, he has not had much direct influence on social architecture, public policy, or public management. The dynamic conservatism that he has encountered is much stronger than he expected. Paquet would also say, however, that he now understands the depth of change that is required on the part of elites (especially the public and academic ones close to home) who have felt "in control" and responsible for much of societal stewardship for so long, and as a result he can appreciate (if not share) the inability of many to see or accept that they can and should play a different role.

As a result, for Paquet this period is one of gradually closing in on how to accelerate the emergence of good governance in today's world, in light of the blockages that must be faced. He has come far enough along the way to feel a degree of comfort (at least intuitively) in talking about the likely governance future of advanced democracies, and what remains is to put the ideas forward in ways that are likely to generate the intelligent conversations that may lead to progress.

Professional Scholar

One measure of Paquet's commitment to scholarship comes from the books that continue to flow from his pen. Two, one in French and another in English, were published in 2005 arguing lucidly and carefully for distributed governance. The review of one, *The New Geo-Governance: A Baroque Approach* (2005b), written by George A. Frederickson (2006), a leading thinker in public administration, hails the work as a "conceptual tour de force" (:1). Paquet and Wallot co-authored another entitled *Un Québec moderne 1760–1840*, which sets out the fruits of their long collaboration and was published in 2007.

In 2008, Paquet tackled an assessment of French Canada in the last half of the twentieth century in a book entitled *Tableau d'avancement: Petite ethnographie interprétive d'un certain Canada français*. The same year saw publication of the results of years of reflection on cultural diversity in Canada as *Deep Cultural Diversity: A Governance Challenge*. These last two could easily be argued to add to his reputation as a public intellectual as well as providing scholarship of high quality.

Three more books will be published late in 2008 and in 2009 (and hint at what is to come): *Gouvernance: Mode d'emploi*; *Crippling Epistemologies and Governance*

Failures; and *Scheming Virtuously: The Road to Collaborative Governance*. In the first of these, Gilles sets out what may turn out to be a shorthand version of his organizing ideas and concepts about societal governance that makes what Drath and Palus (1994) call "public meaning"—that is, it helps to make sense of today's world in ways that are useful and to incite commitment, especially for practitioners and analysts. In it, Paquet says that "The reconstructed setting (for societal governance) is the world of reflexive governance. . . . What is required is the design of a capacity for the organization (up to and including the society itself at the national level) to learn. [This requires] . . . knowledge integration and learning by doing; capacity for long run anticipation of systemic effects; adaptivity of strategies and institutions; iterative experimental and participatory definition of broad directions; and interactive strategy development . . ." (2009a, 265–66).

Perhaps one of the most revealing of his characteristics with respect to his professional scholarship, however, is contained in something that Paquet prepared in 2006 for Campus 20/20 (an inquiry into the future of British Columbia's post-secondary education system). Calling it a "think piece," he explains at the beginning that "The crucial role of a think piece is to generate discomfort, and to initiate an intelligent conversation"; however, "if this piece should not generate vibrant discussions and rich multilogues, the interested reader should feel free to continue the conversation with the author whose coordinates are available on his website www.gouvernance.ca." It is quintessential Paquet.

Public Intellectual

Paquet's investment in the role of public intellectual continues unabated. His work on Radio-Canada in 2002–03 (*Indicatif présent*) included twenty "columns" that formed the first versions of a book entitled *Pathologies de gouvernance: Essais de technologie sociale*, published in 2004. Readable and accessible, it makes complex and abstract ideas understandable, and relevant to people's everyday lives.

In the same way, the short book that Gilles co-authored with Ruth Hubbard entitled *Gomery's Blinders and Canadian Federalism* (2007) has played a part in sustaining his public intellectual persona. Accessible in tone and style, it appeared at a time when the advertising scandal that was the subject of an inquiry by Justice John Gomery was still a hot topic, and it planted the seeds of a possible scenario for a more collaborative and less state-centric Canadian federalism.

As editor in chief of *Optimumonline*, Paquet has managed to significantly increase the magazine's readership, and the magazine has developed a reputation for its combination of quality and interesting ideas from a wide variety of writers on public administration, human resources, new business models, and government online. The managing editor, McEvoy Galbreath, has contributed to this volume.

Testimony to his ability to offer interesting views on and ideas about practical issues is that Paquet was asked to chair a mandate review of the National Capital Commission in 2006 and to prepare a background paper in 2007 for the Task Force on Governance and Cultural Change in the RCMP.

Classical Educator

Paquet is no longer involved routinely in teaching at the university. Nevertheless, he is often approached to contribute to sessions offered by it for graduate students and executives. They are invitations that Gilles always accepts if he is available and if he is free to "educate" while doing so.

At the same time, he continues to find new ways of designing and leading interesting and relevant intelligent "safe space" conversations on important topics, including public policy and management, that deal with wicked problems. One ongoing example is the series that Gilles, together with Ruth Hubbard, and in partnership with APEX, offers for federal executives in the National Capital Region.

In fact, slowly and in ways that cannot be predicted, his governance message is beginning to spread. For example, Paquet is currently taking part in teaching at the Collège des administrateurs at Laval to work on certified training for work on boards (something that will soon be required in Quebec) as well as the doctoral program in *gestion* at the Université du Québec à Montréal.

Putting It All Together

In his seminal work *Democracy and Education*, John Dewey remarks on a little-referred-to strain of belief of Jean-Jacques Rousseau that he asserts tends to acknowledge intellectually that the idea of the state as agent necessarily constrained the eighteenth-century philosophy of the individualistic ideal and "reintroduced the idea of the subordination of the individual to the state" (1916, 60). As Dewey observes, "there are many sayings of . . . [Rousseau's] which point to the formation of the citizen as the higher [ideal than that of the human] and which indicate that his own endeavour as embodied in the Emile [*Emile: Or, on Education* (1762)], was simply the best makeshift the corruption of the times permitted him to sketch" (60).

The profound changes undergone by the modern world—and that are still rapidly appearing—are beginning to raise important questions about the continued viability of the state as the agent in advanced democracies (never mind its desirability). It is possible that differences in political ideology will eventually evolve into differences of opinion about the nature and scope of its role as a player that, while crucially important, can only occupy the side of the societal stage.

Recently, for example, Charles Sabel (2004) published a paper titled "Beyond Principal-Agent Governance: Experimentalist Organizations, Learning, and Accountability" that looks at an emerging class of networked, experimentalist organizations that assume provisionality of goals and argues persuasively that experimentalist institutions are at least potentially democratizable. As Frederickson (2006, 2) points out in his review of Paquet's book *The New Geo-Governance* (which is included in its entirety as one of the contributions to this volume), "there are enough examples of effective geo-governance (i.e. the ways in which effective coordination is effected in a world where resources, knowledge and power are distributed through geographical space) found in the works of (well-known scholars) . . . and the network theorists to confirm Gilles Paquet's claims [that 'collaboration is the new categorical imperative']." Frederickson adds, however, that "It is . . . the fundamentals of geo-governance that really challenge traditional public administration" (2).

Paquet's enduring faith in democracy as a way of life and as a way of humans relating to each other, perhaps unknowingly even to Gilles, seems to have underpinned his evolution as a professional scholar, as a public intellectual, as a classical educator, and indeed as a person. It might be that this faith has not just allowed but also encouraged him to see the external world as fundamentally changing earlier than others, in clearer terms with respect to the implications for good societal stewardship than many, and to be quicker to shout it from the rooftops than most.

True to the extreme openness of intellect that Bollinger (2005) argues characterizes the best professional scholars, Paquet can imagine a world that makes the best use of every individual's ability and willingness to contribute to societal governance while, at the same time, acknowledging that progress in that direction will be slow, painful, and meandering. Democratic societies such as Canada may not get very far by neglect, or accident, or by choice—by choice because the view that bets heavily on citizens rising to the challenge of governing their own society to the greatest extent possible might remain contested into the indefinite future. In fact, citizens in countries such as Canada may continue to choose an approach that places more faith in the state to decide for them in more circumstances—a greater degree of subordination of the individual to the state—as their preferred kind of democracy.

For his part, Paquet argues that, in order to accelerate the emergence of a governance regime that is better aligned with today's realities, new civic institutions ought to be put in place that are based on being vigilant against corrosive centralizing and homogenizing actions of the state on civil society; exercising patience and compromise; and using transversal and subversive leadership that is opportunistic. In fact, together with Ruth Hubbard, Paquet is now working on a book about federalism that, like wikipedia, would be an "open source" where all citizens are free to tinker with Canada's governance system with as few constraints as possible, with the state as backup. At the same time, however, what matters to him just as much (perhaps even more) is that people engage in an "intelligent conversation" about the future and possibly be moved to try to influence it in some small way.

Many who have heard Paquet—fans and detractors alike—will disagree with the picture that he paints of our likely governance future. Nevertheless, it is his determination to play his part in making the world a better place—and to do it his way—that helps to explain why more than thirty people from many walks of life have felt moved to celebrate this anniversary of the beginning of a long and fruitful academic career, and to look forward to his continued contributions in the years to come.

The Contributions

The contributors are scholars in a variety of disciplines, practitioners in public as well as private arenas, and media experts. They write about Paquet from the vantage point of having interacted with him as teacher, as associate, as colleague, as mentor, or as someone whom they got to know because he influenced the world in which they worked directly. A few have interacted with Gilles over several decades, most for a number of years, while others have met him only relatively recently. For some, he has changed their whole world. For others, he has triggered a fresh way of approaching things that are dear to their hearts. For still others, he has been noticeable and helpful at the boundaries of their worlds.

INTRODUCTION

Their essays range in length from a few pages to the limit that the editors imposed. They are written in different styles and carry different tones. We have chosen to organize them in three sections.

Section I groups together a number of essays that deal with Gilles as a person. Following a brief introduction are contributions that view him as educator (from Tony Going, Meyer Burstein, and Pedro Arroja), as colleague (from Tom Brzustowski, Wojtek Michalowski, and Monique Bégin), as associate (from Pierre Bergeron and Robin Higham), and as fellow traveller (from Jean-Pierre Wallot and John Meisel).

Section II deals with the impact that Paquet has had in different situations and at different times. In it are essays that focus on repositioning (from Don McEown and Blair Neatby, Jac-André Boulet, and Bernard Bonin), on influencing (from Jeffrey Roy, Caroline Andrew, and Chris Wilson), and on engaging (from Jim Mitchell, Ruth Hubbard, David Zussman, and McEvoy Galbreath).

Section III contains contributions dealing with specific issue domains. It brings together essays treating organizing ideas and concepts that Paquet has developed (from H. George Frederickson, Monica Gattinger, Paul Laurent, David Wolfe, Christian Navarre, and Michael Skolnik), interpretations of his ideas (from Pierre Fortin, Ralph Heintzman, and Riel Miller), together with two that touch on linkages to his ideas and interests (from Thomas Courchene and Leroy Stone).

Taken together they make up a collection that can be thought of as a kind of kaleidoscope, allowing you to catch glimpses of Gilles Paquet from a variety of different vantage points. What we hope, however, is that, set against the backdrop offered in this introduction and with the conclusion to tie them together, they are also like the single images from the first moving pictures, which (if riffled quickly) tell a story. We hope that a story emerges from this volume about the contributions of a man for whom "doing the best I can in the circumstances"—the best that any of us can hope for—has added value modestly but importantly to the world of scholarship as well as the world at large. A story celebrating a man who is well worth celebrating.

Note

[1] A brief bio-bibliography is appended to this volume. For a more detailed account, including all of his publications, go to his website at www.gouvernance.ca.

References

Bast, M. R. (1999). "Two Types of Creativity: From the Research of Dr. Michael Kirton." www.breakoutofthebox.com/kai.htm [consulted August 14, 2008].

Bollinger, L. C. (2005). Cardozo Lecture on Academic Freedom. www.columbia.edu/cu/news/05/03/cardozo_lecture.html [consulted August 1, 2008].

Boulding, K. E. (1970). *A Primer on Social Dynamics*. New York: Free Press.

Dewey, J. (1916). *Democracy and Education*, ch. 7, "The Democratic Conception in Education.". Stilwell, KS: Digireads.com Publishing, 49–60.

———. (1935). *Liberalism and Social Action*. New York: Putnam.

Drath, W. H., and C. J. Palus. (1994). *Making Common Sense: Leadership as Meaning-Making in a Community of Practice*. Greensboro, NC: Center for Creative Leadership.

Faucher, A. (1978). "Présentation de M. Gilles Paquet par M. Albert Faucher, de la Société royale du Canada." *Discours d'acueiller à la Société royale du Canada, 31–32*, 103–08.

Frederickson, G. A. (2006). "The New Geo-Governance." Review of *The New Geo-Governance: A Baroque Approach*, by G. Paquet. *Public Administration Times, 29.6*, 1–2.

Friedman, J., and G. Abonyi. (1976). "Social Learning: A Model for Policy Research." *Environment and Planning A, 8*, 927–40.

Gilles, W., and G. Paquet. (1989). "On Delta Knowledge." In *Edging toward the Year 2000*, ed. G. Paquet and M. von Zur-Muehlen. Ottawa: Federation of Deans of Management and Administrative Studies, 15–30.

Granatstein, J. L. (1998). *The Ottawa Men: The Civil Service Mandarins, 1953–1957*. Toronto: University of Toronto Press.

Laurent, P., and G. Paquet. (1998). *Épistémologie et économie de la relation: Coordination et gouvernance distribuée*. Lyon: Vrin.

Lightman, A. "The Role of the Public Intellectual." http://web.mit.edu/colmm-forum/papers/lightman.html [consulted January 8, 2008].

Lithwick, N. H., and G. Paquet, eds. (1968). *Urban Studies: A Canadian Perspective*. Toronto: Methuen.

Paquet, G. (1968). "The Economic Council as Phoenix." In *Agenda 1970: Proposals for a Creative Politics*, ed. T. Lloyd and J. McLeod. Toronto: University of Toronto Press, 135–58.

———, ed. (1972). *The Multinational Firm and the Nation State*. Don Mills, ON: Collier Macmillan.

———. (1978). "Un appel à l'indiscipline théorique." *Discours de réception à la Société royale du Canada, 31–32*, 109–18.

———. (1985). "The Optimal Amount of Coercion Is Not Zero." In *Social Sciences Research in Canada: Stagnation or Regeneration?* ed. J. P. Souque and J. Trent. Ottawa: Science Council of Canada, 98–115.

———. (1988). "Two Tramps in Mud Time: Social Sciences and Humanities in Modern Societies." In *The Human Sciences: Contributions to Society and Future Research Needs*, ed. B. Abu-Laban and B. G. Rule. Edmonton: University of Alberta Press, 29–57.

———. (1992) "The Strategic State." *Finding Common Ground*, ed. J. Chrétien. Hull: Voyageur Publishing 85–101.
———. (1993). "Sciences transversales et savoirs d'expérience: The Art of Trespassing." *Revue générale de droit, 24.2*, 269–81.
———. (1994). "Reinventing Governance." *Opinion, 2.2*, 1–5.
———. (1999). *Governance through Social Learning*. Ottawa: University of Ottawa Press.
———. (2004). *Pathologies de gouvernance: Essais de technologie sociale*. Montréal: Liber.
———. (2005a). "The RSC as Public Intellectual." *Optimumonline, 35.4*, 3–29. www.optimumonline.ca [consulted January 15, 2009]
———. (2005b). *The New Geo-Governance: A Baroque Approach*. Ottawa: University of Ottawa Press.
———. (2006). "Savoirs, savoir-faire, savoir-être: In Praise of Professional Wroughting and Writing." Think piece prepared for Campus 20/20.
———. (2008a). *Deep Cultural Diversity: A Governance Challenge*. Ottawa: University of Ottawa Press.
———. (2008b). *Tableau d'avancement: Petite ethnographie interprétive d'un certain Canada français*. Ottawa: Presses de l'Université d'Ottawa.
———. (2008c). *Gouvernance: Mode d'emploi*. Montréal: Liber.
———. (2009a). *Crippling Epistemologies and Governance Failures: A Plea for Experimentalism*. Ottawa: University of Ottawa Press.
———. (2009b). *Scheming Virtuously: The Road to Collaborative Governance*. Ottawa: Invenire Press.
Paquet, G., and R. Hubbard. (2007). *Gomery's Blinders and Canadian Federalism*. Ottawa: University of Ottawa Press.
Paquet, G., and J-P. Wallot. (2007). *Un Québec moderne 1760–1840*. Montréal: Éditions Hurtubise HMH ltée.
Sabel, C. (2004). "Beyond Principal-Agent Governance: Experimentalist Organizations, Learning, and Accountability." In eds. E. Engelen and M. Sie Dhian Ho. *De Staat Van de Democratie. Democratie Voobij de Staat*, WRR Verkenning 3 Amsterdam: Amsterdam University Press 173–195.
Schön, D. A. (1971). *Beyond the Stable State*. New York: Norton.
Sim, E. R., and G. Wright. (2002). "A Comparison of Adaption-Innovation Styles between Information Systems Majors and Computer Science Majors." *Journal of Information Systems Education*, 13.1, 37–50 http://findarticles.com/p/articles/mi_qa4041/is_200201/ai_n902784/pg_3?tag=artBody;coll [consulted August 19, 2008].

Section I

The Person

On renonce d'abord à l'impossible, ensuite à tout le reste.
—Henri Thomas

This section looks at Gilles Paquet from the perspective of those who have known him from the vantage point of former students, colleagues, associates, and fellow travellers.

While the threads of professional scholar, public intellectual, and classical educator are woven throughout, each essay also provides a little glimpse of this very private person. They cover his professional career from his earliest years at Carleton University to the present day.

We see the man who always makes learning fun and who sees it as aimed at more learning as well as learning by more people. We see the man who not only loves to find messages buried in the books of all kinds that he devours but also delights in seeing what happens when these messages are put together.

At the same time, we see the passionate, energetic, and energizing man who has shown himself to be a good neighbour, a loyal and principled partner, and a fundamentally decent, reliable, and honest person. In short, someone who is one of "the good guys."

Part One
The Educator

Chapter 1

The Al Pacino of Carleton University

Tony Going

In the Beginning

I was in my third year at university when I first met Gilles Paquet. He was a professor of economics at Carleton University, and I was a new recruit to the Department of Economics. I had initially enrolled in political science, and like a lot of young people then and now I hadn't the slightest idea of what I wanted to do (when I grew up). I had chosen political science for the brilliant reason that a number of my friends were enrolling in the program.

As it turned out, however, my pursuit of a degree in political science was relatively short-lived. The end came within days of starting a course titled the Canadian Political System, a course that you had to take in order to qualify for graduation. I remember sitting through the first two or three classes. It was torture. Whether it was the subject matter, the course material, the professor, or a combination of all, I just knew I wouldn't last through to final exams.

Fortunately, I had elected to take a number of economics courses as part of my studies. This allowed me to switch to an economics major, and by enrolling in the honours program I wouldn't lose a year of study. Everything went very well until one day I found myself facing another required course, Canadian Economic History. Would this course prove to be the same disaster as the Canadian Political System? If so, I hadn't the slightest idea of what other area of study I would try next.

Canadian Economic History

I didn't know who Gilles Paquet was at the time, only that he would be teaching Canadian Economic History. It was not until quite later that I came to understand just how accomplished he was in so many fields. The course was held in a large classroom to accommodate the substantial number of students who had enrolled in it.

I want to say that the course was held in one of the lecture halls where you sat in elevated rows of seats looking down on a stage, a similar setup to the old movie houses. While this may or may not have been the case, after only a few lectures there was no question that Paquet could have been on stage.

By himself, with no props, in front of over 100 students, he would give a captivating performance. He had exceptional abilities to engage with his students; to take a subject such as Canadian economic history and make it come alive; to reveal the personalities, the struggles, the intrigues that made Canada what it is today. He easily transported us back to the beginnings, to the fur trade and the coureurs de bois who helped to open up the Canadian frontier. He would make us marvel at the energy and ambitions of these early pioneers and the essential role that they played in the development of Canada as a nation.

Week after week, Paquet would exhibit the same energy and charisma. There were very few seats ever left empty. I eagerly tackled his voluminous reading list anxious to participate in whatever debate might ensue. He made you want to engage. He made you want to do your best, to give him back as much as we felt he was giving us.

It was not just me who felt this way about Gilles. Most of my fellow students had the same reaction. Former students whom I met years later talked about their experience in the same manner. I have several friends who were taught by Gilles who fondly remember their time in his classroom and the positive impact that he had on them. Nor was this confined to economics students. Two of my closest friends were enrolled in accounting, and they too were enthralled by Gilles and his lectures. Many made a point of keeping in touch with him, decades later still meeting him for lunch or having a quick coffee. I seemed to be too busy to do so, but I have run into Gilles dozens of times, and he has always remembered my name and stopped to ask how things were going.

What was it about Gilles that impacted us so deeply? For me, he was the best of what our university should have been all about. He was a leading-edge thinker and writer on Canadian economic history. He was enthusiastic about the subject, and he projected that enthusiasm onto his students. He was a magnificent teacher; he had such an effortless way of conveying information and ideas. He was eloquent, charming, and elegant. He was the epitome of a professional and at the top of his game, dedicated to enlightening those who wished to explore Canada and its economic history. He educated us and made the learning fun.

And his engagement did not end at the classroom door. He always made himself available to us. On more than one occasion, I needed to seek his advice. No matter how busy he was, he always found the time to meet with you and make you feel that you were as important to him as any matter he was dealing with, even when he was dean of the economics faculty.

Al Pacino

In the process of writing this article, I was reminded of another experience that, in some ways, paralleled the one I had with Gilles. I was in New York and had booked a ticket to see an off-Broadway production called *American Buffalo* starring Al Pacino. I found the theatre where the play was being held and on entering saw a small semicircle of bleachers that were to seat fewer than 100 attendees. There was no backdrop, no scenery, no props … just Pacino giving one of the most powerful performances I have experienced. It was there in the theatre that I first realized why actors such as Pacino commanded and deserved the money that they were paid.

When you think about it, both Al Pacino and Gilles Paquet are in the field of education and entertainment. And, just as Al was at the top of his game, so too Gilles was at the top of his when I had the privilege of being one of his students. His remuneration was obviously nowhere near the same as that of Pacino, and it makes you wonder why our society does not place a higher value on the contributions that professionals such as Gilles make in the field of education. Certainly, his contribution to my education and his positive impact on my life and hundreds of others whom he has taught far surpass any contribution that Al might have made.

Chapter 2

High Noon

Meyer Burstein

When the "Friends of Gilles Paquet" asked me to prepare an entry for a book about Gilles, I accepted with pleasure. Although more than thirty-five years have passed since I was a graduate student at Carleton University, I still count myself among his disciples and am still influenced by his opinions and thoughts, some recent, others dating back to the time we first became acquainted. Writing about Gilles allows me to acknowledge my debt to him and, at the same time, to express my appreciation for his friendship and my deep affection for him.

How to assess his impact? My own career has been in the federal government heading up various policy, planning, and research organizations in the area of immigration and citizenship. In recent years, Gilles has become increasingly interested in diversity and how it should be managed, but, policy making being what it is, an assessment of his impact on policy outcomes would inevitably understate his contribution. To get the (policy) measure of Gilles, it would be better to look to his impact on policy makers rather than policies. More specifically, to reflect on his impact on an individual policy maker, namely me.

Gilles will likely find humour in the fact that many of the contributions to this volume, including my own, resemble obituaries in *The Economist*. This is no accident. There is a summative quality to a book such as this one. In part, it is due to the retrospective nature of the undertaking. But, more fundamentally, it originates in the implicit premise that the individual's greatest achievements have been wrought. And that we are able, at last, to do our sums because the heaviest lifting has already been done. To quote Gilles himself on this point, "At my age, you no longer plant trees." Yet anyone talking to him, or reading his latest tract, must surely be struck, as I am, by his energy, his intellect, his disregard for convention, his courage, and the wicked and entertaining way he expresses his views. This book is timely, but it will be important to leave space for several more chapters.

I first met Gilles in 1969 as a lackadaisical economics student in the fourth year of an honours program at Carleton University. My interest in economics was practical—a route to a degree and a job—but my curiosity was not engaged—that is, until I participated in his Canadian Economic History course. Gilles was new to the department and not known to the majority of students, but from the very first lecture I became his acolyte. Economics had been an abstraction, a system to be mastered and spewed back. What dawned on me, however, as I struggled with his prodigious reading list and listened to his lectures was that the ideas I was acquiring could be put to work; they could be used to tackle the issues that mattered to a student in the 1970s. Thirty-five years later I still have my binder with the articles and notes from that class. It marks a rite of passage.

I went on to earn a master's degree at Carleton, with Gilles agreeing to be my thesis supervisor for a paper on the economics of ghettos. I cannot remember anymore the reasons for this choice except that I was much taken by the idea of public goods and the logic that this provided for institutional design and collective action. Gilles encouraged me to read widely and to borrow ideas from other disciplines: sociology, anthropology, and political science. I was inspired, and I began applying to graduate schools to pursue a doctorate with the idea that I might become a university professor.

Since Gilles was always present and available—his office was right beside the graduate student study room—I talked to him about my plans. He was supportive, as always, but suggested that I consider a brief stint in government to help me figure out what I wanted to focus on in my doctorate. What made his advice especially credible was his evident appetite for public policy and the fact that his lack of a doctorate had not impeded him in any way. Within six months, I knew that my interest in policy development and government trumped my interest in academia. It was a decision that I have never regretted. Years later Gilles "confessed" that he had been duplicitous and knew where his advice would take me. He also claimed to have known that I was well suited to working in government. Coming from others, this could have been a slight; coming from Gilles, it was a compliment.

My association with Gilles did not end with my shift to government. His interests are remarkably wide ranging, and no matter what topic I was involved in I could count on Gilles for advice as well as breakfast at Fathers and Sons on Osgoode Avenue beside the University of Ottawa. Rarely did a conversation end without a half dozen references being passed on and, as likely as not, an article that Gilles himself had written. I also began, from time to time, to engage him more directly in projects for which I was responsible—high-level consultations to evolve immigration and citizenship management principles; strategic and visioning exercises of a policy or organizational nature; recommendations pertaining to policy and practice; and animating workshops and conferences involving ministers, senior officials, international representatives, and sundry experts.

That Gilles is accomplished no one would doubt. His body of work, both in volume and in span, speaks for itself. But to list his accomplishments—the articles he has written, the workshops he has chaired, the speeches he has delivered—somehow does not do justice to the man himself. For one thing, it fails to recognize his charm. A conversation with Gilles is fun. He immediately takes you into his confidence, and he personalizes the conversation. "The man is an idiot," he says, and you are only too ready to agree. He has that sharpster's trick of assuming your compliance with his ideas and opinions, all the while treading new ground and setting a foundation that makes you thankful you didn't set out your own opinions first.

There is a confidence about Gilles that is deeply appealing. And it does not fade with proximity. If he were a wine, he would not only exhibit a heady initial bouquet but also complex tones and a remarkably smooth, robust, and long-lasting finish. Perhaps it's his style: clear language, big ideas, bold prescriptions. Perhaps it's his penchant for work—24/7 for as long as I have known him. Or perhaps it's the fact that he is better acquainted than anyone you've met with the academic literature across a range of disciplines. To walk into his office and be confronted by stacks upon stacks of books and papers, not only in shelves but also arrayed on the floor, is both amazing and intimidating, especially when it dawns on you that the material is annotated, ordered, and accessible.

But to focus on scholarship alone would miss the essential essence of the man. Gilles is not some bookish recluse to be disinterred on February 2nd, encouraged to mutter dire prognostications, and then set aside until some subsequent appearance is required. He likes to set the agenda, and he is deeply conscious of the manner in which he expresses himself, in writing and in speech, in English or in French. Gilles is a brilliant performance artist, and his interjections and observations are designed to resonate and produce action. He enjoys the *bon mot*, and he wields analogies more effectively and subversively than anyone I have known. He is also the master of the two-by-two table, an insidious device that narrows the world to two dimensions and four choices, only one of which stands up to scrutiny. Guess who champions the only reasonable choice?

I remember as a graduate student Gilles telling me that what mattered was not only the message but also the manner in which it was expressed. Because the endgame, the one that really mattered, was not just peer-reviewed publication but also action. Hence the need for persuasion. It was this, I think, that allowed me, and others like me who ultimately chose public service, to form a bond with Gilles that was different from our relationships with other professors. And it is this attitude that led us—led me—to remain connected to Gilles over the years and to seek out his opinions. My work with the Metropolis project—an initiative that brings academic scholarship to bear on policy development—taught me only too well the difference between policy recommendations served up as scraps and bones after the real meal was consumed and digested, and real policy analysis that starts by understanding the context and the stakes and tries to evoke a course of action that creates opportunities for new and better solutions. It is obvious where Gilles is situated.

Still, all of these gifts would hardly matter if he were nothing more than some impossibly gifted, silver-tongued, academic impresario. He would, of course, still have entertainment value—think of the two-by-two table with entertainment and utility as the two axes—but would have long ago fallen victim to his other condemnatory assessment, "The man's a clown." (As I write this, I can hear Gilles uttering the phrase before he sweeps his hand through his hair and embarks on his mission of selling his point of view.) Clowns and idiots are not simply people with whom Gilles disagrees. They are posers (*poseurs*). People who conceal their laziness and unwillingness to think behind lofty, *faux* analyses. More importantly, they disregard the needs of the constituencies affected by their pronouncements. There is a disregard for fairness and reasonableness in this that offends Gilles. I am with him!

It is tempting in a tributary essay such as this to end with trumpets. I'd prefer to finish on a more whimsical note. What ultimately solidifies the appeal of Gilles is that he is a romantic. He believes in a better future. He believes that things can, and should, be improved. That ideas matter and can be put to work. That colleagues and students can be mobilized to do the right thing.

I think of Gilles as an academic Clint Eastwood. Noon approaches. The bad guys are out slouching against posts. Gilles strides out. Who are these idiots and clowns? Time to set them straight. Bang, bang. They should have done their homework. They should have known better. Perhaps they do now. On to the next issue. But first a glass of wine. And a conversation. There is always time for friends. Good on you, mate.

Chapter 3

Courtesy of Gilles Paquet

Pedro Arroja

It was in the early 1980s, and I was a lecturer at the Faculty of Administration (today the Telfer School of Management), University of Ottawa. For some time, there had been talk among academic staff and students about the appointment of a new dean, who would head the faculty for the next seven years, but the identity of the chosen candidate remained uncertain.

My duties were concentrated on teaching several economics courses at both the undergraduate and the MBA levels, such as macro- and microeconomics, economic policy, and public finance. By that time, I was writing my PhD dissertation in economics at Carleton University. I had come to Canada in late 1978 to do graduate studies in economics, on leave from the University of Porto, Portugal.

One day word made the rounds that Gilles Paquet would be appointed as the new dean of the faculty. For some time, he had been considered one of the most serious candidates for the job. I had already heard about him even though I had never met him since, at the time, he was the dean of Graduate Studies at Carleton University. People familiar with his work in this area were unanimous in their opinion that he was a very dynamic, innovative, academic *gestionnaire*.

The first time I met Gilles was in his office for what seemed to be a routine interview. He asked me about my work, my academic interests, and my academic career intentions and prospects. As I answered his questions, he took notes. Later I would learn that in his position as dean, Gilles was willing to decentralize all areas of decision making except two: human resources and finance. That first interview was thus part of a round of routine interviews in which he made a point of meeting and knowing each member of his academic staff personally.

I did not meet Gilles again for the next four to six months. I was too busy with my PhD work and my heavy teaching load. Immersed in a daily and demanding routine, I was surprised when I got a phone call from his secretary one day. The dean wanted to see me.

In retrospect, I must admit that I was a little nervous at the prospect. I had been teaching to the best of my ability, in both French and English (foreign languages to me). To support my family, I depended on the income that I earned from my junior, non-tenured position at the faculty. Coming from a culture where hierarchy is taken very seriously, being called to the dean's office was not the best thing that could have happened to me that morning. I braced for the worst.

"Pedro, the reason I want to talk to you is that I have heard through your students that you are a very good lecturer and a very effective communicator," Gilles told me as I entered his office.

"Thank you, sir," I replied timidly.

"I also heard that you are a little bit too much of a liberal economist," he continued.

I felt somewhat embarrassed at this remark. I was then in my mid-twenties, and it was in Canada that I became familiar with the works of economists such as Ludwig von Mises, Friedrich Hayek, and Murray Rothbard and became immersed in the works of Chicago School economists such as Milton Friedman, George Stigler, and Gary Becker. In my economics courses at the Faculty of Administration, I often defended libertarian positions before extremely interesting and stimulating, sometimes excited, audiences of MBA students.

On the other hand, Canada was then in the process of pioneering some social policies to assist the poor and immigrants, and I had learned that Gilles Paquet had been involved in some of them, such as the Minimum Guaranteed Income some years before. As a result, his remark about my libertarianism could have been a challenge to a fellow economist, very much his junior, although I wasn't sure.

Gilles then told me that he was not that bad at teaching either, which I already knew from his reputation on the Carleton campus. He added that he had been too busy with administrative work during the first few months of his tenure as dean and had not had the time to teach a course at the faculty. But he intended to do so in the coming spring term.

He then said, "There is a course in Economic Policy at the MBA level in the spring. Would you teach that course with me?"

"Sure. You do the teaching, and I act as your teaching assistant, I presume ...," I answered uncertainly.

"No. I mean the two of us teaching the course at the same time," Gilles said.

His words came to me as a shock. "What do you mean by the two of us teaching the course at the same time? Do you mean that you teach one session, and I teach the following one?"

My shock became more intense as Gilles explained his plan to me. "No. The course has twelve weekly sessions of three hours each. In each session, we discuss a theme, the themes being announced one week in advance to the students. Each one of us will make a presentation lasting between thirty and forty-five minutes. Then we put it up for discussion between the two of us and the students. Is that OK for you?"

"Sure," I said with mixed feelings.

We agreed that we would meet the following week to choose the twelve themes to be discussed in the course.

During the weeks that preceded the course, I worked hard at the library to prepare myself for what I regarded as the most serious professional and personal challenge of my short academic career. When word went around the graduate department about the format of the course, a number of graduate students came to register.

On the first day of classes, Gilles and I stood before the audience. "Pedro, your proper place is on my right," Gilles announced, and the audience laughed.

I believe that Gilles made his presentation first, and some students were discreetly smiling at me, the same students who had spread the word that I was a good lecturer and a libertarian economist, as if to suggest that I now had the opportunity to prove the worth of my ideas against a heavyweight.

Looking back from a distance of more than twenty-five years, I can distinctly remember my feelings of apprehension. I was a junior economist, and Gilles was about twenty years my senior. I was starting my academic career, while he was by then a well-respected academic. Most important of all, at least from my point of view, I was a lecturer at the Faculty of Administration, and he was the dean. Coming from a profoundly Catholic country, and having been raised and educated under an authoritarian regime, this hierarchical difference raised a lot of concerns in my mind. Could I express my ideas freely? How would the dean react if I contradicted him? After all, the renewal of my one-year contract at the faculty depended ultimately on his signature. Last but not least, as we stood before the audience, I could not fail to notice the contrast between the imposing figure of Gilles Paquet and my own.

We started the course as planned. I would do my presentation on the selected theme, and Gilles would do his own, or vice versa. Then there would be a break lasting from ten to fifteen minutes. We would come back to the classroom for more than one hour of open discussion between the two of us and with the whole MBA class.

The themes discussed in the course focused on Canadian economic policy issues, such as budgetary policy, monetary and fiscal policies, and different sorts of social policies. Three weeks into the course, some students were asking us if they could bring family and friends. Soon there were people watching the show packed in the back of the room. After the first few sessions, my confidence had greatly increased, and for the first time in my life I tasted the real meaning of academic freedom.

A few weeks later we had to move to a larger classroom to accommodate the increasing audience. The debates at times were fierce, and our positions were often radically opposed. Needless to say, my solutions to Canadian economic and social issues could be said to belong to the political right (some would say the far right), Gilles's solutions belonging to what could be considered the moderate left, with students equally divided in their support of those respective solutions. On several occasions, signs of exhaustion were visible in our faces at the end of each session.

By mid-term, it was clear to me that this was becoming the most interesting and stimulating teaching and learning experience in my life, a sentiment that was shared by many of the participants. From the very beginning, I put an enormous amount of time and work into the preparation of our weekly sessions. The students were well prepared for the discussions since the relevant materials were handed out to them one week in advance. And Gilles, true to his reputation, would always bring an innovative, surprising, at times shocking new perspective to any old problem.

On the last day of classes, after twelve consecutive sessions of genuinely open, intensive, enthusiastic, and free intellectual debate, we were standing up before the audience as we always did (with me still on Gilles's right-hand side) when the people in the audience rose from their seats and presented us with a prolonged, standing ovation.

I had just lived the most memorable experience of my academic life and had learned its most enduring lesson: namely, that when it comes to the discussion of ideas there are no hierarchies. Indeed, on no occasion during our many sharp disagreements on matters of economic theory and policy did Gilles ever use his seniority or his deanship to counter my arguments or to devalue them. For twelve consecutive weeks, ours were debates between equals, with only the value of ideas mattering and nothing else.

This experience had a lasting effect on my life. For the first time, I looked at the university as the institution *par excellence* for the unrestrained discussion of ideas, regardless of consequences. This was the appropriate setting for the expression of that Greek, unlimited, sometimes wild type of rationality as opposed to the prevailing technical or amputated rationality of the Kantian tradition.

Over the next few years, I had the opportunity to share other academic experiences with Gilles Paquet, teaching courses both inside and outside the university, debating policy issues of the day, and participating in his famous weekly program at Radio-Canada, which enabled me to learn a lot more about him as an academic and an intellectual, actually one of the few public intellectuals I have ever met.

I was impressed first by his social engagement, his strong belief that ideas are not things to stay within the walls of the university; rather, they are to be discussed with the public at large. That ideas are instruments to change the world for the better. It is not enough to conceive them. It is up to the intellectual to persuade the general public about their goodness and the practicality of their implementation. As a result, Gilles never missed an opportunity to reach the general public, writing newspaper articles, participating in public debates about the social issues of the day, hosting his Montreal-based Radio-Canada weekly program for years.

I was also impressed by his subversive creativity. Wherever there is a social problem or a policy issue, Gilles is there with a new perspective, a new grammar, and a new lexicon to read the problem anew and to propose an original solution—often a subversive one. This subversiveness has earned him a well-deserved reputation of *provocateur*, and through his long career it has earned him a number of intellectual adversaries. I sometimes wondered how a subversive intellectual such as Gilles could occupy institutional positions at universities and elsewhere so often, since every institution that he has touched was an institution slated to change—and change drastically.

I saw it for myself in the early 1980s at the Faculty of Administration, University of Ottawa. Two years after his arrival there, it had changed drastically in the number and quality of its publications, in the quality of its teaching, in the interpersonal relations of academic and other staff, as well as in the provision of expert services to the community. The reason for this seeming paradox, I believe, is that despite his subversive proclivities Gilles is a gentleman and an immensely caring human being.

Finally, I was impressed by his love for his country. Gilles is a great Canadian, probably one of the best the country has ever produced. He is known for his works in the socioeconomic history of Canada and, in particular, that of Quebec. But there is hardly any social issue or topic in Canada, at the micro-, meso-, or macrolevel, that has not received some thought and a new proposal by Gilles. He has written extensively on multiculturalism, local government, multinational companies, budgetary policy, governance, ocean policy, federalism, immigration, corporate management, linguistic policy, citizenship, social ethics, and a multitude of other topics, always from a Canadian perspective and with the goal of contributing to and improving Canadian society. Canada has always been the well-loved laboratory for his ideas, and observing him at his work I sometimes had the feeling that I was watching a man helping to build a country.

By the mid-1980s, I had completed my PhD at Carleton University, I had been promoted to assistant professor at the Faculty of Administration, and I had accumulated valuable academic experience in Canada, especially as a result of my close contact and work with Gilles. In 1986, after eight years in Ottawa, I decided that it was time to go back home. I had to perform my military duties in Portugal, and a position of assistant professor was still waiting for me at the University of Porto as the counterpart for the support that the university granted while I studied in Canada.

In January or February of that year, I entered the dean's office and said, "Dean Paquet, I am sorry to tell you, but in September I am returning to Portugal to pursue my academic career there."

He looked at me with some surprise and said, "Well, Pedro, I regret it, but if that is your decision...." And then he added in a prophetic tone, "But let me tell you that, if I know you well, you will not survive there."

The university as the institutional setting for the free discussion of ideas by independent people with no distinction as to age or rank—that was the most cherished lesson I had learned from Gilles Paquet, and I had seen him practising that lesson many times, ever since that first course we taught together, with me watching at his side. I did not realize at the time that this was the greatest of all the subversive ideas that he had succeeded in instilling in me. Looking at the history of the institution, it becomes crystal clear that "the university" is nothing of the sort. Rather, it has been from the beginning, and largely remains today, exactly the opposite: that is, an institution of indoctrination.

Less than two years after returning to my home country, Gilles's prophecy was fulfilled when I resigned from the university. From then on, although I still kept teaching courses and arranging conferences at several universities, I concluded that his influence had made me such a subversive element within the institution that, for my own well-being, I had better change my career. And so I did.

I started out my adult life wanting to make a career as a speculator in ideas. I ended up as a speculator in the stock market. (Let me add that the move was an extraordinary improvement from a financial point of view.) In large part, courtesy of Gilles Paquet.

Part Two
The Colleague

Chapter 4

Getting to Know Gilles Paquet, an Unexpected Pleasure

Tom Brzustowski

Gilles Paquet was at the core of an unexpected pleasure that awaited me when I retired from the National Sciences and Engineering Research Council of Canada (NSERC) and joined the School of Management at the University of Ottawa.

I had known of Gilles for some years, probably from a time soon after my arrival in Ottawa in 1995. My first memory of him was his voice on CBC Radio one morning. He was making some subtle and not-so-subtle comments about a local issue of the day and the people involved. Subtle or not, his comments struck me as interesting, and I remembered the name. I learned that he was at the University of Ottawa. I heard him on the radio many more times since.

Gilles next found a place in my memory when he was president of the Royal Society of Canada. At that time, I could put a face to his name but still didn't know him. I clearly remember several dozen distinguished fellows putting away an undistinguished lunch while packed into a small restaurant on Somerset while Gilles was holding forth on his plans for reforming the RSC. I was still at NSERC at the time and apparently invited ex officio. The plans made sense to me and led to notable improvements. Then I met Gilles on another occasion when we both sat on a prize committee at the university. His comments once again covered the whole spectrum of subtlety. In such ways, I was gradually coming to know Gilles better but still at a distance.

Then one day early in October 2005 I arrived at the School of Management with a licence to reinvent myself as a professor after an eighteen-year absence from university life. One of my challenges was to find places to publish. I thought that

I had some useful things to say about research and innovation in Canada, but I found the academic journals in my new field forbidding. I wrote some draft papers and circulated them to colleagues for advice, and one of them came back with a suggestion. Why not think of submitting them to *Optimum Online*, an Internet journal run by Gilles Paquet, a professor emeritus at the school?

The rest is history. Gilles and I met (first by accident in the mail room), talked, and agreed on much. He impressed me with the readership of *Optimum* both in terms of numbers and in terms of who the readers were. They were exactly the people I wanted to write for. There were more conversations on a broad range of subjects, and eventually Gilles squeezed a book out of me. He didn't squeeze very hard, so it was only a little book.

Now I feel that I know Gilles well enough to tell him what I most admire in him. I can sum it up in three words: depth, breadth, and energy. And what I most enjoy is that conversations with him are always interesting.

An unexpected pleasure to have a colleague like that.

Chapter 5

Fifty Books per Year and Counting

Wojtek Michalowski

"Ha ha ha, ha-ha…. Hoo, h', hoo, far, far and away, a mermaid sings in the silky sunlight." An idiot cooed to himself on the park bench that stood at the crest of the hill. Below him the greensward stretched down to the running track. In the middle distance the hospital squatted among the houses, a living ziggurat, thrusting out of a crumbling plain. The idiot's hair had been chopped into a ragged tonsure. He wore a blue hooded anorak and bell-bottomed corduroy trousers, and rocked as he sang. As I passed by I looked into his face; it was a face like the bench he sat on, a sad, forlorn piece of municipal furniture—although the morning sun shone bright, this face was steadily being drizzled on.

This epigraph comes from *The Quantity Theory of Insanity*, by Will Self, one of the first novels Gilles Paquet gave to me to read. It was also a first step on a reading path that I took with Gilles and hope will continue.

It was about twenty years ago when I heard about Gilles for the first time. I was a newly minted faculty member at the School of Business at Carleton University and was put on a committee developing a graduate program. Our mandate was to position this program in such a way as to "beat our competition at Ottawa run by *this* Paquet."

Fast-forward to 2001, and both Gilles and I were faculty members in the Faculty of Administration at the University of Ottawa. When I first went to his office to thank him for his support and encouragement for the move from Carleton, two observations really struck me in terms of what his office looked like: it had a huge abstract painting on a wall (the kind of painting that is difficult to figure out what it represents), and there were thousands of books overflowing shelves, his desk, and the floor. Surprisingly, not all of these books were about governance or management, so I asked Gilles if he happened to read novels. "Sometimes" was his tongue-in-cheek reply, followed by a recommendation to read Will Self's book. As I quickly discovered, this "sometimes" translated into reading about one novel per week, and Gilles manages to accomplish this on top of the usual weekly reading of articles and the writing of papers, books, and reports.

From that first visit, I immensely enjoyed popping into his cramped office to talk about books that he (and sometimes I) had read or was planning to read. These conversations often allowed me to take a completely unexpected look at a plot and interpret it from some unusual perspective. Gilles has a very intriguing capacity to find *hidden messages* in almost every text and to relate them to some current events. Thus, I discovered that a plot to acquire Breugel's unknown but important painting beautifully described in Michael Frayn's *Headlong* is really a powerful metaphor for the politics at the university or that a story about a medieval travelling troupe of English actors that takes a fugitive priest as one of them (*Morality Play* by Barry Unsworth) is simply a masterful allegory of contemporary machinations in the Canadian political system—especially the part where the actors embark on the quest to uncover a murder committed at the court of a powerful lord.

In my opinion, Gilles's passion for literature influenced his own writings. Essays on the Gomery inquiry, Montfort Hospital saga, or the NCC (to name a few) were not necessarily novels in form, but each was rich in a captivating plot, had an interesting cast of characters, and almost always reached a very unconventional ending. These are the necessary ingredients for a first-class novel! Is Gilles going to write such a real novel? Not as long as the follies of our political and socioeconomic lives provide him with the opportunities to work on another paper, report, or book. He is analyzing them with incredible passion, intelligence, and fantastic political instinct for uncovering all things bizarre, wrong, or simply stupid. This is exactly what we expect from a person who reads (and enjoys) Flaubert, Solzhenitsyn, Plato, or Mulroney. I am sure that we will hear more from Gilles on different but never boring topics.

As an academic, I am accustomed to writing pieces that always finish with some conclusions. I wondered how to conclude this short essay about Gilles and what I should put into a nice summary paragraph. Unfortunately, all my attempts ended in the trash can icon on my Apple computer. Then I asked myself: if I had a chance to ask Gilles one question, what would it be? And the answer was immediate: Gilles, please tell me how you manage to find the time to read fifty novels a year?

Chapitre 6

En hommage à Gilles Paquet

Monique Bégin

J'ai rencontré Gilles Paquet il y a au plus une dizaine d'années. Nous n'avons pas été doyens de facultés au même moment à l'Université d'Ottawa, quand il était le grand patron de la Faculté de gestion et que je faisais mes armes comme nouvelle professeure d'université et qui plus est, en Études des femmes. Il avait été doyen et professeur à Carleton des années avant que je n'y arrive. En d'autres mots, il avait déjà derrière lui une longue et brillante carrière universitaire alors que je débutais. Et pourtant j'ai le sentiment de l'avoir toujours connu, de commencer une conversation comme si nous nous étions quittés la veille et comme si nous comptions de nombreuses batailles communes. Ma chance, c'est d'être devenue un jour sa voisine de corridor dans le vieil édifice Vanier de l'École de gestion, et c'est comme voisine que je veux lui rendre hommage.

Mais qui est Gilles Paquet ?

Jusqu'à tout récemment, maintenant que ce sympathique petit restaurant de bonne cuisine familiale a fermé ses portes, il avait sa table le midi au Bistrot 115, rue Murray. On pouvait aussi le voir Au Clair de Lune en fin de journée, mais là aussi le restaurant a fermé ses portes. (Il se cherche en ce moment une nouvelle adresse sympathique.) On aurait pu tomber dessus en Provence l'été, dans l'arrière-pays près de Grasse. En fait, un été en particulier, il y a loué une grande maison, y a invité les amis en leur promettant le boire et le manger, mais à condition qu'ils fassent leurs chambres et sortent les vidanges. Tout le monde a fait la fête car Gilles Paquet est aussi un bon vivant. On voudrait en savoir plus. Je l'envie de ne voyager qu'en taxi, et d'avoir à toutes fins pratiques son chauffeur attitré. Je suis sûre qu'il y a là calcul de l'économiste qui sait très bien que c'est non pas la solution la plus écologique, mais bien la solution la plus économique par rapport à l'achat et l'entretien d'une voiture. Tomber sur Gilles dans un corridor, au coin de la rue ou même en descendant les escaliers du pavillon Desmarais pendant une fausse alarme d'incendie, ou arrêter un moment à la porte de son bureau, c'est recevoir la bouffée d'air frais d'une fenêtre grande ouverte sur le monde et sur la vie.

Ce qui m'a mise en confiance dans nos rapports, c'est qu'on peut lui dire franchement sa pensée sur tel ou tel propos, événement, actualité, fait divers, à chaud, sans qu'il juge. Il est fondamentalement tolérant. Il écoute avec empathie, voire sympathie, car il sait écouter. Il s'anime et en remet ou il offre un point de vue contraire. À moins qu'il n'enregistre et réfléchisse quitte à revenir sur le sujet plus tard. Il questionne. On peut tomber sur un moment où la sottise humaine vient de le mettre en rogne. Il a même quelquefois des tristesses sur des occasions ratées de bons coups institutionnels ou sociopolitiques qui auraient pu être. Il aime les êtres et voudrait tellement qu'ils donnent le meilleur d'eux-mêmes. Il parle, il explique, il décortique, il soulève les différents rideaux de fonds de scène, il communique, il dialogue.

Son bureau offre un environnement pas tout à fait comme ceux des professeurs Tournesol de la terre, car l'incroyable quantité de livres, posés élégamment en piles successives sur le pupitre, les tables, les étagères, les rebords de fenêtres et le plancher — piles qui tiennent debout en dépit des lois de la physique — est répartie dans un ordre précis que lui seul connaît. Son univers de travail ne participe donc pas du tout du chaos, mais il surprend à prime abord. Et puis on s'habitue car ces piles de livres se révèlent fort amicales. Comme Gilles Paquet est un être généreux, j'ai à mon tour lentement construit une pile de ses écrits, livres et documents divers, laquelle tient en porte-à-faux dans mon bureau, résultat de cadeaux sans cesse renouvelés de mon voisin, cadeaux précieux et dont je suis bien fière.

La définition concise la plus juste du témoignage de vie publique de Gilles Paquet demeure la citation lue lors du doctorat honorifique en Lettres que lui a décerné, en 2005, la jeune Thompson Rivers University, de Kamloops (C.-B.). Ce qui suit n'en est qu'un extrait :

> ... *books which blended transdisciplinary research and applied, experiential knowledge. These highly popular books crossed the academic threshold to be widely taken up by a mainstream audience which used his ideas to frame*

public debate. Since then, he has regularly been in the media as an interviewer or commentator, and has been present on radio and television every week since 1978.

Et ce sont ces années 1978-1990 de la radio à la Société Radio-Canada dont il chérira toujours le journalisme d'enquête au jour le jour, touchant à tout et à tous. Outre sa collaboration à l'émission *Le Magazine économique*[1], il y a couvert une vaste actualité, seul ou avec d'autres (dont Denise Bombardier), ayant interviewé, entre autres personnalités littéraires, Paul Auster sur ses romans new-yorkais ou Josyane Savigneau sur sa biographie de Marguerite Yourcenar ! Inattendu. Tout ça pendant qu'il est Doyen, préservant fidèlement ses jeudis pour parler au monde. Toutes ces années « au ras du sol » comme il dit ont changé dramatiquement sa vie intellectuelle et sa vision de l'université. Il a compris une fois pour toutes l'importance d'être à l'écoute, les gens ayant tant à dire.

Un exemple plus récent de son talent de popularisateur : il a fait descendre dans la rue — sans mauvais jeu de mot — le très ancien principe de la doctrine sociale de l'Église dit « de subsidiarité » repris dans le Traité de Maastricht (1992) selon lequel les décisions prises (ici dans l'Union européenne) le soient au niveau le plus pertinent et le plus proche possible des citoyens. L'échelon supérieur ne garde donc en tant que décideur que les arrêtés que le ou les échelons inférieurs ne pourraient effectuer que de manière moins efficace.

Qu'il ait reçu en 1982 la médaille Jacques-Rousseau (ACFAS) pour son importante contribution à la recherche multidisciplinaire m'enchante. Je me souviens bien du grand botaniste, généticien et ethnologue de réputation internationale, Jacques Rousseau, et Gilles Paquet l'aurait aimé. Je vois encore Jacques Rousseau, sans aucune prétention, grand érudit, moqueur, « de tempérament bouillant et doté d'un insatiable appétit de vivre » d'après ses biographes, et pour qui mes parents avaient beaucoup d'admiration, dans les rues de Notre-Dame-de-Grâce, à Montréal, avec sa belle tête déjà couronnée d'une abondante chevelure blanche. Tout comme Gilles, il ne faisait pas confiance aux idées reçues, allait directement aux sources, observait, discutait et se faisait « sa petite idée ». Et comme Gilles, il a traversé les barrières disciplinaires en passant des plantes aux gens qui vivaient avec elles, dans son cas dans le Grand Nord canadien.

Que les écrits ou les déclarations de Gilles Paquet attisent les passions est un fait facile à vérifier. Dans un sens comme dans l'autre ; on est « contre » ou on est « pour » le phénomène Paquet. Il est par trop prolifique, donc ce qu'il avance ne peut être soutenu par des recherches. Drôle de logique ; et s'il était un travailleur infatigable et discipliné ? Un « agent provocateur » ai-je lu ou entendu quelques fois. Un pamphlétaire — quelqu'un a ici besoin d'un dictionnaire ! Il dérange ; c'est vrai de quiconque remet en question les dogmes établis. Personnellement j'aime bien l'expression d'« intellectuel public » — *public intellectual* — expression que je lui réserve car elle m'est une récente découverte linguistique.

L'Amicale des anciennes et anciens du Petit séminaire de Québec lui a ainsi décerné, en 2006, son prix de reconnaissance avec cette étrange mention : « Ce prix souligne la carrière diffuse et échevelée d'un intellectuel public dont la pensée critique est marquée par un grand intérêt pour la pathologie administrative, un certain goût pour la subversion et une bonne dose d'ironie ». Sans commentaires, car je suis sûre que la mention se voulait un compliment.

Sa marque de fabrique est l'esprit de finesse. Il possède aussi cette vaste culture générale trop souvent absente dans notre Nouveau-Monde. Il n'en fait pas étalage, mais ses écrits connectent merveilleusement son savoir à ceux de générations de penseurs d'univers divers. Il est très rare de voir un discours offrant un solide cadre d'analyse économique tenir aussi compte, et plus qu'à la périphérie, des connaissances démographiques, historiques, sociologiques, culturelles, de celles des sciences politiques et des sciences de la gestion, sans oublier la philosophie morale ou l'éthique. Et, devrais-je ajouter, de la science de la gouvernance. Les économistes, d'habitude, sont très réfractaires « aux autres » des sciences humaines. Paquet, lui, détient ce don peu commun de comprendre du dedans la logique interne non seulement de disciplines intellectuelles autres que les siennes propres, mais de chacun des univers auxquels il se frotte.

Il abhorre le simplisme ; on ne s'en surprendra pas. On pourrait citer à son égard la célèbre phrase du critique social américain H.L. Mencken : « *For every complex human problem there is a neat simple solution, it's just that it's wrong* ». D'aucuns confirmeront que Gilles Paquet semble souvent faire des jugements à l'emporte-pièce, mais quand on y regarde de près, on voit qu'il le fait pour attirer l'attention de l'auditeur ou du lecteur. Un peu comme les trois coups avant l'ouverture du spectacle. Puis il plonge dans une analyse nuancée et détachée des facettes de la réalité qu'il est en train d'explorer et d'essayer de comprendre. J'en veux pour exemple son dernier livre, *Tableau d'avancement : Petite ethnographie interprétative d'un certain Canada français* (2008) que je viens d'acheter. Le titre est un tantinet piquant. Qui plus est, la couverture est illustrée du fameux bas-relief en pierre situé à Québec représentant un chien couché rongeant un os, accompagné du quatrain que l'on sait[2], lequel remonte au Régime français mais qui fut rapporté par des officiers britanniques de Wolfe durant l'occupation de Québec en 1759-1960. Je me suis dit : Ça va barder. Et j'ai eu tort. C'est un livre extraordinaire, dont le titre accrocheur se veut tout bonnement comme les trois coups avant le lever du rideau.

Ce livre s'attaque à l'image d'Épinal de la « Révolution tranquille » arrivée d'un coup sec un beau jour de 1960 et faisant basculer le Québec de « la grande noirceur » dans la modernité. Il le fait de façon très riche et non définitive. Après tout, comment écrire l'histoire alors que les événements n'ont même pas 50 ans d'âge ? Nous ne recevons pas dans cette œuvre un bel argumentaire linéaire et bien ficelé. Non, l'auteur nous prête plutôt son kaléidoscope et notre histoire, toutes en couleurs, nous offre alors des facettes nombreuses pour en enrichir la lecture. Ses propos sur Duplessis, Lesage, Daniel Johnson (père) ou Bourassa sont des plus éclairants. Même conclusion pour André Laurendeau (pour qui il a manifestement beaucoup d'affection), Hubert Guindon, Marcel Rioux ou Fernand Dumont. J'ai bien aimé ses analyses institutionnelles (Québec Inc., les Caisses Desjardins, Pépin-Robarts, l'hôpital Montfort). Ce livre documente et critique la poussée d'intrusion gouvernementale de la dite Révolution tranquille dans le tissu social québecois, tout en observant comment l'ancienne société civile, à sa manière fort dynamique, tente de se redéfinir et de reconquérir son espace social.

Il déteste donc le manichéisme, cette maladie de l'esprit que l'on retrouve dans la politique et le monde médiatique moderne et, en général, dans l'intelligentsia. La vue des choses en noir ou blanc. Quand il écrit, par exemple que : « Droite et gauche sont des mots fumeux qui constituent pour l'économiste des notions évasives bien davantage utiles pour construire des slogans que pour faire avancer l'analyse[3] », j'applaudis car je l'ai vu, je l'ai vécu, j'en suis victime pour ainsi dire. Point n'est besoin d'ajouter qu'il se méfie des élites culturelles. Il est à l'aise dans le monde moderne car il se meut dans un univers de complexité et pas dans un univers machiniste (comme dirait un autre intellectuel public, Thomas Homer-Dixon) ou mécaniciste. Il n'aime pas les gens en poste, ceux qui ont une charge publique, quand ils sont bardés d'absolus, pas plus qu'il n'aime ceux qui flottent dans un relativisme nébuleux. Pour en arriver à une saine gouvernance, et en l'absence de théorèmes tout faits nous indiquant le chemin à suivre, il prêche les délibérations dans le forum public, celles « qui ne se contentent pas de confronter les argumentations mais cherchent à reconstruire une meilleure compréhension[4] ». Dans ses nombreux textes, il reprend ses idées, il peaufine, il va plus loin, il revient à la charge.

C'est un plaisir de le lire car sa langue française est merveilleuse et je prends pour acquis que l'anglaise l'est tout autant. Il a le sens du verbe.

Je lui ai une fois demandé s'il se concentrait complètement sur un thème donné quand il potassait un sujet ou qu'il écrivait, ou s'il pouvait passer d'un sujet à un autre et revenir et ainsi de suite. Il m'a répondu : « Je suis le Père Ovide de la recherche »!, l'homme à tout faire des *Belles histoires des pays d'en haut*[5]. Le (faux) dilettante qui passe d'une question brûlante à une autre sans vouloir perdre une miette de tout ce qu'il y a à explorer et à comprendre autour de lui.

Comme d'autres qui ont travaillé fort tout au long de leur vie, il se trouve chanceux. Il reconnaît avec simplicité les occasions extraordinaires qu'il a eu de participer à de nombreuses et importantes aventures de recherche en politiques publiques, de journalisme (surtout radiophonique), de consultations, de rencontres internationales. Comme jeune consultant, il a collaboré au Comité sénatorial (David Croll) sur le vieillissement ; à la Commission de l'assurance-chômage ; au Comité spécial du Sénat (Maurice Lamontagne) chargé de la politique scientifique, et d'autres. En 1988, Gilles Paquet faisait une sabbatique à l'Institut de recherche en politiques publiques (IRPP).

Il reconnaît la chance qu'il a eue de tomber sur un Albert Faucher, son premier maître, puis sur un John Meisel à Queen's en sortant de Laval, et plus tard, sur un Stephen Kaliski et un Scott Gordon, à qui dit-il devoir sa langue anglaise si châtiée.

Évidemment, ce qu'il a écrit sur la gouvernance m'intéresse au plus haut point. Pourquoi la gouvernance ? Avait-il eu une épiphanie, un moment, un écrit, quelqu'un ? Pas vraiment, m'a-t-il répondu. C'est le fruit d'une longue gestation, pas vraiment consciente, mais s'il faut déterminer un moment précis, ce serait à la fin des travaux auxquels il participait pour le comité créé par Marcel Masse dans la seconde moitié des années 1980 pour repenser les défis énergétiques (comme une partie importante du processus Energy Options/Confluence énergétique). Il y a exploré l'idée de gouvernance à travers l'apprentissage collectif. « Il n'y avait personne en charge ! » a-t-il compris avec stupéfaction en étudiant le secteur.

(Tout comme dans le système des soins de santé, me suis-je dit.) Il découvrait plutôt la présence d'un équilibre plus ou moins stable résultant d'une constante renégociation entre quelques acteurs-clés du pouvoir. On peut être certain que les consommateurs, les clients, les contribuables ou les simples citoyens (ou les patients) n'y sont jamais présents. Aucun des grands acteurs ne peut seul contrôler et faire marcher le secteur, mais chacun peut le bloquer.

Peut-on conclure que Paquet est un esprit morose, voire un pessimiste ? Non pas ! Sceptique, moqueur, ironique, oui par moments, mais toujours réaliste, bien ancré dans les réalités sociales, dynamique, nous poussant à la réflexion, à la discussion et à l'action. Son rôle de critique nous est inestimable, de même que son sens de l'histoire. Et quoi de plus précieux qu'un voisin ami dont la porte est toujours ouverte ?

Notes

[1] Magazine de vulgarisation économique de la Société Radio-Canada animé par Réginald Martel et réalisé par Jean-Claude Lebrecque et Mario Cardinal. Plusieurs collaborateurs participent à la création de son contenu, reportages et entrevues, dont les journalistes Jacques Ouvrard, Jean Giroux, Gilles Paquet ou encore Jacques Véronneau.

[2] Je suis un chien qui ronge l'o – En le rongeant je prend mon repos – Un temps viendra qui n'est pas venu – Que je morderay qui m'aura mordu.

[3] G. Paquet. « La droite, cet objet économique mal identifié », dans N. Michaud, dir., *Droite et démocratie au Québec : enjeux et paradoxes*, Québec, Presses de l'Université Laval, p. 97-119.

[4] G. Paquet. « L'éthique est une sagesse toujours en chantier : réflexions sur l'éthique et la gouvernance » dans *Gouvernance : une invitation à la subversion*, Montréal, Liber 2004, p. 129-156.

[5] Téléroman populaire de la SRC d'après le roman de Claude-Henri Grignon publié en 1933.

Chapitre 7
Le journaliste et le communicateur

Pierre Bergeron

Demander à un éditorialiste, collègue, émule, et néanmoins ami, de décrire la contribution de Gilles Paquet au monde du journalisme relève davantage de la haute voltige que du témoignage. En effet, comment concilier le travail du professeur et du chercheur universitaire avec celui du commentateur, de l'éditorialiste, du journaliste et de l'animateur ?

La première question qu'il faut se poser quand on essaie de décrire le sujet est de savoir si Gilles Paquet peut être considéré comme un journaliste de plein droit. Pas question ici de présenter une carte de membre de la Fédération des journalistes professionnels du Québec ou de quelque autre confrérie journalistique. Pas question de diplôme en la matière. En fait, Gilles Paquet est inclassable dans le métier pour la simple raison qu'il a touché à toutes les facettes du métier à la fois comme professionnel de la chose, comme praticien du métier, comme commentateur public, comme spécialiste et, surtout, comme communicateur. Peu importe la façon, c'est le résultat qui compte. Gilles Paquet communique comme il respire. S'il n'arrive pas à convaincre, il ébranle. S'il ne provoque pas l'interrogation, il force la pause. Peu importe la manière, toujours il divertit. Et quand il choque, c'est si bien amené qu'on en redemande.

C'est pourquoi Gilles Paquet a compris dans sa nature même que le métier de journalisme en est un d'information, de formation et de communication. Il apprend, il enseigne et il livre la marchandise. N'est-ce pas ce que l'on recherche chez un professionnel de l'information ? Dans l'empire de l'éphémère, ce sont les journalistes et les communicateurs qui ne laissent personne indifférent, qui laissent les impressions qui durent, les mots qui restent, les images qui frappent, ou les sons qui s'entrechoquent. De toute évidence, Gilles Paquet y a réussi en mariant très efficacement une carrière académique aux nombreux métiers de l'information et de la communication.

Car la carrière du professeur Gilles Paquet est indissociable de sa contribution très féconde au journalisme écrit et électronique. L'une ne va pas sans l'autre. Les deux ne sont pas des extensions de l'une par rapport à l'autre. Le journaliste et le professeur sont plutôt les deux faces de la même médaille, ce qui donne à Gilles Paquet un avantage marqué quand vient le temps de communiquer le résultat de ses travaux universitaires, de les intégrer à une réflexion sur une question d'intérêt public, de commenter l'actualité ou de donner son avis, ce dont il ne se prive jamais. Et qui le lui reprochera ?

Bien sûr, il y a quelques pièges à éviter quand on demande à un journaliste, éditorialiste et éditeur de donner son avis sur un personnage unique qui a su si bien marier la carrière de professeur à celle de journaliste sans rien compromettre des particularités de l'une par rapport à l'autre, tout en profitant d'un talent qui permet à l'une de féconder l'autre. Pour la petite (et la grande) histoire, j'ai déjà « congédié » Gilles Paquet lors du débat sur la survie de Montfort. Il m'en a bien voulu, un peu, beaucoup, passionnément, mais cela lui a bien servi pour me le rappeler à temps et à contretemps lorsque nous nous sommes retrouvés sur les mêmes plateaux. Cela ne m'a pas empêché d'avoir un profond respect pour le personnage, une grande admiration pour ses qualités de penseur et de communicateur ainsi qu'une grande connivence à chaque fois que j'ai pu compter sur la proverbiale disponibilité.

Toujours est-il qu'il y a, dans la carrière de Gilles Paquet, cette intégration à peu près parfaite entre une pensée cohérente et articulée et cette capacité unique de pouvoir dire les choses dans un langage coloré, intéressant, imagé et structuré. Car la qualité de sa langue, dans les deux religions linguistiques officielles du pays, en fait un communicateur des plus efficaces et dont les avis sont recherchés car ils ne laissent personne indifférent. C'est le moins que l'on puisse dire. On peut ne pas être d'accord, et c'est fréquent, mais on ne peut jamais lui reprocher de ne pas avoir développé, articulé et exprimé avec efficacité une pensée ou une opinion qui parfois dérange sans dénigrer, qui souvent stimule sans provoquer d'antagonisme.

L'indifférence et l'unanimité ne sont jamais au rendez-vous quand Gilles Paquet se prononce. Il veut provoquer. Il provoque. Il fuit l'unanimité. L'unanimité le fuit. Les bien-pensants n'ont qu'à bien se tenir. Si l'iconoclasme de la pensée est l'antidote de la langue de bois, des idées reçues et de la pensée magique, Gilles Paquet en boit à grands traits.

Toujours conscient d'un certain effet, parfois un peu théâtral dans la manière, Gilles Paquet affirme souvent qu'il n'hésite pas à émettre des opinions qui choquent pour faire avancer la réflexion, la lancer dans de nouvelles directions, en dehors des sentiers battus de l'unanimité et de l'indifférence.

Sa première véritable incursion dans le monde du journalisme, il l'a faite en 1978 à la radio de Radio-Canada à l'époque glorieuse du *Magazine économique* à la suite du départ de Joan Fraser, devenue sénatrice, et de Florian Sauvageau. Un jour par semaine, il prenait l'autobus pour Montréal pour aller apprendre sur le tas et sous la férule de Mario Cardinal les rudiments du métier de journaliste. Une journée par semaine, il descendait de la tour d'ivoire universitaire (il était alors à l'Université Carleton) pour devenir « manœuvre » de l'information et apprendre à parler pour que les gens comprennent. Il n'hésite pas à affirmer que Radio-Canada a été une ressource extraordinaire qui lui a ouvert ses portes et qui lui a permis de côtoyer d'excellents journalistes (comme Jacques Ouvrard) pour apprendre la différence fondamentale entre l'académique et le communicateur. Il a donc fait ses classes, à tous les jeudis pendant une dizaine d'années, en se rappelant un vieux principe de base que lui rappelait John Dewey : « *In the beginning is the issue* ». Savoir identifier le problème avant de poser les question et de passer les jugements.

De ses années à Radio-Canada, il se rappelle en particulier une série qu'on lui avait demandé sur l'histoire économique du Canada en 25 heures, une expérience qui a été un véritable succès et où on lui avait donné carte blanche et bien de la corde pour se pendre : « On va te laisser parler de n'importe quoi pourvu que ce soit compréhensible. On va te laisser faire de l'éducation économique sans aucune forme de censure ». « Je faisais du théâtre », se rappelle-t-il ajoutant que Mario Cardinal lui avait dit un jour que « Le droit à être écouté est subordonné à celui de ne pas être emmerdé ».

Gilles Paquet fait partie de ces trop rares « académiques » dont le parcours médiatique est l'extension naturelle de la pensée, de la recherche et de l'enseignement. Ses publications se comptent par centaines, ses interventions médiatiques et journalistiques par milliers. Les chefs de pupitres de nos grands comme de nos moins grands médias trouveront toujours en Gilles Paquet le collaborateur recherché et le commentateur coloré qui n'a jamais eu peur de ses opinions et qui ne craint jamais de les exprimer, même quand elles vont à l'encontre ou à la rencontre de l'unanimité ou de l'uniformité. Cela ne lui vaut pas que des amis mais cela ne l'empêche pas d'émettre des opinions iconoclastes qui surprennent et qui forcent la réflexion et le débat.

Gilles Paquet, le communicateur, est aussi un travailleur acharné comme en font foi ses activités dans les médias écrits qui se comptent par centaines : 128 articles de magazines dont 87 chroniques et 41 articles, 5 vidéos, 212 articles et éditoriaux et 2 lettres d'information. C'est cependant à la radio et à la télé que Gilles Paquet a apporté sa remarquable contribution. À la radio d'abord où il a fait pas moins de 1500 entrevues au *Magazine économique*, de 1978 à 1989, une centaine de chroniques à l'émission *Transit* de 1991 à 1994, et une vingtaine de collaborations à l'émission *Indicatif présent* en 2002 et 2003.

À la télévision, il a mené une soixantaine d'entrevues à *Aujourd'hui dimanche* en 1990 et 1991 et participé à pas moins de 400 sessions de *Studio Two*.

Toutes ces collaborations ne doivent pas faire oublier que Gilles Paquet est un habitué des forums et des émissions d'information qui trouvent toujours en Gilles Paquet un collaborateur « qui donne de la bonne copie » car il a le sens de l'image, de l'effet théâtral, une grande capacité d'intégrer ses opinions aux grands enjeux de notre société, sans craindre de déboulonner les mythes et, il l'avoue lui-même, d'être « un peu effronté ».

En plusieurs occasions où nous nous sommes retrouvés sur le même plateau, j'ai toujours été fasciné par la remarquable capacité d'adaptation et la grande générosité de Gilles Paquet pour ses interlocuteurs. Pour lui, une bonne discussion est une occasion de mettre sur la table toutes les facettes d'une question, de les présenter, de les défendre et de les confronter car « *In the beginning is the issue* »! Je le sais très sincère quand il n'hésite pas à jouer l'iconoclaste et à remettre en question les idées reçues, les unanimités et la pensée magique. Cela lui vaut une étiquette de « droite » si tant est que ses opinions naviguent sur toutes les eaux sans ne jamais perdre de vue le rivage du centre. Un peu effronté, parfois beaucoup et très consciemment, Gilles Paquet est un conférencier très apprécié car il sait marier une érudition politique, sociale et économique à une capacité innée d'intéresser, de provoquer et de divertir, tout en informant.

Alors qu'il était président de la Société royale du Canada, il n'a jamais craint de présenter des débats sur ce qu'il est convenu d'appeler certains sujets « tabous » ou bien de grandes unanimités de notre société comme les PPP (partenariats public-privé), le créationisme ou la diversité culturelle. Comme commentateur, écrivain et universitaire, il n'a pas craint de soulever des interrogations sur la vérificatrice générale Sheila Fraser, les universités ainsi que les limites à la diversité culturelle dans la foulée des travaux et des conclusions de Gérard Bouchard et Charles Taylor sur les accommodements raisonnables. Ce sont autant de sujets où Gilles Paquet devient intarissable et sait facilement forcer la réflexion sans pour autant forcer l'adhésion à ses opinions parfois tranchées. Il y a dans la « méthode Paquet » de communication une capacité innée de faire valoir un point sans pour autant vous l'enfoncer dans la gorge. Pourtant, on n'est jamais vraiment confortable lorsqu'on se retrouve aux antipodes de ses positions. Force est d'admettre qu'il sait intégrer avec une habileté remarquable les fruits de connaissances étendues, présentées avec clarté et démontrées avec une conviction ... qui laisse toujours des portes ouvertes. « À tout le moins, parlons-en » ! La langue de bois et la pensée magique deviennent parfois des murs infranchissables de silence quand vient le temps de discuter de questions qui dérangent ou qui déstabilisent.

En fait son expérience de journaliste lui fait juger sévèrement jusqu'à quel point le monde universitaire peut être « plate » lorsque vient le temps de porter sur la place publique le fruit de ses connaissances. « C'est lorsqu'on passe de l'académique au monde des communications qu'on se rend compte comment on était plate avant » ! « Je n'avais plus d'intérêt à me prosterner devant les idoles de l'académie ».

Par exemple, dans les années 1990, le sujet de la gouvernance a pris de plus en plus d'espace sur la place publique. Gilles Paquet s'est investi dans le sujet en constatant publiquement ce que tout le monde remarquait sans trop en parler, c'est-à-dire que plus personne n'est en charge, plus personne n'est responsable, en particulier dans la fonction publique, parce qu'« il n'y a plus dans le système un sens critique très aigu ». Mais pourquoi ?

On constate jusqu'à quel point Gilles Paquet, le commentateur, croit fermement à la nécessité de la critique, sociale, économique ou politique, dans toute organisation sans que cela ne passe pour de la déloyauté ou de la trahison. « Il ne faut pas que toute forme de critique soit considéreé comme une forme de trahison », même quand cela va à l'encontre des idoles ou des idées reçues. Par exemple, lorsque la vérificatrice générale Sheila Fraser affirmait à propos du scandale des commandites que l'on a transgressé toutes les règles dans le livre, Gilles Paquet s'insurge. « De quel foutu livre s'agit-il » ? Au fond, la question fondamentale que soulève Paquet, c'est de savoir dans quelle mesure, quand on évolue sur le terrain de l'opinion, du commentaire, de la prise de position ou de la politique, il existe vraiment « un livre » qui puisse servir de référence absolue ou de grille de lecture. Il existe bien certains principes à partir desquels on peut émettre une opinion, éclairée certes, mais qui demeure une opinion.

Ceux qui, comme moi, ont subi les foudres de Gilles Paquet à l'occasion de la lutte pour la survie de l'hôpital Montfort n'ont pas eu que des mots d'appréciation à son endroit. Ce n'est pas que son côté iconoclaste, provocateur ou effronté qui nous a mis souvent en nette contradiction. C'est parfois la manière. Nous avons tous les deux nos propres « convictions » sur le sujet. Je suis d'accord avec Gilles Paquet qu'il aurait été sain de pouvoir débattre de questions délicates touchant l'avenir de l'hôpital Montfort et même sur la stratégie à suivre pour en éviter la fermeture ou pour s'assurer des meilleurs services de santé (et en français) dans tous les hôpitaux de la région. Un débat ouvert aurait peut-être mené à des conclusions différentes. Par contre, la stratégie employée était défendable car elle visait à opposer un front commun qui ne tolèrerait aucun recul, fût-il stratégique, face à une décision à la fois administrative et politique. En fait, Gilles Paquet souhaitait ouvrir le débat sur une telle question et débarrasser l'opinion publique de ses œillères. On peut arguer que cela aurait servi d'argument au gouvernement Harris pour justifier sa décision en soulignant la division des francophones de l'Ontario sur le sujet. La suite des événements et l'essor subséquent de Montfort ont démontré qu'il était alors justifié de démontrer que l'institution était très performante, jouait un rôle prépondérant dans la formation de professionnels de la santé en français et servait bien les intérêts de la collectivité.

On ne peut reprocher à Gilles Paquet sa capacité innée à provoquer pour forcer la réflexion et le débat. C'est ce qu'il a fait comme journaliste et comme commentateur tout au long de sa carrière. Pourfendeur de l'unanimité, on sent chez Gilles Paquet un ardent désir de se démarquer, d'ouvrir les débats de société ou de déboulonner les statues. De toute évidence, on n'érigera jamais de statue au journaliste ou au professeur Paquet. Il ne nous le pardonnerait jamais.

Toujours de son temps, Gilles Paquet a été un précurseur de ces universitaires qui ont compris que l'enseignement et la communication sont les deux déclinaisons du savoir. Il ne prend son sens que dans la mesure où il se partage, où il se donne. Gilles Paquet n'est donc pas communicateur par devoir, par obligation ou par nécessité. Il est communicateur par définition. De le savoir également journaliste est pour notre métier une source de valorisation unique puisque nous savons qu'il voue à notre métier un immense respect et un engagement qui ne fait aucun doute. On dit souvent que le journalisme mène à tout, à condition d'en sortir. On constate également que nombre de journalistes sont arrivés au métier via une formation universitaire différente du métier tel qu'il s'enseigne. Gilles Paquet est toujours resté fidèle à l'un comme à l'autre tout en respectant et l'un et l'autre avec leurs différences, avec leurs limites et, surtout, avec leurs possibilités.

Il faut le voir comme analyste à la fois décortiquer l'événement, le décrire avec beaucoup de couleur et, bien sûr, faire passer son message. La controverse est un outil de communication dans la mesure où elle favorise le choc des idées et l'avancement des choses. Il faut savoir doser l'effet, ne pas faire passer l'interlocuteur pour un imbécile et savoir communiquer ses idées avec rigueur et couleur. Gilles Paquet a toujours su communiquer sans diminuer … au risque de provoquer l'inconfort de son interlocuteur.

J'ai suivi de près le déroulement du panel de la Revue du mandat de la Commission de la capitale nationale que Gilles Paquet a présidée, et réalisée, en 2006. Il avait reçu ce mandat du ministre des Transports, de l'Infrastructure et des Collectivités et responsable de la CCN, l'honorable Lawrence Cannon. C'est dans cet exercice de sept mois que Gilles Paquet a mis à bon escient son expérience de journaliste, d'universitaire et de communicateur. Sans aller dans les détails, on peut affirmer qu'il est allé droit au but, comme il l'entendait, sans jouer le jeu des groupes de pression qui n'allaient pas rater une occasion de se manifester et d'essayer d'influencer le travail du panel. C'était bien mal connaître Gilles Paquet et surtout bien mal connaître son extraordinaire capacité d'analyse, de synthèse et de « clairvoyance » des idées, des suggestions et des programmes de ceux qui croyaient profiter de cette plateforme pour se faire du capital politique sur le dos de commissaires patients et compréhensifs. Il n'en fut rien.

La publication de son rapport fut un bel exemple des talents de communicateur de Gilles Paquet et de sa connaissance intime du monde des médias. Car il ne suffit pas de publier un « beau rapport » dans les temps requis et en deçà du budget, encore faut-il le communiquer, savoir mettre l'accent sur les points importants, faire un travail de sensibilisation et assurer le suivi. C'est sur ce dernier point que la patience de Gilles Paquet a été mise à rude épreuve. Une fois le rapport remis, il ne lui appartenait plus. Il ne se faisait pas d'illusion sachant toutefois que seul le temps ferait avancer les choses, petit à petit. Pas assez vite, mais petit à petit. Son expérience de journaliste lui a appris à bien lire le contexte. Ainsi, les recommandations portant sur les améliorations à la gouvernance de la Commission de la capitale nationale ont été endossées d'emblée par le gouvernement. Bien sûr, Gilles Paquet est un homme pressé et qui n'a pas la langue dans sa poche. Réaliste, on le sent quand même impatient quand le gouvernement tarde à bouger. Mais le communicateur est aussi un libre penseur qui sait mettre la pression quand on se traîne les pieds. C'est sans doute l'aspect de son mandat qu'il a trouvé le plus difficile à tolérer.

On peut donc se demander si, dans le fond, Gilles Paquet est un journaliste dans l'âme qui s'est égaré dans le domaine académique ou un universitaire pressé qui a compris la valeur du monde de l'information comme extension de son travail de professeur et de chercheur. Le respect qu'il commande, son érudition hors du commun et son extraordinaire capacité à ne pas trop se prendre au sérieux en ont toujours fait pour moi un exemple du mariage parfait entre l'« académique » et le journaliste, les deux se définissant par la communication. Son sens de la répartie, de l'histoire et de l'image en ont toujours fait pour moi un communicateur hors du commun.

Si, en plus de 30 ans de métier, Gilles Paquet se demande encore ce qu'il est vraiment, de l'universitaire ou du journaliste, je dis : Tant mieux ! Laissons-le à cette interrogation existentielle et instable. Car c'est de cette instabilité « confiante » qu'il se nourrit et qu'il est pour nous tous, simples journalistes, une source d'inspiration, et un éternel délinquant.

Part Three

The Associate

Chapter 8

Unbundling Paquet

Robin Higham

I first met Gilles Paquet while completing the final months of thirty-five years with the Department of Foreign Affairs and International Trade. Recycled as the "diplomat in residence" at the University of Ottawa's Institute for Canadian Studies, I had few acquaintances at the university. But Gilles was omnipresent on campus, and it wasn't long before our paths crossed. I was pleased to find a home and took up his invitation to join his nascent Centre d'études en gouvernance. It was soon evident that I had a tiger by the tail and that my new colleague was a force of nature not just on campus among students and fellow professors but also within the considerable public policy community in the federal public service.

In the weeks that followed, I learned that, throughout his long career as an academic, the uniqueness of his work placed Gilles in high demand as a lecturer and conference participant, as a media commentator on a wide range of social, economic and political questions, and as a consultant to all three levels of government in Canada. His discourse could be unorthodox and disconcerting, but his conclusions and recommendations never failed to surprise with their self-evident logic. It was also increasingly apparent to me that the Paquet brand of inescapable logic was only self-evident after he debunked the so-called embedded assumptions that so often keep other colleagues and scholars from locating *le nerf de la guerre*, the heart of the matter.

When I joined in the mid-1960s, Canada's external affairs and foreign trade services were renowned at home and abroad for a capacity to think and strategize long term, to collaborate with like-minded allies, to build compromise, and to serve as honest broker between parties where communications were in difficulty. Both the Departments of External Affairs, and Trade and Commerce were even known to take risks! Lessons learned at the knees of senior and more worldly foreign service colleagues in those early years taught innovative policy development habits and rigorous assessment of long-term national interests. From under Gilles's penumbra, I was beginning to understand that my earlier programming had been eroded during those later career years of the 1980s and 1990s. It was a refreshing flashback to rediscover what seemed to me at the time "the way we used to do things." At his Centre on Governance, we talked about governance!

But of course there was something more to Gilles than just a return to those imagined golden years. The more I saw him at work, in tireless conversing, reflecting, lecturing, reading, and of course writing, the more I became intrigued with his method of problem analysis and public policy development—what I came to call *la mèthode paquesienne*. I wanted to understand how this mere university professor (with practically no foreign affairs experience after all) could be so consistently insightful on such a broad and varied spectrum of governance and public policy issues. There are many others, of course, who know and admire his work—and many critics as well. But disciple or heretic, all recognize that Gilles employs a uniquely effective approach to policy analysis and policy development. My question was simple. "How does he do that?"

The answer, if there is one, is of course more complex. His closest associates, while as intrigued as me about what makes this man tick, were wisely unwilling to even attempt an exploration of the secrets of *la méthode paquesienne*. But for me, unbundling Gilles Paquet had become both a casual puzzle project and a desire to learn more from my enigmatic new colleague.

As I became a dedicated Gilles watcher, one early impression was a sense that *la méthode* takes much of its inspiration from his years of practising a certain *esprit de contradiction*. Gilles, it seemed to me, was taking an almost perverse pleasure in asking "Who says?" or "What if?" in challenging those embedded assumptions. *La méthode* seemed to me to start with a conclusion—that conventional embedded assumptions are, by their very existence, the most likely reason for the failed policies under review. Gilles always needs to know up front what the protagonists claim the issue is all about. For him, whatever is taken for granted in most public policy challenges is probably just not so. He instinctively goes back to ground zero, the starting assumptions, to launch his naively innocent questioning.

You can find examples of that *petite astuce* in much of his writing. In the 1999 book *Oublier la Révolution tranquille*, for example, you will recognize the "What if?" question early on. What if historians and policy makers have been wrong in describing the core issue regarding social and economic development in Quebec? He argues that major changes in Quebec society were going on for many years before the so-called *Revolution tranquille* of the 1960s was singled out as a seminal event. When you remove that favourite icon of modern Quebec nationalist discourse, the Quiet Revolution, the story of Quebec's remarkable evolution of 400 years takes on a much different, much more sustainable, and self-confident character. Consequently, the set of best policy options and priorities for going forward comes out much differently as well. Paquet argues that, because of that faulty and contrived national narrative, the narrative of victimization and failure, many Quebeckers have been focusing on the wrong enemy and the wrong weak spots—and the wrong responses.

Gilles made a similar challenge in a more recent discussion regarding contemporary governance in Canada. He questioned an assumed need for more and stronger leadership from the centre at the federal government level. His conclusion was that it is not centralized leadership that is the missing piece of the puzzle. What is problematic is the assumption itself—that government needs to be both centralized and led from the centre. That assumption, he claimed, has us all waiting for someone to take charge of governing us. But set aside that apparent precondition for governance from the centre, and we discover something new. It looks as if our democratic institutions, the division of power and responsibility, as well as the existing institutions and administrative mechanisms, are essentially in place. It seems that we are already well equipped to function and make policy as a decentralized, learning, and dynamic society. From that perspective, from a relocated ground zero, where no one is in charge but us, responses to new policy challenges are quite different.

Gilles likes to insist that, once these kinds of misguided assumptions are exposed, we can usually escape the mental prisons that frustrate our search for "the core issues." Doing so may entail asking how we fell into those traps in the first place. Did those constraining perspectives prevail because certain stakeholder groups succeeded over others in defining the core issue in ways that served them best? Did it serve Quebec nationalism to argue that the province has suffered 250 years of economic and social decline, and that the only answer is to escape the bonds of those who were being held responsible for that decline? Is it those who crave centralized power who are arguing most vociferously that we need a strong leader at the centre in Canada? Clear away the faulty framework, and the rationale for current or entrenched policies often vanishes.

I often see Gilles standing back like that, isolating cause-and-effect linkages, without partisan government policy experts or other stakeholders to distract him. He understands, of course, that his freedom as a disconnected and independent observer is a strategic advantage. This freedom of thought is a luxury too often out of reach for policy-making officials who must live and work with those very stakeholders whose arguments they might otherwise challenge. Gilles is acutely aware that it is not always easy, but it is always essential, to resist one's own tendency to self-censure, to rejig analysis in order to maintain peace with the stakeholders who see danger in a revised perspective on the core issues—the new and perhaps troublesome context. Hence the controversial nature of so much of his work.

More than once I have heard Gilles say that it is a crucial step to flush out which of the embedded assumptions cannot be explained or justified under rigorous examination. In his recent book about governing for deep cultural diversity, for example, he dares to suggest that there are limits to reasonable accommodation, that it is an error to make policy as though we can have deep diversity and social cohesion too. The political correctness and human rights champions who believe in "multiculturalism without borders," and who have succeeded in embedding that notion as a core value of Canadians, tend to get pretty annoyed with him on this point. Nevertheless, in that deep diversity governance treatise, Gilles fearlessly notes how the left often blocks constructive public discussion by labelling as racist or as human rights offenders those who dare to question limitless multiculturalism. For Gilles, it is that omnipresent political correctness rule book that is Canada's downfall, our open-debate blocker of choice.

But Gilles would be the first to insist that *la méthode* is not only about confronting unfortunate truths. *Au contraire*, it is about exploring the terrain for workable policy options. That exploration involves his search for a "reconciliation of frameworks": locating the spaces where stakeholder interests and perceptions are in agreement. Where do those frameworks overlap? He reminds us that the incompatibility of those various stakeholder frameworks is why we have a policy problem in the first place. It is clear that he views the role of the policy analyst and policy maker as more than just isolating those incompatibilities. This role is also about locating common ground and designing responses to capitalize on that platform. I have watched Gilles open this phase of his inquiries with the disarming question "Where can we/you agree?" The collective initial response can be tiny, but it is almost never "Nowhere." For example, the variety of perspectives in the national debate on governing multiculturalism in an environment of deep diversity is so great that about the only thing we can get agreement on is that current policies are unsustainable and that we have to talk about it. It is not a lot, but it's a start.

But, Gilles warns us, to do that, to get the overlap with which we can work, we may have to reframe the issue itself. And here he employs another secret weapon, a capacity to "say it sharply" (I quote), to describe the new context or framework with a short phrase or even a single attention-getting label.

Gilles once confided that he carries in his back pocket his own version of the list of four characteristics inspired by John Friedman and George Abonyi that any policy recommendations must deliver: (1) they must be technically feasible, (2) they must be socially acceptable, (3) they must not be overly destabilizing to the political environment, and (4) they must, of course, be implementable. That is why he found so risible the recommendation of the recent Taylor-Bouchard Commission to remove the crucifix in the Quebec National Assembly. Measure that idea against the second and third benchmarks above.

Gilles also wants us to be much more diligent at capitalizing on the capacity of our decentralized democracy to act as a learning society. He wants continuous recycling of the public policy debates, those conversations that never end. What can we learn from our mistakes? What conclusions can we draw from what we have learned? What are the new or emerging false assumptions and erroneous perceptions that must be exposed yet again?

Employing his bitingly wicked wit, Gilles acknowledges that *la méthode* requires a willingness to be blunt, what he calls positive subversion. Very un-Canadian, no fence-sitting allowed. Put on your helmet, declare your conclusion, and *en fonction de ça* propose a response, he insists. Even if you know that it will generate discomfort. Your task is good policy first.

Perhaps a viewer warning is needed here. Gilles would be the first to acknowledge that these are techniques and processes that are not always career enhancing when practised by the uninitiated, particularly if they are public servants or working in any other hierarchical organization. Some of my colleagues at the university view *la méthode* as a leadership formula. That may be true, but effective and sustainable leadership requires more than uncompromised pragmatism. Gilles works primarily in the realm of an *independent* policy analyst here—the supplier of advice to those would-be leaders.

But there is another *petite astuce* at work here. It is about where to find relevance in the inevitable oversupply of data, information, and knowledge that we will uncover in our researches. Job one in *la méthode* is about tagging what is really pertinent to the discussion and what is not important. Doing so requires a capacity for distinguishing "what is" from what others believe "ought to be." When Gilles talks about what ought to be, he means, of course, how the various stakeholders want us to see their problems. What he is looking for here is an analysis that is unencumbered by trying to take into account the often messy and distracting human factors such as "Is the boss, or the minister, going to like this?" As his co-authored book on the Gomery inquiry reminds us, it is the "speak truth to power" thing.

But if you can do that, if you can find the relevant buttons to push, if you can really cut through the fog, there is a good chance of finding blue sky ahead. Gilles knows that, and I have often speculated that this is why he finds such glee in employing his innocent political incorrectness. Watch as he quietly sets aside corporate or cultural assumptions or feigns ignorance of the imponderables—"positive subversion" at work again. *La méthode paquesienne* is about having the courage to accept the conclusions and directions suggested by your research and analysis, your acquired knowledge and understanding. It is at that tipping point where knowledge metamorphoses into wisdom.

Of course, there is much left to unbundle here, but perhaps these reflections can qualify as a loosening of the binder twine.

Part Four
The Fellow Traveller

Chapitre 9

Notes sur une longue et fructueuse collaboration

Jean-Pierre Wallot

Il me semble plus exact de voir l'histoire nationale et l'histoire globale comme deux récits qui s'enrichissent mutuellement

—Anya Zilberstein

On peut s'engoncer dans la liberté au point de s'en étouffer. On peut aussi engloutir ses lecteurs dans le tsunami mortel des épanchements de confidences. Ces deux dangers, comme tant d'autres, nous confrontent au moment de survoler plus de 40 années de collaboration suivie et, somme toute, fructueuse. Encore faut-il faire gaffe si l'un des deux larrons (en l'occurrence, moi-même) écrit sur l'autre (Gilles Paquet) : entre autres, le danger de confondre l'objet d'étude et l'auteur de ce chapitre[1]. De plus, que dire de nos propres carrières personnelles et parallèles ? Bref, on ne peut charcuter la réalité trop finement ni éluder les pièges d'une telle entreprise. Mais en même temps, il faut partager pareille expérience, surtout quand elle implique un être riche comme Gilles Paquet : philosophe en constant éveil, économiste à la recherche d'un élargissement à toute la société, administrateur efficace, architecte social, passionné de l'évolution du Canada, du Québec et du pluralisme, autant de caractéristiques parmi d'autres qui auréolent cette personnalité exceptionnelle. J'ai appris beaucoup de ce commerce et j'aimerais en esquisser ici quelques grands traits.

Les chantiers

La vie nous réserve toutes sortes de surprises. On pourrait rêver de voyages exotiques ou encore d'heureux possibles (bonheur, ciel, parousie, pour reprendre certaines des catégories anciennes). On peut s'enflammer de visions d'amours folles, d'amitiés sans nuage ou de découvertes fondamentales. Y a-t-il quelque sort sublime, quelque parcours sans obstacle, quelque apport imprévisible ? Ou faut-il s'incliner docilement devant des malheurs qui nous flagellent parfois sans interruption ? L'humain façonne-t-il son destin ou le destin conditionne-t-il largement le sillon à creuser ? Peut-on lorgner le pré du voisin avec envie — ou reconnaissance ? Les réponses à nos besoins et à nos désirs surgissent-elles, inattendues, comme les secousses imprévisibles d'une tempête ou comme une accalmie apaisante ? Suffit-il de patienter pour que tout « vienne à point à qui sait attendre » ? Doit-on pousser sa pensée et son action jusqu'au « boutisme » ou s'accommoder plus ou moins bien de situations complexes ? Éternelles questions parmi d'autres qui hantent les humains et qui voltigent, comme des papillons, sur le fil ténu entre un extrême et un autre.

Tel était en tout cas mon état d'esprit au début de la trentaine, après l'obtention de mon doctorat. Je cherchais à me « décorseter » de la chape idéologique dont on m'avait coiffé à l'Université de Montréal. Certes, il serait faux de conclure ici à une condamnation lapidaire de ma formation (excellente d'ailleurs) dont je suis redevable à mes « maîtres ». Mais toutes les universités adhèrent à des théories ou à des problématiques plus ou moins fermes : c'est l'une des raisons d'ailleurs pour lesquelles les bons professeurs incitent souvent leurs étudiants(es) à fureter à droite et à gauche. Orphelin de père depuis l'âge de 19 ans, j'avais dû persévérer dans la même institution car je devais travailler à temps partiel pour payer mes études. Or voilà qu'en 1965-1966, je fais application au Musée de l'Homme (aujourd'hui, le Musée canadien des civilisations) et y suis accepté. Je ne connaissais pas encore la fresque historique de Fernand Ouellet (qui ne paraîtra que plus tard en 1966), mais avais pratiqué cet historien de façon assez suivie. Je disposais par ailleurs d'une banque de documentation socioéconomique amassée entre 1960 et 1965, d'où mon désir de maçonner un indice des revenus et des prix à la consommation. J'écrivis donc à Gideon Rosenbluth, alors en charge de la rencontre annuelle de l'Association canadienne d'économique et de science politique, qui me conseilla d'approcher un jeune chercheur récemment engagé à l'Université Carleton. Il s'agissait du professeur Gilles Paquet, que je n'avais pas encore rencontré. Cependant, je venais de signer un compte-rendu élogieux de l'un de ses articles majeurs paru dans *Recherches sociographiques* (1964) relatif à l'émigration des Canadiens français aux États-Unis. De plus, il était économètre, spécialité fort prisée dans le contexte où je trimais.

Je pris rendez-vous avec « Gilles » — nous nous appellerions très rapidement par nos prénoms. Je lui expliquai mon problème. Empêtré dans une foule de données statistiques importantes, mais complexes, il me fallait construire une courbe des prix et des revenus entre 1791 et 1812. Pouvions-nous travailler ensemble ? Aujourd'hui, l'affaire peut sembler aller de soi. À l'époque, j'étais un nationaliste québécois, associé aux travaux de l'École historique de Montréal (Séguin, Brunet, Frigault, etc.) — une école à forte saveur « nationaliste » —, mais plongeais aussi mes racines dans un passé canadien et européen (du côté de mon père). Gilles Paquet, lui, venait de Québec, plus précisément du « pied de la pente douce » : il était le produit des « sciences sociales » de Laval mais aussi associé à un groupe moins formel — l'École historique de Quebec — plutôt anti-nationaliste (Faucher, Ouellet, etc.) ; ses collègues et amis comptaient de nombreux membres au sein de l'« École historique » de Québec dont au moins un, Fernand Ouellet, enseignait aussi à Carleton.

L'existence de certaines continuités, à ce moment, ne pouvait empêcher la poussée de ce que l'on qualifiait la rupture dans l'évolution socioéconomique et culturelle au Québec. Malgré une sympathie spontanée et certaines affinités de méthode (quoique selon une variété de degrés et d'approches) pour scruter une évolution concrète — la « science », les faits, un ou des modèles théoriques[2], la situation aurait pu être délicate pour l'un et pour l'autre. Pourtant, au lieu de nous asséner des diktats ou de peaufiner des discours creux, nous nous sommes immédiatement impliqués dans l'action : examen de la documentation ; son organisation rationnelle ; recours à des éléments théoriques ou à une problématique pertinente. À l'origine, nous envisagions un projet de durée moyenne de quelques années peut-être. Attitude d'autant plus normale que Gilles comptait emprunter des données sur la longue durée à Fernand Ouellet, l'un de ses collègues et amis. Ce dernier refusa de pactiser avec « l'ennemi » — en l'occurrence moi-même qui ne le connaissais pas encore.

Quoi qu'il en soit, de fil en aiguille, les premières interrogations et les conclusions préliminaires nous ont fait dériver vers des voies sans cesse élargies. La réalité sociale embrasse un ensemble de forces et de freins qui interagissent entre eux. Il fallait toucher plus profondément à l'économique (d'où le concept d'« économie généralisée » emprunté à l'économiste français François Perroux), à la démographie, au social, au politique, au mental, etc. D'où ce long périple de recherches diverses qui se sont révélées finalement inévitables et fécondes tant les questions et les méthodes variaient d'une approche à une autre, tant les éclairages croisés révélaient des perspectives nouvelles. Cette collaboration interdisciplinaire rare a nourri une cosmologie de rechange dans la compréhension du Canada français. Gilles a beaucoup exploité ces conclusions, y compris dans la remise en question de la Révolution tranquille et de son caractère central. Ces travaux ont été l'œuvre de pionniers.

Très tôt, le tourbillon des recherches et des congrès nous a emportés. Trois temps forts ont marqué ces débuts. D'abord, le Congrès d'histoire économique de Léningrad (Saint-Pétersbourg) et le Congrès des sciences historiques de Moscou se succédaient sur deux semaines (en août 1970). À cette époque, il n'y avait pas de micro-ordinateurs. On s'esquintait sur la machine à calculer (avec un ruban pour vérifier !). Quelles soirées qui pendant des mois s'éternisaient dans la nuit, alors qu'au petit matin, il fallait reprendre le collier après quelques heures de sommeil. Nous avons produit un texte de 100 pages, vérifiées et corrigées jusque dans l'avion. Par ailleurs, il ne faudrait pas oublier le premier colloque du GRISCAF (Groupe de recherche sur les idéologies dans la société canadienne-française) à l'Université de Montréal qui attira, entre autres, Robert Palmer et Jacques Godechot, les propagandistes de la thèse de la « Révolution atlantique ». Ce premier colloque fut suivi d'un autre à Concordia (encore Sir George Williams University), en 1971, auquel participa Albert Soboul. À cette occasion, les regards se braquèrent davantage sur les groupes sociaux et les idéologies. Enfin, il ne faut pas oublier non plus notre chapitre de 1969 sur l'évolution de l'histoire économique au Canada.

Je me rappelle aussi la fièvre de la rédaction de l'article sur la « crise agricole », à l'été 1972 (à Vancouver), puis celle du texte sur les groupes sociaux et la lutte pour le pouvoir dans le Bas-Canada qui paraîtrait en 1974. Parallèlement, depuis la fin des années 1960, nous avions commencé à explorer les niveaux de vie et de bien-être de cinq groupes sociaux (seigneurs, marchands, artisans du bois, artisans du fer, habitants) dans le Bas-Canada. Il s'agissait d'une compilation monstre de toutes les données (y compris les données nominatives) dans les inventaires après décès (1792-1812). Plus tard, nous déborderions jusqu'en 1835. Peu en reste, nous avions aussi « spectrographié » le commerce international du Bas-Canada grâce à diverses compilations (détaillées et synthétiques) des entrées et des sorties au port de Québec. Une mouture (encore préliminaire) de tous ces fronts a nourri notre livre *Patronage et pouvoir* (1973) et bien d'autres publications : là encore, on pigeait dans les résultats de plusieurs de ces enquêtes parallèles qui s'interpénétraient toujours davantage. Quant à Gilles, tout au long des décennies, il poursuivrait ses interventions souvent provocantes sur une foule de sujets, en particulier l'émigration des Canadiens français aux États-Unis, la gouvernance, l'évolution des programmes sociaux, l'avenir des sciences humaines, la Révolution tranquille, etc.

Il serait fastidieux de raconter en détail nos « sueurs » et notre production (une cinquantaine de communications, de textes et de livres). Mais le mouvement toujours plus englobant de nos préoccupations nous a inspiré de nombreuses remises en question ou des compléments d'information au cours des années, entre autres : la restructuration et la modernisation de la société québécoise au tournant du XIXe siècle ; la prétendue crise agricole ; le système financier et le régime monétaire bas-canadiens ; l'historiographie socioéconomique de l'évolution du Québec et du Canada ; l'exploitation des inventaires après décès pour cerner les niveaux de richesse des cinq groupes sociaux mentionnés entre 1792 à 1835, Québec et Montréal ; les rentes foncières, les dîmes et les revenus paysans ; les villes comme technologie sociale ; l'impact du marché sur les campagnes canadiennes ; la Nouvelle-France, le Québec et le Canada : un monde d'identités limitées ; les discontinuités socioéconomiques dans l'histoire du Québec/Bas-Canada ; la propriété foncière et les niveaux de richesse dans les campagnes, voire la stratégie foncière des habitants des régions de Québec et de Montréal ; une spectrographie des genres de vie dans les campagnes ; la culture matérielle ; le crédit et l'endettement en milieu rural bas-canadien ; les archives notariales comme révélatrices de la trame socioéconomique ; la Coutume de Paris et les inégalités socioéconomiques au Québec ; etc.

Les « leçons »

On pourra s'étonner que les premiers paragraphes relatent certains détails couvrant quelques années, alors que la suite embrasse trente ans en un paragraphe. En réalité, ce chapitre ne vise pas tellement à mettre en valeur nos « épopées », souvent insérées dans des enquêtes d'histoire comparée de la France de l'Ouest, du Québec/Canada et, plus tard, de la Suisse. Il vise plutôt à répondre partiellement à deux questions : d'abord, que peut-on tirer d'un si long cheminement ensemble, d'une fréquentation avec un être extraordinaire comme Gilles Paquet ? ; puis, comment avons-nous pu travailler aussi longtemps sans nous colleter, sans rouspéter sur qui fait quoi, etc. ? Combien de fois certains collègues nous ont aspergé de pareilles questions, identifiant même l'auteur (supposé) de telle ou telle partie d'un texte. On nous a reproché également de sombrer dans les sables mouvants de la « théorie » : arme à deux tranchants s'il en est une, car elle met en cause soit l'énonciation des éléments théoriques et leur pertinence (responsabilité des auteurs), soit le manque de familiarité avec les éléments théoriques ou la paresse (responsabilité des lecteurs), etc.

Quoi qu'il en soit, un certain nombre de leçons émanent de cette longue fréquentation (plus de 42 ans). Elles méritent qu'on les énumère car elles dessinent certains traits essentiels à une collaboration scientifique productrice. D'abord, il faut pouvoir partager des éléments et des méthodes complémentaires qui s'enrichissent et acculent les chercheurs à explorer de nouvelles avenues. S'il n'y a pas de « valeur ajoutée », le jeu n'en vaut pas la chandelle. Mieux vaut rester « amis », se voir occasionnellement et boire de bons vins. D'autant que dans un vrai partenariat, le travail s'avère beaucoup plus ardu pour chacun : il faut spécifier le ou les problèmes à clarifier, définir le rôle de chacun, manipuler le matériau comme une pâte fragile sertie de pièges et de joyaux souvent secrets au premier abord, se convaincre mutuellement — tâche souvent pénible compte tenu de points de départ aussi divers —, savoir se délester de présupposés trop souvent inconscients, procéder à plusieurs rédactions, ensemble et séparément, etc. En ce domaine, Gilles était et demeure le roi. Comme il le dit fréquemment, il faut « être des chercheurs d'or, non des trouveurs d'or ».

Avant ou assez tôt après un tour d'horizon, nous cherchions une problématique ou des éléments théoriques articulés qui permettraient d'organiser le dossier documentaire. L'histoire, ont dit tant d'historiens, ne se réduit pas à un ramassis de faits. Son vrai rôle est d'expliquer, de faire comprendre un savoir complexe d'événements, de personnes, de forces de toute nature interagissant dans le temps. Tâche impossible sans le recours à une problématique, officielle ou non, explicitée ou non. « Je pense, donc je suis », disait Descartes. Les « scientifiques » affirment aussi penser : ils devraient donc exploiter les données directes et indirectes, fouiner le cas échéant dans des sources peu amènes, interpréter et non seulement raconter. Bref, ils doivent donner un sens à l'aventure humaine, qu'elle soit de petite ou de grande échelle. Or les données, les « faits » historiques, ce sont les historiens qui les identifient et les qualifient de tels. D'où les interminables débats sur l'« objectivité » de l'histoire et des autres sciences sociales, sans parler des sciences dites pures. Aussi la présence de deux regards aiguisés et entraînés à questionner la documentation différemment, sans gommer leur caractère partiellement subjectif, ne peut que rehausser la qualité finale du produit.

Il est arrivé aussi que certains thèmes ont sommeillé plus ou moins longtemps dans nos classeurs : l'un ou l'autre ressentait un malaise et n'était pas prêt à accoucher sans une réflexion plus poussée. Il faut donc s'en remettre au principe que l'on ne publie qu'une fois l'accord réalisé. L'amitié est précieuse. Mais l'intégrité, la recherche de la vérité, la clarté, la qualité du texte, la nécessité de se coiffer du chapeau de chef de l'opposition à certains moments, autant de principes et de pratiques auxquels il faut recourir. Mieux vaut rester sur sa faim que de publier un texte insatisfaisant. Là-dessus, Gilles était d'une probité et d'une ténacité extraordinaires. Il répétait souvent qu'il fallait faire confiance à l'avenir ; qu'il convenait de recourir parfois à une franchise « brutale ». Je pense notamment à l'article sur la crise agricole, à celui sur les groupes sociaux, à celui sur l'apprentissage du pouvoir, à celui sur le système financier bas-canadien, etc. À cause de cette approche, ces textes ont pu enrichir l'historiographie.

Comment avons-nous pu cheminer ensemble (et séparément aussi) pendant plus de quatre décennies ? Il est possible que le hasard aurait pu se pointer : mais Gilles a changé d'université et j'ai moi-même voyagé entre Montréal et Ottawa. Pas une année ou deux ne s'est écoulée sans que nous produisions telle(s) ou telle(s) œuvre(s), y compris notre « somme » de 2007[3] et notre travail actuel sur le « foncier » (avec Jean Lafleur). Nous avons aussi coopéré avec la « SRC » — entendons : la Société Radio-Canada (survol de l'histoire économique du Canada) en 1980-1981 et la Société royale du Canada (aujourd'hui, Les Académies des arts, des lettres et des sciences du Canada) à diverses occasions durant la présidence de Gilles et la mienne (à la fin des années 1990 et au début des années 2000). Nos explorations communes ont même alimenté nos ré-interprétations sur le passé récent du Québec. Comme me l'expliquait Gilles récemment, « Un Québec moderne est pour moi un accomplissement important, impossible à réaliser seul ».

L'amitié entre hommes comporte presque toujours une part de pudeur. On peut se connaître 20, 30 ou 40 ans. Par confidences directes, généralement étalées dans le temps, surtout par observation ou par des rumeurs, on peut deviner les avatars d'une vie, le sens possible de certaines décisions, la clé d'une saute d'humeur. Mais on ne pénètre dans cet univers qu'à petits pas, sans se livrer à des assauts trop directs. Parfois, les circonstances s'y prêtent mieux, mais chacun protège une part de son intimité. Éventuellement, les passions et les désirs s'estompent, la familiarité s'insinue peu à peu. Si les personnes ont quelque grandeur d'âme, on doit leur faire confiance, surtout dans les coups durs. Ce qui ne suppose nullement une reddition sans condition.

Gilles Paquet est une personne d'une très grande qualité, d'une intelligence aiguisée, d'une vivacité sans pareille, qui aime d'ailleurs (parfois) les combats pour eux-mêmes ou s'affiche spontanément « chef de l'opposition » pour nous acculer dans nos derniers retranchements. Cette qualité suppose une capacité à revoir toutes les options, à les jauger, à arrêter l'approche la plus juste pour avancer nos positions, pour arrondir leurs angles trop pointus le cas échéant. Son écorce parfois dure cache mal une loyauté à toute épreuve, une fidélité à certains principes de base (documentation abondante, probité, vérité, nuances, honnêteté, mention des sources secondaires, etc.), un grand respect des « anciens » qu'il critique d'après ses données, mais sans y prendre plaisir (sauf exception !), bref un être à qui ses collègues — et le public plus large — ont pu décerner postes de direction, honneurs et causes désespérées ! C'est pourquoi j'ai eu l'immense honneur de travailler avec lui si longtemps et d'apprendre les rudiments concrets de l'interdisciplinarité.

Notes

[1] Malgré les apparences, il ne faut pas céder à l'illusion toujours possible que l'auteur se glorifie à travers un autre.
[2] Ainsi, Gilles Paquet atténuerait considérablement la portée de la « Révolution tranquille ». Voir son livre *Oublier la Révolution tranquille*, Montréal, Liber, 1999.
[3] G. Paquet et J.-P. Wallot, *Un Québec moderne 1760-1840 : Essai d'histoire économique et sociale*, Montréal, HMH, 2007.

Chapter 10

An Intimate Vignette

John Meisel

The major focus of a festschrift is invariably the body of work that its hero has contributed to the world, work that calls for being defined and applauded by his or her friends and admirers. Since there is nothing at all *invariable* or predictable about Gilles Paquet—the *raison d'être* for this volume—this paper addresses not so much the *œuvre* as the *œuvrier*, to coin a pun.

My first idea for this very personal reflection was to attempt an utterly unconventional piece befitting so non-conformist and original a *rara avis* as Paquet. In the 1950s and early 1960s, I had become quite friendly with professor Albert Faucher, the celebrated ornament of Laval's fine economics department. He was a brilliant scholar and an utterly lovable human being. And he also turned out to have been Gilles's mentor at Laval. Albert alerted me to his student's intention to go to Queen's for graduate studies. I was, in a sense, introduced to Gilles by Albert, for whom I had immense respect and affection. Any friend of Faucher's was a friend of mine. A few years later I was not surprised to find that the excellent entry on Faucher in *The Canadian Encyclopedia* was penned by Gilles.

Faucher was not a number-crunching economist but an economic historian who clearly saw how economic, social, and political realities penetrated one another and together defined the contours of societies. His probes into Quebec's past were seminal and influential, affecting, *inter alia*, Gilles's outlook and perceptions. Knowing this, and knowing how much Gilles admired his old "Mr. Chips," I had the idea that a nifty paper for this book would be to engage in an exercise of postdicting (the opposite of predicting) his mind as a young Québécois *before* he arrived at Queen's and to gauge what, in his persona, reflected salient features of Quebec, as delineated by Faucher. The rare methodological device of postdicting had been applied to elections in Canada by Jean Laponce (1972), a free spirit whose mind in some respects resembled Paquet's in resourcefulness and originality.

An equally daring postdicting notion would have been to reconstruct Paquet's childhood characteristics from the young man whom Gilles had become once he left his home province. In the end, sanity prevailed, and I realized that it would be madness to out-Paquet Paquet. I abandoned the two postdicting experiments and instead turned to a less hazardous project: namely, identifying some of his essential traits based on the many interactions that I have had with Gilles the person rather than the pure public intellectual, writer, media personality, or policy wonk.

The first magnet drawing us together was, not surprisingly, my then major research interest, a project exploring the use of statistics in analyzing elections. A little before Gilles arrived at Queen's, I had launched studies of recent elections in the Kingston federal and provincial constituencies. They provided the basis of my first serious academic paper in the field, on the role of religious affiliation in voting (Meisel 1956). Methodologically, they drew on a wide range of approaches, inspired by such diverse scholars as André Siegfried in France; R. B. McCallum and his Nuffield College colleagues in the United Kingdom; and Columbia's The People's Choice team under Lazarsfeld in the United States.

Although my work was well received, several friends observed that it would have benefited from the application of available statistical tests. Steve Kaliski, now in the Queen's economics department (but then at Carleton), was one of these friends. Gilles was a bright graduate student at Queen's with quantitative skills, and I enlisted him as a research assistant. He and I eventually wrote a paper together (Meisel and Paquet 1964) that became something of a classic, primarily because it was one of the earliest efforts exploring ways to buttress with statistical tools Canadian political analysis and because, as such, it illustrated the primitive stage of Canadian so-called political science at the time. It also prompted an excellent and suggestive commentary from Muni Frumhartz in the same book as Meisel and Paquet, pp 32-38. Ten years later it would have been considered a laughably oversimplified and unnecessary exercise. We presented it to a special session on statistics held by the Canadian Political Science Association at its annual meeting in Hamilton (McMaster), and it was published with other contributions to two statistical panels of the CPSA.

Our paper was not of lasting scientific significance, but while the result of our collaboration may have been a shade less than earth-shattering it was respectable enough, and it provided a truly stimulating, pleasant, and sometimes amusing collaboration among our team. The team consisted not only of Gilles and me but also of Charles Gordon and Nancy Thain. The two eventually married and attained fame in their respective *métiers*, journalism and international aid, in part, I tell myself, because of the experience that the four of us enjoyed in producing something of an experimental paper. It was hard and intensive work but also much fun because all of us approached our task in a light-hearted manner and because we felt something of a *frisson* from being pioneers.

The primary focus of our efforts was to explore how, in the absence of surveys (which, at the time, were still prohibitively expensive; see Meisel forthcoming), various ways of determining the strength of correlations made it possible to be more precise than heretofore when measuring the effects on electoral behaviour of a wide variety of demographic variables. One factor—the impact of economic conditions on the voter—caused us particular trouble but was obviously so important that it could not be neglected. Our basic approach in most of the paper was to superimpose electoral districts on census tracts, or vice versa, and to use the rich material contained in official statistical data drawn from the census to obtain correlations between socioeconomic and demographic conditions and voting choice. To our chagrin, we discovered that income data—essential to our purposes—were ascertained only in the decennial full census and not in the smaller mid-term snapshots of the Canadian population that were more appropriate for our purposes. The latter did, however, report on the number of lodgers in each census tract. We hypothesized that, the lower the proportion of people renting their homes, the higher the incomes and vice versa. This highly circuitous approach (and slightly tongue-in-cheek assumption) amused us to no end and endowed our testing of what we termed "the lodger hypothesis" with much humour. Despite the frivolous dimension of the enterprise, we applied a series of statistical tests to it, including regressions that, at the time, were still seen by some political scientists as daringly innovative. The expected relationship held in Toronto but less well in Montreal.

This long song and dance about what we were about provides the background for the ensuing account of why I was so favourably impressed with Gilles and how this brief interaction shed so much light on him and on the manner in which his life later unfolded. Space for research was always scarce in those days, but Queen's managed to come up with a laboratory in Ellis Hall, the home of civil engineering, quite close to my office. It was likely this unusual working space that later led Gilles to refer to this episode as "*ce séjour comme apprenti dans son laboratoire.*" Since the team functioned mainly in the summer, we were in no one's way and were free to spread ourselves all over the innumerable workstations in the lab. Our quartet of psephologists was almost lost in this brightly lit vastness, but the sense of humour and cheerful disposition of its occupants overwhelmed the institutional and somewhat sterile setting. Gilles, although a little older than Charley and Nancy, and coming from a different culture, got along famously with them and did not seem to be at all put off by the slight skepticism with which they—particularly Charley—viewed his statistical armoury. All three were predisposed to intercultural fraternization. The Quebecker was in the minority but had not a whit of a minority complex and became totally integrated into the team in no time. This capacity to easily bridge Canada's linguistic and ethnic divides has been one of his outstanding gifts, one that Gilles has used throughout his life to strengthen the performance of some of our major educational, governmental, research, and media institutions. He has unerringly placed emphasis on the function of any organization or group and not on the ethnic, linguistic, or religious dimension, unless these dimensions impinged on its goals or purposes.

The most astonishing aspect of Paquet's involvement in our project, and then again in his career, was his willingness—an economist in training at first and then in earnest—to stray from the narrow confines of his discipline into the much broader and more fluid area of politics. The Queen's economics department was and still is heavily weighted toward parsimonious economic theory, model building, and the like rather than the less formal domain of social and political studies. And even some aspects of economic history, Albert Faucher's for example, play a lesser role in its universe than in that of some other departments. Gilles, I believe, found this focus rather dry and welcomed an escape into the more congenial domain of electoral politics and the application to it of some of the probes more widely employed, at the time, by economists rather than political scientists. His career strongly supports this impression since, though never completely pulling his big toe out of the economics pool, his professional interests focused largely on public administration, management, and the whole spectrum of decision making, mostly in the public sector, as well as on the place of ideas in society, not to mention just about every aspect of life, whether related to economics or not. So, in a sense, Gilles strayed from a monastic commitment to economics before he even completed his formal training in that discipline.

In a recent miniature self-portrait, Gilles refers to himself as a student of governance and a "practitioner of what Lon Fuller called—eunomics—the study of good order and workable social arrangements, and what others call the economics of governance," a field that has little to do with what hard-nosed university economists teach their students (Paquet 2008c, 30).[1]

This slight non-conformity was an early indication of the approach to many of the challenges and issues that Paquet has confronted ever since. A broad problem-focused perspective is always preferred over the adherence to some disciplinary or ideological adoration of the saints. His freewheeling urge to see and try to resolve problems without being fettered by a specific dogma, though its roots cannot be uniquely ascribed to the "lodger hypothesis" days, has characterized much of his work and has given it its unexpected, surprising character. If there is a hint of orthodoxy, it is that Gilles likes to be something of a contrariant. Conventional wisdom is seldom safe under his gaze.

Our quantitative analysis of election results was a precursor to another of his predilections: the use of new technology in the service of one's craft. While statistics was hardly new, its application to electoral analysis was still rare in those days and needed to be improved and popularized in Canada. Gilles liked that. Years later, as a pioneer in quite a different new technology, the electronic dissemination of knowledge and analysis, he adopted and magnificently utilized electronic publishing in the exciting and rich *Optimum Online: The Journal of Public Sector Management*, of which he is the founding editor. It continues the high standards of its printed predecessor but vastly expands its scope and reach by exploiting the flexibility of the web.

The aforementioned paper containing a brief self-portrait deals with linguistic minorities and attests to his enduring interest in language use in Canadian society, and in relations between francophones, anglophones, and allophones. An early exposure occurred when Gilles landed at Queen's and joined the little band of toilers in Ellis Hall. That tiny group, although only four in number, represented the three linguistic traditions so characteristic of Canada. Throughout his career, Gilles has been a student of this defining feature of our land and someone actively engaged in preventing this situation from exacting undue social costs and, on the contrary, positively enriching our collective experiences. It is no accident that Gilles played critical roles in both of Ottawa's great universities, Carleton and Ottawa (one English speaking, the other bilingual but principally French speaking), and that he eventually settled into the latter, Canada's quintessential academic linguistic crossroads. He would, needless to say, have confronted that challenge even without having been plunged into it while in Kingston, but I like to think that this experience started him on the way, although none of us was even dimly conscious at the time of that dimension in our intercourse and of its implications.

That Gilles expanded so effortlessly and so early from economics to political analysis and turned to pastures non-economic is not at all surprising in light of the subsequent evolution of his thought processes. A striking and delightful aspect of so much of his writing is its eclecticism and its frequent evocation of works, ideas, and examples from diverse cultures, disciplines, art forms, and times. Gilles is familiar with a rich world of diverse myths, literatures, traditions, art forms, and cultures. Consequently, exotic and hence striking allusions and examples lace his substantive analyses, adding nuance and colour to his arguments, and unexpected references and images to his titles.

Having squeezed the foregoing out of my recollections of one happy collaboration with Gilles, I can move on to touch upon a couple of other highlights. The first is extremely personal and should probably not even be considered within so formal and exalted an enterprise as a festschrift. But, again, I justify taking huge personal liberties here on the ground that Gilles has demonstrably and consistently been happy, and perhaps even driven, to defy the expected, the usual, and the "normal." After all, the title for this book is *Gilles Paquet: Homo Hereticus*. He may therefore welcome being on the receiving end of non-conformist treatment. For my part, I follow the famous advice that it is better to give than to receive. This is a big build-up for a relatively small thing, but it is anything but small in my mind.

In 1982, a couple of years after I went to Ottawa to head up the Canadian Radio-television and Telecommunications Commission, I was asked by the rector of the University of Ottawa whether I would accept an honorary doctorate from the university. This was a complete bolt out of the blue, totally unexpected and literally awesome in its impact. The thought had heretofore never entered my head that I was in this sort of league. I confess that since then I have been fortunate to be similarly honoured by a number of other universities, and the surprise that I should be considered worthy of such an accolade wore off a little, although each subsequent invitation still elicited a colossal sense of gratitude and an unseemly touch of pride. But the University of Ottawa was the first, and its impact was thus unrivalled. That it was also as close as we have ever come to a bilingual and bicultural institution in Canada appealed to me to no end since this was a cause for which I had metaphorically shed a lot of blood.

Universities sometimes bestow *honoris causa* degrees on wealthy folks, or those with a lot of influence, in the expectation that some financial or other tangible benefit will follow. No such *revanche* could have been expected of me, a threadbare academic masquerading in mandarin clothing. I did not lose much sleep over why I had been chosen or how the award had come about and just assumed that my involvement with language accommodation was being recognized by a "language-sensitive" institution. After more experience with honorary degrees, both as a recipient and as a member of committees involved in the decision-making process, I came to realize that these treasured diplomas do not grow on trees and that in most cases some champion lurking in the background toils and lobbies on behalf of a candidate. Enter Gilles Paquet. I did not tumble onto this at first, but should have, since my citation was delivered by the dean of the Faculty of Administration—G. P. himself—and bore unmistakable marks of his pen. I have been too discreet ever since to ask whether my hunch was right but am sure of it.

Again a long palaver to make a point. It leads to the discovery that Gilles, the national figure, professional giant, and public intellectual, also harbours beneath his official robes the heart of a warm, private person, to whom human relationships and friendships *are* important, the outward, curmudgeon-like persona notwithstanding. The citation for my ceremony, while touching the usually required bases, also touched my heart for its warmth and a very generous acknowledgement of my part in our joint publication twenty years previously. Paquet, the *Mensch*, is sometimes unseen but is present more often than is usually perceived and acknowledged, perhaps even by Gilles himself.

Since in many respects we moved for years in more or less the same circles, our paths crossed repeatedly over the years, usually at academic conferences and symposia or at gatherings where profs and officials mingled over some issue or problem. A much sought-after speaker, Gilles occasionally had scheduling problems, but my memories contain a whole flow of events in which we chewed on the same bone and in which I was invariably stimulated by his ideas. I cannot now distinguish the specific venue of any one such encounter but do recall one particular organization where our paths often overlapped, although we did our heftiest lifting within it at different times. It is the Royal Society of Canada—now renamed, thanks in part to Gilles's efforts, RSC: The Academies of Arts, Humanities, and Sciences of Canada.

Gilles was without doubt the modern era's foremost pooh-bah of the society, at various times serving as the president of its Académie des lettres et des sciences humaines, honorary secretary, honorary treasurer, and president. He also, among other initiatives, launched a series of joint meetings at different universities, characteristically named by him Conferences on Taboo Topics. During my presidency, 1992–95, he happened not to hold any office, but he sympathetically observed my fruitless efforts to put the RSC on a sound financial footing. A few years later, when Gilles was president, he made a massive effort to the same end, radically changing the structure and even the name of the venerable old academy but, insofar as the kitty went, without any greater success. The Royal Society of Canada was founded in 1882 and is one of the country's oldest and most respected institutions among both of the country's linguistic communities. The kudos that it enjoys are illustrated, among other things, by its president being an *ex officio* member of the committee deciding who is to be inducted into the Order of Canada. To propose fundamental structural changes, new criteria for eligibility and a new name, and to make significant changes in the election process, are all extraordinarily bold and far-reaching changes, transforming the organization. It remains to be seen what the effects of the new order will be on the society and its capacity to perform the role of an autonomous intellectual leader in Canada. Whatever its merits, however, Gilles's spear-heading the process that brought about these tectonic shifts took extraordinary self-confidence and courage. Irrespective of the final outcome, one must admire the cool-headed resolve and energy that in effect created the new national academy.

In one of the classics of crime fiction, Dorothy Sayers's *Murder Must Advertise* (1933), Miss Meteyard says to Lord Peter Wimsey, "Things have to happen. You're one of the sort that pushes round and makes them happen. I prefer to leave them alone. You've got to have both kinds."[2] During most of his life, Gilles has sought to push things around indirectly by teaching, writing, and broadcasting. His presidency of the Royal Society of Canada and some of his consultancies reveal that, when the occasion arises, he can be daring enough to sully his hands in action, even when the consequences are of the greatest moment.

It is a telling commentary on his hierarchy of values that Gilles devoted so much time and energy to one of Canada's premier intellectual associations. He highly prizes its commitment to excellence, its transcendence of disciplinary ghettos, and its national scope. He saw in the society, *inter alia*, a potentially powerful instrument for the infusion into policy and other applied fields the products of the country's best independent minds. That its potential was inadequately realized was, without doubt, a primary motive in his efforts to energize and remake it. His indefatigable striving to this end did not, in my view, achieve anything like all the results he wished for. But they attest to a fundamental tenet of his being: that imperfection calls for being tackled, that the citizen should not merely tolerate things that aren't right but should seek to improve them. Gilles is too much of a realist to expect perfection but, *au fond*, despite a somewhat misanthropic mien, believes that people and hence institutions are amenable, when the will and the skill are present, to being improved to better serve the public good.

Flash! An Addendum

No sooner had I finished this piece, which was to end here, when a parcel arrived at my door from a publisher containing not one but two volumes of spankingly new books by Gilles. They offer screamingly loud testimony to his going full blast ahead, little fatigued by the antecedent forty-five years of toil. The book in your hands will have to be only the first volume of an ongoing series.

The parcel led to another gratifying insight: my interpretation of where Gilles wishes to place his intellectual marbles, as sketched above, is confirmed and reinforced. One book, *Deep Cultural Diversity: A Governance Challenge* (Paquet 2008a), is an iconoclastic re-examination of much current conventional wisdom on the subject that has, as I indicated, engaged Gilles off and on for a long time. The subtitle of the introduction says it all: "Diversity as Weasel Word and Multiculturalism as Questionable" (1). The other, *Tableau d'avancement: Petite ethnographie interprétative d'un certain Canada français* (Paquet 2008b), takes us right back to Albert Faucher, with whom I started this chapter. Indeed, Albert is referred to on the first page of the text proper. The theme of the work is a new interpretation of Quebec's history, going beyond the currently fashionable overemphasis on the unique role and primordial importance of the Quiet Revolution. It points to the relevance of other political, intellectual, and institutional factors, and it contains fascinating chapters on a number of profoundly formative other causal actors and events. It is a succinct invitation to the reader to rethink Quebec's history in a fresh light. Paquet here goes back to his old master and carries on his work. Can you hear Faucher clapping in the wings?

Notes

[1] For an essay that sees eunomics as the fusion of the values of law with the empirical data and methods of the objective sciences, see Lazar (1963).
[2] The quotation is from my 1959 paperback edition in the New English Library (254).

References

Laponce, J. (1972). "Post-Dicting Electoral Cleavages in Canadian Federal Elections, 1949–1969." *Canadian Journal of Political Science, 7.2*, 270–86.

Lazar, J. (1963). "Eunomics and Justice." *Duke Law Journal, 2*, 269–80.

Meisel, J. (1956). "Religious Affiliation and Electoral Behaviour: A Case Study." *Canadian Journal of Economics and Political Science, 22.4*, 481–96.

———. (Forthcoming). "Clio, Psephos, and Calculi: How We Started." In *Four Decades of Canadian Election Studies: Learning from the Past and Planning for the Future*, ed. Mebs Kanji, Antoine Bilodeau, and Thomas Scotto.

Meisel, J., and G. Paquet. (1964). "Some Quantitative Analyses of Canadian Election Results." In *Conference on Statistics 1962 and 1963*, ed. J. Henripin and A. Asimakopulos. Toronto: University of Toronto Press, 1–31.

Paquet, G. (2008a). *Deep Cultural Diversity: A Governance Challenge*. Ottawa: University of Ottawa Press.

———. (2008b). *Tableau d'avancement: Petite ethnographie interprétative d'un certain Canada français*. Ottawa: Presses de l'Université d'Ottawa.

———. (2008c). "Vitality of Linguistic Minorities in Canada: Two Perspectives." *Optimum Online, 38.2*, 30-46. www.optimumonline.ca [consulted January 15, 2009]

Sayers, D. (1933). *Murder Must Advertise*. London: Victor Gollancz.

Section II

The Impact

[I]l y a des cas où l'imagination fait le bonheur de la tactique.
—Jacques Perret

This section looks at Gilles Paquet in terms of the impact that he has had over the decades.

Here we see the threads of professional scholar, public intellectual, and classical educator somewhat more clearly. At the same time, albeit in a small way, the contributions themselves add a little more to a picture of the man himself.

We see his impact in terms of organizational repositioning—setting out with courage and determination to enable others to make the highest and best use of the possible in facing the future. We see his impact in terms of inspiring the thinking of others. And we are treated to a broad range of views of Gilles engaging others with new concepts and frames, always in pursuit of better societal stewardship.

Part Five
Repositioning

Chapter 11

Dean of Graduate Studies and Research, Carleton University, 1973–1979

Don McEown and H. Blair Neatby

When Gilles Paquet attended his first meeting as dean in September 1973, it was announced that the doctoral programs in chemistry and economics had received qualified assessments as part of the sector assessments undertaken at the provincial level by the Advisory Committee on Academic Planning (ACAP). It was the first time that a university system decision had a negative impact upon the university. While there is no record in the Senate minutes for that meeting of a reaction to the news by the new dean, there is in later minutes a copy of a document entitled "Speculative Notes about ACAP and Planning: For Internal Discussion Only," dated fall 1973. Dean Paquet began these notes with the following statement: "Much of what follows is based on some assumptions about the nature of ACAP for it is less important to try to cope with its activities of yesterday than to be prepared to make the highest and best use of its activities of tomorrow."[1] This statement shows his approach to the problems that he was asked to solve. Paquet wanted his colleagues to expend their energies in preparing for the future and not to waste their time trying to find answers to the problems of the past. In a period of constant change and adjustment, his approach was the most practical. He would often find it difficult to convince others to accept that approach.

In 1973, the new dean of Graduate Studies at Carleton was faced with two major and very complex problems. The first was to fit Carleton into the provincial university system so that it could maximize its talents and opportunities. The second was to sustain growth, both in quality and in quantity, of graduate studies and research in a time of retrenchment and despair.

In the decade prior to his appointment, university growth in Ontario was explosive. From a few universities of modest size, Ontario quickly evolved to a university system of fourteen provincially assisted institutions varying from small to large and from new to old. In that decade, the environment in which these universities operated also dramatically changed from self-governing institutions that received annual government grants to provide a university education to a small set of the population, to a government-funded system of self-governing institutions of mass education. One of the significant engines of this growth would be the expansion of graduate studies because more students required more professors. Since the rest of the world was experiencing the same growth, the new professors could not be provided by the universities of the United States and Europe. Ontario would have to train many of the faculty that it would need.

It was around the management of graduate expansion that a provincial system for the universities began to evolve in the province and in which each university's dean of Graduate Studies became a critical player. At the beginning of the period, the existing universities and the Ontario government came to an agreement that, if the government funded the expansion of the universities so that every qualified student would have a place while maintaining the autonomy of each institution, the universities would undertake the necessary growth to handle the demand. This agreement did not provide the necessary mechanism for the planning and coordination of such growth. It soon became apparent that, to make the program work, some coordination among the universities particularly at the graduate level was necessary, so a commission known as the Spinks Commission was appointed to study the issue. Its recommendation to create a University of Ontario was rejected by the government and the universities, but its analysis of the various forces at play drove the universities and the province to give greater definition to a structure that had been evolving as a product of the general growth.

It had three parts. The first was the Council of Ontario Universities (COU), whose members were the universities in the province and represented by the president of each institution and a faculty member elected by each institution's Senate. The second was the Ontario Council on University Affairs, whose members included the public at large, government officials, and academics appointed by the government and serving as a buffer body between the universities and the government. The third was the Ministry of University Affairs, which administered the funds granted by the government to universities and their students. COU soon recognized that, unless it took some action to coordinate graduate work, the government would, so it established the Ontario Council on Graduate Studies (OCGS), on which each university's dean of Graduate Studies was a member, and it in turn established two subcommittees. One was the Appraisals Committee, which had the task of overseeing the conduct of appraisals of graduate programs in terms of their quality. The other was the Advisory Committee on Academic Planning (ACAP), which oversaw the conduct of assessments of graduate work by sectors to identify which graduate programs existed and their capacity to meet the needs of the province. It was the first set of ACAP assessments that greeted Dean Paquet at his first Senate meeting.

The dean of Graduate Studies had an important and difficult role to play in this process. COU was a collection of individual, self-governing institutions and operated by consensus. Any rules that it adopted had to be accepted, grudgingly or otherwise, by most if not all of its members. The rules governing assessments and appraisals had been set by OCGS and approved by COU. Each appraisal and assessment was vetted and commented upon by OCGS before being considered and acted upon by COU. No university was bound by the decision in that it could continue or begin a graduate program without COU approval, but because there would be no grants for students enrolled in such programs, as a practical matter, lack of COU approval meant that an institution was unlikely to mount or keep such graduate programs.

Each dean faced unique problems. Because graduate work and the accompanying research activity comprise the stuff of any university's reputation, their advancement is critical to its development of any institution, especially in an era of financial constraint. The Ontario university system consisted of basically three types of institutions: larger and older full-range institutions with some established graduate program, and the ambition and confidence that they should have a lot more; younger and medium-sized institutions with the beginnings of graduate programs in certain areas and the ambition to become larger with more graduate work; and the new universities, which had little graduate activity and that limited to master's work. Each dean thus had to find solutions to problems that would work and be acceptable to colleagues found at the provincial level yet satisfactory to an anxious clientele at home. Assessments and appraisals of doctoral programs were the primary area of concern.

This provincial role for the dean of Graduate Studies was still undefined when Dean Paquet took office. Few at Carleton understood it, and even fewer appreciated its significance to the operation of the university. It became critical that the role of the graduate faculty and its dean, being the interface between the system and the university, be changed from what it was in the past. Traditionally, the Faculty of Graduate Studies through its dean was to control quality, and the instruments used were the process of admissions and the conduct of examinations, especially the thesis exam. Now the facts of competitive growth and being part of a system meant that there needed to be much more planning and coordination of the university's graduate work and in turn its research activities. Thus, one of the first tasks that professor Paquet undertook as dean was the restructuring of the Faculty of Graduate Studies.

It was not an easy task to persuade others to change their ways. In the documents that were in play leading up to the changes that were finally realized, Dean Paquet describes the attitude of the members of the university in the following manner: "Carleton is less paralyzed by tradition than by a belief that small decisions originating from the different constituencies will be harmonized by an 'invisible hand' automatically. Consequently it is always very difficult to persuade the Carleton community of the need for concertation [*sic*] and planning. Moreover, each constituency is jealous enough of its autonomy that each has proved rather hostile to most attempts to construct federated bodies for the purpose of harmonizing policies."[2]

There was also a need to provide a research administration function at the university. The question often raised (after the question of whether the university should have such an office or not was solved) was whether it should be separate from, or part of, Graduate Studies. In time, without much discussion, it was agreed that it was an activity that should be undertaken as a function of a Faculty of Graduate Studies and Research. In describing what he thought the faculty should do, the dean wrote,

> However it should be clear that if these functions and concerns (research and graduate studies) overlap to a great extent, they do not overlap completely. On the graduate studies front, the Faculty of Graduate Studies and Research shall have to focus on *monitoring* and *planning* functions designed to ensure and maintain the highest standards of instruction

and the highest quality relationship between graduate students and their supervisors. On the research front the Faculty of Graduate Studies and Research will focus on *information*, *service* and *animation* functions to help members of the community make the highest and best use of the potentialities and of the available resources for individuals or group research.[3]

On looking back on the establishment of the Faculty of Graduate Studies and Research, we are surprised that it happened so quickly and without much fuss. University governance had been an explosive issue in the recent past, and the various governing bodies newly constituted were the result of a bitter fight over reforms, and everyone was determined to protect the new jurisdictions. We think that part of the explanation for its relatively easy passage lies with the way in which the dean presented the case for change. His arguments for change concentrated on meeting the challenges of the future, and his proposed organization was widely based so that all could participate in its decisions but was sufficiently focused so that those decisions could be implemented. The other reason for its easy passage may have been that members of the university had their minds on other things.

Growth in the previous decade was not the only factor that changed universities. There was a great deal of social change, particularly as it applied to that age group that populated universities. It was the era of student revolution, and its impact was felt on the institutions in three major ways: how the institution was governed, the form of the curriculum and how it was taught, and student life outside the classroom. By the end of the decade, a major sea change had occurred in the relationship of the student to the university. Now students were members of the board and Senate, arts and social sciences degree programs had less structure, and there were co-ed residences. The university was no longer *in loco parentis* to the student, and there were bars on campus. Deans were no longer the father figure, kindly or otherwise, but tough-minded managers bound by rules dealing with a much more sophisticated clientele than their predecessors.

Carleton's experience of this period was much the same as the others in the system, but Carleton probably had less difficulty making the adjustment than most. Carleton was not fixed in its ways by a long history but old enough to have sufficient maturity and stability to manage change, and students and faculty exhibited great tolerance for, and understanding of, the range of ideas and potentially disruptive forces that permeated the environment. Most of those who worked at the university would probably credit the president of the day, A. D. Dunton, with the quiet success that the institution achieved during the 1960s. A man of great grace and charm, popular with students and faculty alike, he had a light touch at the helm of the university and skilfully made the best of its people to keep the institution on an even keel during a very stormy period.

Carleton, when it changed from Carleton College to Carleton University in 1957, had a full-time student population of about 600. During the 1960s, Carleton University grew on average about one Carleton College a year. Beginning in 1960, with a full-time enrolment of 1,148, it grew to 8,271 by 1970. In 1960, it had just moved to a new campus, with about five buildings in place, and by 1970 it had two campuses with twenty-one buildings on the main campus and three buildings on the St. Pats campus. Its full-time graduate enrolment had grown from 56 to 717.

At the beginning of the 1970s, conditions abruptly changed. The government, with other priorities and other demands on its treasury, had begun drawing its strings on the purse. An embargo on new graduate programs was imposed, funds for new capital projects dried up, the annual increase to the operating formula was set at less than inflation. The government without notice increased tuition fees by $100 for the first time since the bargain had been struck, beginning the shift of the financial burden for post-secondary education from the state to the student. As for Carleton, this scene became more depressing when its full-time enrolment fell, particularly in undergraduate arts, heralding years of fear about substantial operating deficits, and Dunton, after fourteen years as president, decided to leave office.

The environment at the university when Dean Paquet took office was becoming very troubled. The following chart[4] displays some of the factors that made it so.

Carleton's planning had been based on continuing growth, and the sudden reversal in fortunes had created confusion and insecurity. As part of the reforms flowing from the changes in university governance of the late 1960s and early 1970s, the Senate had considered the rules governing tenure and termination for cause, and just as Dunton retired in June 1972 the Senate passed the document. As an afterthought, a postscript was added that the document did not apply to the condition of layoff, so a committee was appointed to design the procedure for this to happen. That fall enrolment fell, and, with the government setting the

Year	FTUG Enrolment	Annual Surplus (deficit) $	Cumulative Surplus (deficit) $	Events
71–72	7,635			Dunton retires, Oliver appointed
72–73	7,459		820,041	Rules for faculty layoff considered at Senate
73–74	7,465	(528,371)	291,670	Debate continues over lay off, consideration of instructional resources allocation formula
74–75	7,573	(302,821)	(11,151)	$4 million deficit estimated for following year, faculty apply for union certification
75–76	7,985	452,514	441,363	First collective agreement with faculty, wage and price controls, administrative staff unionizes
76–77	8,090	377,165	818,528	Second collective agreement with faculty, wage and price controls still apply
77–78	7,680	(84,465)	734,063	Teaching assistants apply for certification
78–79	7,221	(593,327)	140,745	

grant increase at less than inflation, panic began to grow that serious financial problems were around the corner. The continuing debate about layoff rules was the stuff of long Senate meetings, and the public discussion of an instructional resource allocation formula led some to guess that the targets for such layoffs had been identified. President M. K. Oliver, in an honest effort to be open and transparent, too often allowed the worst possible scenario to dominate public planning discussions.

As you can see from the chart above, enrolment growth and the finances of the university were erratic. Oliver had opened up the budget process so that its progress could be monitored by the Senate. This act caused the planners to be extremely cautious and avoid risk taking so that the factors of reduced enrolment and funding support produced an estimate that always displayed the most pessimistic scene, which called for the most drastic action. However, what happened was that external events, such as a special extra formula grant in two of the years and changes to the formula, meant that the immediate impact of dramatic enrolment change was muted, and where deficits were expected there were surpluses and vice versa.

The upshot was that the board and the faculty lost confidence in the president, and this in turn created the conditions necessary for the faculty to overcome their natural conservative instincts and become the first faculty association to be unionized in Ontario. The whole process overwhelmed the management of the university, and the overlay of collective bargaining upon collegial government at the university as it had evolved to the mid-1970s made any change in direction very difficult to achieve. From 1974 on, the university was captured by the process of certification, collective bargaining, and administration of the resultant contracts.

We think that it is to his credit that against this background Dean Paquet did much to lay the groundwork for things that came to fruition in the next decade. He was lucky that it was not until the end of his appointment that he became directly involved in union negotiations and could promote activities based on merit instead of entitlement. He was a free spirit in an environment that had been overcome by process and structure.

Below is a table[5] displaying full-time graduate enrolment during his term of office.

Year	Enrolment
73–74	684
74–75	769
75–76	996
76–77	982
77–78	966
78–79	975
79–80	951

These increases were achieved when the competition was tough and other universities were much better off in terms of the financial resources that they could bring to bear. Paquet corralled all the funds that he could find from whatever source and offered financial support to far more graduate students than those funds provided. He knew that all the offers would not be taken, and he was prepared to risk being overextended rather than have funds left over. In a time of financial stringency, his calculation of risk was absolutely correct. My impression is that he was also very careful to deploy that money, when he could, so as to maintain and encourage development in the areas of strength and potential strength.

The importance of this activity was not obvious, but it was critical. It represented one of the few positive actions taken by Carleton at the time. Many of the young faculty hired in the previous decade were now maturing as scholars and researchers, and along with the deans of the undergraduate faculties Paquet tried to create opportunities for these scholars to flourish. While many at the university were at best struggling to adapt to the changing times and at worst merely shifting the deck chairs about, Paquet used change to build and sustain the graduate and research enterprise at the university.

Professor Steve Wilson, then chair of the Department of Religion, offered this assessment of Dean Paquet's role.

> Two things characterized Gilles Paquet in our memory. First, he explicitly promoted research and rewarded those (and only those) who had done or were doing it. This ruffled a lot of feathers, since the Carleton tradition up until then had been inclined to reward everybody the same way, regardless of their level of achievement. Second, he showed considerable flexibility and creativity in ensuring that units and individuals could achieve their ambitions in the areas he controlled. If this meant bending the rules or bypassing the obstacles, whether internally or externally imposed, then so be it. Some thought this cavalier, but many have reason to be grateful for his unwavering, sometimes ingenious, support.

In the documents supporting the establishment of the Faculty of Graduate Studies and Research, Paquet dealt with Carleton's relationship with the University of Ottawa and described it and its potential this way.

Carleton was allowed to develop according to its own spirit without having to use all its resourcefulness. There was little need felt for policy and no taste for coordination, even between neighbours; a slow shift from hostile to peaceful coexistence can best define Carleton's evolving relationship with the University of Ottawa up to late 1960's. It has become more obvious that there must be more planning and that the latitudes available to Carleton must take fully into consideration the planning of the University of Ottawa. Carleton and the University of Ottawa share to a large extent the same terrain and even if their overall tonus is bound to differ, there is no reason not to take advantage of the possibilities offered by diverse forms of collaboration, cooperation or joint ventures.[6]

When Paquet took office, there were still some in the senior administration who had been in the university during the time when there was a hostile coexistence, so in addition to the argument that coordination and planning were essential it was important to give notice that the university of Ottawa was no longer the enemy but a potential ally. His involvement in, and his encouragement of, joint consultations and activities at all levels were important to later development of a wide range of joint programs and collaboration at the graduate level. It was an important development to undertake, and it paid off generously during the 1980s.

We have been intimately associated with university life for fifty years, and we are persuaded that the decade of the 1970s was the ugliest for anybody who was a university administrator during those fifty years. While that was true everywhere in the system, we think that it was especially true at Carleton. It was the product of many factors, but its principal manifestation was being the first institution in Ontario to have a faculty union, and to be the pioneer in collective bargaining and the administration of contracts. It is to his credit that Dean Paquet was not a mere administrative housekeeper, as was sometimes the salvation of others, but accepted the challenge of change and met it with innovation, imagination, and persistence. In a time when change was difficult, he persuaded the university to establish the Faculty of Graduate Studies and Research, and such was his wisdom in its design that it has changed little in structure to this day. He encouraged the expansion of graduate enrolment. Full-time graduate enrolment grew from 682 to 951, and in the same period part-time enrolment grew from 532 to 818. The doctoral program grew from 158 full-time students and 73 part-time students in

1974 to 202 full-time students and 80 part-time students in 1979. Paquet began the process of managing research activities at the university level. He was the first senior university official to actively encourage collaboration with the University of Ottawa. It was a very creditable record for a graduate dean in that six-year period.

It is more difficult to assess what impact Paquet had as a participant in the provincial system. His writings indicate an early and accurate assessment of the forces that would direct actions of the system. His later appointment as one of the academic members of the government-appointed Committee on University Affairs suggests that he held the esteem of his peers at the provincial level since the government of the day was not likely to appoint someone whose credibility would be challenged. Such credibility in Dean Paquet's case may have had much to do with his performance as a member of the Ontario Council of Graduate Studies.

His final years as dean had the added complication of being a member of the Search Committee to find a successor to Oliver. The known candidate and the favourite of many was John Porter, who had recently been appointed vice president academic and, during Oliver's many absences, acting president. The Search Committee numbered six—three appointed by the Senate, two faculty, and a student—and three external members of the board. Of all the members of the committee, the best known to the university community was Paquet. When the surprise announcement was made that W. E. Beckel was the unanimous recommendation of the committee, many within the university blamed Paquet that their favourite hadn't been picked. We think that this was unfair. Porter in the eyes of the board members on the committee had too many of the attributes of Oliver, and we don't think he was ever a serious candidate in their eyes. They wanted a proven university administrator, and that is what they got in the person of Beckel.

Most deans during this period did not stand for reappointment, many did not want to, and others knew that the general environment was such that reappointment was unlikely whatever their successes may have been. At the conclusion of his term as dean, Gilles Paquet returned to the economics department and then left the university to take up an appointment at the University of Ottawa. It was not a surprise, but it was a great loss to Carleton.

Notes

[1] Carleton University Archives, *Senate Minutes,* April 8, 1974, Appendix V to Appendix B, 1.
[2] Carleton University Archives, *Senate Minutes,* April 8, 1974, Appendix B, 4.
[3] Ibid., 6.
[4] The enrolment numbers are taken from page 26 of the *Data Book 1997* published by Carleton University and found in its archives. The financial numbers are found in successive budget documents associated with the reports of the Finance Committee in the Minutes of the Board of Governors from 1973 to 1979.
[5] The enrolment figures are found in the Carleton University *Data Book* for each of these years.
[6] Carleton University Archives, *Senate Minutes,* April 8, 1974, Appendix B, 3.

Chapitre 12

Gilles Paquet et son rayonnement au sein de l'ASDEQ

Jac-André Boulet[1]

La contribution de Gilles Paquet à l'Association des économistes québécois (ASDEQ) mérite d'être particulièrement soulignée. Que ce soit à titre de conférencier, de commentateur ou d'organisateur, son sens de l'efficacité, son dévouement et son expérience, ont permis à Gilles d'inculquer de solides principes de gouvernance à l'Association. Par ses dons de communicateur, il a contribué à sa visibilité ; par sa notoriété, il lui a légué une profonde respectabilité ; et par son attachement indéfectible à l'Association, il en est devenu un véritable pilier.

Ses réalisations

Gilles Paquet arrive à point nommé à la présidence de l'ASDEQ, en 1989, à l'invitation de Gilles Beausoleil qui venait d'être nommé au nouveau poste de directeur exécutif.

Fondée en 1976[2], l'Association atteignait alors ses 14 ans. Adolescente, elle vivait tous les soubresauts qui accompagnent cette vibrante période de la vie. Gilles Paquet est élu président, à ce moment critique de son évolution. Il en devient alors son quatorzième président.

Il aide l'Association à traverser cette étape « tumultueuse » en redonnant vie, tout d'abord, à une structure de gestion du Conseil d'administration (CA) à trois présidents : le président en titre, le président désigné et le président sortant. Ensuite, en collaboration avec Gilles Beausoleil, il procède à une réorganisation interne de l'Association pour donner plus de poids à ses trois sections régionales :

Montréal, Québec et l'Outaouais. Désormais, le président de chacune des trois sections régionales et leurs directeurs respectifs sont, d'office, membres du Conseil d'administration national. Il est aussi convenu que les présidents du Conseil d'administration national seront nommés en alternance entre les régions. Ceci permet de remédier à la situation passée dans laquelle les membres du Conseil national étaient choisis indépendamment des Conseils d'administration régionaux. Les uns n'avaient donc pas de comptes à rendre aux autres et il en résultait des relations plutôt floues et déconnectées. Gilles Paquet, de concert avec Gilles Beausoleil, permet à l'Association de renforcer ses liens internes, en mettant toutes les instances de décision à contribution et en les orientant vers un objectif commun. Il en a résulté une bien meilleure cohésion entre l'ASDEQ nationale et ses trois régions, une plus grande stabilité et une plus grande continuité dans ses processus décisionnels.

Il est également important de souligner que pendant son mandat à la présidence, Gilles a redonné vie à un projet que l'Association n'avait réussi à concrétiser que de façon sporadique : celui de la publication des Actes des congrès annuels. Sous sa présidence, leur publication prend un véritable essor et se maintiendra pendant dix ans (jusqu'en 1999). Notons que c'est grâce à son travail soutenu et acharné que cette activité a pu être menée avec diligence et de façon systématique pendant cette période. Une telle publication présentait un grand intérêt tant du point de vue universitaire que professionnel (retombées en termes d'élaboration de politiques). En 2000, en raison de l'ampleur du phénomène de mise en ligne des publications à travers le monde, et suite à l'acceptation de plus en plus grande des milieux académiques de cet instrument de diffusion, la publication des Actes change de format. Les Actes sont désormais accessibles en ligne, sur le site Internet de l'ASDEQ.

Notons enfin au chapitre des réalisations de Gilles, pendant son mandat, sa très forte implication dans l'organisation du Congrès de 1990 sur le thème « Éducation et formation à l'heure de la compétitivité internationale ». Les Actes de ce Congrès figurent parmi les plus populaires de la série. Gilles récidive en 1999, en participant étroitement à la préparation du Congrès annuel qui porte cette fois-ci sur « Les défis de la gouvernance à l'aube du XXe siècle ». Bien sûr, il accepte à nouveau, comme il l'avait fait plus d'une fois au cours des Congrès précédents, de rassembler les textes et de publier les Actes.

Son engagement

Lors de la création de l'Association en 1976, Gilles Paquet, sans en être l'un des pères fondateurs, n'en est pas moins aux premières loges. Dès le premier Congrès, et en raison notamment de la notoriété et de la respectabilité qu'il avait déjà acquises, on fait appel à ses talents pour donner le ton à la rencontre. Ceci dit, inviter Gilles à une rencontre pour y faire une présentation est aussi laisser libre court à l'un de ses penchants favoris : la polémique. Gilles aime provoquer son audience, la faire réfléchir, la faire sortir de ses retranchements. Il veut l'inciter à aller le plus loin possible et à toucher les abysses tout comme les sommets de la démarche intellectuelle. Au cours de ce premier Congrès, Gilles dénonce ce qu'il qualifie de « psychose des économistes » et s'associe par là même à un mouvement de « contestation » qu'il voit émerger au sein de l'Association.

Nous devons nous rappeler que l'ASDEQ est née, pour reprendre le langage tellement imagé de Gilles, « d'un mouvement de contestation et de subversion ». Lorsqu'en mai 2007, l'Association lui décerne le titre de « Membre honoraire », il en est particulièrement gratifié parce que, à ses yeux, l'ASDEQ est une organisation fondamentalement subversive. C'est-à-dire que l'Association fonctionne dans un état d'esprit propre et selon des modalités qui s'éloignent des sentiers battus et qui se rapprochent des siens.

Cet appui indéfectible de Gilles Paquet à l'Association, nous le devons donc en particulier au fait qu'elle s'est définie dès le départ comme une organisation professionnelle. Les préoccupations premières de l'ASDEQ sont une meilleure connaissance pratique de la réalité économique et un apport éclairé au déroulement des débats de politiques publiques. Pour Gilles Paquet, qui considérait que la science économique était devenue aseptisée et déconnectée de la réalité, il s'agissait bien de contestation et de subversion.

L'ASDEQ devient ainsi pour lui une âme sœur, une associée, une autre tribune susceptible de lui permettre de poursuivre son travail de vulgarisateur de la science économique. Ce travail, il l'accomplissait déjà à la radio, à la télévision et auprès d'autres associations. En demeurant toujours bien ancré dans le monde universitaire, il a placé la science économique au cœur des préoccupations sociétales et lui a donné à un ascendant et une crédibilité qui rejaillissent sur l'Association.

Ce talent de communicateur, de vulgarisateur, de stimulateur, de provocateur, voire d'iconoclaste, qui le caractérise si bien, a été mis à profit plusieurs fois à l'ASDEQ : ici, en Outaouais, dans le cadre de nos activités régionales, mais aussi dans le cadre des congrès annuels de l'Association qui se déroulent en alternance en Outaouais, à Québec et à Montréal. Gilles fut tantôt conférencier d'honneur, tantôt conférencier principal dans le cadre de séances plénières d'ouverture, ou de séances plénières de clôture. Il a été souvent conférencier dans un atelier ou animateur de sessions, sans oublier les nombreuses fois où ses talents de conseiller (contenu des programmes ou choix des conférenciers) sont venus éclairer nos décisions.

Une appréciation

Nombre d'économistes, et en particulier ceux qui gravitent au sein de l'ASDEQ, sont impressionnés par la vivacité intellectuelle de Gilles, sa rapidité à saisir un problème et en évaluer l'importance, et son efficacité à proposer des pistes de solution.

En peu de mots, Gilles Paquet est un intellectuel brillant et un travailleur acharné qui ne se perd pas dans des considérations purement théoriques. Lors de la création de l'Association en 1976, il déplorait déjà « la tendance des économistes universitaires à sombrer dans l'étude de la syntaxe économique au prix d'un abandon de la sémantique des problèmes quotidiens ».

Pour nous, l'énorme contribution de Gilles Paquet à l'ASDEQ est aussi due en grande partie à la capacité qui lui est propre de créer des liens et à la générosité, qui l'honore, d'en faire profiter les autres. Elle relève aussi d'une vaste connaissance qu'il a accumulée, que ce soit à travers ses lectures, les centaines d'entrevues qu'il a conduites au cours de ses activités journalistiques, ou suite à la rédaction de ses ouvrages historiques.

La reconnaissance de l'ASDEQ

Suite à l'incidence que Gilles Paquet a exercé sur l'ASDEQ et la société en général, l'Association lui a décerné, lors de son Congrès annuel de 2007 à Québec, le titre de membre honoraire.

Un membre honoraire de l'ASDEQ est un économiste qui a marqué la profession, notamment par la diffusion et la vulgarisation des connaissances économiques, qui a joué un rôle important dans l'économie du Québec et dont la contribution professionnelle aux activités de l'Association a permis à celle-ci de grandir et d'atteindre la crédibilité et la visibilité qu'on lui connaît aujourd'hui.

Gilles Paquet devenait le septième récipiendaire de ce titre, au cours des 32 ans d'existence de l'Association. L'avaient précédé, Robert Bourassa (1992), Jacques

Parizeau (1992), Pierre Fortin (1995), Bernard Landry (2000), Gilles Beausoleil (2003) et André Raynauld (2006).

Lors de la cérémonie, l'ASDEQ a tenu à souligner non seulement sa contribution à l'Association, mais également celle qu'il a apporté à la profession, son rayonnement à travers ses divers engagements professionnels et les diverses distinctions qu'il a reçues au cours de sa carrière.

Parmi ses divers engagements professionnels, nous avons tenu à souligner sa participation à titre de président de la Fédération des sciences sociales du Canada, de l'Association canadienne-française pour l'avancement des sciences (ACFAS) et de Les Académies des arts, des lettres et des sciences du Canada.

De plus, en raison de l'importance accordée par l'ASDEQ à la vulgarisation de la science économique, les contributions de Gilles Paquet en tant que journaliste dans les réseaux de radio et de télévision, ses éditoriaux et ses apparitions fréquentes à la télévision pour commenter les questions d'importance nationale ont été aussi dignes de mention.

Notes

[1] J'aimerais remercier Gilles Beausoleil, Charles Carrier et André Downs qui m'ont été d'une précieuse aide pendant la préparation de cette note.

[2] Le congrès de fondation de l'ASDEQ a eu lieu les 9 et 10 avril 1976 à Québec. Ses fondateurs, Jacques Brind'Amour, Denis Fugère, Mario Ste-Croix, Régis Bouchard et François Turenne avaient amorcé les travaux de création un an plus tôt, en juin 1975.

Chapitre 13

Un passage marquant à la présidence de la Société royale du Canada

Bernard Bonin

Gilles Paquet ne laisse personne indifférent. Certes, il n'a pas toujours raison mais on ne s'ennuie jamais en sa compagnie. Doté d'un esprit critique peu commun, il aura inévitablement heurté certains au cours de sa carrière. Mais heureusement pour lui et pour nous tous, cet esprit critique se double d'un admirable sens de l'humour qui lui permet généralement de désarmer l'opposition.

Au fil des ans, Gilles Paquet a été très actif en ce qui a trait au « service à la collectivité », universitaire ou autre, troisième volet du triptyque servant à évaluer la contribution d'un membre de la communauté académique. Pour ma part, je me souviens encore de l'époque où il était trésorier de l'Association canadienne d'économique/Canadian Economics Association.

La présentation du rapport annuel d'un trésorier est rarement l'occasion de multiples éclats de rire venant de l'assemblée. Gilles, qui s'adressait alors, il y a déjà presque quatre décennies de cela, à cette auguste assemblée de « maximiseurs » avait soulevé l'hilarité générale en tournant en dérision notre politique de placement des fonds de l'association dans laquelle on retrouvait des titres dont le rendement était bien en-deçà des rendements courants du marché.

La Société royale du Canada (SRC) se range aussi parmi les institutions qu'englobe le « service à la collectivité ». Gilles Paquet en devient le président alors que l'on entend fréquemment des appels de gens aussi éminents que le Gouverneur général de l'époque, Son Excellence Adrienne Clarkson, l'invitant à devenir plus représentative de la société canadienne, mieux ancrée dans cette société, et plus ouverte, plus accueillante aux manifestations culturelles peu présentes en son sein jusque là. Gilles Paquet n'est pas du genre à refuser un tel défi. On admettra sans peine que l'entreprise est risquée. À l'automne 2003, début de la présidence Paquet, la Société royale du Canada existe déjà depuis plus de 120 ans. Elle a subi avec succès l'épreuve du temps, et il est donc permis de croire qu'elle repose sur des assises solides. À l'examen, il est vite apparu qu'il n'en était rien. Outre que l'inertie guette souvent une institution plus que centenaire, la pertinence de la SRC est trop souvent remise en cause pour que l'on puisse ignorer les critiques dont elle fait l'objet ; par ailleurs, les fondations financières sur lesquelles elle repose sont friables.

Les raisons pour lesquelles la modernisation de la Société s'impose
Dans une communication qu'il transmet aux membres le 10 septembre 2004, Gilles Paquet explique le déroulement du processus de modernisation de la Société royale du Canada et les raisons pour lesquelles une telle restructuration paraît s'imposer.

a) La Société ne peut se passer du support financier du gouvernement. Or, ce support ne viendra pas à moins que la Société devienne plus visible, plus pertinente et plus efficiente.

b) La Société « ne peut espérer obtenir de support financier à long terme en tant qu'institution nationale de la part du gouvernement canadien à moins de se doter d'une gouvernance bilingue et à moins de montrer qu'elle se gouverne d'une manière qui donne voix à la société canadienne ». En un mot, elle doit devenir davantage représentative de la société canadienne.

c) Le système de nomination et d'élection à la Société laisse à désirer. Non seulement une forme de malthusianisme est apparue par suite d'une interprétation parfois fort restrictive de certains critères de nomination, ce qui a eu pour effet d'exclure un grand nombre de Canadiens dont les réussites intellectuelles (ou artistiques) sont pourtant indéniables, mais l'équilibre hommes-femmes, linguistique et régional a souvent été remis en cause.

d) Sans une gouvernance bilingue et sans un processus électoral plus souple, la Société « ne pourra pas devenir le leader incontesté des Académies canadiennes des sciences et elle ne sera pas reconnue et financée comme tel ».

e) Le nom même de la Société royale du Canada est un irritant dans ses activités, en ce sens qu'il ne communique pas vraiment la nature de l'organisation à la société canadienne et « colporte même un petit côté archaïque », selon le langage, coloré mais franc, que le président Paquet utilise à cette occasion. La modernisation de la Société passe donc par un changement de nom, ou tout au moins, par la promotion d'une appellation qui communiquerait mieux aux citoyens le sens de ses activités.

En résumé, la Société doit faire les efforts nécessaires afin de devenir :

1) plus représentative et donc plus légitime, c'est-à-dire assurer une meilleure représentation des champs intellectuels et une meilleure balance homme-femme, disciplinaire et régionale ;
2) plus pertinente et socialement utile, c'est-à-dire en arriver à une meilleure focalisation sur la résolution des problèmes de la société canadienne ;
3) plus fonctionnelle, efficace et vraiment canadienne, c'est-à-dire parvenir à un meilleur alignement sur les familles de disciplines, à un vrai bilinguisme institutionnel et adopter un nouveau nom qui reflète mieux ce qu'est la SRC.

Ces constats émanant des travaux du Comité Wallot créé par le président de l'époque Howard Alper (et dont Gilles Paquet faisait partie), devaient conduire plus tard à une refonte en profondeur des statuts de la Société, que les membres ont acceptée par la suite lors d'un scrutin dont le résultat a été sans équivoque.

La restructuration de la SRC sous la présidence de Gilles Paquet

Dans le but de rendre la SRC plus fonctionnelle, il a semblé opportun d'adopter une nouvelle appellation qui refléterait mieux la nature de la Société. En conséquence, ce qui était connu jusque là sous le nom de Royal Society of Canada/Société royale du Canada pourra dorénavant mener ses activités sous les appellations suivantes : RSC : The Academies of Arts, Humanities and Sciences of Canada/SRC : Les Académies des arts, des lettres et des sciences du Canada.

Ce changement devait marquer le fait que la SRC est une des sociétés savantes du Canada, en réalité la plus ancienne, et n'a pour but que de « contribuer au développement du savoir et de la recherche et de reconnaître les contributions remarquables apportées dans les arts, les lettres et les sciences ». Il convient de noter ici le désir de mieux accueillir les contributions originales venant des milieux artistiques, ce que la modification d'un certain nombre de statuts dont il sera question plus loin, viendra renforcer.

Les efforts en vue de rendre la Société plus pertinente et socialement utile se traduiront par l'inclusion, parmi ses activités, de l'évaluation indépendante et savante des enjeux contemporains d'intérêt public et importants pour le Canada, offrant de ce fait une tribune publique pour les discussions sur ces grandes questions. Ceci, en plus de la préparation et la publication de rapports et de recommandations au sujet des arts et des sciences au Canada, que l'on retrouvait déjà dans les anciens statuts, devait contribuer à mieux ancrer la Société dans la vie canadienne.

Une redéfinition des membres élus à titre spécial allait dans le même sens. Ces personnes œuvrant « dans le domaine public » ont aidé « de façon exceptionnelle la Société à atteindre ses objectifs ». Comme il était dit « qu'être élu à titre spécial est un honneur rarement accordé », on ne devait pas craindre un abaissement des normes de qualité requises pour l'élection à la SRC. Cependant, il devenait évident que la Société pourrait s'enorgueillir de compter dans ses rangs des personnes dont les contributions étaient autres que celles d'une belle carrière dans l'enseignement ou la recherche, universitaires dans la très grande majorité des cas.

La restructuration des académies a sans doute été la mesure la plus radicale et la plus controversée de l'effort de modernisation entrepris sous la gouverne de Gilles Paquet. Elle a été entreprise dans le but de mieux asseoir la légitimité de la SRC et de parvenir à un meilleur alignement sur les familles de disciplines. En même temps, elle venait concrétiser l'accueil des artistes et le désir du président de parvenir à « un vrai bilinguisme institutionnel ».

Lors de l'accession de Gilles Paquet à la présidence, l'Académie 1 regroupe tous les membres francophones du domaine des arts, des lettres et des sciences sociales. L'Académie 2 regroupe tous les membres anglophones des mêmes disciplines et champs d'étude. L'Académie 3 se compose de quatre divisions : génie et sciences appliquées ; sciences de la terre, de l'océan et de l'atmosphère ; sciences de la vie ; mathématiques et physique.

Après la restructuration, l'Académie 1 comptera trois divisions : 1) Humanities ; 2) Lettres et sciences humaines ; 3) Arts/les arts, soit une division pour les anglophones, une autre pour les francophones, et une division bilingue pour les artistes, cette dernière solution ayant été préférée à la création d'une quatrième académie pour les arts. L'Académie 2 comptera deux divisions : 1) Sciences sociales ; 2) Social sciences. De ce point de vue, l'Académie 3 ne subira aucune modification puisqu'elle comptait déjà quatre divisions. Par la même occasion, il fut décidé d'accroître le nombre de membres réguliers pouvant être élus chaque année : de 30 à 39 pour l'Académie 3, et de 10 à 24 pour l'Académie 1, alors que l'Académie 2, reflétant ainsi la nouvelle structure, verrait le nombre de nouveaux membres éligibles passer de 20 à 15.

Trois constatations s'imposent ici. D'abord, dans l'ensemble, le nombre de membres éligibles chaque année passe de 60 à 78. Ensuite, en disant que la moitié de ces nouveaux membres pourrait venir de l'Académie 3, on se trouvait à respecter assez bien la proportion existant avant la restructuration. Enfin, en conservant des divisions francophones aux Académies 1 et 2 on reconnaissait qu'il existe différentes « communautés de pratique » pour reprendre les termes que Gilles Paquet a utilisés dans sa communication du 10 septembre 2004.

Parmi les critiques ou les craintes qui furent adressées à cet effet de modernisation de la Société, il faut faire une place à celle qui s'est exprimée probablement avec le plus de vigueur : c'est celle de l'amenuisement du rôle des francophones au sein de la Société royale du Canada. Fidèle à ses habitudes, le président Paquet a donc pris son bâton de pèlerin dans le but de désarmer l'opposition. Il faut dire qu'il ne manquait pas d'arguments contraires à faire valoir.

On était en droit de s'attendre à ce que le nombre de francophones ne baisse pas et puisse même augmenter ; on peut dire la même chose au sujet de la proportion des membres francophones. On se rappellera que l'ancienne Académie 1 était francophone ; l'ancienne Académie 2, anglophone. Dorénavant, les francophones allaient se retrouver au sein d'une division francophone dans chacune des nouvelles Académies 1 et 2, selon leur discipline et champ d'étude, respectant en cela les « communautés de pratique ». Mais en plus, l'Académie 1 allait compter une nouvelle division bilingue destinée à accueillir les personnes des milieux artistiques, dont à n'en plus douter des gens dont l'activité s'exprime en français. De ce point de vue, l'Académie 3 ne connaissait aucun changement, la « communauté de pratique » étant à forte prédominance de langue anglaise. Toutefois, on peut être à la fois un scientifique francophone et publier en anglais : en invitant l'Académie 3 à prêter une attention particulière à un meilleur équilibre linguistique, on était en droit de s'attendre à l'élection d'un plus grand nombre de francophones.

Gilles Paquet pouvait aussi faire savoir à ceux qui craignaient cet amenuisement de la présence des membres francophones que la tradition — non incluse dans les Statuts — de l'alternance de la présidence de la SRC entre un membre francophone et un autre anglophone allait être préservée et qu'il y avait tout lieu de croire que la présidence ne pourrait être occupée désormais que par une personne bilingue. De plus, l'esprit de la réforme était certainement que chacune des académies devrait se doter d'une gouvernance bilingue. À cet effet, les deux principaux dirigeants d'une académie sont censés provenir de communautés linguistiques différentes c'est-à-dire que si le directeur est anglophone, le secrétaire sera francophone et vice versa. Enfin, le bilinguisme sera davantage affirmé à la permanence de la SRC. Mais cela nous amène à la deuxième grande initiative de la présidence de Gilles Paquet.

L'assainissement de la situation financière de la SRC

C'est là, en effet, l'autre grand volet de la réforme entreprise au cours de son mandat. Lorsqu'il prend place à la barre de la SRC, celle-ci se trouve dans une situation financière délicate. Les déficits sont fréquents, les revenus courants ne suffisant pas à couvrir les dépenses courantes ; la Société doit puiser dans son fonds de développement pour couvrir les dépenses courantes. Ces déficits sont encourus en dépit des efforts considérables faits dans le but de réduire les dépenses. Par exemple, la permanence est anémique et la Société n'a pas de directeur général depuis plus d'une décennie. Qui plus est : les conditions dans lesquelles la Société doit travailler ne laissent entrevoir aucune amélioration. C'est ainsi que logée gratuitement par le gouvernement fédéral depuis cinq ans, il devient évident que la Société ne pourra espérer bénéficier de telles conditions à perpétuité. Il semble donc assez clair que la Société royale du Canada devra trouver de nouvelles sources de revenus, car les cotisations que lui versent ses membres chaque année ne suffiront pas à assainir sa situation financière.

Gilles Paquet propose que l'on crée un nouveau type de membres : les membres institutionnels. L'article 5 des Statuts définit les membres institutionnels en ces termes :

> Les membres institutionnels sont des institutions ou des organisations privées ou publiques dont la nomination à titre de membre institutionnel a été approuvée par le Conseil de la Société. Chaque membre institutionnel désignera un représentant à la Société et jouira du statut de membre institutionnel pour un mandat d'au plus trois ans, renouvelable indéfiniment. Les membres institutionnels auront les droits et privilèges de la Société selon les dispositions des Statuts.

À ce jour, la très grande majorité des membres institutionnels sont des universités, mais un certain nombre « d'organisations publiques » (centres de recherche par exemple) se sont aussi prévalues de ce statut. Les membres institutionnels s'engagent à verser une cotisation de 10,000 dollars par année ou 25,000 pour trois ans et la Société a pu en recruter suffisamment pour lui permettre d'embaucher un directeur général, d'étoffer sa permanence, de payer son loyer et de cesser de couvrir ses dépenses courantes en puisant dans son fonds de développement. Cet assainissement financier, la SRC le doit indiscutablement à Gilles Paquet qui aura parcouru le pays tout entier dans le but de convaincre le plus grand nombre possible de membres institutionnels d'adhérer à la Société. On notera que ces efforts de recrutement n'ont pas encore été étendus aux « organisations privées » comme les Statuts le permettent.

En contrepartie de leur contribution financière, les membres institutionnels obtiennent un certain nombre de privilèges. En premier lieu, la Société s'engage à organiser chaque année quelques symposiums sur les sujets d'actualité mais controversés. Ces rencontres scientifiques se tiendront surtout dans les universités et seront organisées en collaboration avec les administrations universitaires en prenant bien soin de couvrir sur quelques années, l'ensemble du Canada.

Au cours de l'année qui a suivi l'intégration des membres institutionnels, le président Paquet a tenu promesse et a patronné personnellement des symposiums sur des sujets aussi variés que la diversité culturelle, le nucléaire, l'eau, pour ne mentionner que ces trois là.

En deuxième lieu, et cela vaut surtout pour les universités, les membres institutionnels se voient accorder le privilège de soumettre le nom de l'un de leurs professeurs parmi les nominations à l'élection. À noter qu'il n'y a pas là l'assurance d'une élection du candidat dont le nom aurait été soumis par un membre institutionnel ; ce mécanisme comporte seulement l'assurance que ce candidat sera porté à l'attention des comités de nomination. Puisque le processus normal exige qu'une candidature soit patronnée par des gens qui sont déjà membres de la Société, obtenir une première élection à la Société peut être un obstacle difficile à franchir pour une institution universitaire. Cet effort vise donc à faire en sorte que la SRC s'assure que des candidatures de qualité, autrement ignorées, seront portées à son attention.

Les membres institutionnels se voyaient aussi offrir la possibilité de nommer deux représentants au Conseil de la Société et un au Comité exécutif (ou de direction). Enfin, on leur conférait un statut privilégié lors du banquet qui couronne chaque année la cérémonie de la présentation des nouveaux membres. La première mesure a été partiellement mise en vigueur : deux représentants d'institutions de taille différente sont en effet devenus membres du Conseil, bien que ces personnes, en pratique, n'ont que rarement participées aux réunions. La deuxième mesure n'a pas été mise en vigueur. Quant à la troisième, on peut dire qu'elle a été pleinement appliquée, car nombreuses sont les institutions ayant jugé opportun de réserver une table, spécialement lorsqu'un collègue est parmi les nouveaux membres honorés à cette occasion.

Conclusion

La réforme en profondeur d'une institution plus que centenaire comme la Société royale du Canada était, avons-nous dit, une entreprise risquée. Quelques années déjà après avoir été faite, cette réforme continue de soulever des questions. Il n'y a pas lieu de s'en étonner, mais le constat n'est pas sans importance. Au terme de ce bref hommage à Gilles Paquet, faisons écho à trois de ces questions : La réforme Paquet survivra-t-elle ? Faut-il y voir le prélude à un nouvel élargissement de la participation aux activités de la Société ? Assisterons-nous à une nouvelle « ouverture » sur la société canadienne ?

La première question peut surprendre à prime abord ; elle est néanmoins fort légitime. L'encre des nouveaux Statuts n'était pas encore sèche qu'on entrevoyait déjà des modifications. (Ici, il faut y voir rien d'autre qu'une figure de style, puisque les Statuts n'ont pas encore été publiés.)

En un sens, il n'y a pas lieu de s'en offusquer, car cela signifie que la SRC est une institution vivante. Cependant, si les changements proposés (et adoptés dans certains cas) avaient frappé au cœur de la réforme Paquet, ils n'offriraient pas le gage d'une grande stabilité. Heureusement, les deux grands volets de la modernisation dont il fut question ici (restructuration des académies ; membres institutionnels), n'ont pas encore été remis en cause. Le recul dont nous disposons est encore insuffisant, mais la réforme tient le coup !

Cette réforme est-elle le prélude à un nouvel élargissement de la participation aux activités de la Société ? Si celle-ci désire obtenir un financement à long terme du gouvernement canadien il lui faudra « montrer qu'elle se gouverne d'une manière qui donne voix à la société canadienne », pour reprendre les termes que Gilles Paquet utilisait dans sa communication du 10 septembre 2004. Or, à cet égard il faut bien reconnaître que les gestes posés jusqu'à maintenant n'ont eu qu'une portée fort modeste. Les membres institutionnels existent, et sont d'ailleurs de plus en plus nombreux. (On en comptait 33 en septembre 2007, ce qui est certainement un beau couronnement de l'effort entrepris par Gilles et continué sans relâche par celle qui l'a remplacé à la présidence, Patricia Demers.) Nous leur avons consenti une participation aux activités du Conseil, mais nous n'avons pas encore mis en vigueur leur participation au Comité de direction, alors que nos Statuts permettent une telle participation. On s'interroge également sur la possibilité pour les membres élus à titre spécial d'occuper des postes de direction à la Société. Et puis, les membres institutionnels ne comprennent encore aucune « organisation privée », pourtant incluse par définition. Dire qu'on doit s'attendre à de fortes résistances à l'endroit d'une telle inclusion, reviendrait sans doute à énoncer l'euphémisme de l'année !

Assisterons-nous à une nouvelle « ouverture » sur la société canadienne ? Là encore, les progrès accomplis ont été modestes. Certes, les symposiums sur des sujets d'actualité sont la concrétisation de cette ouverture ; tout comme l'accueil des artistes. Pour diverses raisons, l'accueil des artistes s'est d'ailleurs révélé plus difficile que prévu. Le principe en a été établi pendant le mandat de Gilles Paquet, et la nomination de la première cohorte a été faite sous sa gouverne, mais c'est Patricia Demers qui a eu la tâche de voir à la nomination du second groupe d'artistes et à la première élection véritable du troisième contingent selon le processus normal de la SRC.

Comme elle avait présidé le groupe de travail qui devait suggérer à la Société de se montrer plus accueillante à l'égard des artistes, on comprendra facilement que ce projet lui tenait à cœur.

Pourtant, un certain nombre d'artistes méritoires ont jugé préférable de décliner l'invitation de joindre les rangs de la SRC, soit parce qu'ils ont jugé ne pas avoir beaucoup d'affinités avec celle-ci, soit parce que disposant de leurs propres milieux d'accueil, ils ne voyaient ni l'opportunité, ni la capacité d'en ajouter un autre.

Et, la création du Conseil des académies canadiennes (dont la SRC est co-fondatrice), a changé les perspectives en ce qui a trait à l'organisation de panels d'experts destinés à répondre aux questions que le gouvernement canadien soulève dans ses mandats. On ne voit donc pas encore clairement ce que la SRC pourrait faire afin de devenir « plus pertinente et socialement utile ».

Ces quelques interrogations montrant que la réforme de la Société royale du Canada est une « symphonie inachevée », ne viennent absolument pas entamer l'admiration que l'on doit avoir pour le chemin parcouru sous l'égide de Gilles Paquet. Les progrès accomplis au cours d'un mandat somme toute assez bref (deux ans) nous autorisent à parler d'un passage marquant et remarqué à la présidence de la Société royale du Canada. Contre vents et marées, il a su relever le défi que représentait pour lui la modernisation de cette institution plus que centenaire. On ne célébrera jamais assez les efforts qu'il a dû faire pour y arriver.

Part Six

Influencing

Chapter 14

Paquet and Jacobs: On Sectoral Relations and a Search for Common Ground

Jeffrey Roy

A leader is someone who steps back from the entire system and tries to build a more collaborative, more innovative system that will work over the long term.

—Robert Reich

Introduction
In late August 1991, I arrived at the University of Ottawa's Vanier Hall for an orientation program offered to new MBA students. At one point, each faculty member teaching a required course in the program was asked to say a few words about the course and how it fit within the overall scheme of things.

Gilles Paquet did not disappoint. While most other instructors provided general flavours for the topics and coverage of their courses, Gilles assured everyone in attendance that, while not unimportant in precise ways, most of what we had just heard was really about plumbing—and what was missing (what he would thus provide) was a sense of the big picture of how business existed (and as we shall see below co-existed) within a much more dynamic and complex institutional environment. His course, Government and Business Relations, was a mandatory course in the second year of what was then a two-year program. Having a few course exemptions in hand, I was fortunately able to sign up in my first year, a seemingly modest advantage that would carry major repercussions for not only my graduate studies but also my entire career.

The premise of Gilles's teaching in this course was that business did not operate in a vacuum—that is, within the strict confines of the marketplace—but that private sector structures and corporate strategies were shaped by a broader social and political environment that, all too often, company managers failed to recognize, much less understand. To be effective in an increasingly complex world, it was thus necessary to have a modicum of understanding of the government and the non-profit sectors and, more importantly, their impacts on and interdependencies with business.

As I will elaborate below, timing is an essential part of this story. The tone of business-government relations in 1991 was far different from anything found today, especially in the Anglo-Saxon world where Conservative and Republican governments had only just begun to soften their ideological stances of the previous decade that emphasized a stark delineation between state and market (most of the time espousing views of the latter as good and of the former as bad).

I was a new graduate student, and the timing of the message was exceptional in that I had chosen an MBA at the University of Ottawa as a compromise between my growing interest in the public sector and a more pragmatic view at the time of an MBA as the most portable and least limiting choice for graduate studies. Having Gilles's course in the first term of the program would indeed provide a unique vantage point to rise above the various trees (of business methodologies and management tools), and begin to gain a sense of the fuller and richer forest that does indeed constitute the more meaningful plateau for graduate work, career development, and perhaps most importantly a more generalized love of learning.

Social Learning and the Boulding Triangle

At the heart of Paquet's problem solving and decision making (and thus what would come to be regarded as a governance philosophy) is the notion of embracing complexity over simplicity. As other contributors have invoked in this volume, Gilles is fond of saying that for every complex problem there are simple solutions that are both elegant and wrong.

This viewpoint, often provided to amuse, underpinned a more serious distinction between his MBA course on Government and Business Relations and most other courses in the curriculum that Gilles would often chastise as being overly narrow and precise. This is not to say that the tools of accounting and finance do not contribute in fundamental ways to organizational performance; rather, management is more art than science. At the end of the day, leaders grappling with corporate strategy or government policy (or interactions of the two) require frameworks for critical thinking in surroundings where uncertainty and imperfect information are norms and not exceptions.

In a world of such complex and multifaceted problems, it is thus only through a robust and open process of social learning that practical and sustainable decisions are likely to emerge. Equally important, as such decisions must be adapted over time to changing circumstances, learning is not static but dynamic and ongoing (a key insight that would explain Gilles's gravitation toward learning and evolution-based economics). Here again Gilles would become an early pioneer of "collective intelligence" formulations of governance that are today further strengthened by an increasingly interactive and participatory Internet-based era (which many of late have labelled a web 2.0 ethos).

With respect to boundaries and relations between business, government, and the non-profit and voluntary worlds, Gilles leveraged the work of institutional economist Kenneth Boulding in devising a template to illustrate the "co-evolution" of these three partially distinct and yet overlapping spheres of human and organizational life (Paquet 1997, 1999). This co-evolutionary perspective of private, public, and civic spheres (the latter also referred to as civil society, the non-profit or third sector[1]) respects the need for sectoral boundaries while also emphasizing the manner by which sectors are also interdependent—not only influencing one another according to their own specific agendas and structures but also engaged in concerted processes, the resilience of which determines the collective governance performance for a jurisdiction as a whole.

Central to co-evolutionary performance is therefore social or collective learning, a process of mutual adjustment as decisions and events in one sector impact the others. The Boulding triangle was thus construed as follows:

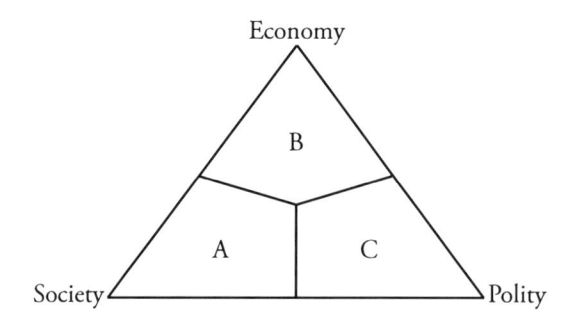

Paquet explains that boundaries separating the sectors—and thus the intersection of these boundaries—are in constant flux from impacts both large and small in any given jurisdictional environment. For instance, a natural disaster of one sort or another can dramatically, albeit hopefully temporarily, cause the market sector (economy) to contract, in favour of government action (polity) and/or the self-organizing capabilities of citizens and communities (society). Often more subtly, democratic elections, economic growth, and policy shifts driven by either foreign or domestic circumstances can alter the relative sectoral balance.

Paquet's depiction of these interdependencies is particularly apt in portraying the systemic governance challenges of a jurisdiction as a set of many different types of organizations and institutions. Indeed, while today the term "governance" is nearly ubiquitous in applications to both intra- and interorganizational processes of one sort or another, Paquet's pioneering work in Canada drew attention to the need for a country, or a domestic, subnational jurisdiction such as a province or city, to foster productive working relationships between sectors (1997, 1999; Hubbard and Paquet, 2005). Within such relationships is a constant need for conversation and active engagement, a basis for learning through harnessing "the magic of dialogue" (Yankelovich 1999).

As a student, I quickly developed an affinity for such an approach for numerous reasons. First, I had abandoned economics after undergraduate studies largely due to an overquantification of what I had essentially selected as a social science. After learning the basics of economics from some truly gifted instructors during my first and second years of university study, most everything about economics soon became the pursuit of mathematical precisions that seemed increasingly out of step with real-world problems and policy challenges. Gilles would subsequently validate my disillusion.

Second, with respect to sectoral orientation, especially in terms of the appropriate roles of business and government, it was reassuring to be told not to feel compelled to choose between one or the other as an ideological or professional home (obviously, Ottawa is an ideal locale to foster such cross-over, and though I was not alone in feeling this way it was often an inherently tough sell within an MBA program—as I would soon discover teaching this course within the same program).

Third, there was a political overtone as well. Prior to coming to Ottawa, I was a student delegate working on behalf of Paul Martin in the lead-up to the 1990 leadership convention, persuaded in part by then-candidate Martin's invocation of the need for partnership between industry and state. Such a sentiment was reinforced when in 1992 Gilles was invited to the Liberal policy conference in Aylmer, Quebec, a forum of prominent speakers from around the world that would underpin their initial Red Book manifesto for the 1993 federal election campaign.

Gilles's address in what became an edited volume from the conference was entitled "The Strategic State," and it served as an important linchpin between my early political tendencies and my tenure as a graduate student. Of course, anyone who might have mistaken this convergence between ideas and policies as indicative of his partisan affiliation with the Liberal Party would be corrected time and time again in the years that followed! Working with Gilles as a research assistant, we then sought to apply this foundation of sectoral relations in various guises that would soon bring about an interesting mix of interactions with the ideas and persona of Jane Jacobs.

Paquet and Jacobs: An Elusive Middle Ground

In a co-evolutionary world of fluid boundaries and important synergies between business and government, Jane Jacobs proved particularly instrumental not only in Gilles's own writings but also through some of our early collaborative efforts to apply the co-evolutionary framework to contemporary Canadian governance challenges. While most readers of her considerable body of scholarship tend to associate her first and foremost with the workings of cities, she also tackled what she viewed as distinct moral foundations underpinning the private and public sectors, with important consequences for how they should (or should not) interact.

In terms of Jacobs's long-time interest in cities, one of her main premises centred on the importance of diversity and the dynamic interactions of different elements of an urban ecosystem as the lifeblood of development: "At the root of her convictions was the belief that a city was constituted not by buildings or even the spaces between them, but by the rich mix of people—their individual and collective energies, actions, and desires—who brought the city to life" (Przyblyski 2006, 18). In this regard, Jacobs's conceptualization of urban life is co-evolutionary and, just as important, highly localized, and it fit well with Gilles's own outlook in many respects. In addition to emphasizing interdependence across sectors, in fact, much of his own writing (e.g., the aforementioned strategic state piece) has continued to be devolutionary in emphasizing the importance of bottom-up innovation (see, e.g., chapters in this volume by Caroline Andrew, Chris Wilson, and David Wolfe).

In 1992, Gilles and I had "co-written" (graduate student and research assistant that I was, I invoke this term tentatively where my own role is concerned) two reports on Canadian prosperity, and the need for more bottom-up policies and strategies for economic development. We argued for more flexible and localized planning models conducive to public and stakeholder engagement, and thus collective learning. The underpinning philosophy was one of innovative milieus organically grown by local communities themselves rather than ordained via what Gilles has often termed the "centralized mindset" of a federal government apparatus (especially in the realm of industrial and regional development).

The political mood of the country had also begun to shift in this direction, as witnessed by Gilles's own contribution to the Liberal Aylmer initiative as well as the then-Conservative government's so-called Prosperity Initiative. Although the latter was focused on federal government action, it nonetheless represented a departure from a Mulroney-era ideology of free trade and open markets, embracing the notion of a strategic role for the state (around the same time, regional development agencies in Atlantic and western Canada were decentralized into more regional, autonomous structures in order to work more collaboratively with provincial and local authorities and stakeholders).

Through Gilles's own association with the Canadian Centre for Management Development (now the Canada School of Public Service), a decision was made to create a short learning video on prosperity in Canada based in part on our reports and the contributions of other informed commentators from across the country. Our aim was a mix of scholars and practitioners, and was bolstered by Gilles's calling card; my job was to line them up and get them on board.

Jacobs answered the call—literally, in what I recall as a brief and pleasant phone conversation in which she spoke fondly of Gilles and his contribution to the topic at hand. She agreed to participate in the video, and provided her insight on localized diversity and innovation in urban and regional settings. Her own perspective strengthened the cause and fit well with others who agreed to lend their time to the project (in large part due to a respect and admiration for Gilles), notably Marcel Coté, who had just published his own manifesto of localized, bottom-up development, *Growing the Next Silicon Valley*.

Yet this intellectual alignment between Paquet and Jacobs would not endure as her next significant project would prove to become one of his favourite targets in the classroom and in his writing in subsequent years. Her 1992 book entitled

Systems of Survival is a forceful attempt to portray business and government as separate and distinct domains or "syndromes," to use her chosen term.[2]

The book is written as a dialogue among a group of diverse individuals who come together to explore the moral underpinnings of modern societies. A central tenet of the book is the presentation of the private and public spheres as two independent worlds, depicted and contrasted as the guardian and the commercial syndromes. In each case, a set of principles and values defines the purpose and behaviour of actors, be they individuals or organizations, operating within institutionalized boundaries. The result is a form of covenant governing the actions of each group that, in turn, translate into market-driven versus government-based incentives and choices.

The following traits summarize Jacobs's two syndromes:

A. COMMERCIAL MORAL SYNDROME	B. GUARDIAN MORAL SYNDROME
Occupations associated with it concern commerce, production of goods, services for commerce, most scientific work. The classic bourgeois values and virtues.	Occupational groups: armed forces and police, aristocracies amd landed gentries, government ministries and their bureaucracies, commercial monopolies, law courts, legislatures, religions (especially state religions.
The condition characterized by these "symptoms" is viable commercial life.	The condition is the work of protecting, acquiring, exploiting, administering, or controlling territories.
Shun force Come to voluntary agreements Be honest Collaborate easily with strangers and aliens Compete Respect contracts Use initiative and enterprise Be open to incentiveness and novelty Be efficient Promote comfort and convenience Dissent for the sake of the task Invest for productive purposes Be industrious Be thrifty Be optimistic	Shun trading Exert prowess Be obedient and disciplined Adhere to tradition Respect hierarchy Be loyal Take vengeance Deceive for the sake of the task Make rich use of leisure Be ostentatious Dispense largesse Be exclusive Show fortitude Be fatalistic Treasure honor

Two important assertions arise from this depiction and its discourse-based application to modern governance systems. First, individuals are naturally drawn and more suitable to one sphere of activity (and not both); second, and as a result, mixing individuals and organizational activities from both spheres is inherently dangerous, leading to what Jacobs terms "monstrous hybrids." As a result, a key message derived from this narrative is the importance of separateness between business and government, in large part due to inappropriate mixing or collusion.

Taken at face value, Jacobs's presentation can merely serve to reinforce the important contrast between public purpose and private gain. It bears noting, however, that this seemingly obvious message came after a decade of largely conservative rule in Anglo-Saxon countries during which the rise of new public management strongly encouraged the importation of business practices and values (and in many cases people) into government, whereas within the private sector the growing movement toward sustainable development was based on embracing the guardian-like responsibilities of business organizations to exercise greater ecological sensitivity (Hawken 1993).

For Gilles, however, the central and fatally flawed proposition put forth by Jacobs is that individuals must choose or that most everyone is inherently suited to a role within either the commercial or the guardian syndrome. There is precious little room for overlap in Jacobs's world: indeed, it is not entirely an exaggeration to say that for her all governance failures stem from overlapping roles or individuals employed in one sector when their behavioural traits dictate that they should be in the other (e.g., an overly entrepreneurial public servant compromising the public interest by bending rules in the name of policy or program innovation).

Initially, I had no difficulty embracing Gilles's critique as it seemed to me both intuitive and desirable that well-educated individuals should be expected to have the cognitive and moral capacities to navigate across the different terrains of the Boulding triangle. Critiquing Jacobs's dichotomy, furthermore, flowed quite naturally along with a defence of co-evolution and the necessary cross-fertilization of ideas, people, and institutional learning across sectoral boundaries. The Public Policy Forum had set up shop, lending further legitimacy to the notion of collective benefit from better intersectoral awareness and interaction. The tide thus seemed steadily against Jacobs, at least in my own world, and critiquing her approach became a central theme of a joint textbook that Gilles and I prepared on the topic of business-government-society relations. To this day, I continue to use Jacobs in the classroom and encourage students to find examples rebuffing her underlying claim that governance hybrids are unworkable and dangerous.

Yet at the same time, perhaps influenced by too much time spent in Ottawa and accumulating scandals of inappropriate fusions of private and public interests (coupled with a growing interest in IT partnerships, where corruption is less an issue than mismanagement, overly rigid procurement processes, and an absence of sufficient empathy and learning across sectors—i.e., less than optimal co-evolutionary skills and capacities), I could never shake off the notion that Jacobs had a point—that to partner successfully across sectoral boundaries, one first had to appreciate where such boundaries lie and what purpose they serve: the elusive goal being to align the best of both sectors rather than fuse them.

With such thoughts in mind, I decided in 2006 to write a short, updated text on business-government relations that would (1) underpin my teaching of Government and Business Relations in a new setting at Dalhousie University; (2) emphasize digital governance challenges in line with my growing interest in this realm; and (3) pay homage to Gilles by acknowledging his foundational guidance and by making use of what I had hoped would be a clever enjoining of Paquet and Jacobs in explaining sectoral interactions in Canada.

Such was not the case, however. The common ground that seemingly emerged in my head was less apparent to Gilles, and true to form he had no difficulty letting me know in some pointed feedback on the book itself (which no doubt came in the form of a still restrained note). In fairness, again true to form, Gilles listened patiently to my case and gave me ample freedom to complete the book as I saw fit (a book that was much better as a result of the feedback and revision but no doubt left Gilles unconvinced in many places as well).

My own interpretation is a compromise of sorts. I continue to believe—hope at least—that my book is on reasonably solid ground in making the case for appreciating sectoral uniqueness and boundaries and the different ethos underpinning industry and government (my limited treatment of society or the so-called third sector was another justifiable critique of the book by Gilles, but we will not go there). The book concludes by making a case for the necessity of governance hybrids and by acknowledging Canada's limited progress in bridging the sectoral gulf to the detriment of the country's productivity and governance performance (here Gilles's more recent works on Canada's economic performance as well as his collaborative efforts with Ruth Hubbard on the necessity of governance innovation point the way; Hubbard and Paquet 2005, 2006).

To confess, then, at times I still see not commonality but value in bridging the separate but potentially complementary messages of Paquet and Jacobs. Just as the mixing of public and private interests has arguably become more common—perhaps unavoidably so in light of today's governance complexities—so too is there a need to (1) ensure that safeguards are in place to govern individual and organizational conduct both within and across each sphere; (2) design and implement appropriate mechanisms for evaluation and learning; and (3) foster awareness of and dialogue on where the appropriate boundaries lie between commercial and guardian endeavours in light of changing socioeconomic, political, and technological circumstances (Roy 2007).

Yet at the same time, I've come to regard the aforementioned point about an individual's ability to transcend sectoral and thus behavioural limitations as a key (though surely not the lone!) irritant for Gilles and not without reason. My own book did not go far enough in addressing this point, and the social and cognitive aspects of sectoral interactions that are indeed fundamental to complex and collaborative governance systems (and much of Gilles's more recent interest in social technologies that facilitate learning and collaboration in a manner that is both institutional and personal). Indeed, notions of human cognition and institutional learning, important themes in much of his most recent writing on governance systems, have largely remained off my radar likely because they are beyond my grasp in terms of rigorous scholarship. By contrast, the breadth of contributions of this book speaks to the range of dimensions contemplated by Gilles in both innovative and integrative manners.

Anticipating Collaboration and Governance

The Canadian discourse on collaborative governance and public-private partnering is owed in large measure to a small group of Canadian pioneers in this regard, chief among them Gilles Paquet. Much of what he espoused through the late 1980s and early 1990s to many unreceptive and skeptical audiences is now taken for granted as mainstream thought—just as surely as much of what he currently writes and conveys offers insight into what is to come. In a similar manner, Gilles anticipated the explosion of interest in governance matters more generally and how good governance would come to be both a common and at times a shared challenge across the public, private, and non-profit sectors.

What has no doubt been a good deal more difficult for Gilles to accept is the resilience of Ottawa's centralized mindset, and here I use the term, in part unfairly where geographical and municipal boundaries are concerned, in reference to the federal government, when, as his own considerable efforts with the cities of Ottawa and Gatineau and the perhaps-not-quite-localized-enough National Capital Commission demonstrate, governance is inherently multilevel. From his early writings on the "strategic state" to more recent efforts with Hubbard on "Gomery's blinders" and the reformation of federalism, his importation of the European principle of subsidiarity into the Canadian scene underscores the truism that positive change is much more likely to be a bottom-up process led by cities, communities, and (smaller and perhaps richer) provinces.

By contrast, the federal government has hardly served as a bastion of innovation in recent years, plagued as it has been by scandal and the resulting compounding of centralized management and political control. Even the mild-mannered Public Policy Forum (2007) weighed in with an unusually strong condemnation of the federal apparatus and its inability to adapt to the challenges ahead. Disappointingly, I suspect, for Gilles, Harper's arrival often seems to have reinforced traditional federal-provincial tensions and an increasingly centralized federal government apparatus. Indeed, in a typically provocative manner, supported by the likes of Senator Hugh Segal, Gilles has also pointed to elements of the Ottawa-centric federal public service itself as being less than entirely loyal to a new team seeking new ways of governing.

Of course, the centralized mindset is hardly unique to Ottawa alone. It exists in most countries sharing Westminster democratic structures and to varying degrees within all Canadian provincial capitals (e.g., in Cape Breton there is a twofold centralized mindset to lament in both Halifax and Ottawa!). While Gilles is a proponent of decentralized governance and stronger municipal capacities, his forceful participation in debates about a fiscal disequilibrium is also partly reflective of what Caroline Andrew (2002) has called this country's "obsession with federal-provincial relations." I've often thought in recent months observing the strikingly similar governance challenges of the cities of Halifax and Ottawa that it would be wonderful to see Gilles return to the field of urban affairs and offer a retrospective consideration of amalgamated municipalities that seem to have struggled in fostering effective collaborative capacities, both internally and across sectors, that are necessary for social learning and resilient governance and development.

In sum, as technological, service, and policy interdependencies grow, it is clear that the case for collaborative governance intensifies both within and across jurisdictional and sectoral boundaries. Nobody in the country has done more than Gilles Paquet to prepare the intellectual groundwork for this important shift while also taking the message directly to current and future leaders via classrooms at all levels of study. Within all segments of Ottawa's increasingly diverse communities, Gilles personifies his belief in bottom-up change by always welcoming conversation, debate, and especially new ideas. And on that note Jane Jacobs would no doubt concur.

Notes

[1] There is no uniform definition for this other sector (often referred to as the third) that is nonetheless meant to encompass the many forms of formal organizations and informal movements that are neither private sector corporations nor public sector bodies.

[2] A useful review of this book by Professor Mary Ann Glendon of Harvard University is available at www.firstthings.com/ftissues/ft9312/reviews/glendon.html [consulted September 28, 2008].

References

Andrew, C. (2002). *What Is the Municipal Potential?* Regina: Saskatchewan Institute of Public Policy.

Hawken, P. (1993) *The Ecology of Commerce*. New York: HarperBusiness

Hubbard, R., and G. Paquet. (2005). "Betting on Mechanisms: The New Frontier for Federalism." *Optimum Online, 35.1*, 2–26.

———. (2006). "Re-inventer notre architecture institutionnelle." *Policy Options* (September). Montreal: IRPP, 55–63.

Jacobs, J. (1992). *Systems of Survival*. New York: Random House.

Paquet, G. (1997). "States, Communities, and Markets: The Distributed Governance Scenario." In *The Nation-State in a Global Information Era: Policy Challenges*, ed. T. J. Courchene. The Bell Canada Papers in Economics and Public Policy 5. Kingston: John Deutsch Institute for the Study of Economic Policy, 25–46.

———. (1999). *Governance through Social Learning*. Ottawa: University of Ottawa Press.

Przyblyski, J. (2006). "The Life of Great American Cities after the Death of Jane Jacobs." *SPUR Newsletter* (June). San Francisco: San Francisco Planning Urban Research Association.

Public Policy Forum. (2007). "Canada's Public Service in the 21st Century" (discussion paper). Ottawa: Public Policy Forum.

Roy, J. (2007). *Business and Government in Canada*. Ottawa: University of Ottawa Press.

Yankelovich, D. (1999) *The Magic of Dialogue: Transforming Conflict into Cooperation*. New York: Simon & Schuster.

Chapter 15

Urban Governance, *à la* Paquet

Caroline Andrew

Introduction

I begin by stating my perspective in this chapter: I can be described as a "frequent flyer" on Gilles Paquet's definition of governance. I have used it to think about a variety of policies and programs of urban and local governance in Canadian cities, women in cities, equity-seeking groups in Canadian cities, urban francophones in Ottawa, and immigration policy, again in Ottawa.

I start this chapter by distinguishing my use of Paquet's definition of governance from his definition so as to be clear about both the borrowing and the changes through the borrowing. I realized in preparing this chapter that there is at least one major point (perhaps there are two) where I have departed from his definition of governance as the effective mechanisms of coordination in situations where power, resources, and information are widely distributed.

The first surprised me: I had forgotten that Paquet's definition talked of effective mechanisms, whereas I had always used the definition simply as mechanisms. One less word but also a rather different perspective. His writings are basically around analyzing, exhorting, and presenting arguments about how to improve governance and being critical of a full range of practices that Gilles argues impede good governance. My aim is different; I want to understand which mechanisms of coordination have developed—whether they turn out to be effective or not.

The second point of departure concerns the definition given to the term "mechanisms," at least in some circumstances. In a very interesting article by Ruth Hubbard and Gilles Paquet (2005), "Betting on Mechanisms: The New Frontier for

Federalism," the word *mechanisms* refers to broadly defined types of behaviour that could bring needed flexibility into Canadian federalism by creating the conditions for working cooperatively. Two things are needed: a space to work together and conditions that create a situation in which all parties gain from the collaboration. These two conditions lead to four mechanisms: forums for discussion, reporting mechanisms, ways to generate trust, and fail-safe mechanisms. These are high-level conceptual spaces, aimed (in that particular article) at corresponding to the problems identified in current Canadian federalism.

My use of "mechanisms" is at a much more detailed and perhaps more practical level. I want to understand the forms used to bring about coordination across the barriers of widely dispersed power, resources, and information. I want to do so in order to understand how governance systems operate, who is involved, and who has developed the particular forms of cooperation. I want to understand who has been excluded. I will briefly develop a case study of immigration policy and governance in the City of Ottawa and then, using this example, evaluate the usefulness of my borrowing Paquet's definition of governance.

Starting from the definition of governance as the mechanisms of coordination in situations where power, resources, and information are widely distributed, I will look first at the questions of power, resources, and information before focusing on the mechanisms of coordination that currently exist.

Immigration Policy and Governance in Ottawa

One of the levers of power is constitutional jurisdiction, and immigration policy is a joint responsibility of federal and provincial governments. However, constitutional jurisdiction is simply one element of power, and the relative activity of different government levels has varied considerably across time despite the fixed nature of constitutional authority.

At the present time, the federal government is clearly still the primary actor in immigration policy (Biles et al. 2008), but provincial activity is a growing factor. Ontario joined the provincial activism relatively recently, and the federal–Ontario agreement of 2005 is currently rolling out greatly expanded activity. Important innovation exists in the federal–Ontario agreement; municipalities were explicitly mentioned for the first time in a federal–provincial context, and, although this was clearly related to the importance of the immigrant population in Toronto, it has opened up space for municipalities across Ontario and therefore for Ottawa.

Civil society also has elements of power in the immigration field. One of the major characteristics of Canadian immigration policy in the recent period is the use of third-party delivery agencies (Tolley forthcoming). This has meant the development of an important sector of immigrant-serving agencies. In Ottawa, the agencies have created a *table de concertation*, LASI (Local Agencies Serving Immigrants), which brings together the executive directors of the most important agencies. LASI is a coordinating structure that has created an independent agency, LASI World Skills, which is extremely active in the area of immigrant employment. LASI World Skills was one of the founding members, with the United Way, of Hire Immigrants Ottawa, a program that brings together a council of employers, along with the immigrant sector, to promote employment of immigrants.

All this indicates that service provider organizations do have some power. They are constrained, of course, by the fact that their funding comes from federal and provincial project funding, often with highly particular criteria, objectives, and funding arrangements. But they do have power in that they speak for the immigrant sector and in that government policy is dependent on their successful implementation of policy directions.

Resources are also widely distributed, particularly if we think in terms of human resources as well as financial resources. Indeed, thinking in terms of human capital, social capital, and financial capital further complicates the distribution of resources. At all levels of government, and across sectors of civil society, there is human capital invested in the immigration area: teachers of ESL and FLS, federal policy analysts, municipal recreation directors and managers, volunteer human resources people sitting on advisory committees and boards, and one can continue. Social capital can also be mapped across the region: geographical communities, ethno-specific communities, communities of practice, networks of identity.

One example is the City for All Women Initiative/Initiative: Une ville pour toutes les femmes (CAWI/IVTF: see Andrew 2005; and Andrew and Klodawsky, 2006), a partnership organization between the City of Ottawa and community-based women's groups. CAWI has created social capital in an organization thanks to many factors, including the community development skills of the coordinator, Suzanne Doerge. It has been successful in mobilizing women from recent immigrant groups to articulate their needs and their demands at City Hall, and the city, at least parts of it, has appreciated the fact that CAWI brings new voices to the city's deliberations. Its success is also linked to the social capital created, both bonding (women) and bridging (cross-race and ethnicity, cross-language, cross-religion).

Financial resources are widely, and very unequally, distributed. Within the public sector, the federal government has far more resources than the local government. Much has been written about the financial problems of urban governments in Canada, and clearly such problems comprise one of the important constraints on municipal activity.

Information is the third category in Paquet's description of the wide distribution of assets among multiple actors. Information can be kept or distributed according to different strategies. For example, the ten-year-old Metropolis initiative has had a particularly active strategy of producing and distributing information (Shields and Evans 2008). Knowledge exchange is at the heart of this initiative. The City of Ottawa would be toward the other end of a continuum; it has almost no tradition of wide distribution of information, and the information that it generates internally usually remains internal.

Informal information flows among all the actors: information about sympathetic teachers and schools, housing owners who are sympathetic to immigrants, neighbourhoods to choose or avoid. The informal information flows co-exist with a variety of more formalized information, from websites to information brochures, from training manuals to press releases. Thinking about information also raises the category of missing information, and one of the important governance questions around immigration policy in Ottawa has been the reflection on generating more information on the strategies of immigrant integration in the newly diversifying second- and third-tier Ontario communities. The codification of tacit knowledge is a policy lever.

So immigration policy in Ottawa is a governance question. No one actor alone can take action; coordination is necessary. Inspired by Paquet, I will focus on the identification of the mechanisms of coordination and their characteristics. The kinds of coordination mechanisms will be categorized first of all in terms of whether the mechanism was created by the state or by civil society. This is fundamental in terms of understanding governance as processes involving multiple actors and in terms of situating governance processes in relation to state, market, and civil society.

The analysis of governance depends on clearly understanding the initiators of various mechanisms so that coordination does not become a word to blur the actual process. I am also interested in the funding, institutionalization, and current composition of the coordinating mechanism in order to understand the current positioning in terms of state, market, and civil society, but the fundamental criteria for this analysis are the initiating actors.

Starting with LASI, which I have briefly described, it has been initiated by civil society and remains within civil society. It remains relatively informal, with no dedicated staff. It operates on the basis of trust among the executive directors of the immigrant-serving agencies. Although LASI itself has no staff, its "spin-off" company, LASI World Skills, does. The lead roles are played by the executive directors of the two largest agencies, Hamdi Mohamoud of OCISO (Ottawa Community Immigrant Serving Organization) and Carl Nicholson of the Catholic Immigration Centre.

Other coordinating structures within the immigrant sector are COMPAC, which has worked with the Ottawa police to strengthen links between the immigrant community and the police as well as to move the police to be more sensitive to, and representative of, the immigrant and visible minority communities. MOST is another organization that has brought the immigrant community together on a broad basis. For both organizations, leadership is shared between Carl Nicholson of the Catholic Immigration Centre and Yew Lee of Axiom Consulting. Again, both are relatively informal, with no dedicated staff. LASI is currently interested in making proposals and getting funding for positions to build its capacity to better coordinate the work of the immigrant-serving sector.

CAWI has also been initiated by civil society but is composed of representatives of civil society and the City of Ottawa. CAWI has chosen not to try for city funding, although it is now receiving an amount of money from the city for a specific project, the creation of a multifocal lens. CAWI has chosen instead to get funding from sources outside the city (Status of Women Canada, Trillium, United Way) in order to conserve a relationship with the City of Ottawa that can be based on the idea of partnership rather than defined by city funding.

These civil society-initiated mechanisms of coordination are therefore motivated by the desire for the autonomy of civil society. However, they must all then deal with the problem of capacity and the dilemma of financing the structure of enhanced civil society capacity. Different solutions have emerged, but the underlying tension remains; autonomous action by civil society requires either extraordinary volunteer activity or resources to structure enhanced capacity.

The next type of coordinating mechanisms consists of arrangements set up by civil society actors because state funding was available. We can see them as different from the first type because the mechanisms would not exist if state funding was not present. An important example in the area of immigration is Hire Immigrants Ottawa, a program of United Way Ottawa, with LASI World Skills and a Council of Employers, from both the public and the private sectors. The program is funded by the Ontario government, the Ministry of Citizenship and Immigration. The aim of the program is to engage employers with the immigrant community in the question of immigrant employment. The program has full-time employees and implies the volunteer time of the Council of Employers.

Another interesting example is the regional network set up within the francophone immigrant community as a result of a call for proposals by the Ontario Region of the federal Department of Citizenship and Immigration. Three networks were funded in Ontario (in the north, east, and south), and the network for eastern Ontario was created by the francophone immigrant settlement agency, le Conseil économique et social d'Ottawa-Carleton (CESOC). The intention is to bring together the full range of the groups within the francophone immigrant community to enhance the capacity of this community to access federal funding. The network is run by civil society but for objectives determined by the federal government. This is not to say that building capacity within the francophone immigrant community is not an objective felt by that community, but the decision to create these networks was not an initiative of civil society.

The third category of coordination mechanisms is comprised of those created by the state but composed of civil society actors. The advisory committees of the City of Ottawa are examples of this kind of mechanism, particularly the Equity and Diversity Advisory Committee (EDAC). Another example is at the provincial level: the federal Department of Citizenship and Immigration's Ontario Region Francophone Advisory Committee, which does include some local and regional Ottawa civil society representatives. This committee deals generally with francophone immigration to Ontario, but it also considers local and regional issues.

A final category would be state-initiated coordination among instances of the state. One example would be the linking across municipalities that was funded by the Ontario government to create municipal web portals on immigration. The City of Ottawa, as one of the municipalities funded to create a portal, participates in this coordination.

There are, of course, more formal state coordination mechanisms, starting from the federal–provincial–territorial (FPT) ministerial meetings. These meetings in the area of immigration are at a relatively preliminary stage of development, as illustrated by the fact that this committee does not at the present time have a provincial co-chair, something that exists in other FPT policy areas.

This has not been a complete inventory of the coordinating mechanisms that exist and that impact on immigration policy in the City of Ottawa. Its aim has been twofold: to illustrate the multiplicity of the coordination mechanisms and to illustrate the differential positioning of these mechanisms in the governance triangle of state, market, and civil society. This positioning has been done in a simplistic manner, focused on the initiating actor, but this positioning could be analyzed in a much more detailed and nuanced fashion. Some specific names have been mentioned in order to illustrate that individual agency plays a vital role in governance systems.

The Usefulness of Paquet's Governance Definition

Rather than trying to evaluate the success of the Ottawa immigration governance system in terms of policies, programs, and activities, I will attempt to evaluate the usefulness of the Paquet definition of governance for understanding local policy in Canadian cities. The benefits seem to me to be triple: it puts all levels of political and social action on the same footing, it does the same for individual and institutional actors, and the categories of power, resources, and information allow for an analytical understanding of the politics of governance.

The Paquet definition allows for an interscalar understanding of immigration policy in that all levels of political and social actions are included. This means that specific empirical research determines who intervenes in the City of Ottawa's immigration policies. It is not a prior determination of what is municipal government that determines how the city's policies really evolve; it is from looking through the governance mechanisms that we can determine which political and social actors play the most important roles, and at which level or levels of political and social action different elements of overall policy are determined.

In addition, the Paquet definition does not prejudge whether individuals or groups are the actors of the governance system, and this once again allows for theorizing that stems from empirical investigation. This is particularly important in terms of municipal immigration policy in that there is no formal role for municipal governments in this area; Canadian municipalities have limited resources and a limited pro-action policy tradition in the twentieth century (not so in the nineteenth century, but that's another story), so we know little about the actual role of municipal and local actors in the broadly defined policy area of immigrant settlement and integration. We know that certain areas of municipal policy have potential importance for immigrant integration, but we know little about the ways that this plays out.

Finally, the categorization of power, resources, and information is a theoretically useful way of moving forward our understanding of governance and urban policy. It allows us to link to the important issues around governance—is it simply neoliberalism with a new face? Does it allow a genuine space for civil society, and, if so, does it allow alternative visions of collective futures, or does civil society simply reproduce existing views? Who comprises civil society, and why do some parts intervene and others not? If civil society does simply reproduce existing ideas, is this because of the weight of existing institutions, path dependency, reliance on state financing, or agreement with existing policy directions? Power, resources, and information cover both structures and relationships between the various actors.

Therefore, for me, the usefulness of the Paquet definition of governance is that it pushes toward both empirical research and theorizing. Who is networking, and are there unexpected people and/or organizations in the networks? And, at the same time, who is benefiting from the policy, and who is losing out? And how is this linked to the nature and the forms of the coordinating mechanisms that function in the policy area being examined?

The Benefits of Avoiding High-Level Generalities

Although the definition of "mechanisms" used by Paquet as set out in the article that I referred to earlier helps with respect to some of the tensions and contradictions in Canadian federalism, I would also argue that this definition might sometimes operate at a rather high level of generality. To this extent, there are some lessons that can be developed by using "mechanisms" in the more practical and detailed way that I have tried to outline in my example of the City of Ottawa's immigration governance system. Specifically, the trade-offs and tensions that are continually being negotiated in governance systems can perhaps be better described by being concrete.

I will use one example: the tensions around the institutionalization of voluntary efforts and the impact on the role of paid staff in relation to board members. This issue is taken up by Hubbard and Paquet (2007) in their text "The Governance of Solidarity Organizations: An Exploratory Essay." The text is rich and complex, full of insights. Hubbard and Paquet are fully aware of the tensions involved in trying to achieve multiple and conflicting goals, but there is an implicit preference for the "honour cats," those whose motivation is "rooted in a sense of *me-all* obligation based on status, on a sense of pride and competence" (9), and an implicit condemnation of the increasing institutionalization of the solidarity organizations. Near the end of their text, they articulate what they see as two major consequences of the growing "hybridization" of solidarity organizations:

> First is a growth of hyper-competition as a natural consequence of the takeover of the solidarity organizations by staffers and bureaucrats. But they are not alone. In this age of growing distrust of the state, citizens are choosing to get involved in *impolitical* ways, and solidarity organizations are a magnificent instrument for ideologues to mobilize emergent publics.
>
> Second, this triple helix (hypercompetition, bureaucratic efforts to replace politics with administration, and some hijacking of solidarity organizations by radicals) has made the governance of solidarity organizations much more complex and may explain why solidarity organizations have often lost their sense of purpose and ceased to be the agents of prototyping and serious play (24).

This does point out two important questions: the institutionalization of honour and the role of staff in relation to board members, and the fuzziness of accountability structures in governance systems. However, it also simplifies the tensions that I described earlier in my profile of coordinating mechanisms in Ottawa's immigration policy.

LASI is limited in its capability because it works on the volunteer time of the members, who are themselves staff, the executive directors of the immigrant settlement agencies. The same logic applies to a City for All Women Initiative, albeit in a somewhat different form. The members of the Steering Committee are in the majority women who have been active at a community association level but who are not knowledgeable about the processes of more formal politics. More than this, they start from the position of feeling that they have no place in formal politics and that therefore there has to be a process of building confidence, carefully preparing them to participate, and supporting this participation.

This takes human resources that go beyond volunteer capacity. Yet these are honour cats in Hubbard and Paquet's terms—the women are wonderful examples of "me-all" and a sense of honour—triggered in part by the lack of recognition that they have had in Canada (for their educational credentials, their work experience, and their capacity for social action), and in part by their vision of a more socially just and equitable world for all, including themselves (and which is linked, of course, to their own personal decisions and/or trajectories to Canada). Bringing new categories of citizens into active governance seems to me to be impossible without staff capacity because of the reasons described above but also because active governance will not work unless there is a certain degree of success in achieving goals seen to be important to the newly active actors.

This point also applies to LASI. The organization holds together because of practical advantages (reducing competition, sharing information) but also for reasons of honour. The heads of the agencies believe in a more inclusive Canada for recent immigrants and for themselves—they too are honour cats, but they want to see results for their efforts, and doing it all themselves does not bring results commensurate to their visions.

Conclusion

There are consequences, of course, to institutionalization, and Hubbard and Paquet are clear about them. But defining governance in terms of effective mechanisms of coordination seems at least to call for a more balanced acknowledgement of the tensions involved in choosing to enhance volunteer activity with paid staff. Indeed, these questions should probably lead to a more extended reflection of the notion of "mechanisms." What is the appropriate level of analysis, and does a more high-level approach yield more important answers than the very practical level that I have been describing here?

But this question goes beyond the objective of this chapter—to recognize my intellectual debt to Gilles Paquet by illustrating why I find my version of his definition of governance useful both to focusing empirical research and to facilitating theorizing around the practices of local politics and development in Canadian cities. For that, *un grand merci*.

References

Andrew, Caroline. (2008). "Gendering Nation-States and/or Gendering City-States: Debates about the Nature of Citizenship." In *Gendering the Nation-State: Canadian and Comparative Perspectives*, ed. Yasmeen Abu-Laban. Vancouver: UBC Press, 239–251.

Andrew, Caroline, and Fran Klodawsky. (2006). "New Voices: New Politics." *Women and Environments 70-71*, 66–67.

Biles, John, Meyer Burstein, and James Frideres. (2008). *Immigration and Integration in Canada in the Twenty-first Century*. Montreal and Kingston: McGill-Queens University Press and Metropolis.

Hubbard, R., and G. Paquet. (2005). "Betting on Mechanisms: The New Frontier for Federalism." *Optimum Online, 35.1*, 2–25. www.optimumonline.ca [consulted January 15, 2009]

———. (2007). "The Governance of Solidarity Organizations: An Exploratory Essay." *Optimum Online, 37.4*, 2–22. www.optimumonline.ca [consulted January 15, 2009]

Shields, John, and Bryan Evans. (2008). "Building a Policy-Oriented Research Partnership for Knowledge Mobilization and Knowledge Transfer: The Case of Metropolis Canada." Presentation at the Canadian Political Science Association meetings in the Congress of the Humanities and Social Sciences, Vancouver, May 2008.

Tolley, Erin. (forthcoming). "Multi-level Governance in Immigration and Settlement: An Introduction." In *Multi-level Governance in Immigration and Settlement*, ed. Erin Tolley. Montreal and Kingston: McGill-Queens University Press.

Chapter 16

Building Cooperation through Conversation

Chris Wilson

Introduction

Robert Wright (2000) argued that the history of humankind could be characterized by what he called the "vector of life," the tendency of human beings to evolve larger and more complex systems of social cooperation. The direction of this arrow of history, he said, points clearly toward increasing interdependence and the adoption of *non-zero sum* relationships. Despite the long and obvious human history of *zero sum* relationships typified by win-lose interactions, social Darwinism, conflict, and war, this very competitiveness, Wright argued, continues to move humanity toward greater cooperation, to the point where today it struggles with cooperation at a species level and on a global scale. That said, cooperation remains an epic struggle to take advantage of the forces that are driving us together while mitigating the forces that togetherness inspires that also drive us apart.

Within this context, Gilles Paquet has made important contributions to enabling us to accelerate this trend of human and organizational cooperation within a modern context. He is an astute observer of the dynamics of governance (which he describes as effective coordination when information, resources, and power are widely distributed) as well as a relentless commentator on public policy and administration.

His 1999 book *Governance through Social Learning* is a compilation of many of his ideas regarding relational governance, and it presents governance as a lens through which one can observe the dynamics of organizational cooperation. Despite his "official" retirement some years ago, Paquet continues to contribute to a growing collective narrative about the need to find better ways to live and work together, and especially about how to do so.

With respect to a recent book of Paquet's on governance, *The New Geo-Governance: A Baroque Approach*, published in 2005, H. George Frederickson (2006) commented in *Public Administration Times* that Paquet "creates a word-picture of the highest quality, and his portrayal of our likely governance future is a conceptual tour de force". Frederickson went on to say that Paquet had advanced the work of leading thinkers and observers, such as Robert Axelrod, Harlan Cleveland, and Peter Drucker, on collaborative governance, especially in the area of public administration, through his emphasis on the technologies and mechanisms of geo-governance, by which Paquet means the many ways in which (1) individuals and institutions (public, private, and civic) manage their collective affairs in space, (2) diverse interests accommodate and resolve their differences, and (3) these many actors and organizations are involved in a continuing process of formal and informal competition, cooperation, and learning in space.

There is no doubt that Paquet's work continues to underscore Wright's theme. At the same time, his special contribution has been in the area of mechanisms of cooperation, reflecting a degree of pragmatism uncharacteristic of many of his peers and unusual for a non-practitioner.

Governance Today

Today's fast-paced, globalized world demands that people in advanced democracies such as Canada find better ways to cooperate in life and work. For the past while, Paquet's message, much like that of Block (1993) and Cleveland (2002), has consistently challenged the popular myth that "someone is in charge" while encouraging organizational leaders to embrace cooperation and shared governance like a surfer riding a wave—adapting through small movements and social techniques that over time cumulatively begin to shift management paradigms and practices.

The importance of this approach became clear to me the first time I met Paquet, in late 1995, at a tax policy convention for the Conservative Party after its ignominious defeat in 1993. Paquet had been invited as a sort of *éminence grise* to advise party officials on possible changes to its taxation platform.

The social contract between citizens and government has been steadily weakening since the early 1970s, as evidenced by the steady decline in the public's trust in government. That trust hovers now as it did in 1995 around thirty percent (Graves 2008; Wilson 1998). Paquet urged the Conservatives to stem this tide by finding ways to engage with citizens in a collective conversation about the means and ends of government intervention. Such a conversation was likely not only to encourage greater tax compliance, he said, but also to contribute to better policy effectiveness and social coherence.

Paquet appreciated that citizens needed to understand the real trade-offs involved in making policy choices to be able to take stock of the consequences themselves. "If the cost is zero," he used to say, "the demand will always be infinite. Unfortunately, the supply is always finite." Yet he believed that discussions about trade-offs had to go beyond the ballot box and the phoney consultations where governments pretend to listen and citizens pretend to have made a difference. Paquet asserted that, to restore government legitimacy, citizens needed to become more actively engaged as partners in their own governance. He pointed to the successful efforts of the Quebec finance minister to help people save on taxes as a means of increasing legitimacy and bringing them into a conversation. Such was my introduction to the Paquet school of social learning, moral contracting, and cooperative mechanisms, the centrepiece of his writing and teaching in the decade since.

Why is there a greater need today for Canadians to find better ways to live and work together? Because big G Government in countries such as ours is increasingly out of sync with the need for small g governance as a process for resolving many issues of importance to citizens (Paquet 2006). Big G asserts that a small group of experts can effectively be "in charge" of resolving the country's most important and complex concerns. While this approach of elite accommodation behind closed doors has been discredited, as for example in the constitutional failures of Charlottetown and Meech Lake, it remains the default governing process, especially in public administration. On the other hand, small g, which encourages groups of stakeholders to take ownership of problems and to learn their way out of them, is becoming increasingly common.

The complex, "wicked" problems/issues of relevance here that have responded favourably to small g approaches include some public policy challenges, problem solving in the face of rapid technological change, and fostering unique socioeconomic-technical advantages for geographically based clusters. This means that, among other things, communities (broadly defined) need to bet on establishing a *cooperative advantage* in order to tackle the increasing number of chronic socioeconomic problems that they face if they would like to have a greater chance of achieving success.

Whether public policy challenges relate to matters such as poverty, safety, health, or climate change, the difficulty in resolving these issues is a direct result of their being "collective action" problems (Heath 2001). That is, they will not be solved *for* us as much as they will be solved *by* us working cooperatively. These are not someone else's problems. They are *our* problems. As such, they demand that we take greater ownership of both problem and solution by contributing to our own governance.

With respect to problem solving in eras of fast-paced technological change, Best (1990) observed that interfirm cooperation increased and was crucial during such periods: "firms not only compete, but they can also cooperate to provide common services, to shape the 'rules of the game,' and to shape complementary investment strategies" (17). In other words, the formation of "communities" of firms offered a means of improving collective efficiency and providing cooperative defence against external threats.

At the same time, cooperation among local actors can provide a basis for competitive advantage that results from the cultivation of socioeconomic-technical characteristics that can be ascribed to some communities and not to others. For example, Porter (1990) has observed that regional industrial clustering generated trusted relationships between producers and suppliers, and created a source of efficiency that could enhance national competitiveness. Similarly, Saxenian (1994) found that close relationships between firms, universities, and other local institutions could generate regional innovative advantages that were not easily duplicated. Some communities can effectively generate social capital (Putnam 2000), and so reduce transaction costs among firms and instill increased confidence in public sector administration (Rothstein 2005). More recently still, Florida (2002) has suggested that the nature and quality of communities can encourage or discourage the clustering of talent, the principal economic resource in an era of knowledge-based industry.

Barriers

Despite the reduction of the physical constraints of distance and language today, the drive to achieve this *cooperative advantage* is not widespread, rapid, or unidirectional.

The reasons are undoubtedly many; fundamentally, as Paquet (2005) points out, there is no satisfactory recipe for the practice of good governance.

Many theorists and practitioners of administration have promoted the use of more rules, structures, and standardized processes or the reification of values to exert better control over more complex and distributed governance arenas. Paquet, on the other hand, has encouraged the use of mechanisms such as dialogue, moral contracting, mutual accommodation, experimentation, and shared learning. "When the ground is in motion," says Paquet (1999, 220), "organizations can only govern themselves by becoming capable of learning both their goals and the means to reach them *as they proceed*." Here there are no fixed rules, only creative people, their commitment to change, and the relationships of trust among them.

A key barrier to accepting this "social learning" approach to more collaborative governance relates to resistance to the underlying notion that "no one is in charge." It is possible that as individuals we refuse to accept this more realistic but scarier notion of authority largely because of its corollary. If no one is in charge, then "everyone is in charge" (Cleveland 2002), implying that we must take ownership of, and responsibility for, our own futures. However, following that path can be fraught with risk, as every entrepreneur knows, so for the pretense of safety and predictability we abdicate our judgment and freedom to choose to would-be leaders, assuming religiously that they will save us from ourselves.

At the same time, governments that inhabit a world of positional and coercive power have particular trouble turning away from the use of rules, structures, standardized processes, and reified values. The reality of complex and distributed governance arenas is either denied (Hubbard and Paquet 2008) or subjected to reinterpretation (Bradford 2007) for the old tools of control to remain plausible.

In fact, the state architecture epitomized by the agency model of Westminster-style democracy may well be wholly inadequate (Hubbard and Paquet 2007). A new social contract, one that directly engages the citizenry, has become compulsory. According to Paquet, this new contract emphasizes collective obligations as much as individual rights, constant negotiation and institutional tinkering (what he likes to call *bricolage*) over grand schemes, and strengthened democracy and stewardship over centralized leadership. It adds up, he says, to a new institutional architecture, "the strategic state," capable of directly engaging communities and citizens together with their governments (Paquet 2001) in an ongoing conversation.

Canadian governments (especially but not only at the federal level) are behaving somewhat schizophrenically in this regard, increasingly embracing partnerships in practice while maintaining that power sharing beyond the public sector could not and should not happen (Gow 2007).

On the one hand, there is an unmistakable trend to more broadly distributed, polycentric governance with its loose arrangements and guiding principles, presenting what Paquet has often described as "a game without a master." It is not just governments that are governing but also companies, voluntary organizations, neighbourhood groups, and, yes, individual citizens. For instance, in a recent survey by the Crossing Boundaries (CBNC) initiative (Lenihan et al. 2006), a near consensus of public sector managers in Canada (over 98.4% of respondents) indicated that they believed partnerships were both necessary and legitimate in the context of public sector policy making and program delivery.

On the other hand, Canada's state apparatus has remained "fundamentally Hegelian," where state functionaries continue to view themselves as having "moral purposes that transcend those of its individual citizens" (Hubbard and Paquet 2007, 100). Even when confronted with evidence to the contrary, in pilots such as the Vancouver Agreement (Auditor General of Canada 2005), or the Action for Neighbourhood Change (Gorman 2007), or the Community Futures program in Nova Scotia (Hodgett 2008), that experience is marginalized and inoculated from influencing government more broadly.

No wonder the CBNC survey also observed that public servants did not have "a common understanding of the term 'partnership'" and that "Canada—particularly at the Federal level—is lagging behind other Commonwealth Countries and the United States in the development and use of innovative partnering arrangements" (Lenihan et al. 2006, 3). So while Canadian governments are pushed by circumstances to pursue collaborative strategies with private, not-for-profit, and other government partners more frequently, their paternalistically challenged sense of public interest inhibits their understanding of good partnership practice.

In their recent book *Gomery's Blinders and Canadian Federalism* (2007), Hubbard and Paquet suggest that there continues to be a sense permeating the public sector, and the federal government in particular, that *only* public officials are competent to define and protect the public interest. The public—the citizenry, business, and non-governmental organizations—is consistently dismissed as being incapable of understanding complex issues, prioritizing options, comprehending trade-offs, negotiating strategies, or coalescing around decisions.

This claim to competence would be laughable if it weren't so dangerous. As one former senior federal bureaucrat instructed me, "politics is not about solutions. Focusing on problems is a luxury for government. Positioning trumps solutions every time." Governments only rarely implement solutions to complex problems because of the time that it takes to sort out what's going on and to generate internally coherent responses. Results take commitment and persistence over time. Positions, on the other hand, can be determined with the outcome of a poll, cost little to implement, and can be as flexible as the wind. Therefore, in a public sector context, competency as defined by results is a *non sequitur*.

Strangely, the necessity that governments feel to engage in partnerships fails to dissuade them from the belief that they are in full control of all the elements to achieve their policy and program intentions. More realistically, when governments choose to rely on others to deliver their mandates, "they voluntarily relinquish their status as sole arbiter of the collective interest" (Wilson 2007). Public interest becomes intertwined with partnership interests as governments temporarily "become members of an issue circumscribed commons." In such relationships, public interest and the interests of public organizations ought to be congruent with the achievement of the partnership agenda, and partnership success naturally depends on the ability of the participants to act as effective partners.

Cooperative Advantage and Collective Conversations

Peter Block tells us that "[c]ommunity is fundamentally an interdependent human system given form by the conversation it holds with itself. The history, buildings, economy, infrastructure and culture are [artifacts] of the conversations and the social fabric of any community" (2008, 30).

Mary Jo Hatch has written about how new ideas become part of cultural norms through a bidirectional conversational process. "What is essential," she says, "is that a critical mass of appreciation for a new [cultural] artifact be built up so that diffusion takes hold within retroactive realization processes" (1993, 668). Hatch also quotes T. P. Wilson: "We do not build up a pattern of society from descriptions of single actions [in an additive way] . . . but rather develop an account in a hermeneutic fashion, forming ideas about overall patterns on the basis of particular events and then using these same ideas to understand more clearly the particular events that gave rise to them" (quoted in Hatch: 675).

Building on this notion of how new ideas become part of cultural norms, it is possible to set out the dynamics of community culture as presenting two opportunities for conversation: (1) to evolve community-based paradigms, assumptions, and values by referencing the many individual activities that feed into a community through innovation, affirmation, and dialogue (*clockwise*); and (2) to understand the relevance and utility of new ideas and practices by referencing the community's broad understanding of an issue through a provision of context, the diffusion of new knowledge to sectors and organizations, and the assimilation of knowledge and "best practice" by individuals (*anticlockwise*). When both of these conversations reach a "critical mass," new ideas, practices, and products gain acceptance within a newly formed and accepted community paradigm (the dynamics are set out in Figure 1).

The *cooperative advantage* of community—something that, as noted earlier, offers the hope of tackling many socioeconomic problems effectively—is generated by reduced transaction costs from trusted relationships; innovation and adaptability through social learning; coordinated actions from shared commitments; and effective infrastructures and streamlined regulatory regimes from common purposes.

Note the underlying thread of conversation that delivers that cooperative advantage. It is through the many conversations among community members that relationships and social capital are built; that social learning occurs; that commitments become shared; and that purposes can be understood as common. And, while it is true that communities have encouraged and made space for individual freedom, excellence, creativity, and competition, they also demand participation in a collective conversation through which each member, each organization, and each institution can acknowledge its interdependence and contribute to a shared agenda, acting as "an investor, owner, and creator of [a] place" (Block 2008, 3).

If the collective narrative is open and welcoming, if it is directed to future opportunities and not the wrongs of the past, if it gives meaning and expands our sense of self, if it promotes ownership and accountability among community members, if it is all these things, then people can grow into an evolving story by contributing their knowledge, resources, and commitments. What may have been unthinkable in an older narrative becomes possible in another.

If, on the other hand, as Block (2008) has suggested, the narrative marginalizes hope, if it waits for someone else to take charge, if it seeks accountability through control and coercion, if it seeks to find fault and market fear, if it seeks entitlement

Figure 1: Dynamics of Community Culture

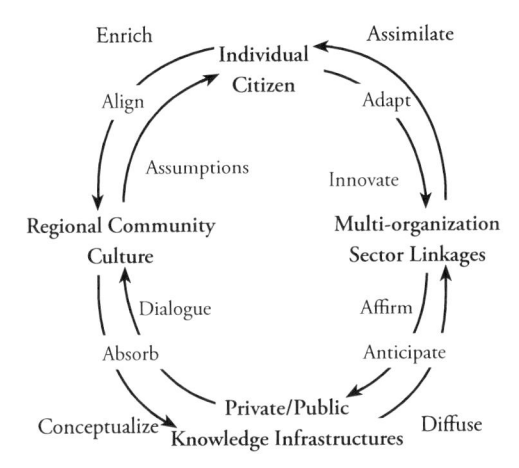

over commitment, if it demands more rules, laws or regulations, and if it minimizes the value of citizens' contributions, then it will fail in creating community change and only affirm the collective action problem: "we can't do it alone, but we can't do it together either."

Such narratives promote cynicism, dependency, free rides, social fragmentation, unaccountable leaders, an absence of citizenship, and ultimately despair in the belief that people can make a change. They also give rise to ideational "zombies"— ideas held to be true within the community despite their lack of evidence or even evidence to the contrary (Provincial Centre of Excellence for Child and Youth Mental Health at CHEO 2006).

This suggests that the quality of a community's collective narrative is not only an essential thermometer of community health and resilience but also acts as a tool for altering the structures, social fabric, and form of the community itself. This in turn suggests that community well-being may be improved if conversations can be modified to take better advantage of the forces that drive people together while mitigating those that drive them apart. Nonetheless, redirecting a community's conversation will likely require changing its initial dynamics fundamentally and a great deal of patience.

It begins with the small things. Whom do we include in those conversations? Are we inclusive enough of diverse perspectives yet small enough to allow everyone to fully participate? Where do we hold them? On neutral ground, or do we host them in-house? Do we set up to lecture people, or do we use round tables to facilitate dialogue? Do we listen or just present our own ideas? Do we utilize champions and brokers? Is the conversation that we try to initiate reflective of the broader conversation that we would like to have?

As Block points out, "The key to creating or transforming community, then, is to see the power in the small but important elements of being with others. The shift we seek needs to be embodied in each invitation we make, each relationship we encounter, and each meeting we attend. For at the most operational and practical level, after all the thinking about policy, strategy, mission, and milestones, it gets down to this: *How are we going to be when we gather together?*" (2008, 10; emphasis added).

Changing the nature of a conversation also takes patience. Not appreciating this simple truth and trying to rush into collective action is a recipe for failure. Many times I've been in meetings where partners continually ask "What am I doing here,?" or "Where are we going with this,?" or "What am I supposed to contribute?"—even after several meetings at which this has been discussed and/or where the questions were supposedly answered before the group ever got together!

In part, this is because the group has not yet succeeded in getting the attention of participants; in part, it is also because people are used to someone else telling them what to do. Just shifting to the idea that they are responsible for answering these questions takes time. Yet with patience, as anyone who has worked in a collaborative process knows, there comes a time when suddenly everything just seems to click. People begin to take ownership of the collective agenda, their language changes from "I" to "we," and suddenly the debate becomes a conversation much like that among friends after dinner. If things are really clicking, then people begin to feel a collective sense of positive energy similar to what Mihály Csikszentmihalyi calls "flow" (2003).

With groups, this kind of flow is prompted by the interactions among people, usually their conversations together, and might be characterized by the following:

(1) clear group goals and targets, not "win-win" goals but a single "win" commonly understood;

(2) the development of a common language/lexicon that bridges diverse perspectives;
(3) the use of prototyping, straw dogs, and visualization;
(4) the adoption of shared ownership and identity and a shift away from "us" and "them" to "we";
(5) the accommodation of different perspectives even if agreement is not present; and
(6) heightened concentration and creativity where group members no longer feel bound by their native paradigms.

With luck, a sense of expansion or of "everything fitting into place" emerges as members begin to appreciate a wholeness that is more than the sum of their individual contributions, and they may begin to feel a sense of excitement and altered time, something that accompanies an individual experience of flow.

Peter Senge and his colleagues (2005, 12) have described this group experience. They say, for example, that, if "we penetrate more deeply to see the larger wholes that generate 'what is' and our own connection to this wholeness, the source and effectiveness of our actions can change dramatically." They believe that the process involves using conversation (in the broadest sense of interacting with one's environment) to shift attention away from the established patterns of meaning and behaviour, and toward opening it up to future possibilities. That openness they term "presencing." The term, says Senge colleague Otto Scharmer (2002, 1), "is a learning that is not based on reflecting the past, but rather on feeling, tuning in to, and 'bringing-into-the present' all future possibilities. . . . Presencing means: liberating one's perception from the 'prison' of the past and then letting it operate from the field of the future."

Unfortunately for those wedded to management science, presencing and flow do not conveniently emerge on demand but do so organically and in due time. One sets up some initial conditions and lets go, something like diving, having faith that the people and the conversational process will yield a desirable (even if not the intended) result.

Returning to the principles and mechanisms espoused by Paquet, these are in effect guides for intervening in the conversational pathways. Some principles that have proven helpful, as Paquet points out (2005, 78), include "price-cost relations, competition, subsidiarity, maximum participation, [and] multistability." He emphasizes, however, that a focus on mechanisms and what he refers to as social technologies (forms of coordination arrangements that are rooted in particular physical support but that shape social relationships), while initially appearing to be less effective and more "messy" than principles, rules, or structures, may turn out in the long run to be more practical (299–317). Paquet notes as well that they have the advantage of lending themselves to the necessary improvisation and experimentation that accompanies tackling complex collective problems effectively.

Some of his ideas for improving cooperative governance include the following:

(1) *lowering entry and exit barriers* to reduce the risks of cooperation, increase participation, and reduce the likelihood of active or passive subversion;
(2) *facilitating conversation* by using round tables over consultations, dialogue over debate;
(3) *presenting real options* to inspire learning and innovation but also recognizing that trade-offs need to be made because there is no free lunch—everything has a price;
(4) *developing a common knowledge base* and lexicon instead of debating the merits of the existing ones;
(5) *reframing exercises* to facilitate collective learning about future possibilities rather than past mistakes;
(6) *using fail safes*, the undesirable processes or conditions that automatically come into play in the event that cooperation breaks down; and
(7) *establishing informal feedback* processes, such as the use of neutral brokers, personal meetings, dinners, coffees, etc., to build partner relationships and confidence between partners.

Conclusion

The above ideas are not cooperative behaviours per se, but they do encourage cooperation while discouraging free rides and other uncooperative behaviours. They contribute to an atmosphere of trust, honesty, openness, transparency, mutual accountability, and mutual benefit that has been associated with effective cooperation.

While Paquet has never been much of a practitioner, he has always had a keen ear for the stories of practitioners. As time passes, his repertoire of stories of successful collaboration continues to grow, but there is one that he uses in *Governance through Social Learning* (1999) that is particularly revealing of the type of conversation that he has sought to inspire, a conversation that is likely to enable and enhance good community governance and collaborative partnership. It is from a story by John Womack about Gildaro Magana (who took over the Mexican Revolution after the assassination of Zapata). Womack says of Magana that "What he learned was to mediate: not to compromise, to surrender principle and to trade concessions, but to detect reason in all claims in conflict, to recognize the particular legitimacy of each, to sense where the grounds of concord were, and to bring contestants into harmony there. Instinctively *he thrived on arguments, which he entered not to win but to conciliate*" (quoted in Paquet 1999: 40; emphasis added).

References

Auditor General of Canada. (2005). *2005 Report of the Auditor General of Canada—November—Chapter 4—Managing Horizontal Initiatives*. Ottawa: Minister of Public Works Canada.

Best, M. (1990). *The New Competition: Institutions and Industrial Restructuring*. Cambridge, MA: Harvard University Press.

Block, P. (1993). *Stewardship: Choosing Service over Self-Interest*. San Francisco: Berrett-Koehler.

———. (2008). *Community: The Structure of Belonging*. San Francisco: Berrett-Koehler.

Bradford, N. (2007). *Whither the Federal Urban Agenda? A New Deal in Transition*. Ottawa: Canadian Policy Research Networks.

Cleveland, H. (2002). *Nobody in Charge*. San Francisco: Jossey-Bass.

Csikszentmihalyi, M. (2003). *Good Business: Leadership, Flow, and the Making of Meaning*. Toronto: Penguin Books.

Florida, R. (2002). *The Rise of the Creative Class*. New York: Basic Books.

Frederickson, H. G. (2006). "The New Geo-Governance." Review of *The New Geo-Governance: A Baroque Approach*, by G. Paquet. *Public Administration Times, 29.6*, 1–2.

Gorman, C. (2007). *Final Reflections from the Action for Neighbourhood Change Research Project*. Ottawa: Caledon Institute of Social Policy.

Gow, I. (2007). "Whose Model Is Realistic, Whose Unrealistic?" *Optimum Online, 37.4*, 36–41. www.optimumonline.ca [consulted February 2, 2009]

Graves, Frank. (2008). *Canadian Values: Understanding Our Values in a Global Context*. Presentation to Connecting with Canadians–Canadian Policy Research Networks Leadership Summit 2008, Ottawa, February 13.

Hatch, M. J. (1993). "The Dynamics of Organizational Culture." *Academy of Management Journal, 18.4*, 657–93.

Heath, J. (2001). *The Efficient Society: Why Canada Is as Close to Utopia as It Gets.* Toronto: Penguin Canada.

Hodgett, S. (2008). "Unintelligent Accountability and the Killing Off of Optimism." *Optimum Online,* 38.2, 47–57. www.optimumonline.ca [consulted January 15, 2009]

Hubbard, R., and G. Paquet. (2007). *Gomery's Blinders and Canadian Federalism.* Ottawa: University of Ottawa Press.

———. (2008). "Cat's Eyes: Intelligent Work versus Perverse Incentives." *Optimum Online,* 38.3, 1–20. www.optimumonline.ca [consulted January 15, 2009]

Lenihan, D., et al. (2006). *Transformational Changes and Policy Shifts in Support of Partnering—Within, Across, and Outside Government.* Ottawa: Crossing Boundaries National Council.

Paquet, G. (1997). "Slouching Toward a New Governance," *Optimum,* 27.3, 44–50.

———. (1999). *Governance through Social Learning.* Ottawa: University of Ottawa Press.

———. (2001). "The New Governance, Subsidiarity and the Strategic State." In OECD, *Governance in the 21st Century, Forum for the Future.* Paris: OECD.

———. (2005). *The New Geo-Governance: A Baroque Approach.* Ottawa: University of Ottawa Press.

———. (2006). "From Government to Governance: Implications for Delivery of Public Service Work and the Federal Public Service." Address to the Sixth Annual Managers National Professional Development Forum, Managing the Iceberg: Service to Canadians in a New Era, St. John's, April 30–May 3.

Porter, M. (1990). *The Competitive Advantage of Nations.* New York: Free Press.

Provincial Centre of Excellence for Child and Youth Mental Health at CHEO. (2006). *Knowledge Exchange: A Review of the Literature from the Perspective of Child and Youth Mental Health.* Toronto: Provincial Centre of Excellence for Child and Youth Mental Health.

Putnam, R. (2000). *Bowling Alone: The Collapse and Renewal of American Community.* Toronto: Simon and Schuster.

Rothstein, B. (2005). *Social Traps and the Problem of Trust.* Cambridge, UK: Cambridge University Press.

Saxenian, A. (1994). *Regional Advantage: Culture and Competition in Silicon Valley and Route 128.* Cambridge, MA: Harvard University Press.

Scharmer, C. Otto. (2002) "Presencing: A Social Technology of Freedom." *Trigon Themen,* Feb.

Senge, P., O. Scharmer, J. Jaworski, and B-S. Flowers. (2005). *Presence: An Exploration of Profound Change in People, Organizations, and Society.* New York: Doubleday Currency.

Wilson, C. (1998). "Quo Vide: A Matter of Public Trust." *National,* 7.2, 20–27.

———. (2007). "Facilitating Contingent Cooperation." *Optimum Online,* 37.1, 27–34. www.optimumonline.ca [consulted January 15, 2009]

Wilson, T. P. (1987). "Sociology and the mathematical method." In *Social Theory Today,* A. Giddens & J. Turner (eds), 383–404. Stanford, CA: Stanford University Press.

Wright, R. (2000). *NonZero: The Logic of Human Destiny.* New York: Vintage Books.

Part Seven

Engaging

Chapter 17

Paquet as Ironist and *Agent Provocateur*

James R. Mitchell

Introduction
This short paper explores one of the most interesting (and indeed virtually unique) characteristics of Gilles Paquet as a scholar and theoretician of public policy and public management. I refer to his capacity, informed by long experience, a vast intellectual range, and an immense body of creative work, not simply to analyze issues and problems, but actually to promote change in institutions through the deliberate use of irony, hyperbole, dramatic metaphors, and what can fairly be described as an aggressive "shotgun" approach to the application of new concepts and conceptual frameworks.

Through these techniques, Paquet challenges and expands the reader's understanding of both policy problems and the range of possible solutions. He also offers serious, practical suggestions—in some cases almost too many suggestions—to give effect to those solutions in public sector organizations. This, I argue, is among his most valuable contributions to Canadian intellectual life and to public policy. His success in this regard rests in part on his deliberate role as ironist and intellectual *agent provocateur*.[1]

In describing Paquet as an ironist, I must begin by acknowledging that I am in a sense distorting the meaning of the term. "Irony" was originally understood to refer to a kind of mock modesty, the deliberate *under*stating of one's own capacities and insights for argumentative effect. (This was the technique used to such telling effect by Socrates in Plato's dialogues.) However, Paquet—a modest man in person—is quite the opposite in print, and the ironic tools that he employs represent a different sort of didactic dissimulation, one that provokes the reader into an awareness of serious issues through the deliberate use of flamboyant language and almost overlayered argumentation.[2] His is the irony of *over*statement. While this approach can sometimes appear exaggerated, it is always to a deliberate purpose. Gilles is never self-indulgent, and while his criticisms of institutions and actors can be severe he is also profoundly respectful of the institutional framework that defines this country and its governors.

Stirring the Pot

In thinking about Paquet's application of colourful language for deliberate effect, we might take as an example his use of ironic description in his 2006 essay on the BC post-secondary education system. There Paquet both praises what that province has done in integrating its higher-education system and decries the "apartheid" that still divides the university sector from the college and university college sectors. Here, as in so many of his other papers, he uses deliberately exaggerated language to provoke the reader's attention to a very real problem—in this case the systematic failure in British Columbia to balance what he describes as the three basic goals of education: namely, the pursuit of knowledge (*savoir*), the acquisition of skills (*savoir-faire*), and personal development (*savoir-être*). His purpose is clear, and his argument is, in my view, successful: to meet the needs of both the labour market and society as a whole, governments must pay more attention (and show more respect) to *all* these elements of post-secondary education.

Another recent example of scholarly hyperbole justified by good policy intentions comes from a paper titled "Super-Bureaucrats and Counter-Democracy" (Paquet 2008b). Here Paquet focuses on the growth of unelected and essentially unaccountable independent office holders who are both expected and empowered to address perceived problems in public policy and public management, in part because Canadians mistrust established institutions, including Parliament. Here, however, his impulse for the dramatic and his desire to stir the pot get him into some conceptual trouble.

For dramatic effect in making his argument in this paper, Paquet (2008b) lumps together everything from officers of Parliament to agency heads to at least some deputy ministers and calls them all "super-bureaucrats." He refers to them as "newly minted crusaders," "Knights Templar," and "saboteurs" who "proclaim that in our present age of distrust, they are the only line of defense capable of protecting citizens" (1). In thus depicting and labelling what he describes as "a far-reaching process of counter-democracy," Paquet draws attention, in a dramatic way, to two quite distinct problems of governance in Canada today. The first is the erosion of the traditional relationship of trust between officials and ministers; the second is the increasing resort by politicians and the public to office holders independent of government who carry substantial powers to "protect" the public interest.[3] As Paquet rightly observes, there is an increasing impulse today to go around apparently discredited institutions and cut through traditional lines of democratic authority through recourse to these independent office holders. This impulse is not a healthy one for our democracy, and Paquet is right to draw it to our attention. But it is not, as he appears to think, the same issue as the relationship between ministers and the senior officials who serve them.

In reality, these are two distinct matters, each worth an essay or a book on its own.[4] Yet in an excess of rhetorical zeal, Paquet conflates them through the use of a flamboyant taxonomy that groups all these senior office holders into a single category, the "super-bureaucrat." This oversimplification is effective, but it is deeply misleading. Officers of Parliament play a role entirely different from that of a deputy minister: notably, they do not in any sense serve or report to a minister. Yet Paquet (2008b, 2) writes as though these different sorts of office holder are all of a type: "it only requires a small fraction of these officials to consider themselves authorized to be disloyal to their ministers in the name of the higher interests of the country—especially if we do not know who they are—to completely transform the relationship between ministers and super-bureaucrats. If one out of twenty is potentially passively or actively disloyal (and no one knows who belongs in that category), the general ministerial paranoia becomes understandable: one no longer knows whom to trust!" A similar confusion is evident in his claim that "the majority of senior public servants and super-bureaucrats (who loyally serve the government) cannot help but be frustrated and discouraged by the climate of distrust which has been implanted . . ." (3).

This kind of language—overdone for effect and doubtless used with every good intention—betrays a serious confusion in roles and thus in categories. Officers of Parliament do not serve the government; they serve Parliament. Heads of regulatory agencies and quasi-judicial tribunals have statutory authority and legal independence from government that are essential to their function. They do not serve the government — they serve Canadians. Deputy ministers, however, are quite the reverse: their authority derives from that of the minister; they serve the government directly and Canadians only indirectly.

All of this is to say that, while there is clearly a purpose to be served by this kind of stirring-the-pot language, it also carries with it the risks of excess. It appears that for Paquet that is a risk worth taking. How much more boring it would be to write or read a paper carefully distinguishing different types of senior office holder and pointing out the difficulties that arise when their respective roles are distorted in practice, whether by the people filling the jobs, or by the politicians and political scientists who mistakenly look to them as remedies for weaknesses in government. How much more effective it is to point the reader to real problems in governance through powerful language and perhaps oversimple categories that grab one's attention and spur one to further reflection. This, however, is the vocation of the *agent provocateur*, and it works.

Changing the Way Problems Are Understood

The manner in which Gilles Paquet has defined, described, and analyzed issues has in many cases changed how the public policy community sees (or ought to see) those issues. In this respect, his role as *agent provocateur* has sometimes been played out less through provocative language or hyperbole than by means of cool analysis that is provocative simply in that it goes sharply against the prevailing currents of thought in Ottawa or in academe.

For example, Paquet's criticisms of the reaction to the Sponsorship Affair and his analysis of the shortcomings of the two Gomery reports were among the most forthright and insightful expressed in print. In a paper titled "The $100 Million Mirage: A Cautionary Note" (2004), Paquet points out that public and political reaction to the misdeeds identified in sponsorship was in certain respects overblown, that not every activity under that program was ill intended or inappropriate, and that a good deal of what Canadians deserved to know about the program was revealed neither by the government nor by the inquiry. His paper was a call not to dramatic action but to sober analysis and reflection, and to a balanced appreciation of the realities and challenges that governments face. As he says, "The $100 Million metaphor [i.e., as shorthand for the money 'stolen' under sponsorship], plus the statement that 'all the rules in the book have been broken' may make good headlines but they also appear to be excessive statements at a time when considerable prudence was required" (3). In a related paper with Ruth Hubbard

(2006), Paquet combines a reasoned skepticism about the immediate impact of the Gomery reports (essentially not much) with a more provocative insight into what he sees as an unintended consequence of the Gomery recommendations, namely (what he sees as) a long-overdue rebalancing of the federation through a lifting of "the shadow of over-centralization and top-down federalism" (4). It is too soon to tell, but he may be right. Here again he is provocative without any resort to irony or hyperbole.

Some would argue that Paquet has too many ideas, that he introduces too many new concepts,[5] and that he is too quick to generate and apply new conceptual frameworks to what is actually a fairly limited set of public management issues. I do not agree. Rather, I would argue that Paquet is inclined to deliberately overstate both the issues and the elements of his solutions. He does this partly to paint them in dramatic terms ("to get the reader's attention") and partly in the knowledge that, even if only a few of his ideas were taken up, they would make a significant difference to government and governance. This is what I would call "deliberate dissimulation," and at least in some cases he uses it to achieve not so much a scholarly purpose as a public interest one.[6]

Making a Difference

Paquet has never hesitated to tilt at the favoured ideas of the day. Nor has he been reluctant to criticize the players, whether politicians, officials, or members of the press. But he is not simply a critic; he is clearly someone who wants his ideas and his arguments to have an impact on public policy and on the institutions of government.

Given the immense volume of Paquet's scholarly output and the wide range of his interests, the question that must be answered, therefore, is whether this *ironiste provocateur* approach has actually resulted in fruit. Has it made a difference? It is my view that it has, both in how the public policy and public management communities understand the issues on the public agenda, and in what has been done to policies and institutions as a result of his work.

For example, his analysis of, and recommendations for, a new governance structure for the RCMP (Paquet 2007) were adopted in principle by the Brown Task Force, as were his recommendations for an integrated mechanism for grievance and redress. Similarly, his views on the need for an integrated approach to higher education, and the importance of building on what is there already, are reflected in the BC government's approach to its post-secondary education system.

There are issues that, for political or bureaucratic reasons, people in government or the media find difficult to address. Yet Paquet has never lacked the courage to go where his insights take him. A good example lies in his comments to the 2006 APEX symposium, titled "A Curmudgeon's Commentary," where he reminded a less-than-sympathetic audience of the need to look at issues of diversity in Canada rationally and dispassionately rather than as matters of ideology. In a similar vein, he has more recently analyzed the challenges of meaningful citizenship in a multicultural, globalized society by putting out ideas and proposals for "degrees of citizenship" that were bound to stir controversy and debate (see Paquet 2008a).

These are areas of public policy where Paquet's provocative approach to analysis and prescription has yet to produce any direct effect on policy. Yet they are all dimensions of his constructive role as *agent provocateur*.

Conclusion

It would be unfair to portray Gilles Paquet's brilliant career as simply that of ironist and *agent provocateur*. Paquet is first and foremost a scholar of remarkable accomplishment who has worked with distinction in both official languages at both of Ottawa's major universities. But it is clear from his writing, and from the range of issues on which he has been engaged (at all levels of government), that his scholarly vocation has always been aimed at the larger public interest. As much as any member of Canada's public management community, Paquet has been trying to make a difference—to bring issues to public attention and to change things wherever necessary. His choice of terminology may not always have represented the most diplomatic approach to the public policy environment of the moment.[7] But he has, beyond any doubt, succeeded in doing what every social scientist dreams of—bringing his ideas to a wider audience than just the community of scholars.

A written style and scholarly technique that may have seemed over the top twenty-five years ago have surely found their proper application today, in a public environment where issues too often are treated more as entertainment than as matters of serious concern to the country. In the information-intense environment of today, one has to paint with bold strokes to be seen, and to speak out loud and clear to be heard. Gilles Paquet has done this time and time again, and he has done it very well. He has been provocative because that was required, and that is what has worked. There are few other scholars who have had a major impact in both public policy and public management, and even fewer who have managed to say so much on so many topics, with such dramatic impact and such substantive effect. For that, we owe him our respect and our thanks.

Notes

1. This aspect of his work is exemplified in the work that he did on "governance and cultural change" for the Brown Task Force on the RCMP (Paquet 2007); his papers on the Gomery commission ("The $100 Million Mirage: A Cautionary Note" [Paquet 2004] and "Gomery: Missed Opportunity or Blessing in Disguise?" [Hubbard and Paquet 2006]); his work with Ruth Hubbard on public service reform ("The Myth of the Public Service as a Lump of Guardians" [Hubbard and Paquet 2007]; and his paper "Toward a Baroque Governance in 21st Century Canada" (Paquet 2000), in which he identifies irony as a national characteristic, essential for our future success.
2. Many of Paquet's written contributions to learning can best be described as think-pieces. In a 2006 paper entitled "Savoirs, savoir-faire, and savoir-être: In Praise of Professional Wroughting and Wrighting," Paquet defines a think-piece as an essay that is "meant to provoke reflection and also to generate positive and negative reactions from the readership with a view to breaking out of the box of conventional thinking and producing innovative avenues that might not have been explored otherwise as fully as they should have" (2). A think-piece, he says, is something written "to generate discomfort, and to initiate an intelligent conversation" (2). This description can justly be applied to much of his work on public policy and public management.
3. The 2006 *Federal Accountability Act*, for example, creates five new (or nearly new) independent officers with this kind of mandate.
4. Savoie (2008) is a recent major work on the issue of the relationship between ministers and officials that takes up some of these concerns.
5. E.g., "super-bureaucrats," "super-professionals," "the paranoid organization," "delta knowledge," to name but a few of hundreds of colourful terms coined by Paquet in his many publications.
6. I would argue that this is particularly so in his papers on issues of current controversy such as sponsorship.
7. My own reaction, when I first heard him pronounce from outside government on the issues with which I was engaged inside the bureaucracy, was that this was an awfully clever fellow, infuriating but always thought-provoking and courageous.

References

Hubbard, R. and Paquet, G. (2006). "Gomery: Missed Opportunity or Blessing in Disguise?" *Journal of the Financial Management Institute of Canada, 17(3)*, 21–23.

———. (2007). "The Myth and the Public Service as a Lump of Guardians." Available at www.gouvernance.ca [consulted February 5, 2009]

Paquet, G. (2000). "Toward a Baroque Governance in 21st Century Canada." Available at www.gouvernance.ca (2000)
———. (2004). "The $100 Million Mirage: A Cautionary Note." Available at www.gouvernance.ca.
———. (2006). "Savoirs, savoir-faire, and savoir-être: In Praise of Professional Wroughting and Wrighting." Report prepared for Campus 20/20—An Inquiry into the Fitire pf British Columbia's Post-Secondary Education System. Ottawa: Centre on Governance, University of Ottawa.
———. (2007). "Background Paper Prepared for the Task Force on Governance and Cultural Change in the RCMP." http://www.publicsafety.gc.ca/rcmp-gre/-fl/eng/backgroundpaper.pdf (accessed _____).
———. (2008a). *Deep Cultural Diversity: A Governance Challenge*. Ottawa: University of Ottawa Press.
———. (2008b). "Super-Bureaucrats and Counter-Democracy." Available at www.networkedgovernment.ca.
Savoie, D. (2008). *Court Government and the Collapse of Accountability in Canada and the United Kingdom*. Toronto: University of Toronto Press.

Chapter 18

Looking Past the Dots

Ruth Hubbard

An ability to make distant analogies unlocks a world of potential.
—Fred Stratton (CEO, Briggs and Stratton)

Introduction
People sitting in front of a computer screen filled with the comings and goings of randomly generated dots can stare at them until they get a headache. As I discovered, however, if they force themselves to look past the dots, they begin to see something different. As time passes, they start to notice a few relatively stable shapes emerging, made up of individual dots that come and go—constantly replaced by others that appear in roughly the same place.

To my mind, Gilles Paquet is one of those rare people who is not only able to look past the dots but can also notice linkages that elude others, thereby observing a broader range of the evolving patterns. The result is that, with a career of forty-five years and still counting, he is now able to offer promising ideas about social architecture that are both novel and workable.

The very nature of what he sees, however, is controversial because it forces people to question some of their explicit and/or implicit fundamental beliefs and assumptions. At the same time, acceptance of his view by some is made even harder by a few of the very traits that have made his journey possible—such as seeking to engage through provocation and being a contrarian at heart.

This short paper is a thank you to Gilles for what he continues to give to us as a self-confessed practitioner of what Lon Fuller calls "eunomics" (the study of good order and workable arrangements) in the field of modern societal stewardship.

The Journey

The relationship between citizens, their government, and their future has been of interest to Paquet since the beginning of his professional career in the early 1960s. Four and a half decades of experience have brought him to believe that strategies for government intervention in countries such as Canada that are more likely to succeed will be very profoundly different from those presumed effective in the postwar decades of the 1950s and 1960s. Briefly tracing a few highlights of his journey illustrates both the evolution of his thinking and the various pathways that have made it so fruitful.

Starting, Adjusting, Then Shedding

Gilles began his professional career in 1963 with the tools in good currency at the time. It was an era in Canada that for at least the next twenty years was unable to shed federal government domination of social architecture despite the growing maturity of regional governments.

It was a time when governments were still trying to deal with the devastating effects of the Great Depression and World War II, heavily influenced by mainstream (Keynesian) economics. In this approach to intervention, governments did everything, including delivering the services themselves. There was a focus on planning starting in the 1950s and 1960s, and a heavy reliance on modelling, built on assumptions of perfect knowledge and rationality.

Canada's federal government used this approach for problems in which there was incontrovertible evidence of public need (e.g., when it was clear that the aged—some in real financial need—were living longer and that baby boomers would soon flood an unprepared labour market). The government also applied it to "wicked" problems such as urbanization (i.e., problems with less clear and/or contested goals and uncertain and/or unknown means–ends relationships).

Shortly after beginning his professional career, Paquet became a consulting economist on policy files dealing with both kinds, including the Senate's examination of aging, urbanization, Quebec's exploration of health care, and federal manpower and unemployment insurance (UI).

In addressing policy concerns related to health care (1965–66), as Gilles himself observed much later, the frame of straightforward technical response that he was using meant that he was "aiming too high" (Paquet 2008a, 85–86). He was to discover that, like urbanization, it was a different kind of problem—one that we now call "wicked"—so that, to be effective, government interventions needed to be tackled differently.

In fact, urban studies provided Paquet with an opportunity to use a different approach for an issue domain in which "the complexity of the problem has been acknowledged in scores of books, [but] nowhere does one find a strategy for the analysis of the urban unit in all its complexity" (Lithwick and Paquet 1968, 4). Together with Harvey Lithwick, he directed a series of multidisciplinary seminars in Ottawa dealing with problems of cities and regions between 1965 and 1967 that resulted in a co-edited book that reframed much of the debate and is currently being reissued (Lithwick and Paquet 1968).

His search was now clearly under way for a new way of seeing things. Paquet began to use a more pragmatic approach with more emphasis on innovation because control was not possible and planning not entirely effective.

By 1971, he was arguing for a process-oriented analysis (e.g., experimental "utopias" and simulation techniques) to explore the lateral possibilities that could be derived from original hypotheses, while acknowledging its inevitable downsides, pointing out that it "blurs the traditional difference between innovation and control-monitoring, but . . . appears to be the only effective response to the accelerated change that identifies our temporary society" (Paquet 1971, 60). In fact, Paquet was arguing that policy was ill structured, operating in a turbulent environment, and, as a result, needed to have a formulation that was open, involving continuous feedback (Paquet 1971).

Never someone to be "hemmed in" in his intellectual journeys, Gilles gradually found himself exploring a variety of different avenues to enrich his thinking, to provide sounding boards for his ideas, and to stimulate his creative juices. In effect, they became different kinds of laboratories that he would use to learn about what did or did not go well, and why, as well as (eventually) to effect repairs.

The first was work in economic history with historian Jean-Pierre Wallot in the late 1960s. They explored, enriched, and significantly reinterpreted the socioeconomy of Lower Canada around the turn of the eighteenth century in a way that is still in good currency. This collaboration would eventually span forty years and produce many joint papers, several co-authored book chapters, and three co-authored books.

Another was his journalistic work. In 1978, Gilles began more than a decade as a journalist/interviewer with Radio-Canada on *Le magazine économique*. All told, his national-level radio work lasted almost uninterrupted until 1994. This was an exercise in finding and revealing flaws, in probing to find out why something did not work, and in being deliberately provocative to bring issues to life in ways that would engage the audience.

By the end of the 1970s, Gilles knew that the tools in good currency were not useful and that he needed to find a new set. This was a time when he believed that restructuring (including using proven methods and rich hypotheses in new ways and/or on new terrains) and institution building were the way to go.

Searching, Groping, Soaking, but Not Concluding

His weekly Radio-Canada work eventually involved 1,500 enquiring and provocative interviews. In fact, Paquet would later observe that it turned him into a different person—persuading him that the real influence on public policy was the power of a critical population and not social scientists. In effect, what radio did for him was to get a few of his listeners to start asking questions.

In the mid-1980s, Gilles began to talk about "social learning." He learned about a promising concept first introduced by Friedman and Abonyi in 1976 for stylizing a model of policy research that "combines a detailed analysis of four interconnected sub-processes; (1) the construction of appropriate theories of reality, (2) the formation of social values, (3) the gaming that leads to the design of political strategies, and (4) collective action" (Paquet 1999a, 47). Paquet pushed the concept much further, seeing social learning as intellectually complex and messy with no tools or templates to guide the necessary probing. Later he would describe it as "a useful guide to social architecture . . . [as well as] a radar in an inquiring system trying to design [public institutions]" (1999a, 51). As a result, he set about applying the idea of social learning to some of the big policy issues of the day.

In 1987, Paquet (1999a, 55–77) wrote about the Free Trade Agreement debate as an example of the need for "technical problem-solving to take place within a broader context of reflective inquiry . . . [since] an alternative to positivism now exists and there is a call for it" (74). Two years later (1999a 93–108) he analyzed the approach used by the federal government with respect to energy, and while he praised the non-traditional approach of providing guiding principles to engage in a public consultation he observed that they were defined too narrowly for the turbulent times of the day and argued for an avoidance of a fixation on goals and controls, opting instead for taking a chance on process and a well-managed forum.

"Governance" as an Organizing Idea

During the 1990s, the terms "governance" and then "social learning"—which later became watchwords—were ones that Paquet was using to help reframe the social debate. By now, he was reaping the benefit of his earlier thinking, and by the middle of the decade he had invented a new language for new publics. In his media "laboratory," he began writing weekly editorials for *Le Droit* (1992–95) that taught him about the importance of rewording to reach an audience of people in all walks of everyday life. By 1997, he was pointing out that the federal government (albeit forced by a fiscal crisis) was putting forward the beginnings of an alternative philosophy of governance—one based on the concept of subsidiarity that was implicit in its six program review questions (Paquet 1999b).

Gilles summed up his thinking in two books, one in English titled *Governance through Social Learning* (1999a), and a more ambitious one in French with Paul Laurent titled *Épistémologie et économie de la relation: Coordination et gouvernance distribuée* (Laurent and Paquet 1998). Both used a wide variety of issue domains to illustrate and illuminate the basic ideas expressed in them.

Making Repairs

By the beginning of the new century, Paquet began collaborating with me in what would become another laboratory. We started exploring and writing about social technologies (Hubbard and Paquet 2002), the usefulness of mechanisms aimed at tipping points to kick-start change (2005), and new institutional architecture to support a new approach to Canadian federalism (2006).

In 2002–03, Gilles had the opportunity to present twenty chronicles on Radio-Canada as part of *Indicatif présent*. He subsequently revised them and turned them into a book entitled *Pathologies de gouvernance: Essais de technologie sociale* (2004).

The intellectual underpinning for his media work was set out in *Gouvernance: Une invitation à la subversion* (Paquet 2005a). In it, Gilles described some principles of good social architecture (e.g., subsidiarity, maximum participation, competition, and true cost/pricing) as well as moral contracts as a useful mechanism and incentive-reward systems as important considerations (167–76).

The same year saw the publication of his most ambitious work in terms of scope, *The New Geo-Governance: A Baroque Approach* (2005b). In it, Gilles added more ideas about mechanisms (e.g., dialogue, reframing, and belief-action systems) and made the point that there must be provisions for both active trust and fail-safe systems in case of danger to system integrity or stability (78–79).

Both 2005 books argue for a move away from state centricity. Nevertheless, Paquet has never suggested that there is no further need for the public sector. As he said in the geo-governance book, "the strategic state undoubtedly has a role to play in jump-starting, catalyzing, and steering the process of social learning, while allowing the other two domains [the private and civic sectors] to occupy their terrains as fully as possible" (2005b, 68).

Since 2005, Paquet has continued to explore areas that pique his interest. Among other things, it has been a time for engaging in work to push the non-state-centricity argument further toward an open source, experimentalist stewardship of Canada that stems from the belief that knowledge is, by definition, partly tacit and fragmented so that no one can have it all (Hubbard and Paquet 2007).

Cognitive Dissonance

A little reflection suggests that two interacting reasons probably contribute to the controversy that Paquet's ideas provoke. First, his use of the term "governance" has a subversive nature. As Gilles put it in his geo-governance book, "In modern democracies the sort of citizen participation entailed by . . . [cooperation-amplifying] mechanisms . . . is a challenge to the usual method of representation: it short circuits the usual process through which the collective will is supposedly expressing itself in the polity—the ballot box . . . mechanisms that promote dialogue, partnering, leadership and the like are the very fabric of governance, but they have a subversive impact on the state" (2005b, 313).

Others (e.g., Phillip Bobbitt) have argued convincingly that the nation-state can no longer commit to enhancing the welfare of all of its citizens. Nevertheless, by delving increasingly into the "how" of effective social architecture, Paquet comes perilously close to making it clear that not only is no one de facto "in charge" but also that the idea of someone being "in charge" in today's world is too far fetched to be clung to by most reasonable people.

Even though the strategic state that Paquet describes must be vibrant and has an important role to play, it is hard to imagine something that would be more threatening to societal elites used to a world in which "governance" was the same as "government" and meant elite accommodation behind closed doors. Or in fact to citizens in countries such as Canada who have come to presume that the existence of public services is one of the main foundations of a modern government's legitimacy (Pollitt 2003).

Second, Paquet has virtually perfected the use of provocative (albeit often amusing) language as well as a deliberate contrariness to destabilize his audiences just enough so that they never see things quite the same way again. He does it so well and is so well known in Canada that he is much sought after as a speaker or *animateur* in order to kick-start a period of reflection by those who are assembled or to play the role of a journalist who engages as well as informs.

It seems that many people enjoy being enticed, in entertaining ways, to pause and reflect on something that they can actually see as related to their own situations. At the same time, however, some find it hard to keep their feelings (on behalf of others and/or about themselves) at bay and, perhaps as a result, do not hear the substance of what Gilles is saying. Even for those willing and/or able to temporarily set aside any real or perceived personal criticism in his remarks, the interaction inevitably leads to the hard work of reconciling proposed actions with their own personal values—something that people far prefer to evade or avoid (Yankelovich and Rosell 2008). As a result, the tone that Gilles employs can offer a convenient way out. The reaction has been particularly strong, sometimes even vitriolic, when he has set out ideas that go against the grain of the ideologies in good currency.

Looking Backward
Some of Paquet's most contentious debates are linked to the past, as the following examples illustrate.

The Quiet Revolution is a name given to the six-year period (1960–66) that saw a dramatic change in how Quebec steered itself. Many social scientists now challenge the melodramatic view that Quebec's "dark ages" were finally overcome by that *Révolution tranquille*, a view that saw a relatively backward, conservative society dominated by the Roman Catholic Church freed by the actions of an interventionist state to enable it to become modern and entrepreneurial. Successive Quebec governments and many elites (regardless of their pro- or anti-separation stance) up to the present day have used the Quiet Revolution as a reference point to buttress their views about the need for an interventionist state. Paquet would say that, even today, many Quebec elites argue that an attack on the state is an attack on the very society itself.

As a result, by making the case convincingly that not only was Quebec's Quiet Revolution *not* the turning point that finally set the province free but also that it disastrously diminished the social capital necessary for its economic prosperity and well-being in *Oublier la Révolution tranquille: Pour une nouvelle socialité*, Paquet (1999c) managed to offend both federalists and separatists.

Another example arose with respect to a strategy adopted by a language minority that resorted to using constitutional protection of minority language rights to argue for keeping a hospital open rather than focusing on what was really at stake: a sensible arrangement for the provision of regional health care. The saga began with the work of the Hospital Services Restructuring Commission mandated by the Ontario government to report on the optimal way to deal with tertiary care in the regional health care system of eastern Ontario. Work such as this would always generate huge resistance because someone's ox was bound to be gored. Its final report in 1997 used technical analyses to fend off intense pressure from one hospital to keep what it had but not strongly enough to close the door completely. Collaboration among three key hospitals might have been sufficient to stiffen the spine of the Restructuring Commission, but instead each used its own strategy, and in the case of one, the Montfort Hospital, the judicial route was chosen. The result was that the Appeal Court of Ontario found that there had been administrative negligence but threw out its claim that its status was protected by the *Charter of Rights and Freedoms*.

In writing about it, Paquet (2008b, 173–92) argued that it was not the end (keeping the Montfort Hospital open) that he opposed but the means that had been chosen. He asserted that this approach probably made it harder for the Ontario government to act in favour of minority rights of francophones in the future because it appeared that anything granted to a minority group could be argued to be granted in perpetuity.

Unsurprisingly, his judgment of Franco-Ontario elites was clear and toughly worded. Paquet wrote, for example, that "*les élites franco-ontariennes de l'Est Ontario ont mal servi la communauté: par une négligence condamnable dans les premiers moments des travaux de la Commission, par une naïveté désolante en croyant, comme Josué, pouvoir arrêter le soleil et éviter tout changement et toute restructuration, par une désinformation et une démagogie systématiques désolantes qui ont empêchées un débat serein sur la restructuration, par un manque d'intérêt à collaborer avec les autres communautés quand c'était essentiel, et par une radicalisation, une ethnicisation et une juridiciarisation hasardeuses des débats en bout de piste. Il faut un changement de la garde*" (2008b, 189–90). In fact, this stance cost him dearly, putting an end to his work at *Le Droit*.

Looking Forward

It is in looking forward, however—at imagining new ways of thinking about Canadian federalism—that cognitive dissonance (especially on the part of many societal elites) seems to be at its strongest. At the same time, it is also here where avoidance or evasion of confrontation over ideas seems most prevalent.

My own collaboration with Gilles suggests one possible reason for that dissonance, at least insofar as the federal "tribe" of deputy ministers is concerned. After nearly three and a half decades as a federal public servant and more than a decade as a deputy minister, I began to work with Gilles in 2000. A long-time advocate of federal public service reform and practitioner of it, in the last five years of my tenure as a deputy head I became increasingly convinced that, in a globalized and rapidly changing world, federal deputy ministers needed to begin to actively explore the evolving role of governments in advanced Westminster-based democracies such as Canada if they (including me) were to be able to effectively reposition the professional public service.

Gilles and I have spent nearly a decade examining, reflecting upon, and writing about issues related to public administration that combines the knowledge, experience, and intuition of the academic and the practitioner. The result has led to insights for both of us that almost certainly we would not have had (or would not have identified so clearly) on our own.

For my part, I was forced to confront a number of assumptions that I was unaware of making. By far the most difficult was the idea that societal stewardship did not necessarily involve governments in hierarchical leadership roles.

At first, like the narrator in Edward A. Abbot's two-dimensional "Flatland" before he actually sees a three-dimensional sphere himself, the idea had simply never occurred to me. Once I encountered it, coming to grips emotionally with the idea of non-state centricity proved very difficult. For a long time, it seemed to run against the grain of the deep-seated belief that was planted along with the burden of office that I had consciously accepted as a professional public servant in the late 1970s.

In a classic demonstration of what people such as William Bridges call the difference between "transition" and change, underneath the idea of non-state centricity lay my presumption that accepting it meant that my entire earlier professional life had been a complete waste of time and that there was no role for deputy ministers that was as complex, as interesting, and as exciting as I had known. The first, of course, was simply not true, and the second was just plain wrong.

In Paquet's laboratory, I came to see the "burden of office" framed differently, and it opened new and exciting doorways to public sector reform. I could see how a government department or agency might move forward with a greater likelihood of success than I myself had experienced as a deputy minister, faced with the growing need for a different approach to policy development, regulation, and service delivery. It was like looking at the same landscape from quite a different vantage point.

Nevertheless, explicitly reconciling that frame with my deep-seated belief was both difficult and painful. No wonder people avoid or evade "tough choice" work if they can.

Just how controversial Paquet's view appears to be while never being directly contested may be exemplified by a recent exchange between Gilles and a well-known and respected Canadian academic, Iain Gow, to whom Gilles recently referred as a "defender of strong state-centric governance" (2007, 45). The particular difference of opinion took the form of concern expressed by Gow about the characterization of his model of public administration that appeared in a book co-authored by Gilles and me (Hubbard and Paquet 2007a, 88–94). The result was that Gow (2007) took advantage of the opportunity offered to him to clarify his position to stress that his model had been misrepresented and its architect maligned.

In his rebuttal, Gilles makes it clear that there was never any desire to misrepresent or malign. He observes, nevertheless, with his usual élan, that what is really at stake is a sharp difference of opinion about relative benefits of the notion of basic state centricity that underpins Gow's model. He notes that Gow "has synthesized the broad features of his model . . . [as he has 'found it in the literature' to use his words], reproclaimed that it is effective and should remain intact, and defended it against the emergent alternative model that Hubbard and Paquet's book claims to be more desirable. . . . Specialists in public administration are unlikely to allow the state to be deprived of its rust-proof core without a fierce fight: what would Hamlet be without the Prince of Denmark!" (2007, 45, 48).

Undeterred by the controversy that his work often creates, Gilles continues to try to overcome cognitive dissonance. Building on a profound belief in the power of a critical population to help accelerate the emergence of good societal stewardship in countries such as Canada, he finds imaginative ways to stimulate and provoke conversations on tough public issues.

While president of the Royal Society of Canada (RSC) (2003–05), for example, Gilles launched an initiative that saw the RSC, together with expert organizations and a large network of collaborators, generate forums to tackle thorny issues and "taboo topics" (without itself becoming associated with any particular "partisan" stand). These forums generated a good deal of interest and, while seen as too disturbing to be continued by his successor, are in the process of being rekindled by the new president. The slow, tentative emergence of the RSC as public intellectual that was stressed by Gilles during his tenure as president (Paquet 2005c), and exemplified in part by this bold venture, may yet come to pass.

In the fall of 2006, Gilles and I began a partnership with APEX to create and deliver a series of "taboo topics" for a few dozen federal public executives in the fall and winter of each year. A summary of the results of the first two were published in 2007 (Hubbard and Paquet 2007b) and 2008 (Hubbard and Paquet 2008). Participants have enthusiastically endorsed both the idea and the importance of having "safe spaces" for discussing some of the wicked problems that they face while lamenting their absence within government. The initiative continues today, extending its reach in tiny steps.

In the same vein, 2008 saw the publication of a book authored by Paquet (2008b), titled *Deep Cultural Diversity: A Governance Challenge*, aimed at triggering a discussion of a problem of great importance in Canada (i.e., reasonable accommodation along with a redefinition of citizenship and what it means to be a Canadian). Shortly after its release, Charles Enman (2008) reported on multiculturalism in a local newspaper this way: Paquet "says that the greatest achievement of the recent Bouchard-Taylor Commission in Quebec was [that] it opened . . . a conversation [on what, if any, limits there are to accommodation] in the province." He quoted Paquet as saying, "I want religion, ethnicity, colour, all these things to become as insignificant as the colour of your eyes — so our relationships are based on our behaviour, our intelligence, our characters. But that's not a place we will arrive at soon."

Conclusion

One of the most distinguished public administration scholars of today, George Frederickson (2006), has described the portrayal of our likely governance future in Paquet's 2005 book on geo-governance as "a conceptual tour de force," noting that what advances the work of earlier world-renowned observers and thinkers (especially with respect to public administration) is his emphasis on the technologies of geo-governance.

Paquet's ideas may be controversial when they are first set out. Nevertheless, with time, some have become incorporated subtly into mainstream thinking (e.g., those relating to the need for modernizing the federal public service, which Gilles first began talking about in 1985, long before the clerk of the day, Paul Tellier, launched the first of what have necessarily become continuing waves of reform with PS2000). Because his work increasingly underscores the importance of technologies and because he argues in favour of emphasizing governance *mechanisms* as opposed to principles or organizational structures—things that are by definition less threatening, more practical, and more understandable (if less certain in terms of outcome)—his views (including the more recent ones about Canadian federalism) may well ultimately prevail.

My own belief is that the impact of his thinking about social architecture will be significant and long lasting but that it may well never be substantially acknowledged as such either by the majority of "traditional" Canadian public administration scholars or by the federal "tribe" of deputy ministers who are still valiantly trying to emulate the Ottawa mandarins from a long-ago era—the few people who worked hand in hand with their political masters to dramatically change the country. For many elites, his ideas may just be too painful to confront directly. To my mind, aided and abetted by his own focus on enabling small pockets of the population to be critical, the results of his work will probably emerge in the subversive kind of way that Gilles himself advocates for bringing about significant change.

They say that the proof of the pudding is in the eating. Controversial Gilles Paquet may well be. It is worth remembering, nevertheless, that without his particular ability to make distant analogies we might still have no pudding!

References

Enman, C. (2008). "Redefining a Canadian." Review of *Deep Cultural Diversity: A Governance Challenge*, by Gilles Paquet. *Ottawa Citizen*, June 7, A1.

Frederickson, G. (2006). "The New Geo-Governance." Review of *The New Geo-Governance: A Baroque Approach*, by Gilles Paquet. *Public Administration Times*, 29(6), 1–2.

Friedman, J., and G. Abonyi. (1976). "Social Learning: A Model for Policy Research." *Environment and Planning A*, 8, 927–40.

Gow, I. (2007). "Whose Model Is Realistic, Whose Unrealistic?" *Optimum Online*, 37.4, 36–43. www.optimumonline.ca [consulted January 15, 2009]

Hubbard, R., and G. Paquet. (2002). "Ecologies of Governance." *Optimum Online*, 32.4, 25–34. www.optimumonline.ca [consulted January 15, 2009]

———. (2005). "Betting on Mechanisms: The New Frontier for Federalism." *Optimum Online, 35.1*, 2–25. www.optimumonline.ca [consulted January 15, 2009]

———. (2006). "Réinventer notre architecture institutionelle." *Options politiques, 27.7*, 57–64.

———. (2007a). *Gomery's Blinders and Canadian Federalism*. Ottawa: University of Ottawa Press.

———. (2007b). "Cat's Cradle: APEX Forums on Wicked Problems." *Optimum Online, 37.2*, 2–15. www.optimumonline.ca [consulted January 15, 2009]

———. (2008). "Cat's Eyes: Intelligent Work *versus* Perverse Incentives." *Optimum Online, 38.3*, 1–17. www.optimumonline.ca [consulted January 15, 2009]

Laurent, P., and G. Paquet. (1998). *Épistémologie et économie de la relation: Coordination et gouvernance distribuée*. Lyon: Vrin.

Lithwick, N. H., and G. Paquet, eds. (1968). *Urban Studies: A Canadian Perspective*. Toronto: Methuen.

Paquet, G. (1971). "Social Science Research as an Evaluative Instrument for Social Policy." In *Social Science and Social Policy*, ed. G. E. Nettler and J. Krotki. Edmonton: Human Resources Council, 49–66.

———. (1985). "An Agenda for Change in the Federal Public Service." *Canadian Public Administration, 28.3*, 455–61.

———. (1999a). *Governance through Social Learning*. Ottawa: University of Ottawa Press.

———. (1999b). "Innovations in Governance in Canada." *Optimum Online, 29.2–3*, 73. www.optimumonline [consulted January 15, 2009]

———. (1999c). *Oublier la Révolution tranquille: Pour une nouvelle socialité*. Montréal: Liber.

———. (2004). *Pathologies de gouvernance: Essais de technologie sociale*. Montréal: Liber.

———. (2005a). *Gouvernance: Une invitation à la subversion*. Montréal: Liber.

———. (2005b). *The New Geo-Governance: A Baroque Approach*. Ottawa: University of Ottawa Press.

———. (2005c). "The RSC as Public Intellectual." *Optimum Online, 35.4*, 3–29. www.optimumonline.ca [consulted January 15, 2009]

———. (2007). "Letting the Cat out of Gow's Bag." *Optimum Online, 37.4*, 45–49. www.optimumonline.ca [consulted January 15, 2009]

———. (2008a). "Pour une éthique prospective et reconstructive fondée sur les besoins." *Ethique publique, 10.1*, 83–91.

———. (2008b). *Deep Cultural Diversity: A Governance Challenge*. Ottawa: University of Ottawa Press.

Pollitt, C. (2003). "New Forms of Public Service: Issues in Contemporary Organizational Design." In *The Art of the State: Governance in a World Without Frontiers*, ed. T. Courchene and D. Savoie. Montreal, Institute for Research on Public Policy, 209–235.

Yankelovich, D., and S. Rosell. (2008). "Viewpoint Learning Model." www.viewpointlearning.com/about/model.shtml [consulted February 2, 2009]

Chapter 19

Gilles Paquet and the Federal Public Service

David Zussman

> The people who oppose your ideas are inevitably those who represent the established order that your ideas will upset.
> —Anthony D'Angelo

Introduction

This wide-ranging volume of individual contributions in honour of Professor Emeritus Gilles Paquet is a testimony to a lifetime of scholarship about public policy and democracy in Canada. For almost forty years, Paquet has been an omnipresent observer, teacher, and *provocateur* about all aspects of Canada's ongoing development as a nation.

While the public service per se has never been at the core of his work, Paquet has often dipped his fingers into the vast pool that defines the activities of the federal public service as a way of tying his view about the emerging governance regime in Canada to the practical implementation of his unique governance model. His strong views and pointed accusations about disloyalty, inefficiency, and misguided management measures in the federal government have made him a very popular speaker at departmental retreats and executive strategy sessions. As a consequence of his ongoing and very public interest in the role of the public service in Canada in 2006, the Association of Professional Executives (APEX) of the federal government recognized his unique contribution to public service by awarding Paquet the Public Service Citation for having made "an outstanding contribution to a better understanding of the Public Service."

My association with Gilles is now longer than twenty-five years. We first met while he was dean of the Faculty of Administration (now the Telfer School of Management) at the University of Ottawa and was searching for faculty to teach in the public management side of the faculty. My background as a psychologist in addition to my diverse policy experiences in a number of federal departments tweaked his interest and led to my hiring as a professor of public policy and management in the faculty. As a consequence of our close working association, it wouldn't take long for me to appreciate how much Gilles valued "out-of-the-box thinking" and people who had a different view of the world.

For my sins, I succeeded Gilles as dean of the faculty, and this development cemented our relationship as one of teacher-student. It is within this context that I have prepared this overview of Gilles's lifetime contribution to the public service literature in Canada.

It is important to note that Gilles is first and foremost an economic historian with a strong attachment to using history to explain current events. This approach is equally true with regard to his work on the public service. Since Paquet has never worked in the federal public service, he has relied on his observational skills and has developed some strong views about this venerable and important public institution.[1] He has largely based his analysis on interactions that he has had with public servants as a consumer of federal government services, as an acute observer of public service activities, and through the hundreds of professional development courses and lectures that he has delivered to the public service over the past twenty-five years.

Despite his proximity to the fishbowl in which senior officials operate in Ottawa, over the years Paquet has always resisted the temptation to look at the public service through the lens of the senior mandarins. Instead, he has concentrated his thinking and theorizing on the larger core of the public servants, and that may explain his special affinity with the rank-and-file public servant. Recently, Gilles has departed from his generalized look at the public sector by assessing, with his colleague Ruth Hubbard, the role of the clerk of the Privy Council. However, given his overarching and broad interest in public governance, the actions and motives of senior officials are insufficient for his purpose since they provide an incomplete picture of the real dynamics of managing large organizations. Instead, his research has focused on the middle ranks of the public service, as he thinks that the locus of power and control in large public organizations is found in the "guts" of the organization.[2]

This chapter is designed to provide you with an overview of Gilles Paquet's views regarding the federal public service. While his career spans almost forty years of research and observation, Paquet has largely confined his work to looking at the federal government and the people who have populated this important federal institution. While he wrote passionately about provincial matters and had strong views about the role of Quebec in Canada, his public sector interest centred on the people who worked in the federal government in the city where he lived and taught.

This chapter is organized into three sections. The first section summarizes the contextual matters that describe the environment in which the federal public service operates. Paquet has noted some of these contextual factors, while others are drawn from the contemporary literature on Canadian public administration. The second section examines some of the key issues that have preoccupied Paquet over the decades. When one reads his vast body of material on the public service, it is apparent that his interests have narrowed over the past decade, settling on a number of "key" issues that revolve around good governance and accountability. The third section concludes the chapter with a series of observations designed to summarize the important learnings and to suggest some further work that might become part of Paquet's future research and writing.

Context of His Work

There is a wide consensus that the environment in which the public sector operates has changed dramatically over the years. Everyone who writes about governance, government, and public management has a favourite list of factors that contextualizes the working environment of the public sector today.

Paquet has his own list, and in typical fashion it is slightly different from those of most Canadian academics. For example, in a recent publication, Hubbard and Paquet (2008, 86) observed that "the last three decades have brought new and even more daunting challenges for the public sector: the need to accommodate deep diversity, globalization, and the citizens' rising desires to be 'kept in the loop' have increased the pressure to adjust both more substantially and more rapidly. This has led to public sector reforms throughout the world."

Two others who have recently thought a lot about working in the public sector are Paul Tellier and Don Mazankowski, who have captured the current contextual challenges in their recent Prime Minister's Advisory Committee report (2008). In general terms, they argue that the world in which the federal Public Service operates has become more complex and unpredictable. This new environment is characterized by an aging population, a globalized economic landscape, ever-changing information and communications technologies, the emergence of new horizontal issues and changing public attitudes to government.

All of these factors have led Paquet (2006a, 21) to conclude that "the new global context and the increasing social diversity of modern societies have created both the need for devolution to ensure the requisite flexibility and innovativeness to compete effectively worldwide, and the need for more participative governance regimes to better respond to the needs of the different social groups and mobilize their intelligence." In his view, this is due to "the relative decline in the role of the state, and the state's dis-aggregation into sub-national fragments; the parallel emergence of the multi-sectoral/multilevel governing mechanisms in a world where nobody is in charge; and the illiberal flavour of the state-centric culture of adjudication that attempts, in the face of the new complex situations, to grant ever more arbitration power to state super-technocrats" (2009, 207).

This has been exacerbated by the declining importance of the federal government within the Canadian federation. Driven in part by the growing importance of social programs (e.g., health and education) and in part by the increased fiscal capacity of the provincial and municipal governments, the "relative importance" of the federal government, in Paquet's view, has declined despite its dramatic increase in size since 2000 (Hubbard and Paquet 2005, 7).

One recent concern for Paquet has been the overreaction in the federal government to the work of Justice Gomery in terms of the imposition of a new accountability framework that is blame oriented and unwarranted in the face of the evidence. In his view, legitimate "accountability is conditioned by context: pressures generated by globalization, accelerated technological change, but also, and most importantly, as a result of greater cultural diversity, heightened and diverse citizens' expectations, crises in public finances, new ideologies, and so forth" (Paquet 2008a, 9). However, the "misguided" work of Gomery is based on a number of eroded assumptions such as the notion that the state must dominate governing because the public sector can be presumed to do most things more effectively than the other two, "the fixation on one-size-fits-all and uniformity in the delivery of public services, and the notion of a firewall must exist between the public sector and the rest of society" (9). In addition to the overworked accountability framework,

Paquet has identified other contextual issues that have an impact on public servants. They were the recent trend of policy analysts denying the complexity of their policy issues by seeking simple and inappropriate solutions, gotcha accountabilities where wrongdoers must be identified and punished, and the false belief that government operates in an open and transparent fashion (9).

In practical terms, the federal public service that Paquet writes about today has been undergoing a dramatic transformation that plays directly into his observations about the changing nature of governance in Canada. For example, the public service today is the same size as it was in 1983 when Pierre Trudeau was prime minister. There are 255,000 employees, and fifty-five percent are women. While the number is the same as twenty-five years ago, the profile of the public service is very different. The public service is older, more gender neutral, and more diverse in terms of the ethnic makeup of employees. Over and above these developments, a dramatic change has taken place in the executive group. For example, forty percent of the executive cadre is comprised of women; that represents an increase of thirty-five percent compared with 1983. To compound the challenge presented by this new balanced workforce, the average age of executives is fifty-one, and for assistant deputy ministers the average age is fifty-four. Due to a very comprehensive pension plan, more than fifty percent of executives and twenty-five percent of rank-and-file public servants can retire without penalty by 2012.

As suggested earlier in this section, the major contextual challenge identified in much of Paquet's work for the past fifteen years has to do with his observations about the evolution of governance in Canada. In essence, Paquet concluded about fifteen years ago that the evolving technological, economic, and social dynamisms taking place at the time would require governments to find new ways to ensure "effective coordination in a world where power, resources and information are ever more widely and asymmetrically distributed" (2006a, 3). "While states and nations (and the related notions of citizenship and identity) have traditionally been anchored in territory, of late, they have become much more footloose, 'de-territorialized.' As a result, the hierarchical and authoritarian geo-governance nation-state structures (that have been in good currency for the last century or more) have proved to be rather ineffective in meeting the coordinating needs of socio-technical systems that are continually stirred by new technological advances, external forces generated by the globalization process, greater social differentiation, and higher interdependency" (2009, 209).

In Paquet's view, the institutional order is slowly moving from the dominance of big G Government toward the dominance of small g governance that would have significant challenges for "senior public servants in the trenches, as the ground on which they operate would appear to be in motion" (Hubbard and Paquet 2007a, 2).

Paquet's Particular Concerns

After reviewing his writing and commentaries for the past decade, it appears that Paquet has a discrete number of particular concerns about the federal public service. The first of his issues is that, over time and despite the constraints imposed by a new accountability regime, public servants have become too powerful by taking over many of the oversight functions from political leaders who, over time, have lost their legitimacy.

This has led Paquet to conclude that this transfer of power has allowed or encouraged the public sector servants to act in a disloyal manner in order to preserve their interpretation of the public interest. The disloyalty theme is a large part of his recent work since he believes that "there is a general agreement among observers that disloyalty may have increased over the past decade or two" and that public servants are no longer working in the broad public interest (Paquet 2008a, 10).

Paquet believes that disloyalty pervades all levels of the public service but especially at senior positions, where he has particular concerns about the behaviour of deputy ministers. In his opinion, most deputy ministers do their jobs, but they "(s)ome deputy ministers ... have begun to suggest that their mandate differs from that of simply informing and assisting their ministers. They have declared themselves to be the direct and privileged interpreters of the public interest, and to have the responsibility for standing on guard for the country when facing elected representatives whose legitimacy, according to them, has become questionnable." (Paquet 2008b, 1). Even if one of five public servants acts in a disloyal manner, Paquet believes that this can lead to a situation of general ministerial paranoia at the political level where no one any longer knows who to trust.

Furthermore, the rising culture of adjudication that has emerged over the past while has exacerbated the situation by giving too much more power to super-bureaucrats, such as the Supreme Court, central banks and commissars of all stripes, and has amounted to efforts at regulating democracy (Paquet 2006b). Paquet is also concerned that no one is responding to this development because he believes that the public perceives the current system as corrupt, and as a result it is up to the public service to protect us. In turn, he notes that in effect the public servants have further compounded the situation by demanding that the superior moral authority of super-bureaucrats be recognized as incontestable by granting them additional powers. In his general view, the real tragedy created by the lack of punishment for deception and irresponsibility at the top of the bureaucracy resides in the fact that the majority of senior public servants and super-bureaucrats (who loyally serve the government) cannot help but be frustrated and discouraged by the climate of distrust that has been implanted—a climate which is explicable but is inflicting much undeserved distrust on them.

Paquet further argues that many eminent scholars who were indifferent to the devolution of powers to lower orders of government have celebrated this growth of undemocratic institutions, arguing that "the clutches of professional technocrats in charge of these super institutions are more efficient than the clutches of amateur elected members in legislatures—and have proposed the multiplication of such adjudicatory institutions in various areas, like health and the environment" (2009, 212).[3]

While Paquet would challenge anyone who thought that he or she possessed the "truth" about a given issue, he has argued in many of his publications that public servants "have a duty (as part of their burden of office) to provide their best advice as fully as possible to their political masters" (2008a, 11). Therefore, while he remains very concerned about the issue of disloyalty, he nonetheless champions the need for public servants at all levels to "speak truth to power."

Another theme of Paquet's work is his assertion that, because of the changes taking place in governance and the particular characteristics of the new accountability regimes being introduced into federal government, there is actually no one in charge of managing the public sector. Ironically, just as public servants are assuming more responsibilities for ensuring good government, Paquet notes that fear of failure, a culture of risk aversion, a blame game led by undisciplined and uninformed parliamentarians, as well as unrelenting oversight activities provoked by the *Accountability Act* have created a leadership vacuum in government. All of these factors have created an environment that Paquet believes has led to a decline in open critical thinking (Hubbard and Paquet 2007a, 16) and the failure to experiment with new policy ideas (2009, 219).

More recently, Paquet has turned his attention to the pivotal role played by the clerk of the Privy Council. Based on a historical analysis of the twenty-one clerks of the Privy Council since Confederation, Paquet has concluded that their role has significantly diminished over time. Historically, the role played by the clerks remained fairly constant, although the details of their work varied considerably depending on day-to-day challenges. Paquet suggests that each clerk has to play the roles of cabinet secretary and deputy minister to the prime minister. These roles are to provide information, coordinate horizontal activities, integrate federal-provincial matters, manage crises, and oversee the public service.

However, after a lengthy analysis of the tenures of all the clerks of the Privy Council, Paquet has concluded that the last few clerks have "all proved to be internally focused on overhauling the state, and may be said to have generally failed to meet the challenges of their maven, connector and salesman function. As a result, the job of Clerk has lost its crucial place, and has failed to mount the sort of network of expertise that would help to shape the new Canadian governance. During all these years, the PMO trumped the PCO, and the Clerk's role has been fundamentally eroded" (Hubbard and Paquet 2005, 26). Moreover, more recently, clerks have become *révélateurs* since their role has changed to one of a "maven, connector and salesman" in the ways that Malcolm Gladwell describes in his landmark book *The Tipping Point: How Little Things Can Make a Big Difference* (2000).

With the decline in the power of the state (and the federal government within it) and the emergence of polycentric governance, it has been even more difficult for the clerk to exercise power. According to Hubbard and Paquet, "the role of integrator and steward has been first diffracted, and largely submerged. The elusive authority of the Clerk has ceased to have a determinant impact, and has come to be overshadowed by the role of helpmate to the party in power" (2005, 30).

These developments have led Paquet to conclude that the public service is an obstacle to changing the overall governance structure and that public sector renewal has failed. In summary, he has argued that "the presumed idiosyncrasy of public sector employment has now become one of the most important constraints on the evolution of governance in Canada: it has dramatically stalled the exploration of a whole array of collaborative arrangements between the private, public and social sectors (because this would be likely to erode the almost sacred basis of state employment) and has prevented serious efforts to modernize the public sector whenever it might entail fragmentation of the body of public servants that might be required to operate under different regimes" (Hubbard and Paquet 2007b, 9). Resistance to new ideas has occurred because "every public sector job has been consecrated as one of 'guardian' of the public good or the fabric of society and therefore declared untouchable" (10).

With regard to public sector reform, Paquet believes that governments have failed despite many efforts because they have been "unduly focused on the search for the Big Solution—the recipe that would apply across the board and at all levels, despite the fact that the personnel to whom these reforms are meant to apply experience extraordinary circumstances" (Hubbard and Paquet 2007b, 14). They offer a bold and controversial remedy that would see the public sector partitioned into four different groupings of public servants: super-bureaucrats, guardians, professionals, and employees. In their view, the employees have different responsibilities, and therefore "there are no reasons why they should be treated in an identical manner" (16).

By differentiating the workforce along functional lines, Paquet believes that there is a better chance for reform to be successful by differentiating the work carried out by the public service. In this way, each group would be subjected to different accountability regimes and management practices. Ever the reformer, Paquet has also argued for the replacement of the Westminster model with a "more modern version taking fully into account the multiple loyalties of public servants" (Paquet and Pigeon 1996, 20).

Conclusion

In the end, Paquet has developed a list of recommendations that he believes would bring the public service in Canada back to a more legitimate place with regard to its relationship with politicians. His first suggestion is that the federal government implement "an intelligent" accountability regime that departs from the current system of uncovering wrongdoing and blaming those who have erred. In this context, the public service should soften the notion of accountability by moving away from blanket rules to a regime that relies more on a values-based system that rewards risk taking and administrative learning. Moreover, Paquet believes that the current climate of fear that has been the product of accusatory administrative practices and "blaming" needs to be replaced by ongoing rounds of dialogue among public servants in a safe space so that innovation and experimentation are championed.

Second, Paquet argues that new institutions are needed to deal with the changing nature of governance in Canada. "A monitoring agency that would assess the quality and reliability of information, forums where governments, the private sector, and the not for profit sector can debate important national issues in particular domains and, a council that would make possible promising experimentations (2008a, 12).

Third, Paquet also believes that citizens need to be more involved in decision making through modern forms of engagement. His governance work has impressed on him the need for more public input, not only because it gives legitimacy to the decisions, but also because evidence suggests that their judgments are often better than those of experts. He notes that "James Surowiecki (2004) has explored this process through which crowds elicit effective evolutionary stable strategies and breed surprising outcomes. He has shown that under conditions of diversity, independence and decentralization, much collective intelligence emerges from crowds, and much effective coordination ensues: 'the many are smarter than the few'" (Paquet 2009, 229).

With regard to disloyalty, Paquet believes that, "unless this sort of behaviour (that amounts to betrayal and treachery) is seriously punished, there is no way that trust can ever be rebuilt. Yet the capacity and willingness for the public service system to shield deceivers from any punishment (and even to reward such behaviour by lateral promotions, especially out of the country) stands as a constant re-enforcement of this sort of behaviour" (2008a, 11).

It should be clear from this brief chapter that Paquet has thought deeply about the role of the public service in the evolving governance structure in Canada. More than a decade ago, he held many optimistic views of the future of the public service, but many of his earlier predictions of a smaller, more focused, public service and an increasingly innovative institution have not actually occurred (Lindquist and Paquet 1997; Paquet 1985). Clearly, Paquet is a passionate observer of, and commentator on, the federal public service, although his reliance on historical trends provides conclusions that are at odds with the data-driven approach taken by many of his public management contemporaries.

Regardless of his approach, many executives in the federal public service are voracious consumers of his work since they believe that his observations provoke them to rethink their roles in this large and complex institution, and his invitation to them to "scheme virtuously" is a most appealing one. In this capacity, Gilles Paquet is a willing participant by creating a provocative dialogue that reinforces his passion for teaching and his unrelenting pursuit of truth and justice.

Notes

[1] Despite a strong preference for evidence-based decision making, Paquet has a very eclectic view of what constitutes evidence. This includes single-case instances and single-observer events.

2   It is always difficult to identify where influences originate, but the notion of middle managers being the most important culture carriers in large organizations can be found in a book that Jak Jabes and I co-authored in the mid-1980s entitled *The Vertical Solitude* (1986).
3   For more on this topic, see Blinder (1997); Dror (2001); and Zakaria (2003).

References

Blinder, A. S. (1997). «Is Government too Political?» *Foreign Affairs, 76.6*, 115–126.

Dror, Y., 2001, *The Capacity to Govern*. London: Frank Cass

Gladwell, M. (2000). *The Tipping Point: How Little Things Can Make a Big Difference*. Boston: Back Bay Books.

Hubbard, R. and Paquet, G. (2007a). "Cat's Cradle: APEX Forums on Wicked Problems." *Optimum Online, 37.2,* 2–15. www.optimumonline.ca [consulted January 18, 2009]

———. (2007b). "The Myth of the Public Service as a Lump of 'Guardians.'" *Optimum Online, 37(1),* 9–26. www.optimumonline.ca [consulted January 18, 2009]

———. (2008). "Clerk as Révélateur: A Panoramic View." In *Searching for Leadership: Secretaries to Cabinet in Canada*, ed. Dutil, P. Institute of Public Administration of Canada, Toronto, 85–120.

Jabes, J., and D. Zussman. (1986). *The Vertical Solitude*. Halifax: Institute for Research on Public Policy.

Lindquist, E., and G. Paquet. (1997). "Government Restructuring and the Federal Public Service: The New Search for a New Cosmology." In *Government Restructuring and Career Public Service in Canada*, ed. E. Lindquist. Toronto: Institute of Public Administration in Canada, 71–111.

Paquet, G. (1985). "An Agenda for Change in the Federal Public Service." *Canadian Public Administration, 28.3,* 455–61.

———. (2006a). "The Many Are Smarter than the Few: A Plea for Mobius-Web Governance." *Optimum Online, 36.4,* 21–40. www.optimumonline.ca [consulted January 18, 2009]

———. (2006b). "Une déprimante culture de l'adjudication." *Policy Options, 27.5,* 40–45.

———. (2008a). "A Plea for Intelligent Accountability." *FMI-IGF Journal, Winter 2008,* 9–14.

———. (2008b). "Super-Bureaucrats and Counter-Democracy." *Canadian Government Executive, June 2008.*

———. (2009). "Foreign policy: the many are smarter than the few." In *Crippling Epistemologies and Governance Failures: A Plea for Experimentalism*. Ottawa: University of Ottawa Press, 206–234.

Paquet, G., and L. Pigeon. (1996). "In Search of a New Covenant." Working Paper 96–22. Centre on Governance, University of Ottawa.

Tellier, P., and D. Mazankowski. (2008). "Prime Minister's Advisory Committee Report on Public Sector Renewal." Available at www.pco-bcp.gc.ca.

Zakaria, F. (2003). *The Future of Freedom*. New York: Norton.

Chapter 20

Letter to the Editor-in-Chief of *Optimum Online*

McEvoy Galbreath

Gilles, you started with *Optimum: The Journal of Public Sector Management* in 1994 and began your work creating a safe place for the public discussion of public issues with volume 26–1, summer 1995. The next volume (27–1) saw the journal take on a "modified form and . . . new ambitions." *Optimum* had become the stepchild of three parents: Consulting and Audit Canada (Public Works and Government Services Canada) continued to support the journal financially, though on a declining basis; the University of Ottawa continued to provide and support the services of the new editor-in-chief; and Prospectus, an Ottawa-based contract publishing firm, came on board to assume the duties of transforming *Optimum* into a privately funded venture. Prospectus morphed into The Summit Group in late 1998, which gave me the sole honour of working with you, a task that I (currently managing editor) came to with trepidation but have enjoyed and cherished.

In the first issue of *Optimum* under the new triumvirate, you wrote a very upbeat and optimistic letter in which you explained that "The intent [of the new corporate format] was to ensure the continuity of *Optimum* through a funding base that would immunize it from the pressures of public sector financial stringency." Over the next few years, I saw you rise to the occasion and show your inner fibre as editor-in-chief when it wasn't the pressures of "financial stringency" that threatened *Optimum* but the pressures of political sensitivity.

The case in point I will recall as the Reimer-Kervin papers, which discussed the then hugely sensitive federal initiative called the Universal Classification System. The stance you took as editor-in-chief in this eighteen-month discussion over whether and how to publish Reimer's research paper and Kervin's response has taught me so much about the real meaning of editorial integrity.

Some individuals working for the government partner were nervous about publishing a paper openly criticizing the official position of the Treasury Board Secretariat (an important client of Consulting and Audit Canada). (TBS did not want it published because it was supposedly just a point of view.) As an accommodating move, you suggested that you would gladly publish a companion piece to Reimer's research paper, written by any credible expert suggested by TBS who might provide another point of view. Kervin from the University of Toronto was suggested, and you persuaded him to write a critical/complementary piece. Both pieces were then slated to be published in the forthcoming issue of *Optimum*.

It appears that this arrangement did not entirely satisfy TBS (or at least that was the interpretation of Consulting and Audit Canada) since, unknown to you, the staff at our government partner's office was asked to withdraw the controversial papers (accepted by you as editor-in-chief) and to replace them with another paper accepted for publication but slated for future publication.

This was unacceptable to you, and you wrote a long factum (as lawyers would call it) to the deputy ministers of the Treasury Board Secretariat and of Public Works and Government Services, and to the clerk of the Privy Council (with copies to your editorial board) demanding an explanation and reparation. This action led to a hiatus in the publication of *Optimum* as the matter got sorted out. It was clear in your factum that, if a resolution were not forthcoming, you would go public with a denunciation of censorship.

The issue was sticky, and some zealous bureaucrats used a threatening tone. There was even the possibility of *Optimum* being wiped off the map. Yet your factum was a weighty document, and the matter was finally resolved after a considerable amount of time in an amicable way. The Canadian government did not want to be put in such a situation by zealous bureaucrats and decided to sell *Optimum* to us, the other publishing partners—to fund a transition to an electronic format would be less financially onerous for them. More importantly in the short run, the Reimer and Kervin papers were published in the next issue of *Optimum*. The journal has benefited immeasurably from your guidance and strong hand when it comes to "walking the walk and talking the talk" about discussing difficult subjects in a public way!

Moving to the web was a major threshold. This was something that the twenty-somethings were doing with such joy and excitement, but for me it was fraught with potentially insurmountable problems. But in the end, it was done! In September 2001, we launched the journal via the World Wide Web and delivered www.optimumonline.ca, thanks to the help, technical genius, and extraordinary patience of 76design and Brett Tackaberry. You saw right away the potential that the web held for *Optimum*. I hasten to add that the web has not relaxed the editorial steel behind the journal one iota!

One of the things that I admire most about *Optimum* and your role as editor-in-chief is your never-ending desire to respectfully present and discuss uncomfortable topics. In my role as copyeditor, I have read *all* of what *Optimum* has to offer, each and every issue. With each release, I have come to enjoy the care you take with language yourself and the humour you use to help even the most difficult topics seem more digestible. Through your editorship, you have sought out and brought to the journal the best commentary of the land on issues of public management by the best specialists in Canada. Then, when that got to be routine, you raised the bar by publishing the Taboo Topics series of workshops that you developed in cooperation with the Royal Society of Canada. And you have continued to stir the pot of public discussion of difficult public management issues with the recent reports on the safe-space breakfast series on Wicked Problems that you and Ruth Hubbard have carried out in collaboration with APEX. These discussions have probed very touchy issues and exposed some raw nerves.

Optimum is not only the place to read the best and brightest on Canadian public sector management, but it has also become a place to gain new insights into issues that are boiling below the surface, a place where one always has one's perspectives broadened. To me, this is the hallmark of a truly great publication!

In your "Note from the Editor-in-Chief" in volume 27–1, in which you took great care to outline and clarify your role as the editor-in-chief, you also concluded with a note of optimism, which was very generous of you at the time given your bad experience with former partners and not knowing well your newer colleagues at Prospectus: "We hope that the new *Optimum* compares with a good and aging wine in a new attractive bottle, that the new partnership lives up to expectations, and that *Optimum* become[s] an ever more influential journal of public sector management and carries its message to tens of thousands of professionals and executives before the end of the century."

The move to the web has been a God-send for the journal and has done much toward achieving your objectives. In 1996, I recall printing 5,000 copies of the journal (copies in English and French available), and perhaps 2,500 of them were read. Early in the present century, *Optimum Online* reaches some 10,000 registered subscribers, covering the public and civic sectors of Canada, Australia, New Zealand, the United States, the United Kingdom, and parts beyond!

Gilles, it has been an amazing ride so far, and I look forward to many more issues of *Optimum* as I am sure that I have much more to learn from you!

Section III

The Issue Domains

> [L]'univers sensible ne s'explique que par une équation qui nous oblige à admettre également un univers où les contraires se concilient, la transcendance justifiant le réel, un troisième ordre justifiant les deux autres, la "charité" expliquant tout le problème. . . .
>
> —Alexandre Vialatte

This section looks at Gilles Paquet in terms of many of the issue domains in which he has had an influence, both directly and indirectly.

It is the professional scholar thread that dominates here, but the tack that the various contributors take in this section says something as well about both the classical educator and the public intellectual threads. The chapters also reveal a little about the person himself.

At the same time, the section deals with the contributions that Paquet has made in terms of the organizing ideas and concepts that he has offered and/or shaped, of the interpretations that he has brought forward, and of the linkages to his work that others have seen from their own vantage points and that they wish to acknowledge.

Part Eight

Organizing Ideas and Concepts

Chapter 21

The New Geo-Governance

H. George Frederickson

For those interested in public administration the recent book by Gilles Paquet, *The New Geo-Governance: A Baroque Approach* (2005), is required reading. Paquet's description of our governing institutions and the rapidly changing contexts in which they are embedded is a word-picture of the highest quality, and his portrayal of our likely governance future is a conceptual tour de force. As is often the case with important books, at certain points *The New Geo-Governance* challenges the foundations upon which traditional public administration rests. Paquet particularly addresses the place of territorially based jurisdictions—the Westphalian nation-state and its sub-state jurisdictions—as essential preconditions for effective public administration.

Twenty years ago Dwight Waldo wrote, "we simply do not know how to solve some of the problems government has been asked to solve." Paquet reasons that this is because "the nation state when confronted with the global adjustment processes and the demands of subnational groups, is not unlike Gulliver: unable to deal effectively with the dwarfs of Lilliput or the giants of Bobdingnag." Local forces from within and regional and global forces from without have rendered the territorial nation state and its subdivisions "less congruent with contemporary realities, and less capable of providing an effective governance regime." As a result, "new forms of distributed governance arrangements have emerged based on a more diffused pattern of power"—systems of geo-governance. By geo-governance, Paquet means "the ways in which effective coordination is effected in a world where resources, knowledge, and power are distributed through geographical space."

Many leading observers and thinkers have made essentially the same observations including Robert Axelrod and Michael Cohen; James March and Johan Olsen; Harlan Cleveland; Jean-Marie Guehenno; Walter Kickert, Erik-Hans Klijn, and Joop Kooperman; Peter Drucker; Samuel Huntington; and James Rosenau. But because of his emphasis on the technologies of geo-governance, Gilles Paquet advances the earlier work of these theorists particularly with respect to public administration. To operationalize geo-governance and make it effective, he argues against emphasizing governance principles and rules, organizational structures, management processes, and culture and in favor of emphasizing governance mechanisms, by which he means "the many ways in which (1) individuals and institutions (public, private, and civic) manage their collective affairs in space, (2) diverse interests accommodate and resolve their differences, and (3) these many actors and organizations are involved in a continuing process of formal and informal competition, cooperation, and learning in space." Although Paquet's language is a bit arcane, by "governance mechanisms" he means day-to-day patterns of collaborative problem solving: in other words, public administration. "Collaboration is the new categorical imperative" for public administration.

What, in more precise terms, do the new "mechanisms" of geo-governance look like? They are made up of dispersed and decentralized organizations that "govern themselves by becoming capable of learning both what their goals are, and the means by which to reach them, *as they proceed*, by tapping into the knowledge and information that active citizens possess, and getting them to invent ways out of the predicaments they are in. This leads to more distributed governance and deprives leaders of their monopoly on the governing of organizations. . . . This diffraction of power has evolved because it triggers more effective learning in the context of rapid change, through decentralized and flexible teams, woven by moral contracts and reciprocal obligations, negotiated in the context of evolving partnerships." There are, according to Paquet, interorganizational ligatures that exhibit "the new lightness and fluidity of the increasingly mobile, slippery, shifty, evasive and fugitive power [which] is not completely a-territorial, it is characterized, however, by new forms of belonging that escape the control of the nation-state to a much higher degree than before, by virtual agoras, liquid networks, variegated and overlapping terrains where citizens [and public administrators] can land temporarily."

Such arrangements "lend themselves to improvisation and experimentation. Consequently, it is not that we feel particularly well served by mechanisms, but they are one of the few workable levers we have. Indeed, when one reflects on some of the broad features of the new ligatures that have been found particularly useful in seeking to construct good governance arrangements in practice, mechanisms would appear to be the operational unit most likely to be of use. . . ." Such mechanisms are the "agoras (information sharing places, shared spaces, consultation/negotiation tables, and the like) for clusters of stakeholders in different sectors or regions." Effective mechanisms are continuous, resilient, and have solid interorganizational learning capacities that tend to exhibit vertical, horizontal, and transversal patterns of soft accountability and ethics, as well as pronounced patterns of leadership and trust.

However, as Paquet indicates, there are at least as many examples of the failure to cooperate as there are examples of successful geo-governance. Why? It is "often the case that the required mechanisms are either missing, fail to live up to expectations, or neutralize one another. There is either (1) no place for dialogue and deliberation, or for collaborative arrangements to be negotiated; or (2) no way to neutralize and overcome rivalry and envy; and little possibility of building much partnering and leadership on inexistent trust; (3) or little in the way of intelligent mutual accountability mechanisms; or (4) not much of the requisite enaction, control, and stewardship mechanisms for effective social learning. As a result geo-governance flounders." But there are enough examples of effective geo-governance found in the works of Elinor and Vincent Ostrom, Robert Axelrod, Harlan Cleveland, Earnest Haas, Howard Rheingold, and the network theorists to confirm Gilles Paquet's claims.

It is, however, the fundamentals of geo-governance that really challenge traditional public administration. As Paquet puts it, "The mechanisms that promote dialogue, partnering, leadership and the like are the very fabric of governance, but they have a subversive impact on the state." This is because "[i]n modern democracies the sort of citizen participation [and direct public administration involvement] entailed by the mechanisms sketched out above is a challenge to the usual methods of representation; because it short-circuits the usual process through which the collective will is supposedly expressing itself in the polity—the ballot box."

As formal democratic polities, what role shall the nation, the state, or the city play in modern geo-governance? First, there is much that remains mediated by national, state, and city regimes inasmuch as their polities are deeply territorial.

According to Paquet, "the territorial nation still plays the role of an echo box, through which much must be arbitrated." Traditional democratic politics—office holding, parties, campaigns and elections, law making, revenue extraction—form the backdrop for geo-governance. But geo-governance has at least as much to do with public administration as it has to do with jurisdictional politics. "This new pattern has vested infra-national communities with new powers, has built on new principles of cooperation/competition within and across national boundaries, and has been rooted in new capabilities that are much less state-centered."

If you are ready for a particularly thoughtful and challenging treatment of public administration, read Gilles Paquet's *The New Geo-Governance: A Baroque Approach*, and get a glimpse of your future.

Editors' note: This review of *The New Geo-Governance: A Baroque Approach* (Ottawa: University of Ottawa Press, 2005) by Gilles Paquet appeared in *Public Administration Times, 29.6* (2006), 1–2, and is reprinted with the permission of the author.

Chapter 22

Contribution to Governance Scholarship: Definitions, Debates, and Omissions

Monica Gattinger

La problématique de la gouvernance . . . propose la recherche des moyens d'assurer une coordination efficace quand ressources, pouvoir et information sont vastement distribués et que personne ne peut prétendre avoir la possibilité de faire le travail seul.

—Gilles Paquet

With this deceptively simple definition, Gilles Paquet proposes a conceptualization of governance that may be among the most comprehensive and analytically useful approaches to the term. He has also, through his prolific writing on governance, developed a means of analyzing the concept that elevates it from an abstract, loosely defined term (which is often the case in governance literature), to a veritable—to use his words—*manière de voir*. His application of this *manière de voir* to topics as far-flung as cultural diversity, national defence, corporate governance, health care, and universities has contributed greatly to governance, policy, and administrative studies both in Canada and abroad.

In the face of this broad and impressive body of scholarship, it is daunting—perhaps foolhardy—to contemplate addressing Paquet's contribution to the field in a short chapter. Nonetheless, it is an important and worthy challenge to undertake—albeit with the knowledge that such a brief piece cannot possibly do justice to or capture adequately the man's contribution to governance scholarship. Hence, I have intentionally kept the focus of this chapter narrow, and admittedly this is a very modest attempt at a Herculean task and certainly not the last word on the subject.

I explore Paquet's contribution to governance scholarship in two main respects.[1] First, I examine his contribution to the conceptualization and operationalization of the term. Through an overview of other scholars' work in the field, I identify the novelty and utility of the "Paquet approach." Second, I explore his approach to governance vis-à-vis that of multilevel governance (MLG)—an increasingly important strand of the governance literature both in Europe and in North America. The section begins by briefly highlighting a number of key themes, debates, and areas of convergence/divergence in Paquet's work and this emerging strand of literature. In the spirit of open academic debate, of which Paquet is so fond, this text would be remiss were it not to consider potential weaknesses in the Paquet approach to governance.

I also explore the growing focus on questions of democratic legitimacy and governance in the MLG scholarship, a tendency not found in Paquet's work. I examine whether his approach privileges notions of effectiveness over considerations of democratic legitimacy. The analysis reveals that Paquet's work converges with MLG literature on questions of effectiveness but diverges in the level of importance that it accords to questions of democratic legitimacy. The chapter concludes with final reflections on the importance of Paquet's contribution to governance studies.

Defining Governance: The Paquet Approach

Scholars and students of governance, as well as practitioners in the field, often lament the lack of clarity around the concept of governance. This confusion arises in part because of the multiple purposes or levels to which the concept can be and has been applied. Rhodes (2000), taking a functional approach, notes that the term can refer to governance as corporate governance, as New Public Management, as "good governance," as international interdependence, as sociocybernetic system, as the new political economy, or as networks, each with its own distinct definition. Krahmann (2003), peering at governance through a "level of analysis" lens, notes that it can be applied globally, regionally, or nationally, with differing conceptualizations of the term at each level.

Each of these governance "worlds" can be characterized by differing foci and emphases, centring on internal organizational governance (e.g., corporate governance or New Public Management), extending beyond public or private organizations to encompass these bodies' relations with other public, private, or civil society actors (e.g., international interdependence, networks, or sociocybernetics), or adopting purposively normative conceptions of organizational or interorganizational relations (e.g., good governance or governance as the new political economy).

In this context, definitions of governance abound. Corporate governance analyzes the way in which private sector firms are directed and controlled, and generally centres on openness and disclosure, integrity, responsibility, and accountability (Rhodes 2000, 56). Governance as New Public Management, meanwhile, deals with the introduction of private sector management techniques into the public sector and the marketization of public goods and services (56). The hallmark of policy-centred definitions, for their part, is to draw the distinction between "government" and "governance," with the former referring to hierarchical, state-centric, and state-dominated forms of policy making, and the latter encompassing non-hierarchical, decentralized, and collaborative policy-making approaches, characterized by interdependence, ongoing communication, and the pursuit of shared policy objectives by governmental and non-governmental actors (see, for example, Börzel 1997; Krahmann 2003; and Wolfe and Creutzberg 2003).[2]

Despite the diversity of central interests, what most of this scholarship shares is a relatively common analysis of the factors giving rise to the emergence of the concept of governance: growing complexity in organizational environments and policy making in the context of rapid societal and technological change; globalization; growing interdependence between governmental and non-governmental actors; reductions in the size of the state, its role, and policy capacity in the wake of fiscal pressures and the ideological turn to neoliberalism; and growing interest among, and pressure by, non-governmental actors to be consulted and to influence public policy. In this new milieu, the theoretical and empirical phenomenon of governance has arisen across multiple functions and levels of analysis, so perhaps not surprisingly attempts to develop a single definition of the term are scarce.

Krahmann (2003) undertakes one of the most valiant attempts. After a meticulous empirical analysis of the rise of the term in scholarly journals over the past few decades, and its various uses at national, regional, and global levels, she proposes the following general definition: "social structures and processes that enable governmental and nongovernmental actors to coordinate their interdependent needs and interests through the making and implementation of policies in the absence of a unifying political authority" (331). This definition focuses attention on structures of coordination and processes for policy development and implementation where policy authority is fragmented. It also recognizes the interdependence between state and non-state actors. But while it is certainly valuable, the definition remains only partial in that it does not capture the material contribution of non-government actors to policy (e.g., provision of resources, expertise, information, etc.). Moreover, its focus on the absence of a unifying political authority obscures the important reality that, even *with* a unified political authority, in the current context, this body would not likely possess all of the tools (command of the problem, resources, and capacity to address it, etc.) to effectively address contemporary policy problems on its own.

This is where the Paquet approach to defining governance makes such an important contribution. As noted in the epigraph to this text, he notes that "*La problématique de la gouvernance . . . propose la recherche des moyens d'assurer une coordination efficace quand ressources, pouvoir et information sont vastement distribués et que personne ne peut prétendre avoir la possibilité de faire le travail seul*" (2003, 11). This deceptively simple definition comprehensively addresses the key features of the phenomenon: how to ensure effective coordination when resources, power, and information are highly dispersed and no single actor can resolve pressing issues on its own. The Paquet approach implicitly recognizes that multiple actors bring to the table relevant tools in their possession (resources, power, and/or information) and collectively coordinate to resolve problems through a variety of mechanisms. The absence of explicit reference to public, private, or civil society actors enables the definition to be utilized across multiple functions and levels (corporate governance, public governance, policy development/implementation, etc., at any level of analysis).

The provision of a succinct, comprehensive, analytically powerful, and widely applicable definition of governance is no small contribution to the field and one for which governance scholars should all be grateful.[3]

Debates and Omissions: Contributions and Limitations of the Paquet Approach

The concept of multilevel governance emerged in the 1990s and is a strand of the governance literature gaining increasing prominence in governance studies. Developed in the European context in response to the reconfiguration of political authority in Western Europe (Peters and Pierre 2002), it refers to "negotiated, non-hierarchical exchanges between institutions at the transnational, national, regional and local levels" (Peters and Pierre 2001, 131).[4] While MLG analysis generally focuses on political institutions, it can and does involve examination of non-governmental actors' involvement in these exchanges (Hooghe and Marks 2003; Peters and Pierre 2002). The vast majority of MLG scholarship is empirically grounded in studies of the European Union, but it is increasingly being applied to the case of North America (see, e.g., Brown 2002; Clarkson 2001; Doern and Johnson 2006; Young and Leuprecht 2006).

Similar to Paquet's research, MLG literature is concerned with coordination and means of achieving it in situations of dispersed authority (Hooghe and Marks 2003). The need for coordination owes to a variety of institutional and structural factors, including social fragmentation, the interdependence and dispersion of power, authority, financial resources, knowledge between and among government and non-government actors, and the growing complexity of policy problems (Papadopoulos 2005, 317–18). This diagnosis of the need for coordination (and hence governance) squares with Paquet's analysis of the characteristics of the new sociotechnical systems giving rise to governance: accelerating technical change, globalization, social differentiation, interdependency, and environmental turbulence, all rendering centralized and hierarchical direction ineffective (2005a, 372; 2005b, xii). Both Paquet and MLG scholars also note the important role of negotiation and informal exchanges in achieving coordination (see, e.g., Benz 2003; Paquet 1999, 8). It is this characteristic of informality that gives rise to concerns about the democratic legitimacy of governance processes in the MLG literature, a point to which I will return below.

In many other respects, however, Paquet's scholarship is either divergent from or complementary to MLG analyses. While both are concerned with coordination and mechanisms of achieving coordination, they take differing approaches and place differing valences on the factors, principles, mechanisms, and instruments underpinning coordination. MLG analysis takes a largely neo-institutional approach, examining the pursuit of coordination as the interplay between formal institutional structures and the fluidity of multilevel arrangements that coalesce around particular policy issues. The literature recognizes that the independence of institutional actors is conditioned by the institutional context (Benz 2003), for instance the degree of decentralization within and between public organizations, their autonomy from centralized political control, etc. Conceptual frameworks in MLG scholarship are largely institution based, distinguishing, for example, between intergovernmental versus supranational approaches to coordination, and intermediaries in between, or the oft-utilized distinction between Type I governance ("general purpose jurisdictions"), formalized distributions of authority such as federalism with "system-wide architectures" that are slow to change, and Type II governance ("task-specific jurisdictions"), which is more fluid and flexible and "ubiquitous in efforts to internalize transnational spillovers in the absence of authoritative coordination" (Hooghe and Marks 2003, 238–39).

Paquet's focus, meanwhile, is decidedly not institutional. Indeed, Paquet eschews a focus on institutional structures because to his mind this approach "leaves too much out of the equation" and "has led experts to indulge in much utopian thinking . . . [maintaining] the view that one could count on an institutional and organizational architecture that would be capable of providing legitimacy, norms, implementation processes, and control mechanisms from the very start" (2005b, 40, 5). He warrants instead that the institutional structure is *en émergence* and that "one can only work at helping such a regime to emerge as a gardener helps a garden to evolve" (6). For Paquet, the principal concern is not institutions but the *process of governance* (40).

In focusing on this process, those who are familiar with his work know that he has developed a veritable vocabulary of governance—*un outillage mental*—to conceptualize the context, concepts, principles, mechanisms, instruments, etc., necessary to pursue effective coordination. "Wicked problems," "Boulding triangles," "co-evolution," "distributed governance," "dispersive revolutions," "learning blockages," "social ligatures," "baroque principles," "*métissage*," "*bricolage*"—these and many more form the language and grammar of governance *à la* Paquet. But perhaps more than anything, his approach is set apart by his focus on the central role of "social learning" ("collective intelligence") as "the most helpful lens" through which to examine current governance challenges (2005b, 2). For Paquet, the success of contemporary organizations (public, private, non-profit) and socioeconomic systems writ large depends fundamentally on their capacity to learn and adapt to their ever-evolving environments and to co-evolve with one another in the process (1999, 7). Learning requires the involvement of everyone with relevant knowledge and information as well as the use of decentralized, flexible teams and partnerships (8–9). Trust is also central to learning, a process in which much knowledge is tacit (2005b, 7).

Paquet's exploration of the soft, micro-, and cultural mechanisms underpinning effective coordination extends far beyond solely learning and trust to encompass mechanisms such as moral contracts, social norms (e.g., pragmatism, reasonableness, mutual understanding), coopetition (partnerships and competition), networks, and ethics. This sets Paquet far apart from the MLG literature's focus on the macroinstitutional context of negotiation.[5]

Where MLG scholarship does consider these softer mechanisms of coordination, it does so from a rather different perspective, one that in fact forms a key fault line of debate in the literature. Scharpf's 1999 book *Governing in Europe: Effective and Democratic?* was one of the first to sound an alarm bell about the extent to which the new institutional structures of the European Union responded to the criterion of effectiveness—the main focus of scholarship and political discourse to that point—but perhaps did not respond as well to democratic criteria.

Until recently, effectiveness—whether a policy choice arrived at in a multilevel system resolves the problem at hand and does so in a way that does not violate politically salient interests (Peters and Pierre 2004; Scharpf 1999)—tended to dominate MLG analysis. Indeed, the literature "largely ignored questions of democratic legitimacy" (DeBardeleben and Hurrelmann 2007, 2). This situation has changed, however: MLG scholars are increasingly exploring the extent to which multilevel processes strengthen or thwart democratic legitimacy. The effectiveness/legitimacy fault line forms a key pivot of debate in the literature, with some scholars noting that the decentralization, informality, and technical expertise characterizing MLG processes open avenues for greater inclusiveness, efficiency, and effectiveness in decision making, with others warranting that these characteristics lead to unequal access, reduced transparency, and weakened political accountability (DeBardeleben and Hurrelmann 2007, 5–6).[6] Regardless of which side of the debate one is on, it is undeniable that much MLG scholarship has been devoted to this topic.

While there is no common definition of democratic legitimacy in the literature, four key components comprising the concept can be gleaned from scholarship in the area: transparency, openness and representativeness, deliberative quality, and accountability (see, e.g., Coleman and Porter 2000; DeBardeleben and Hurrelmann 2007; Peters and Pierre 2004; Rhinard 2002; and Skogstad 2002). *Transparency* refers at its core to information and the ability for actors to access relevant information regarding decisions being made. It requires that "all interested observers [can] inform themselves fully on the core questions and tradeoffs under consideration" (Coleman and Porter 2000, 388–389).[7] The concept of *openness and representativeness* moves beyond a focus on access to information to participation in decision-making processes. It refers to the ability for those who are affected or concerned by the policy issue under consideration to attempt to influence the process (openness) and the degree to which those who are involved in decision making represent the full breadth of potentially affected or interested parties (representativeness) (Coleman and Porter 2000, 388–89). These two concepts are distinct but interrelated in that the former can be realized with the establishment of formal or informal mechanisms to enable interested parties to participate, while the latter can extend to the positive requirement of government to ensure that the full breadth of affected stakeholders is represented in policy processes (this could include, for example, institutionalized participation of representative groups, funding to support participation, etc.).

Deliberative quality concerns the nature of communicative exchanges in governance processes. Drawing on Habermas's concept of the "ideal speech situation," it refers to open debate in which all opinions can be expressed and considered in an equal manner: "a system in which, first, differing conceptions of the public interest are allowed into the policy process, and second, those conceptions are given a fair and thoughtful hearing" (Rhinard 2002, 191). *Accountability* refers to the capacity to monitor and sanction agent behaviour in principal-agent relationships. It includes general mechanisms such as hierarchical supervision, judicial review, and parliamentary investigations and extends to the electoral dependence of politicians on citizens (4). It refers, therefore, to principal-agent relationships between citizens and politicians (democratic accountability), and to those between elected and non-elected officials, for instance between the political and bureaucratic executives (which can be referred to as internal accountability). This dual notion of accountability is particularly important in MLG systems, where the complexity of multilevel policy processes challenges democratic accountability because many of the key actors are non-elected officials and where the fusion of political power in decision making makes it "difficult to trace political acts to identifiable agents" (DeBardeleben and Hurrelmann 2007, 7; see also Papadopoulos 2005, 322).

In contrast to MLG scholarship, democratic legitimacy is not given the same weight in Paquet's work. While his scholarship certainly does attend to questions of transparency, openness and representation, deliberation, and accountability, the main focus of his research is on effectiveness, as witnessed, for example, in his definition of governance but also in the various analytical frameworks of governance that Paquet has developed over the years. Where he does consider these concepts, it is not always with the same degree of detail and comprehensiveness as that found in the MLG literature, nor is he necessarily advocating for their maximum realization (in fact, in some instances, quite the opposite, a point that I return to below).

Paquet does recognize that efforts to identify governance mechanisms include a focus on principles such as legitimacy and transparency (in addition to efficiency), but, given the predominance of soft mechanisms (persuasion, flexibility, moral contracts, etc.), he is not sanguine about the realization of these principles, saying that contemporary governance arrangements "can meet only partially and imperfectly the imperatives of effectiveness, transparency, legitimacy, etc. [and] may be the best that can practically be accomplished" (2005b, 4–5). While this view may be in keeping with his pragmatism, it does little to identify potential means of striving for these objectives in what is admittedly an imperfect world.

Indeed, Paquet's approach to the concept of democratic legitimacy is often only partial: Paquet states the importance of "maximum participation," deliberation, "the participation-society," governments' "duty of dialogue," etc., while providing few guideposts for how to operationalize these principles in practice. How does one define maximum participation—opportunities to participate? Numbers of participants? Representativeness of those participating?—and go about evaluating whether it has been realized in practice? How does one identify whether genuine deliberation has taken place, alternative viewpoints have been expressed, and power imbalances have been addressed in some fashion? There remains much ground to till here.

This is particularly important given that the new governance reality so characteristic of Paquet's work—a decentralized, networked, heterarchical, ground-in-constant-motion, world-without-a-master context where informal soft voluntary mechanisms and emergent institutions are the key coordination mechanisms—is precisely the sort of context within which fundamental democratic principles may be vulnerable to erosion (or, stated another way, where practices lacking democratic underpinnings may flourish). In this light, it is difficult to comprehend why a sustained focus on democratic legitimacy is not present in Paquet's scholarship.

This omission may in part be explained by the strong role that Paquet sees for social conventions and norms (trust, pragmatism, reasonableness, mutual understanding, ethics, etc.) in governance processes, but in the absence of these characteristics—many of which Paquet himself readily admits are lacking or in decline at the current time (see Paquet 2004)—it is difficult to see how democratic credentials based on social conventions and norms would spontaneously emerge in governance processes.

Paquet's lack of a comprehensive focus on democratic considerations may also be explained in part by his own discomfort with some of the principles described above—at least as they are conventionally understood. On transparency, Paquet advises a mix of transparency and opacity, warranting that some governance processes should not be subjected to full transparency because they require a certain degree of "shade" to be effective (2004, 237). On participation, he cautions that the maximum is not necessarily the optimum and that the right (not necessarily the maximum) amount of participation is required to avoid "sabotage" of deliberative processes (238). On accountability, Paquet argues for a shift from traditional hierarchical accountability to soft, horizontal, 360 degree accountability (2005a, 384–87). Unfortunately, on all of these counts, few examples of where, why, or how to draw the line are provided, nor are the concepts developed adequately to be operationalized in practice. This leaves the reader with the uneasy feeling that democratic legitimacy may suffer—or is suffering—in this new governance reality.

Conclusion

Paquet's contribution to governance studies is undeniable: his elegant and comprehensive definition of governance, his untiring search for mechanisms to promote effective coordination, and his ongoing research to develop an analytical framework to unpack governance processes have considerably advanced understanding and usage of the concept. While it is perhaps tempting to make of Paquet's work the definitive word in the field, it is important to cast the net wider given that his research bears certain limitations, one of which—the lack of attention to democratic legitimacy—has been examined herein.

Nonetheless, Paquet has firmly established himself as a defender and promoter of governance, particularly in the Canadian arena. His unique approach to the field—as theoretician, diagnostician, pragmatist, applied researcher, and, when the opportunity presents itself, *agent provocateur*—sets him apart from other governance scholars.

The Paquet approach focuses on diagnosis and remediation: using the governance *manière de voir* and *outillage mental* to detect coordination failures, identify sources of dysfunction and poor performance, and intervene strategically to reduce blockages and identify possible organizational redesigns. In his words, governance experts work to avoid two pitfalls: "the illusion of control (for one is rarely faced in the real world with a complex socio-technical system that has a fixed shape and predictable behaviour, and therefore that one can fully control), and the illusion of Candide (for it is equally naïve to believe that the appropriate institutional and organizational arrangements will always emerge organically in the best way). . . . [Governance experts] try to nurture the sort of basic architecture that ensures effective social learning through interventions at both the strategic and operational levels" (2005b, 74).

With this definition, Gilles Paquet is most assuredly a governance expert and one for which scholarship and practice are certainly the better.

Notes

[1] The chapter focuses on four of Paquet's core books in the field: *Governance through Social Learning* (1999); *Pathologies de gouvernance: Essais de technologie sociale* (2004); *Gouvernance: Une invitation à la subversion* (2005a); and *The New Geo-Governance: A Baroque Approach* (2005b).

[2] Within the policy-centred approach, some scholars continue to adopt a state-centric definition, focusing on governance as providing central direction or "steering" to society (see, e.g., Peters 2000).

[3] Unfortunately, this definition has not been employed in the governance literature to the degree that it merits. The reasons are varied but likely due in no small measure to the fact that there is no recognizable "Canadian School" of governance scholars or scholarship to raise the profile of Paquet's work nationally and internationally.

[4] This definition is clearly less conceptually powerful than Paquet's, further underscoring the value of his approach to governance.

[5] Paquet also stands apart in his mesolevel analysis of coordination mechanisms. In his now infamous use of a "lightly modified" Boulding triangle, Paquet divides a triangle into equal segments representing the ideal types of state, market, and society, each

with its own sets of organizations and organizational dynamics: the mechanisms of *quid pro quo* exchange (market), coercion and redistribution (polity or state), and gift, solidarity, and reciprocity (community or society) (1999, 5). This analytical framework is distinct from that of other governance scholars, who often view the third mesolevel integrative mechanism as networks rather than gift, solidarity, and reciprocity (see, e.g., Peters 1998). To Paquet, networks are not a hybrid of state and market but consensus or inducement-oriented arrangements (1999, 10).

6   Peters and Pierre (2004) go so far as to characterize multilevel governance as a Faustian bargain, whereby short-term considerations of policy-making effectiveness and efficiency achieved through informal processes are traded for core democratic values such as transparency, inclusiveness, accountability, and equity.

7   Rhinard implicitly refers to transparency with the principle "intelligible system of decision-making." He states that "citizens have the right to see what interests are represented in the processing of policy, which actors are making decisions, and what procedural steps are taken to arrive at those decisions. [The] political process should illuminate the societal issues at stake and make the multiplicity of alternative solutions clear" (2002, 191).

References

Benz, A. (2003). "Multilevel Governance in the European Union." Trans. of "Mehrebenenverflechtung in der Europäischen Union." In *Europäische Integration*, 2nd ed., ed. M. Jachtenfuchs and B. Kohler-Koch. Opladen: Leske and Budrich, 317–51.

Börzel, T. (1997). "What's So Special about Policy Networks? An Exploration of the Concept and Its Usefulness in Studying European Governance." *European Integration Online Papers*, 1, 16. www.eiop.or.at/eiop/texte/1997-016a.htm [consulted June 16, 2008].

Brown, D. (2002). "Aspects of Multilevel Governance in Australia and Canada." Paper prepared for the Conference on Globalization, Multilevel Governance, and Democracy: Continental, Comparative, and Global Perspectives, Queen's University, Kingston, May 3–4.

Clarkson, S. (2001). "The Multi-Level State: Canada in the Semi-Periphery of Both Continentalism and Globalization." *Review of International Political Economy*, 8.3, 501–27.

Coleman, W., and T. Porter. (2000). "International Institutions, Globalization, and Democracy: Assessing the Challenges." *Global Society*, 14.3, 377–98.

DeBardeleben, J., and A. Hurrelmann. (2007). *Democratic Dilemmas of Multilevel Governance: Legitimacy, Representation, and Accountability in the European Union*. Houndsmills: Palgrave Macmillan.

Doern, G. B., and R. Johnson, eds. (2006). *Rules, Rules, Rules, Rules: Multi-Level Regulatory Governance*. Toronto: University of Toronto Press.

Hooghe, L., and G. Marks. (2003). "Unraveling the Central State, but How? Types of Multi-Level Governance." *American Political Science Review*, 97.2, 233–43.

Kaiser, Robert and Heiko Prange (2002) 'A New Concept of Deepening European Integration? – The European Research Area and the Emerging Role of Policy Coordination in a Multi-level Governance System,' European Integration online Papers 6(18).

Kooiman, Jan (2000) 'Societal Governance: Levels, Modes, and Orders of Social-political Governance,' in Jon Pierre, ed., Debating Governance: Authority, Steering and Democracy, Oxford: Oxford University Press, 138-164.

Kohler-Koch, Beate and Berhold Rittberger, eds., (2007) Debating the Democratic Legitimacy of the European Union. Lanham: Rowman & Littlefield.

Krahmann, E. (2003). "National, Regional, and Global Governance: One Phenomenon or Many?" *Global Governance*, 9, 323–46.

Papadopoulos, Y. (2005). "Taking Stock of Multi-Level Governance Networks." *European Political Science*, 4, 316–27.

Paquet, G. (1999). *Governance through Social Learning*. Ottawa: University of Ottawa Press.

———. (2003). *Gouvernance: Une invitation à la subversion*. Ottawa: Centre d'études en gouvernance.

———. (2004). *Pathologies de gouvernance: Essais de technologie sociale*. Montréal: Liber.

———. (2005a). *Gouvernance: Une invitation à la subversion*. Montréal: Liber.

———. (2005b). *The New Geo-Governance: A Baroque Approach*. Ottawa: University of Ottawa Press.

Peters, B. G. (1998). *Managing Horizontal Government: The Politics of Coordination*. Ottawa: Canadian Centre for Management Development.

———. (2000). "Globalization, Institutions, and Governance." In *Governance in the Twenty-First Century: Revitalizing the Public Service*, ed. B. G. Peters and D. J. Savoie. Montreal: McGill-Queen's University Press, 29–57.

Peters, B. G., and J. Pierre. (2001). "Developments in Intergovernmental Relations: Towards Multi-Level Governance." *Policy and Politics*, 29.2, 131–35.

———. (2002). "Multi-Level Governance: A View from the Garbage Can." Manchester Papers in Politics: EPRU Series 1/2002. Manchester: European Policy and Research Unit.

———. (2004). "Multi-Level Governance and Democracy: A Faustian Bargain?" In *Multi-Level Governance*, ed. I. Bache and M. Flinders. Oxford: Oxford University Press, 75–91.

Rhinard, M. (2002). "The Democratic Legitimacy of the European Union Committee System." *Governance*, 15.2, 183–210.

Rhodes, R. A. W. (2000). "Governance and Public Administration." In *Debating Governance: Authority, Steering, and Democracy*, ed. J. Pierre. Oxford: Oxford University Press, 54–63.

Scharpf, F. W. (1999). *Governing in Europe: Effective and Democratic?* Oxford: Oxford University Press.

Skogstad, G. (2002). "Legitimacy, Democracy, and Multi-Level Regulatory Governance: The Case of Agricultural Biotechnology." Paper presented at the Conference on Globalization, Multilevel Governance, and Democracy: Continental, Comparative, and Global Perspectives." Queen's University, Kingston, May 3–4.

Wolfe, D. A., and T. Creutzberg. (2003). "Community Participation and Multilevel Governance in Economic Development Policy." Paper prepared for the Ontario Government Panel on the Role of Government.

Young, R., and C. Leuprecht, eds. (2006). *Canada: The State of the Federation 2004: Municipal-Federal-Provincial Relations in Canada*. Montreal: McGill-Queen's University Press.

Chapitre 23
Centralité de la mésoanalyse

Paul Laurent

> Le Vrai toujours
> Est ce qui naît
> d'entre nous
> Et qui sans nous
> ne serait pas
>
> —F. Cheng

> […] ; mais le problème essentiel n'est pas celui du pont mais celui du vide qui subsiste actuellement entre les deux.
>
> —A. Barrère

Les analyses traditionnelles dans la plupart des sciences sociales ont comme clé d'entrée soit l'acteur pris isolément (l'individu ou la firme par exemple en microéconomie), soit un ensemble plus large composé de grands agrégats (comme c'est le cas en macroéconomie). Sans être inutiles, ces visions, qui parfois s'opposent, ne rendent pas compte de certaines réalités médianes (une région dans un développement historique, une filière productive dans un pays, un réseau d'acteurs dans la construction d'une stratégie d'entreprise). Dans de nombreux travaux en économie, en management, en histoire ou encore plus proche de nous en matière de gouvernance, Gilles Paquet remet au premier plan ce type d'approche qualifiée de « méso ». Sans être nouvelle, puisque expérimentée déjà en sociologie par Crozier[1], en histoire économique[2] ou encore en économie industrielle, la mésoanalyse met l'accent sur des sous-ensembles pertinents pour l'observation et la compréhension des phénomènes socioéconomiques.

Nous montrons dans une première section en quoi consiste la mésoanalyse en économie ; la deuxième section dresse, à grands traits, les contours de l'économie industrielle considérée comme discipline phare de la mésoanalyse. Puis, dépassant ce cadre, nous illustrons dans la troisième section cette problématique à travers la construction d'un mésoconcept qu'est le réseau centré sur l'organisation d'un tissu de relations sociales, économiques, managériales, technologiques, politiques. À défaut de constituer un nouveau champ scientifique, la mésoanalyse enrichit de façon considérable la compréhension (et donc l'action sur) des (les) défis auxquels sont confrontés les acteurs d'aujourd'hui.

De la mésoanalyse en économie

Nous montrons, en première approximation et de façon générale, ce que constitue la mésoanalyse en économie. Apparaît au tournant des années 1960, un champ de recherche plus ou moins vierge, mais pas nécessairement nouveau — Braudel[3] l'ayant par exemple exploré dans certaines parties de son travail sur l'histoire du capitalisme —, mais dans tous les cas prometteur.

Il s'agit en quelque sorte de faire face aux problèmes posés par le découpage traditionnel de l'économie en deux « morceaux ». La microéconomie d'un côté qui considère les choix de l'acteur pris de façon isolé (LE consommateur, LA firme) et la macroéconomie de l'autre côté qui s'attache à l'étude de grands agrégats. Cette partition ne relève ni du vice versa, ni du recto verso, ni du yin et du yang. Il s'agit de deux façons de *poser* l'économie, d'élaborer un discours scientifique, de privilégier certains aspects de la réalité économique.

Admettons que la microéconomie est « une branche de l'économie politique qui analyse le comportement des unités individuelles considérées comme libres et isolées à propos des opérations de choix et de décision dans la production, la consommation, l'investissement et l'épargne[4] ». Admettons aussi que le sujet de la macroéconomie[5] se trouve dans l'étude de l'économie considérée dans son ensemble, de son comportement général à l'aide des agrégats (ces grandeurs souvent statistiques de l'activité économique). Il en découle que des pans entiers de l'économie échappent alors à l'observation, à l'analyse, au jugement, à la théorisation et à l'action guidée. Or la vie économique est faite de tous les niveaux : il semble qu'il manque un cadre pour l'un d'entre eux.

De cette première instance, on note que c'est par défaut que se construit la mésoanalyse en économie. Elle se veut intermédiaire mais se définit par rapport à ce qu'elle n'est pas (ni de la microéconomie, ni de la macroéconomie) avant de se situer par rapport à ce qu'elle est réellement (par exemple à travers ses objets d'étude) : « méso » signifie au milieu, médian donc. C'est ce que note Barrère « Le terme méso-analyse semblerait, de prime abord, signaler l'analyse de l'intermédiaire, de ce qui n'est appréhendé ni par la micro ni par la macro-analyse[6] ». Elle est alors un compromis, un substitut. Et c'est là que se pose le premier jalon[7] tout autant que la première limite ; comme si il y a nécessité de créer un nouvel espace et que cette nécessité passe par un compromis. Le théoricien et le praticien ne trouvant plus/pas réponse à leurs questions dans la microéconomie et dans la macroéconomie, la mésoéconomie devient-elle le médiateur d'une opposition réelle ?

Nous pensons que la mésoéconomie est plus que cela.

On risque une métaphore : la mésoéconomie serait ce « vide médian, ce grand Trois né du Deux, qui permet au Deux de se dépasser[8] », c'est-à-dire le lieu de création d'un « espace vivifiant » (Cheng) pour la construction du Trois tout comme du Deux. La mésoéconomie concerne bien des unités de dimensions moyennes sachant que l'acteur individuel conserve toute son importance et que l'agrégat joue son rôle dans la décision économique. Il s'agit de passer de l'opposition et du manque à l'articulation et à la construction d'un nouvel objet. La mésoéconomie est une nouvelle unité représentative et qui dépasse l'agrégation de l'unité et la désagrégation du tout.

Sans revenir sur les limites de la microéconomie et de la macroéconomie, nous souhaitons préciser ce qu'est la vocation (ou la vision au sens où Schumpeter utilise le terme) de la mésoéconomie autour de plusieurs dimensions largement explorées par Paquet[9].

La mésoéconomie veut prendre en compte *la diversité*. Cette diversité est celle des acteurs, des comportements, des habitudes, des histoires, des cultures, du local. C'est un processus de « décomposition du "grand-jeu" en un certain nombre de "sous-jeux" séparables. À partir de la composition et de l'imbrication de ces sous-jeux, chacun avec ses règles propres, il est possible d'étudier l'évolution du grand jeu[10] ». Du coup, puisque la diversité existe, elle joue un rôle dans le processus économique et la catégorie devient plurielle. Cette pluralité est exposée à son tour aux jeux des mises en situation.

La mésoéconomie n'est plus définie par défaut mais en tant que telle par son champ, son objet, son projet. Elle « s'attache donc à l'étude des phénomènes spécifiques aux unités économiques complexes, saisies dans leur structure, leur objet, leurs relations et leur fonction, constituant les sous-ensembles d'une unité économique globale représentant elle-même un ensemble intégré. Elle peut être définie comme l'analyse structurelle et fonctionnelle des sous-ensembles et de leur interdépendance dans un ensemble intégré[11] ».

Les unités complexes étudiées sont homogènes et cohérentes, en situation et insérées dans des réseaux de relations eux-mêmes complexes. Mais cette homogénéité et cette cohérence sont mouvantes, fluctuantes au gré des changements imposés par les jeux de relations.

On peut illustrer le propos en reprenant les fondements théoriques des approches stratégiques proposées par Martinet[12]. L'entreprise est considérée comme un agent de production, mais aussi une organisation sociale et un système politique. Elle est « en marché » mais aussi « en société ». L'entreprise est en lutte avec les acteurs présents sur le marché et en lutte-coopération avec l'ensemble des acteurs internes et externes concernés. La logique des facteurs de production est enrichie par la logique des acteurs.

Nous montrons dans la deuxième section comment les développements en économie industrielle constituent un bon exemple de consolidation d'une certaine mésoéconomie.

Propositions autour de l'économie industrielle

L'économie industrielle n'est pas une discipline homogène. Dans une certaine tradition anglo-saxonne elle désigne « la manière dont les activités de production sont mises en harmonie avec les demandes de biens et services de la société à travers un mécanisme d'organisation donné, tel que le marché libre, et dont les variations et imperfections du mécanisme d'organisation affectent le degré de succès atteint par les producteurs dans la satisfaction des besoins de la société[13] ». Arena[14] a raison de souligner que, ainsi posé, l'objectif de l'économie industrielle (« *industrial organization* ») est assez proche de celui de la microéconomie, la distinction provenant d'aspects méthodologiques comme la proximité plus grande de l'économie industrielle avec la réalité, la prise en compte de perspectives historiques ou encore la formulation de nouvelles hypothèses (plus empiriques) ; déjà la brèche est ouverte.

L'économie industrielle se fait alors surtout connaître pour le célèbre triptyque « structures, comportements, performances ». Le point de départ de la démarche consiste à étudier les « conditions de base » du marché du point de vue de l'offre (matières premières, technologie, cycle de vie du produit, conditions syndicales et professionnelles) et du point de vue de la demande (coefficient d'élasticité de la demande par rapport au prix, taux de croissance, présence de produits de substitution, modes d'achat et comportement du consommateur). Ces conditions de base déterminent les « structures » des marchés appréhendées par le nombre des acteurs présents, le niveau de différenciation des produits et des barrières à l'entrée, la structure des coûts, le niveau d'intégration, lesquelles « structures » définissent à leur tour les « comportements » des firmes, on dirait aujourd'hui les stratégies de firmes quant à l'offre, l'innovation, les prix, la communication entre autres choses. Ces « comportements » conduisent à des « résultats » observés et mesurés sur le niveau de production, l'emploi, la productivité, l'allocation des ressources[15]. Quoique très linéaire et séquentiel, sous-estimant les différentes interactions des éléments du modèle, cette démarche constitue une forme intéressante de compréhension d'un secteur donné, mobilisant des dimensions statiques (les structures) et dynamiques (les stratégies) sur un plan mésoéconomique. Se pose alors peu à peu un nouvel objet.

Plus largement encore, l'économie industrielle aurait trois finalités[16] : a) fournir au décideur public des moyens d'intervenir sur le système productif ; b) aider les responsables d'entreprises dans la détermination des stratégies ; c) contribuer à la critique sociale en analysant les effets du développement du système productif sur la société dans son ensemble. Ainsi posé, l'objet et le champ de l'économie industrielle paraissent larges et ambitieux et se détachent de l'« *industrial organization* ».

Cette mésoéconomie industrielle est bien intermédiaire mais ne fait pas que s'intercaler entre la microéconomie et la macroéconomie ; « elle considère les unités comme les éléments d'une globalité qu'elles influencent et dont l'étude de la logique est le seul moyen de comprendre leur propre fonctionnement[17] ». Elle s'ouvre ainsi sur des disciplines connexes comme le management stratégique indispensable pour comprendre le jeu des décisions, des actions, des positions dans une perspective interactive et nécessairement dynamique de ces mésosystèmes complexes.

La troisiéme section qui suit se veut une illustration de l'un de ces mésosystème complexe qu'est le réseau.

Le réseau comme mésosystème complexe

La notion de réseau est très présente dans certains aspects des travaux de Paquet. En histoire par exemple (sujet que nous ne développons pas ici) autour des processus interactifs, des « jeux avec les acteurs, leurs règles, leurs frontières, leur rythme[18] ».

Un réseau est avant tout un ensemble de relations. Des relations verticales, horizontales, ou transversales, qui sont plus ou moins structurées (implicites dans certains cas, très formalisées dans d'autres cas), mais durables et complexes. Les éléments ainsi liés sont des individus ou/et des organisations en interaction.

Le réseau est un processus dynamique d'échanges coopératifs : les membres du réseau échangent des biens, des services, des idées, des connaissances, des informations, des technologies en vue de mobiliser tout ou partie de leurs propres ressources (humaines, technologiques, financières) pour réaliser en commun un projet.

L'appartenance à un réseau procure à l'acteur un avantage concurrentiel vis-à-vis des non-membres ; cependant la construction d'un réseau ne se substitue pas complètement ou définitivement à la concurrence qui peut perdurer à des degrés divers entre réseaux ainsi qu'entre les organisations ou individus à l'intérieur du réseau.

Un réseau, comme mésosystème complexe, est un processus institué d'organisation de l'activité socioéconomique qui peut être viable sur le long terme et source d'apprentissage pour ses membres[19]. Le concept de réseau s'est imposé peu à peu comme instrument d'analyse des nouvelles formes organisationnelles parce qu'il correspondait mieux aux nouvelles réalités socioéconomiques qui se sont développées au cours des dernières décennies[20]. On parle des nouveaux types de concurrence, de mondialisation, de nouvelles technologies de l'information, d'ampleur des investissements et des risques. Dans ce contexte, la notion de réseau met l'accent sur la prise en compte des interrelations coopératives entre acteurs, notion déjà esquissée par Richardson (1972).

Pour fixer les idées, et pour cerner d'un peu plus près la notion de réseau, nous avons proposé de distinguer cinq sous-systèmes composant le réseau[21].

Le sous-système *métabolique* est à l'interface du réseau et de son environnement. Le réseau puise ses ressources dans l'environnement, que ce soit l'environnement immédiat (l'atmosphère) dans lequel baigne le réseau ou l'environnement plus général.

Le sous-système *technologique* fournit la trame du réseau en fonction de l'état de la technologie physique et de la technologie sociale. Les choix et les orientations technologiques affectent et sont affectés par toute une série de jeux d'interdépendances et de synergies au sein du réseau.

Le sous-système *fonctionnel* permet de focaliser l'attention sur le réseau en tant que processus. Il comprend l'ensemble des relations opérationnelles au sein du réseau. Ce sous-système combine des ressources physiques, informationnelles et interpersonnelles dans une dynamique qui favorise l'apprentissage social, l'innovation, la mise en place de règles de fonctionnement, la coopération, les alliances, la confiance, etc., à l'intérieur d'une structure donnée autour des acteurs, des activités, des ressources.

Le sous-système *structurel* est constitué par l'ensemble des relations qui résultent du processus de structuration à partir des opérations du réseau et du système de conduite pré-existant. Ce sous-système va instituer la capacité d'apprentissage du réseau.

Le sous-système de *gouvernance* est composé des relations qui permettent le partage de valeurs communes entre les membres d'un réseau lui conférant son mode dynamique d'interaction. Cet ensemble de relations de gouvernance est en évolution permanente, en perpétuelle construction.

Chacun des sous-systèmes n'a pas toujours le même poids, le même rôle. L'un dominera le réseau à un moment donné, lui imposant une direction, un style. En d'autres lieux et temps, une autre configuration pourra émerger avec une autre répartition des rôles ou des pouvoirs selon un processus d'ajustement de ces sous-systèmes. Les « facteurs qui expliquent l'émergence, la maintenance, l'évolution du réseau sont fonctions des ressources de l'environnement, des ressources interpersonnelles et des ressources issues des interactions des sous-systèmes qui toutes nourrissent les organisations, les relations de pouvoir dans le réseau et donc la compatibilité des ressources intersystémiques à l'interface des sous-systèmes ».

Cette approche par le réseau « mésosystème complexe » illustre bien l'importance de la mésoéconomie comme catégorie au-delà de son aspect intermédiaire. Il s'agit d'un appareil d'analyse propre dont Paquet a souligné l'importance dans ses travaux récents sur la gouvernance[22]. Cette mésoéconomie a l'avantage de la souplesse et, par moment, l'inconvénient du flou. On peut bien entendu critiquer ce niveau mésoéconomique (et le concept de réseau qui l'illustre) en se posant la question de savoir s'il est nécessaire d'introduire un second hiatus (micro/méso et méso/macro) là où il n'y en avait qu'un (micro/macro). Ou encore, on peut se demander jusqu'où va s'arrêter ce processus de « segmentation » des disciplines : on aura la macro-macro, la macro, la micro-macro, la macro-méso, la méso, la micro-méso et ainsi de suite.

Quoiqu'il en soit, le réseau en tant que concept de la mésoéconomie est central pour rendre compte que « la modularité des individus va tisser entre eux une multitude de liens ténus, partiels, fragiles. À côté de liens usuels (horizontaux dans le marché et verticaux dans la politie), il y aura des liens transversaux ou diagonaux qui traversent les divers paliers et lient des partenaires éloignés. Il s'agit d'une nouvelle figure de lien car le réseau n'offre aucune centralité que l'on pourrait attaquer, mais des nœuds aussi divers qu'éparpillés et qui sont animés de mouvements. Ce n'est plus l'acteur qui est nomade en dépit d'un système figé, et contre lui, c'est le système réseautique qui est lui-même nomade[22].

Notes

[1] Michel Crozier, « The Relationship between Micro and Macrosociology », *Human Relations*, 25, (1972), p. 239-251.
[2] A. H. Cole, *Meso-economics: A Contribution from Entrepreneurial History*, 2e serie, vol. 6, n° 1, 1968, p. 3-33.
[3] Fernand Braudel, *Civilisation matérielle, économie et capitalisme*, Paris, Armand Colin, 1979.
[4] Silem Ahmed et Jean-Marie Albertini, éd., *Lexique d'économie*, 9e éd., Paris, Dalloz, 2006, p. 497.
[5] Dornbush Rudiger *et al.*, *Macro-économique*, New York, McGraw-Hill, 1983.
[6] Alain Barrère, « Propositions pour la constitution d'une méso-analyse », dans *Hommage à François Perroux*, Grenoble, Presses Universitaires de Grenoble, 1978, p. 100.
[7] L. Gilliard, « Premier bilan d'une recherche économique sur la méso-analyse », *Revue économique*, vol. 26, 1975, p. 448-516.
[8] François Cheng, *Le livre du vide médian*, Paris, Albin Michel, 2004, p. 8.
[9] Voir par exemple Paul Laurent et Gilles Paquet, *Epistémologie et économie de la relation*, Paris-Lyon, Vrin, 1998 ; Gilles Paquet, *Gouvernance : une invitation à la subversion*, Montréal, Liber, 2005 ; Gilles Paquet et Jean-Pierre Wallot, *Un Québec moderne : 1760-1840*, Montréal, Hurtubise HMH, 2007.
[10] Gilles Paquet et Jean-Pierre Wallot, *op.cit.*, p. 39.
[11] Alain Barrère, *op.cit.*, p. 103.
[12] Alain-Charles Martinet, *Management stratégique : organisation et politique*, New York, McGraw-Hill, 1984, p. 33.
[13] F. M. Scherer, *Industrial Market Structure and Economic Performance*, Chicago, Rand McNally and C., 1980, p. 1.
[14] Richard Arena, « Approches théoriques et économie industrielle », dans *Traité d'économie industrielle*, sous la direction de Richard Arena *et al.*, Paris, Economica, 1988, p. 107.
[15] F.M. Scherer, *op. cit.*, p. 5.

[16] Francis Bidault, « Confrontation ou constitution : les perspectives de l'économie industrielle », dans *Économie industrielle : problématique et méthodologie,* Paris, Économica, 1982, p. 6.
[17] Yves Morvan, *Fondements d'économie industrielle,* Paris, Économica, 1985, p. 194.
[18] Gilles Paquet et Jean-Pierre, Wallot, *op. cit.,* p. 78.
[19] Bjorn Axelsson, et Geoffrey Easton, éd., *Industrial Networks,* Londres, Routledge, 1992; Patrick Besson, éd., *Dedans, dehors,* Paris, Vuibert, 1998.
[20] Nitin Nohria, « Is a Network Perspective a Useful Way of Studying Organizations ? », dans *Networks and Organizations,* Nitin Nohria and Robert Eccles, éd., Boston, HBS Press, 1992, p. 1-23.
[21] Paul Laurent et Gilles Paquet, *op. cit.,* p. 30-33.
[22] Gilles Paquet, *op. cit.,*
[23] A. Cauquelin, « Rassembler le disparate ou : de la communication », dans *Dictionnaire critique de la communication,* Lucien Sfez, éd., Paris, P.U.F., 1993, p. 188-195.

Reference

Richardson, G. B. (1972) "The Organization of Industry" Economic Journal, 82: 883-896.

Chapter 24

Contribution to Civic Governance, Social Learning, and Smart Communities

David A. Wolfe

Introduction
In a core body of writing from the mid-1990s onward, Gilles Paquet analyzed the key processes of governance and social learning that contribute to innovation and growth in the context of local and regional economies. Paquet argued that, due to what he labelled the "paradoxical consequence of globalization," innovation processes were more congruent with mesolevel, regional, and sectoral realities that provided the most effective context for social learning than with those operating at the national level (Acs, de la Mothe, and Paquet 1996). He criticized the preoccupation with the national level as reflecting an obsession with the "centralized mindset," which many view as a holdover of the postwar Keynesian era. In this era, success of the dominant firms was dependent on the extent to which they could produce generic products with economies of scale from a standardized and generally accessible knowledge base. The governance issues that arose from such a mode of production were dealt with primarily at the national level with the economic governance tools at hand: anti-trust regulation, labour relations policy, trade policy, and macroeconomic policy.

The attenuation of the Keynesian paradigm in the 1970s, followed by the beginning of a period of rapid technological innovation in the subsequent two decades, rendered the centralized mindset of the Keynesian era increasingly obsolete. Paquet argued that, in the current era, particularly when many of the factors of production most closely associated with the centralized mindset were increasingly becoming "ubiquified," in Peter Maskell's (1999) felicitous term, learning processes and network dynamics that operate most effectively at regional and local levels were increasingly the critical sources of innovation and value. In this respect, the question of governance assumed an increasingly prominent place in his writing in terms of how governance mechanisms at the local and regional levels were emerging to replace the more centralized ones associated with the early postwar era. An exploration of his intellectual contribution in this regard is particularly timely as the international literature on governance has grown, and the concept of social learning, which Paquet views as closely interrelated, has been afforded increased attention. This chapter examines the development of his thinking with respect to these two interrelated concepts and explores the manner in which he has applied them to questions of governance at the community level.

Changing Patterns of Governance

At the centre of Paquet's perspective on governance is the belief that it has evolved away from the state-centred, bureaucratic, and hierarchical systems associated primarily with the national level of government toward a more distributed pattern of authority that is dispersed over the core elements of the economy, society, and polity. A recurring theme throughout Paquet's considerable body of writing is the need to view relations of governing in terms of the differing mechanisms of coordination found in each of the three spheres of the Boulding triangle: *quid pro quo exchange* (market economy), *coercion* (polity), and *gift, solidarity,* or *reciprocity* (community and society). In the sphere of the market, the forces of supply and demand and the price mechanism prevail, the domain of the state is governed by rules based on coercion and redistribution, while the sphere of civil society is coordinated and integrated according to the principles of cooperation, reciprocity, and solidarity (Paquet 1999, 5). Paquet argues that the current era of globalization and rapid technological change induces a more distributed pattern of governance that disperses power over a wider range of actors within the Boulding triangle. This new distributed pattern of governance tends to invest new degrees of power and influence in communities and what he terms meso–innovation systems because the capacity for learning can best be realized through patterns of decentralized and reciprocal relations built on evolving partnerships (Paquet 1997, 26).

The key distinction between government and governance turns on the recognition that policy outcomes are not merely the by-products of government actions but also depend on the interaction effects among a wide range of social and economic actors, including, but not limited to, subnational and local governments, the private sector and voluntary, business, and not-for-profit organizations. Paquet maintains that governing relations have moved from a vertical pattern associated with the bureaucratic state-managed mode of development in the post-World War II era to a more heterarchical set of relations in the current era. Distributed governance not only entails a new process involving a dispersion of power toward localized decision making within each of the three spheres that comprise the Boulding triangle but also entails a dispersion of power over a wider variety of actors in groups within the overall triangle. It is embedded in a wide-ranging set of organizations and institutions that involve market forces, the state, and civil society. The most important connections involve what Paquet refers to as links that tie these three families of institutions together (1999, 5). "Governability is a measure of the organization's capability for effective coordination within the context of the environment within which it is nested: it corresponds to the organization's capacity to transform, its capacity to modify its structure, its process, and even its substantive guidance mechanism and orientation" (Paquet 2001a, 188).

Paquet's concern with the more flexible and comprehensive processes of governance, as opposed to the more conventional concerns with governing and government, is reflective of a broader shift that has become common in the political science and administrative science literature. For Rhodes, the increasing adoption and use of the concept of governance signifies a broadening and extension of the meaning of government. Governance, as opposed to government, refers to "a new process of governing; or a changed condition of ordered rule or the new method by which society is governed" (Rhodes 1996, 653). In this view, governance ultimately refers to self-organizing interorganizational networks (660). Central to the concept is the development of styles of governing in which the boundaries between public and private actors, and even across different levels of government have become blurred. Governance focuses on mechanisms of governing that no longer rely on the authoritative distribution of resources derived from traditional governmental structures (Stoker 1998, 17). For Peters and Pierre (2004), the underlying novelty of this concept of governance is the emphasis placed on the processes of governing rather than the institutional structures. The common element underlying these different perspectives on governance underlines "the process through which public and private actions and resources are coordinated and given a common meaning and direction" (78).

This closely parallels Paquet's conviction that the ordered distribution of power and authority through hierarchically ordered patterns of bureaucratic relations based on the Weberian principles of super- and subordination are giving way to more flexible and consensual patterns of authoritative relations. Paquet quotes supportively from a paper by Scott et al. (2001) that suggests that governance is now widely deployed to describe the multifaceted aspects of social and economic coordination in an increasingly interdependent world where various tiers of government must collaborate with each other as well as with a range of non-governmental organizations to achieve their goals. They suggest that the governance of city regions in particular must be viewed as part of a larger issue of coordination across multiple geographical scales and levels of jurisdiction. This "sense of the term sees governance as involving a set of complex institutional reactions to the broader problems of economic and social adjustment in the emerging global-local system" (Scott et al. 2001, 22).

However, not all authors are in agreement that the governance perspective necessarily privileges processes over institutions or that it de-emphasizes the role of traditional governmental institutions and bureaucratic structures in governing processes. For Peters and Pierre (2004) the state is still the most powerful actor in society, which in turn raises the question of how the role that it plays in society and the mechanisms by which it exerts authority and redistributes resources are affected by the evolving processes of governance outlined by Paquet and others. The critical question from this perspective is to develop a better understanding of how coordination is achieved among a wider array of governmental and non-governmental actors, and across an increasing range of jurisdictional and geographical scales (Peters and Pierre 2004, 85).

Transversal Governance

Paquet's answer to this question is clear. The current era of rapid economic and technological change undermines the ability of traditional institutional structures and bureaucratic forms of authority to maintain the overall degree of social and political coordination that they have achieved in the past. In the context of emerging governance processes and the formulation of public policies, this necessitates the adoption of more distributed patterns of governance that deny those in leadership positions their monopoly over directing the activity of the organization based purely on the positions that they occupy within the bureaucratic hierarchy. For organizations to be capable of adapting to rapidly changing environments, they must adopt flatter organizational structures and incorporate a broader cross-section of the membership into discussions about future directions of the organization. In other words, organizational decision making must be less bureaucratic and more consensual. When these concepts are applied to the political process in the idea of governing, the implication is that the exercise of power must be dispersed more effectively over a wider range of actors not only within the political sphere but also within the economic and social sectors of the Boulding triangle (Paquet 1999, 8).

This shift in the locus of authority between the political, economic, and social sectors in the development of governance processes is matched by a corresponding shift across geographical scales away from the national level of government that was privileged during the postwar Keynesian era down toward the subnational level. This shift across geographical and jurisdictional scales results in a broader distribution of power and a more dispersed basis of authority involving a broader range of relevant actors, including institutions and organizations from the economic and social sectors as well as those within the state sector (Paquet 1997, 38). As a result of this dispersion of authority and the development of these transversal governance patterns, the governance system becomes coordinated through less coercive and hierarchical relationships, such as those associated with Weberian systems of management or public administration, and is replaced by more associative networks of cooperation built on consensus and inducement-oriented relationships.

The introduction of this transversal dimension of governance into the more traditional state- and market-determined mechanisms of governance introduces the idea of the network paradigm into prevailing governance, processes. The key feature of networks is their emphasis on the voluntary adherence to norms in contrast to the exercise of formal authority that prevails in traditional bureaucratic organizations. The logic of consensus does not mean that the exercise of power is eliminated entirely; rather, it means that it is distributed more widely among key actors in society, the economy, and the polity. This paradigm not only extends to transactions within the social sector but also penetrates the operations of the political and economic sectors (Paquet 1999, 10). Following Cooke and Morgan (1998), Paquet refers to these as associative forms of governance, which also include key elements of what they previously described as the network paradigm (Cooke and Morgan 1993). The emergence of most associative forms of governance based on the network paradigm is intertwined with the shifting roles played by national versus regional levels of government. As noted at the outset, the emergence of regional governments as effective actors in their own right complements the growing importance of regional communities of shared scientific and technical expertise for the development of a sustained innovative capacity among networks of firms. For Cooke and Morgan as well as Paquet, the role of the public sector within this paradigm is to facilitate desired forms of private activity as well as to provide the levels of institutional and policy support necessary to stimulate and sustain the process of innovation.

Governance and Social Learning

Periods of rapid economic and technological change are characterized by a condition of extreme uncertainty. They place a premium on the ability to acquire, absorb, and diffuse relevant knowledge and information throughout the various institutions that affect the process of economic development and change. In addition to effecting a transverse dispersal of authority across a wider range of social, economic, and political actors that requires the adoption of more consensual forms of decision making, periods of rapid economic and technological change fundamentally alter the definition and achievement of organizational objectives. In periods like this, organizations need to become more reflexive and adaptive; in other words, they need to become capable of learning both what their goals are and how to adapt the means to reach them in a rapidly shifting environmental context. The most effective way of doing this is by tapping into the knowledge and capabilities that members of those organizations possess.

The need to draw upon the knowledge and capabilities of all participants in the organization complements and supports the shift from hierarchical to heterarchical relations of authority. A key aspect of this evolving pattern of heterarchical relations is the importance of learning. Paquet defines organizational learning as the capacity to improve present performance as a result of experience through a redefinition of the organization's objectives, and the modification of behaviour and structures as a result of new circumstances (1997, 31). For Paquet, learning remains a social cognitive process. As a consequence, it depends on interaction, and the primary benefits associated with learning processes are derived from the geographical proximity that not only facilitates interaction among a range of actors but also contributes to new processes of learning.

Paquet's emphasis on the centrality of learning processes and the cognitive and interactive nature of the learning process closely parallels the work of Lundvall and his collaborators on the "learning economy." Lundvall stresses the fact that the knowledge frontier is moving so rapidly in the current economy that access to, or control over, knowledge assets affords merely a fleeting competitive advantage. It is the capacity to learn that is critical to the innovative process and essential for developing and maintaining a competitive advantage. However, the broader issues raised by the current period of economic dislocation and technological change require a more inclusive notion of institutional learning closer to that suggested by Paquet, which focuses on the capacity of institutions to sustain economic growth and facilitate the process of adjustment in the context of rapidly changing economic circumstances on a global basis. This concept of institutional learning is critical for the kinds of organizational changes associated with the emerging, knowledge-based economy. Increasingly, the organizational issue is how to pool and structure knowledge and intelligence in social ways rather than access them on an individual basis. The capacity for social learning and increased networking is seen as essential for tapping into the shared intelligence of both the individual firm and the organization. This form of shared or networked learning assumes that neither the public sector nor individual enterprises are the source of all wisdom; rather, the process of innovation and institutional adaptation is essentially an interactive one in which the means for establishing relations of trust and of communicating insights and tacit forms of knowledge are crucial to the outcomes (Wolfe and Gertler 2002).

Local Governance and Smart Communities

Many analysts have noted the strong association between regional and local aspects of clustering and innovation and the dynamic processes of learning that are defined as central to the emerging processes of governance (de la Mothe and Paquet 1998, 10). Some argue that the region is a critical level for innovation and social learning because spatial proximity between economic actors, and the common socio-institutional context that they share, enable the easy circulation of knowledge that underpins innovation (Gertler 2002; Maskell and Malmberg 1999). Given the interactive and social nature of innovation, city-regions seem to provide the ideal space in which social learning processes can unfold. The development of local "untraded interdependencies" strongly shapes the innovative capabilities of firms (Storper 1995). These interdependencies are strengthened by the presence of key infrastructures for knowledge generation and circulation that underpin innovation and creativity in city-regions: specialized educational institutions and research facilities, unique support services for industry, and institutions that build and strengthen network relationships among firms and other key actors to facilitate the circulation of knowledge (Scott 2004).

As I noted at the outset, the "paradoxical consequence of globalization" makes regions and cities more—not less—important as sites of production, distribution, and innovation. Over the course of the past decade, recognition has grown that even the most global economic activities remain fundamentally rooted in regions in general, and urban regions in particular, as critical sites for organizing economic activity (Gertler 2001). Within this context, the social dynamics of city-regions are crucial in shaping economic outcomes. The interactive and social nature of the innovation process makes city-regions an appropriate scale at which the kind of social learning processes discussed by Paquet can unfold. Knowledge transfer between highly skilled people happens more easily in cities. In a country with diverse and strongly differentiated regional economies, relationships between economic actors, organizations, and institutions at local and regional scales are crucial factors affecting national prosperity. And leading urban regions are no longer prepared to be passive objects at the hands of globalizing locational forces associated with the spread of ICTs and the knowledge-based economy but are taking control of their own economic futures through efforts aimed at the "strategic management" of their economies (Audretsch 2002).

The rising importance of cities has also been tied to the global spread of ICTs through the development of the concept of "smart communities." In most definitions of the term, and indeed in the federal government program of the same name, smart communities were associated with the advanced application of information and communication technologies at the urban scale to create an enabled technology infrastructure to provide firms and organizations in the urban agglomeration with the most sophisticated access possible to both broadband communication technologies and the sophisticated layer of "smart" applications that can be built to take advantage of these broadband connections. Paquet argues that smart community initiatives have been widely adopted by a range of governments to help entire communities create improved broadband access to connect local governments, schools, as well as health and social services to introduce or establish new services that will better address local needs and improve collective skills and capabilities.

However, the common tendency to interpret smart communities in strictly technological terms, from both an analytical and a policy perspective, completely misses the point. The critical challenge lies elsewhere than in the technological domain; rather, it depends on the introduction of more effective mechanisms of social learning through the use of collective intelligence. This requires, in turn, governance structures to enable effective coordination among key civic actors in distributed governance settings. Paquet maintains that there is a pressing need to recast the concept of the smart community away from an exclusive focus on the technologies themselves toward a greater concern with the social mechanisms for learning and governance. He links the concept of the smart community back to the dynamics of social learning and defines it simply as one that acts smartly, learns quickly, and learns well. This requires the most efficient and most effective use of the collective intelligence embedded in the community and its available resources. There are several critical prerequisites for the emergence of a smart community: above all, there must be a sense of *community*, a sense of collective belonging, as well as a capacity to chart a new direction and transform its potential. Technology may be an important enabler of this capacity at the community level, but it is far from the determining factor.

> It is through social learning and its resultant collective intelligence that a community may harness its intellectual, informational, physical and human resources to produce a continuous flow of innovative and usable knowledge. Social learning is the interactive process by which individuals and organizations learn from each other, adapt, innovate, and consequently develop new arrangements and conventions among themselves leading to new rules of behavior. *Collective* intelligence refers to the creative and discriminative capacities of a group, organization or community. Effective social learning increases collective intelligence over time (private correspondence with Paquet 2001).

The sort of strategy that Paquet considers appropriate for building smart communities involves the establishment of lighter and more horizontal structures as the basis for networks. These flatter and more flexible civic organizations must put in place appropriate mechanisms to ensure that the requisite degree of consultation and citizen involvement occurs within the community. Civic leaders, often referred to as civic entrepreneurs (Henton, Melville, and Walesh 1997), need to act as animators in a consultative and participatory mode to obtain the appropriate degree of interaction between firms, governments at different jurisdictional levels, and a wide range of community-based organizations. Both social and physical proximity are critical for establishing the preconditions conducive to the emergence and development of smart communities. Proximity is important because it facilitates a higher degree of interaction among key civic actors and organizations, and contributes to reflexive learning by allowing for an ongoing intensive degree of interaction. Institutional "sites" at the local or civic level that facilitate talk and interaction are essential for allowing the kind of social learning that Paquet sees as central to the creation of smart communities.

The focus on civic interaction, dialogue, and reflexive learning is reinforced by Michael Storper's emphasis on the role of "talk" in building the institutions of the learning economy. Storper (2002) sees talk as an essential process for generating the kinds of conventions and shared understandings that underpin these institutions. The value of talk arises from the need for communicative interaction that goes beyond the mere transfer of information between parties to build the conditions essential to achieve mutual understanding and acceptance. "Talk refers to communicative interaction, designed not simply to transmit information and relay preferences, but to achieve mutual understanding. In the case of prospective learning, information from other experiences where learning has worked . . . can be valuable as a stimulus" (140). Talk must be supported by a range of incentives that encourages the parties to maintain their involvement with these institutions. Small, repeated experimental interactions may prove effective as a mechanism for getting the parties to work together in a limited fashion and facilitate institutionalized learning.

The creation of appropriate sites to support this kind of talk and interaction at the civic level can help to provide improved access to critical pieces of knowledge necessary for building smart communities—the kind of knowledge that is generated by facilitating relationships between various economic actors within a community. Consequently, smart communities must be able to create the incentives necessary for the requisite degree of knowledge transfer, which in turn depends on the appropriate degrees of social capital and trust to facilitate the sharing and transmission of knowledge. The installation of an appropriate governance system for the community, one that is more participatory and less technocratic, where all the relevant sectors of the community participate in making the appropriate political, social, and economic decisions, can lay the basis for building this kind of social capital.

The requirements of social learning needed to build successful, smart communities imply that civic actors and local governments need to pay particular attention to the prerequisites that contribute to more effective modes of learning at the community level. Following Dalum et al. (1992), Paquet (2001b) suggests that this requires new forms of government intervention to improve the factors that contribute to more effective learning: the *means to learn* (education and training systems), the *incentive to learn* (public programs to support projects of cooperation and networks), the *capability to learn* (promoting more decentralized organizations that support interactive learning), the *access to relevant knowledge* (bridging the gaps between key agents and relevant sources of knowledge), and finally supporting the appropriate degree of *institutional remembering and forgetting*.

Overall, the governance of smart communities raises a number of conceptual issues to which governance experts have much to contribute. Paquet (2001b) groups them around four key issues: the need for greater collaboration—there is still a need for better understanding of the conditions under which civic actors will enter more effectively into collaborative arrangements; the challenges of coordination—the conditions that are necessary to ensure effective coordination where power, resources, and information are widely distributed is not well understood in a range of different community settings; the challenges of social learning—which requires a new epistemology of practice that underpins the conditions that will contribute more effectively to social learning; the challenges of evaluation—the basis for evaluating whether efforts directed toward building a smart community have succeeded or failed.

When these prerequisites for more effective social learning at the local level are effectively put in place, they can facilitate more effective learning dynamics that will contribute to the building of what Paquet truly views as smart communities. Neil Bradford (2003) has identified three such learning dynamics that occur when the appropriate institutions and processes are in place. The first is a *civic learning* process that results in recognition among the local organizations, be they private or public sector, of the importance of equity, diversity, and interdependence, and the need to accommodate these realities in their collaborations. Equally important, though, is the second dynamic of *administrative learning*, whereby local administrations learn new skills for building relationships, seeking consensus, assessing risk, and measuring performance. Such skills help to foster a government that is effectively engaged in its essential roles of ensuring balanced representation of social interests, addressing systemic differences in the capacity to participate, convening and organizing meetings, establishing protocols for monitoring progress, and maintaining the focus and commitment of social partners. Finally, the culmination of successful civic and administrative learning leads to the third dynamic, that of *policy learning*. Here feedback from the various actors within the governance process at the community refocuses the policy agenda with street-level insights and experiences as well as new goals. The successful implementation of these kinds of learning dynamics will help to realize the kinds of smart communities that Paquet sees as necessary.

Conclusion

A key challenge for policy makers at local and community levels is how to create the conditions most conducive for generating the forms of governance processes and social learning that will contribute most effectively to the growth of appropriate forms of economic activity within the context of a globalizing, technologically driven economy. These circumstances place new demands on civic and community leaders to generate the preconditions described above. The role of civic leadership emerges as central to the design of strategic management policy at the local level and to account for *how* political choices about urban governance are made. Not every community or regional government will succeed in rising to the challenge. Often communities suffer from a deficit of civic capital, an inability to generate sufficient trust or cooperation among key players to generate the supportive institutional arrangements required to promote growth at local and community levels. Regional governments may similarly lack the requisite degree of foresight to provide the level of support that communities need to meet this challenge. This may result in a "governance" failure as opposed to a state or market failure, which arises from the inability to bring key players together to develop new institutions and the required supports.

Nonetheless, the current period of economic and social change demands the transition to the broader conception of governance and social learning described by Gilles Paquet in an interlinked set of books and papers over the past decade and a half. The key organizational issue that he has clearly identified is how to pool and structure knowledge and intelligence in social ways rather than to access them only on an individual basis. This form of shared or networked learning assumes that neither the public sector as conventionally analyzed in the public administration literature nor private enterprise and community-based organizations are the sole sources of needed knowledge. Instead, the process of institutional adaptation and intelligent governance that he prescribes is an interactive one in which the means for establishing supportive social relations, and of communicating insights and knowledge among an inclusive body of social, economic, and political actors are crucial to the outcomes. The issue is whether the institutions and actors involved at all levels of governance are capable of responding to this challenge and engaging in the kind of social and reflexive learning that Paquet has so eloquently prescribed.

References

Acs, Z., J. de la Mothe, and G. Paquet. (1996). "Local Systems of Innovation: In Search of an Enabling Strategy." In *The Implications of Knowledge-Based Growth for Micro-Economic Policies*, ed. P. Howitt. Calgary: University of Calgary Press, 339–358.

Audretsch, D. B. (2002). "The Innovative Advantage of US Cities." *European Planning Studies, 10.2*, 165–76.

Bradford, N. (2003). *Cities and Regions that Work: Profiles of Innovation*. Ottawa: Canadian Policy Research Networks.

Cooke, P., and K. Morgan. (1993). "The Network Paradigm: New Departures in Corporate and Regional Development." *Environment and Planning D: Society and Space, 11*, 543–64.

———. (1998). *The Associational Economy: Firms, Regions, and Innovation*. Oxford: Oxford University Press.

Dalum, B., et al. (1992). "Public Policy in the Learning Society." In *National Systems of Innovation: Towards a Theory of Innovation and Interactive Learning*, ed. Bengt-Åke Lundvall. London: Pinter Publishers, 296–317.

de la Mothe, J., and G. Paquet, eds. (1998). *Local and Regional Systems of Innovation*. Amsterdam: Kluwer Academic Publishers.

Gertler, M. S. (2001). "Urban Economy and Society in Canada: Flows of People, Capital, and Ideas." *Isuma: Canadian Journal of Policy Research, 2.3*, 119–30.

———. (2002). "Technology, Culture, and Social Learning: Regional and National Institutions of Governance." In *Innovation and Social Learning: Institutional Adaptation in an Era of Technological Change*, eds. M. S. Gertler and D. A. Wolfe. Houndsmill: Palgrave Macmillan, 111–134.

Henton, D., J. Melville, and K. Walesh. (1997). *Grassroots Leaders for a New Economy: How Civic Entrepreneurs Are Building Prosperous Communities*. San Francisco: Jossey-Bass.

Maskell, P. (1999). "Globalisation and Industrial Competitiveness: The Process and Consequences of Ubiquitification." In *Making Connections: Technological Learning and Regional Economic Change*, ed. E. J. Malecki and P. Oinas. Aldershot: Ashgate Publishing, 35–60.

Maskell, P., and A. Malmberg. (1999). "Localised Learning and Industrial Competitiveness." *Cambridge Journal of Economics*, 23, 167–85.

Paquet, G. (1997). "States, Communities, and Markets: The Distributed Governance Scenario." In *The Evolving Nation-State in a Global Information Era: Policy Challenges*, ed. T. J. Courchene. Kingston: John Deutsch Institute for the Study of Economic Policy, Queen's University, 25–46.

———. (1999). *Governance through Social Learning*. Ottawa: University of Ottawa Press.

———. (2001a). "The New Governance, Subsidiarity, and the Strategic State." In *Governance in the 21st Century*, eds. W. Michalski et al. Paris: OECD, 183–214.

———. (2001b). "Smart Communities and the Geo-Governance of Social Learning." *Optimum Online*, 31.2, 33–50. www.optimumonline.ca [consulted January 16, 2009]

Peters, G., and J. Pierre. (2004). "Multi-Level Governance and Democracy: A Faustian Bargain?" In *Multi-Level Governance*, eds. I. Bache and M. Flinders. Oxford: Oxford University Press, 75–91.

Rhodes, R. A. W. (1996). "The New Governance: Governing without Government." *Political Studies*, 44, 652–67.

Scott, A. J. (2004). "A Perspective of Economic Geography." *Journal of Economic Geography*, 4.5, 479–99.

Scott, A. J., J. Agnew, E. W. Soja, and M. Storper. (2001). "Global City-Regions." In *Global City-Regions: Trends, Theory, Policy*, ed. A. J. Scott. Oxford: Oxford University Press, 11–31.

Stoker, G. (1998). "Governance as Theory: Five Propositions." *International Social Science Journal*, 155, 17–28.

Storper, M. (1995). "Institutions of the Learning Economy." *European Urban and Regional Studies*, 2.3, 135–158.

———. (2002). "Institutions of the Learning Economy." In *Innovation and Social Learning: Institutional Adaptation in an Era of Technological Change*, eds. M. S. Gertler and D. A. Wolfe. Houndsmill: Palgrave Macmillan, 135–138.

Wolfe, D. A., and M. S. Gertler. (2002). "Innovation and Social Learning: An Introduction." In *Innovation and Social Learning: Institutional Adaptation in an Era of Technological Change*, eds. M. S. Gertler and D. A. Wolfe. Houndsmill: Palgrave Macmillan, 1–24.

Chapitre 25

D'une industrie automobile à gouvernance centralisée à l'invention d'une chaîne de valeur de distribution de services de mobilité à gouvernance distribuée

Christian Navarre

Les utopies d'aujourd'hui sont les réalités de demain
—Victor Hugo

Cet essai est plus qu'un exercice de style sur l'application, à la Gilles Paquet[1], de l'outillage de la théorie de la gouvernance à l'analyse de l'industrie automobile. Commencé dans les affres des figures imposées, ce travail s'est achevé dans la jubilation, celle du chercheur qui a mis la main sur des résultats inattendus, et ce, au moment où la hausse brutale du prix des carburants déclenche un processus délétère qui pourrait mener à l'implosion de l'industrie.

Or en 2008, l'empreinte de cette industrie est considérable :

1. Le parc mondial de véhicules automobiles, en croissance rapide, est estimé à 700 millions d'unités.
2. Il se vend annuellement de l'ordre de 70 millions de véhicules neufs (marché en croissance rapide) et 120-180 millions de véhicules usagés (estimation de l'auteur).
3. Le chiffre d'affaires annuel réalisé par les constructeurs, leurs fournisseurs et distributeurs est estimé (pour les ventes de véhicules neufs) à 1500 milliards $US. À ce total, il faut ajouter le flux d'affaires généré après la vente de la voiture compris entre 3000 milliards $US et 4500 milliards $US (estimation de l'auteur).

4. Quatre-vingt-quatorze pour cent (94 %) de la production mondiale est manufacturée par 20 constructeurs, 11 de ces 20 constructeurs réalisant eux-mêmes 80 % de cette production.
5. L'industrie contribue à hauteur de 4 % á 5 % de l'emploi global dans les pays industrialisés.
6. L'industrie produit de l'ordre de 25 % des gaz à effet de serre du monde occidental.

Traditionnellement, l'étude de l'industrie automobile repose sur l'emploi de quelques microscopes bien connus, par exemple : l'analyse stratégique des firmes à la Porter (Porter 1985) ou encore l'analyse stratégique de « filière » à la française (Bidault 1989).

Le parti pris de cet essai est d'appliquer un macroscope (de Rosnay 1975) à l'analyse de l'industrie automobile ; en l'occurrence, l'outillage de la théorie de la gouvernance développé par Gilles Paquet (2008; 2005; 2004), qui peut être résumée abruptement comme suit :

1. la finalité de l'analyse de la gouvernance d'un système sociotechnique est de cerner la « dynamique de la répartition du pouvoir, de l'information et des ressources entre les acteurs du champ socioéconomique » analysé,
2. ... en repérant les dysfonctionnements et pathologies stables et récurrentes qui affectent les systèmes décisionnels des acteurs et la régulation des systèmes sociaux techniques auxquels ils participent,
3. ... afin de suggérer le réagencement de ces systèmes sociaux pour en éliminer les dysfonctionnements et en améliorer durablement l'efficacité.

Dans cette perspective, l'industrie automobile inclut les acteurs suivants :

1. Les usagers/consommateurs qui recherchent la satisfaction de leurs besoins de mobilité.
2. L'ensemble des firmes actives tout au long de la durée de vie du produit automobile[2]. Les constructeurs y jouent un rôle prépondérant car ils conçoivent, produisent, distribuent les véhicules et les pièces détachées nécessaires à leur entretien. Ils dominent l'énorme accumulation de capital, le « détour de production » (Böhm-Bawerk 1929) nécessaire à la

satisfaction par l'usage de l'objet automobile des besoins de mobilité des consommateurs.
3. Les pouvoirs publics (gouvernements centraux et gouvernements locaux) qui investissent lourdement dans les infrastructures routières, émettent les règlements de sécurité, contrôlent les émissions toxiques et bientôt l'empreinte carbone des véhicules, et qui conçoivent et font respecter l'application des codes de conduites.
4. Les organisations de la société civile (par exemple, les groupes écologistes ou de défense des consommateurs) qui tentent d'endiguer les effets négatifs de l'usage massif de l'automobile (tels que la pollution, l'asphyxie des centres-villes, l'étalement urbain) ou encore de protéger les consommateurs des excès de pouvoirs des constructeurs. Les syndicats qui défendent, lorsqu'ils en ont les moyens, les conditions de travail de leurs mandants sont à classer aussi dans cette catégorie d'acteurs.

On montrera, section II, que la gouvernance centralisée est le mode dominant de gouvernance de l'industrie automobile. La section III listera les facteurs de turbulence qui affectent l'industrie et menacent son existence même. Cet essai reprend à son compte le principe que la gouvernance décentralisée est le mode de gouvernance le plus approprié pour s'adapter efficacement à la turbulence et au tohu-bohu (Leblond et Paquet 1988). La section IV est consacrée à l'exploration d'un scénario de rupture : la réinvention de l'industrie automobile sur le mode de la gouvernance décentralisée. La section I clarifie les besoins satisfaits par l'industrie et sa raison d'être.

I. Quels sont les besoins satisfaits par l'industrie automobile ? À quoi sert-elle ?

Se déplacer et se mouvoir sont aussi vieux que l'humanité. L'ingéniosité de l'homme a été sans limites pour utiliser des sources d'énergie autres que sa propre force musculaire afin d'augmenter le poids des charges transportées, d'alléger le poids des engins de transports, d'allonger les distances parcourues, d'accroître la vitesse de déplacement.

Chacun d'entre nous satisfait ses besoins de mobilité en choisissant parmi les divers modes de transports qui lui sont accessibles : voiture, marche, métro, deux roues, etc. En concurrence, certains d'entre eux dominent selon leur coût relatif, facilité d'accès, efficacité et symbiose avec la culture dominante.

On observe une fracture nette entre les pays occidentaux et les pays émergents :

1. En effet, les pays occidentaux riches[3] recourent plus que massivement à la route pour le transport des personnes. À l'exception du Japon, où le transport des personnes par le train en représente approximativement le tiers, l'usage de l'automobile (80 %) et du bus (10 %) réalisent de l'ordre de 90 % des déplacements des personnes (mesurés en milliards de passagers/kilomètres). Lors de ces déplacements en automobile, en Amérique du Nord, dans 75 % des cas le véhicule est occupé par un passager seul.
2. Les pays émergents recourent marginalement à l'automobile au profit d'autres modes de transports, y compris le transport par traction animale. L'usage de l'automobile y est accessoire et réservé à des usages spécifiques. L'automobile y est encore un bien de luxe accessible aux seuls favorisés de la société.

Dans les pays occidentaux, l'automobile a donc colonisé l'espace de la mobilité personnelle au point d'en quasi-éliminer tous les autres modes de transport. Évidemment, nous sommes très dépendants de l'automobile, pour ne pas dire intoxiqués par elle.

II. La gouvernance centralisée est le mode de gouvernance de l'industrie automobile

Une industrie de masse marquée dès sa création par un management centralisateur
Le succès de l'automobile, fruit d'une grappe d'innovations survenues à la fin du XIXe siècle, est aussi le résultat d'innovations managériales concomitantes :

1. Pour réduire les coûts de production furent inventées, par Ford notamment, des nouvelles méthodes de production en masse de produits uniformes standardisés (machines organisées en chaîne d'assemblage par modèle, standardisation et uniformisation des composants, contrôle statistique de qualité, spécialisation des postes de travail et des emplois,

etc.), elles mêmes supportées par des systèmes de management centralisés et hiérarchiques. En résumé, le management vertical dans son expression la plus pure (Navarre et Schaan 1992).
2. Écouler la production de masse commandait également une distribution et une publicité de masse. Les constructeurs ont rapidement mis en place, au tout début de l'industrie, des réseaux de concessionnaires franchisés indépendants supportés par des campagnes de publicité de masse. Les concessionnaires, des petits entrepreneurs indépendants, investissaient leurs capitaux personnels pour vendre, entretenir et réparer les véhicules permettant aux constructeurs de réduire les investissements de commercialisation afin d'augmenter d'autant leurs investissements dans les moyens de production et de R et D. En contrepartie des risques financiers personnels encourus, des territoires exclusifs étaient accordés aux concessionnaires avec comme conséquence importante que fut éliminée la concurrence résultant de la mise en compétition de canaux de distribution distribuant des produits identiques (intracompétition). Les constructeurs, à peu près à la même époque et sur tous les continents, ayant généralement adopté ce modèle ont donc dès la création de leurs réseaux de distribution choisi, à leur avantage, un système qui limite la concurrence et leur procure une rente au détriment du consommateur.

La répartition du pouvoir, des ressources et de l'information au sein de l'industrie est concentrée au sommet chez les constructeurs

Les producteurs dominent les concessionnaires. La faible taille relative et la dispersion des concessionnaires ne leur permettent pas de résister aux pressions des constructeurs[4]. Il en est de même en amont, avec des fournisseurs fragilisés qui jouent leur avenir au fil des introductions, sans cesse recommencées, des nouveaux modèles. Chaque nouveau modèle est une occasion, pour les constructeurs, de rebattre les cartes entre tous les fournisseurs. De plus, au fil des crises, les constructeurs imposent unilatéralement les baisses de prix qui leur conviennent. Le statut de fournisseur est éminemment précaire.

Le consommateur subit, et surtout paie, tous les dysfonctionnements de l'industrie. Quelle que soit la transaction (achat d'un véhicule neuf ou usagé, réparation, assurance, etc.), il négocie en permanence en situation d'asymétrie d'information et ce n'est probablement pas le fruit du hasard qu'Akerlof (Akerlof

1970) a choisi dans son article fondateur, parmi d'autres exemples, le marché du véhicule usagé pour illustrer le concept.

Les constructeurs contrôlent donc la chaîne de valeur de l'industrie depuis le consommateur jusqu'aux fournisseurs de matières premières et de composants. Cette domination a été propice à la diffusion, à tous les niveaux de la chaîne de valeur, d'un modèle de management commun à tous les acteurs (fournisseurs, concessionnaires, réparateurs), lui-même inspiré du management centralisé, typique de la production de masse. Les états-majors des constructeurs déterminent sans partage la stratégie et contrôlent à leur profit, sans contre-pouvoirs efficaces, la répartition interne et externe du pouvoir, des ressources et de l'information. Ces états-majors jouent également de toute leur influence pour ralentir l'adoption de réglementations limitant leur autonomie.

La formation de vastes marchés régionaux régulés selon une logique de concurrence oligopolistique, renforce la prégnance de la gouvernance centralisée au sein et entre les firmes
Si au début du XXe siècle des centaines de constructeurs étaient en concurrence au terme d'une période de concentration rapide, l'industrie s'est progressivement divisée en deux grands marchés régionaux dominés par un petit nombre de constructeurs différents basés en Amérique du Nord (GM, Ford, Chrysler) et en Europe (VW, Peugeot, Citroën, Renault, Fiat, Rover, etc.). Durant la seconde moitié du XXe siècle, un troisième oligopole s'est créé en Asie autour des constructeurs japonais (Toyota, Honda, Nissan) et plus récemment coréens (Hyundai, Kia).

En raison des barrières des langues, des spécificités des pays, des différences de réglementation, des barrières à l'entrée, des coûts de pénétration et d'investissement dans les réseaux de distribution, ces marchés régionaux sont relativement étanches. Tout se passe selon un ballet bien réglé, celui de la concurrence oligopolistique. Les états-majors scrutent les comportements d'un petit nombre de concurrents, différencient leurs produits (prix, marque) pour éviter la banalisation et la concurrence brutale sur les prix et recherchent les effets de volume (économies d'échelle). De tels enjeux donnent beaucoup de légitimité au sommet stratégique et aux processus bureaucratiques au sein des firmes.

De plus, les constructeurs entretiennent de multiples liens de coopération pour se partager des usines d'organes (par exemple, les boîtes de vitesse), des moteurs, des produits. Si la concurrence la plus féroce règne sur le « *front office* », la coopération subtile entre concurrents directs inspire le « *back office* ».

C'est donc au total un véritable « pouvoir de monopole » sur l'industrie (Houssiaux 1958) que les constructeurs se sont octroyés.

Premières crises pétrolières (1974 et 1980) et premières ratées du modèle de la gouvernance centralisée
Un système de gouvernance centralisée survit dans un environnement stable mais se « déglingue » rapidement lorsque les conditions de l'environnement change brutalement ou que l'instabilité devient la règle. À l'issue des deux premiers chocs pétroliers (1974 et 1980), le prix du baril de pétrole fut multiplié par dix. L'industrie automobile entra en crise : faillite de Chrysler, quasi-faillite de Ford, crise majeure de GM. À la faveur de cette crise, les constructeurs japonais (principalement Toyota et Honda), dont l'offre de petites voitures de qualité trouva rapidement preneurs, ouvrirent une tête de pont en Amérique du Nord qu'ils transformèrent en une implantation durable. La crise fut tout aussi profonde en Europe, mais moins spectaculaire.

Pour se sortir de la crise, le constat dérangeant des chercheurs… il faut plus de transversalité !
Suite aux effets de cette crise, furent engagés aux États-Unis des programmes de recherche visant à mieux comprendre le succès des producteurs japonais :

1. Une première série de travaux autour du MIT démontra que la performance (en productivité, en qualité, en capacité de réaction aux fluctuations de la demande) des chaînes d'assemblage japonaises reposaient sur des principes d'organisation moins hiérarchique, des employés polyvalents « empouvoirés », l'élimination des stocks et le centrage de la planification sur les flux (Kanban), de nouveaux rapports avec les fournisseurs eux aussi « empouvoirés », une philosophie de la qualité non plus statistique mais zéro-défaut, des pièces conçues pour être facilement produites et assemblées, etc. Bref, un système de management reposant sur une distribution des ressources, du pouvoir et de l'information plus décentralisée avec comme objectif d'éliminer les problèmes en les traitant le plus tôt possible, le plus bas possible dans la hiérarchie, le plus proche de l'action et des décideurs qualifiés. Ce système a aussi été reconnu comme le système Toyota (Coriat 1991).

2. Les travaux de Clark et Fujimoto (1991) démontrèrent que non seulement les constructeurs japonais avaient inventé des nouvelles méthodes de production mais aussi des nouvelles méthodes de conception. En effet, des chaînes d'assemblage plus flexibles, capables de produire une plus grande variété de modèles sur la même chaîne tout en baissant les coûts et en diminuant les seuils de point mort ne prennent toute leur efficacité que si parallèlement, sont conçus un plus grand nombre de produits (deux à trois fois plus de véhicules en marché par constructeur), plus vite (en 36-44 mois vs. 60 mois avec un an de retard en moyenne), moins cher (en gros avec une allocation d'heures d'ingénierie réduite de 50 %) pour profiter de l'avantage stratégique de la flexibilité (Midler et Navarre 2004). Ces résultats ont été obtenus en donnant plus de pouvoir aux fournisseurs, en cassant les hiérarchies et les mentalités de « silos » et en forçant les équipes projets à la transversalité en rapprochant notamment les concepteurs et les producteurs (notion de « concourance »), en « empouvoirant » les directeurs de projets, etc. ; bref, la mise en œuvre de formes de gouvernance décentralisée et de transversalité.

La plupart des états-majors des constructeurs occidentaux, une fois digérée la substance de ces recherches, se lancèrent, avec scepticisme, dans des réformes prudentes visant à doter les firmes de plus souplesse. Cela revenait à introduire des îlots de gouvernance décentralisée (les projets, les « groupes transverses » chers à Carlos Gohsn chez Renault SA et Nissan, par exemple) dans un océan de gouvernance centralisée. Inutile de souligner le caractère instable et explosif de la cohabitation. L'incapacité à dépasser cette dualité a eu comme effet de réduire la portée des réformes mises en œuvre, voire d'en annuler les effets.

III. L'industrie automobile sous la pression de la turbulence et dans le tohu-bohu
La question de l'avenir de l'industrie automobile telle que nous la connaissons est bien à l'ordre du jour car les périls s'accumulent.

Le cœur d'activité de l'industrie n'est déjà plus en 2008 la production de véhicules...
Un véhicule neuf, vendu en Amérique du Nord en moyenne 20 000 $US, génère une valeur additionnelle de l'ordre de 40 000 $ á 60 000 $ durant sa durée de

vie (Ealey 1996). Sur les 60 000 $ á 80 000 $ générés au total, le constructeur en contrôle directement moins de 10 % et indirectement (à travers le contrôle des fournisseurs et des concessionnaires) au plus 25 %. Les constructeurs sont littéralement des colosses aux pieds d'argile. La migration de la valeur de l'aval vers l'amont est largement engagée au détriment des constructeurs.

Les consommateurs ont pris le pouvoir
L'usage généralisé d'Internet a profondément modifié le processus de vente des véhicules (Badot *et al.* 2004, Badot et Navarre 2006)[5]. L'asymétrie d'information dont les concessionnaires bénéficiaient a disparu. Le consommateur a pris le pouvoir avec comme conséquence un laminage des marges sur les ventes de véhicules neufs. Le modèle de la distribution par concessionnaires exclusifs jugé trop coûteux et inefficace est remis en question, y compris par les constructeurs.

La nécessaire réduction de l'empreinte CO_2 de l'automobile sur l'environnement et la hausse du prix des carburants se combinent pour accélérer la nécessaire réduction rapide de la taille des véhicules
Récemment, des réglementations ont été adoptées (notamment en Europe et en Californie) pour limiter rapidement les émissions de CO_2. L'objectif est de rendre les constructeurs directement responsables des émissions de CO_2 des véhicules neufs qu'ils mettent sur la route. Le défi est de taille ! Par exemple, advenant sa mise en œuvre, pour se conformer à la législation californienne, un constructeur, aux alentours de 2016, devra mettre en marché en Californie (et dans les 18 États qui ont choisi de s'aligner), sous peine de pénalités substantielles, des véhicules dont la moyenne pondérée des émissions de CO_2, tous véhicules confondus, serait celle d'une SMART d'aujourd'hui ! En 2008, les émissions annuelles des parcs de véhicules mis sur la route sont en moyenne 2,5 fois celle d'une SMART.

Au-delà de ses effets dépressifs sur l'économie globale, la hausse récente, rapide et brutale du prix de l'essence en Amérique du Nord a eu des effets immédiats : baisse rapide et significative des ventes des véhicules énergivores et hausse des ventes des véhicules plus économiques, attrait croissant pour les véhicules innovants à motorisation hybride, augmentation de la fréquentation des systèmes de transports collectifs.

Pour les véhicules propulsés par des moteurs polluants en gaz à effet de serre, la combinaison de ces deux tendances impose une réduction rapide de la puissance des moteurs et du poids des véhicules. Par conséquent, une explosion des ventes de très petites voitures à plus faibles marges, malheureusement pour les constructeurs.

Les oligopoles régionaux pourront-ils contenir les nouveaux entrants ?
De nouveaux acteurs émergent en Chine et en Inde avec l'intention affichée de prendre leur place, toute leur place sur les marchés mondiaux.

La Chine. Depuis 2007, le marché chinois est en volume de vente annuel de véhicules neufs (de l'ordre de 9 millions en 2008) le second marché national après celui des États-Unis (15 millions d'unités en 2008) et devant celui du Japon (6 millions en 2008). La formation d'un noyau de constructeurs chinois, avec comme avantage compétitif des coûts significativement inférieurs à ceux des producteurs nord-américains, japonais et européens[6], est redoutée. Mais la menace réelle pourrait venir d'innovations managériales. Des prototypes de ces innovations ont été repérés dans des industries proches.

Il ressort de la recherche (Fujimoto et Dongsheng 2006) que le développement fulgurant de l'industrie chinoise de la motocyclette[7] s'explique, certes par un avantage de coût, mais aussi et surtout par la supériorité d'un mode d'organisation de la chaîne de valeur basé sur la coopération entre réseaux intégrés de firmes locales d'assemblage, une large autonomie des fournisseurs, l'ajustement mutuel autour de plates-formes et modules définis en copiant (*reverse engineering*) les modèles des concurrents. Le succès des fabricants chinois reposerait sur un avantage de coût et aussi sur les effets positifs d'une large décentralisation des allocations de ressources, du pouvoir et de l'information ; bref, tous les attributs de la gouvernance décentralisée.

Une automobile est bien plus complexe qu'une motocyclette et cela est un obstacle majeur à la transposition d'un tel système à la conception et à la production de voitures. Rien n'interdit toutefois de penser, en se fondant sur ce qui a été observé pour l'industrie de la motocyclette, qu'il y a une spontanéité chinoise, qui avait aussi été observée lors du développement fulgurant de l'industrie textile chinoise, à privilégier la transversalité, la décentralisation, les réseaux si caractéristiques de la gouvernance décentralisée.

L'Inde. Par comparaison avec la Chine, l'Inde est un petit pays producteur (1,8 million de véhicules en 2008). Les grands constructeurs mondiaux se partagent ce marché. La production des producteurs indiens est marginale. Et pourtant, c'est en Inde qu'est lancée, dans le scepticisme le plus total, la voiture à 2 500 $US (100 000 roupies), la déjà célèbre Nano de Tata Automobiles :

1. C'est une innovation de produit. Le plus spectaculaire n'est pas son prix. En effet, la Nano n'est pas une voiture au rabais. Elle est bourrée d'astuces et durant sa conception 34 brevets ont été déposés[8].
2. C'est une innovation de « process » que Tata a baptisé « *Open Distribution* » qui est de fait un système de distribution à gouvernance décentralisée. La Nano est par conception, modulaire, à la fois pour le produit et le « *process* ». La philosophie de Tata est de produire les modules composant la Nano, puis de les livrer à des mini-chaînes d'assemblage satellites réparties sur tout le territoire indien, y compris dans les zones rurales les plus reculées. Tata assurerait la formation, la mise en activité, le contrôle de la qualité. Ces chaînes d'assemblage seraient financées en combinant des capitaux locaux et éventuellement des capitaux publics. L'objectif est d'adapter chaque véhicule aux demandes les plus fines des clients locaux en recourant à des fournisseurs locaux pour enrichir les véhicules de fonctionnalités non prévues par Tata. Cela revient à ouvrir l'architecture de la Nano aux fournisseurs de composants dès lors que leurs produits sont compatibles avec la logique des modules et à ouvrir des espaces d'enrichissement du produit en instituant un mécanisme permanent de « co-conception » qui mobilise systématiquement l'intelligence des clients et des fournisseurs locaux. Cela revient à « produire en masse de la variété à bas coût » par la mise en œuvre d'un modèle de gouvernance décentralisée.

L'exportation de véhicules de Chine et/ou de l'Inde reposera certes sur un avantage de coût basé sur une main-d'œuvre bon marché. Mais ce ne sera pas la menace la plus inquiétante. Bien plus inquiétant serait la diffusion d'un modèle de gouvernance décentralisée qui donnerait un avantage stratégique à long terme aux firmes automobiles de ce pays.

Retour d'une période d'exubérance technologique et d'innovations
Pour cet essai les innovations observées ont été classées en trois catégories :

Innovation de type I. Ces innovations sont actuellement les plus visibles pour les consommateurs :

1. Innovation vers plus d'électronique intégrée aux véhicules. Ultimement, le remplacement des organes mécaniques (volant, pédales, embrayage, etc.) par des systèmes dits « *X-by-wire* » (comme pour les avions) aura comme effet direct de réduire le poids des véhicules et de transformer le rapport de l'usager au véhicule (McKinsey 2003).
2. Exploration de nouvelles motorisations : moteurs hybrides (essence et diesel), moteur à hydrogène, moteur électrique, moteur à air comprimé, etc.

Au total, l'usage du « *X-by-wire* » et du moteur électrique favoriseraient l'émergence de plates-formes de véhicules légers, écologiques, spacieux, radicalement différents.

Innovation de type II. L'automobile comme agent[9]. Le développement de l'électronique automobile transforme progressivement la conduite en retirant au pilote certaines décisions qui sont exécutées par des automates (ESP, ABS, « limitateur » de vitesse, etc.). Lors du déclenchement de ces dispositifs, le pilote perd le contrôle du véhicule dont la trajectoire et/ou la vitesse sont prises en charge temporairement par les automates. L'accumulation de dispositifs électroniques encouragera la mise en réseau d'un nombre croissant d'informations, y compris des informations venant de l'extérieur (aujourd'hui, par une connexion GPS combinée à une liaison téléphonique sans fil) avec comme conséquence que certaines décisions habituellement prises par le conducteur le seront avec plus d'efficacité, par les automates embarqués dans le véhicule, notamment pour des raisons de sécurité ou de confort. Le conducteur sera libéré de la nécessité d'une attention constante.

Innovation de type III. Les innovations appliquées à l'automobile comme élément constitutif de systèmes de transport intelligents. La présence sur la route de millions de véhicules a des effets négatifs dont le coût pour la collectivité est considérable :

pollution et coût des embouteillages, congestion des centres urbains, pollution additionnelle à celle du transport, accidents, etc.

La liberté sans limite de prendre des décisions individuelles microlocales sur la vitesse et la direction, prises en continu par un conducteur en situation d'information très imparfaite, provoque des « effets de foule » indésirables qui se traduisent par des accidents et des périodes de ralentissement, voire d'immobilisation des véhicules. Pour éliminer ces effets indésirables, il faut piloter globalement le débit routier en temps réel et asservir la conduite locale de chaque véhicule à l'optimisation de ce débit. Bref, pour rendre fluide la circulation et réduire les accidents, le conducteur doit perdre le contrôle total des décisions de pilotage. Le développement d'Internet et des communications sans fil introduit une nouvelle vague d'innovations[10]. D'ores et déjà, les véhicules ont la capacité de se situer dans le trafic, de communiquer en P2P avec d'autres véhicules proches, d'être informés sur l'état de la circulation amont et aval en temps réel, d'entretenir un dialogue avec la route et la signalisation routière qui deviendront elles aussi intelligentes et adaptatives. Tout le matériel de cartographie ainsi que la collecte des données de trafic sont mis en ligne depuis longtemps (Yahoo, MSN, Google, etc.) presque toujours gratuitement.

Une voiture communicant avec la route et les véhicules de son environnement pourrait recevoir des systèmes globaux de régulation, à créer, les instructions de limitation et de régulation de la vitesse et/ou de direction qui seraient mises en œuvre par les automates embarqués.

On peut imaginer qu'un tel véhicule communiquerait aussi avec les systèmes de transports collectifs ouvrant la possibilité d'intégrer tous les modes individuels et collectifs de transport et de les optimiser en fonction du programme de déplacement de l'usager.

Au total, vient de s'ouvrir une période cumulative d'innovations aussi décisive que celle du début du XXe siècle :

1. Plus d'innovations de type I accélérera plus d'innovations de type II et transformera l'automobile en un agent autonome spécialisé de plus en plus efficace.
2. Plus d'innovations de type II accélérera plus d'innovations de type III ouvrant la voie à une optimisation intégrée des modes de transport, individuels et collectifs, selon des modes de gouvernance décentralisée.
3. Les technologies mobilisées pour créer et développer ces dispositifs reposent elles-mêmes consubstantiellement sur des dispositifs de gouvernance

distribuée (Internet, réseaux de calculateurs, P2P, compréhension de plus en plus fine des technologies de la coopération) (Rheingold 2002), (Ostrom 1990; 1992).
4. Ces innovations s'appliqueront à des véhicules à propulsion propre, probablement électrique, communiquant, ultralégers, compacts.

Face à ce tohu-bohu, comment le millier de dirigeants des 11 entreprises qui réalisent 80 % de la production mondiale d'automobile vont-ils s'y prendre ? Comment ces dirigeants vont-ils collectivement survivre au tsunami en préparation ? Comment les hiérarchies frileuses de ces firmes, retranchées dans leurs silos, vont-elles se réinventer ? Peut-on d'ailleurs se réinventer au fil des rituels budgétaires ?

Pour l'instant, en dépit des annonces de « véhicules-solutions » (par exemple, la Volt de GM ou les projets de coopération autour de la voiture électrique), force est de constater « plus de la même chose » ! Et pourtant les périls s'accumulent !

IV. Exploration des conditions et des effets d'un renversement hypothétique du mode de gouvernance de l'industrie

Les voies de la réinvention de l'industrie peuvent être ouvertes :

1. Par le millier de dirigeants des 11 entreprises produisant 80 % de la production mondiale en généralisant délibérément les motorisations hybrides, les véhicules électriques, et en amorçant l'industrialisation du moteur à hydrogène, etc.
2. Par les 1500 á 3000 dirigeants des 31 petits producteurs mondiaux, dont Tata Automobiles, aucun ne produisant plus de 600 000 véhicules en 2005 et la plupart moins de 100 000, tous non-occidentaux (à l'exception de Porsche) qui produisent moins de 10 % de la production mondiale en 2005. Par exemple, la Nano de Tata et l'« *Open Distribution* », un véhicule électrique chinois à bas prix, l'adoption du moteur à air comprimé (Tata), etc.
3. Ou encore, selon la thèse de Christensen (1997), la Révolution viendra-t-elle de firmes inconnues[11] ?

La thèse de cet essai est que le passage à un mode de gouvernance distribuée est nécessaire pour tirer parti de toutes les innovations disponibles et à venir. C'est donc à un tel scénario que la section est consacrée.

Changer de paradigme architectural
Il est d'usage de classer les types d'architecture automobiles selon deux dimensions :

1. Le degré d'ouverture. Une architecture est dite ouverte lorsqu'elle est partagée par de nombreux partenaires développant leurs produits ou services dans un cadre commun, par exemple Linux. Au contraire, l'architecture est dite fermée ou propriétaire lorsqu'elle appartient à une firme qui en garde jalousement le secret, par exemple Microsoft et les versions successives de Windows. Jusqu'à présent, les architectures des véhicules sont fermées et propriétaires.
2. Le degré de modularité. Une façon de réduire la complexité d'un produit et de son processus de production est pour chaque fonction de concevoir un composant physique spécifique, un module, de telle sorte que la relation fonction-module soit isomorphe. Idéalement, l'objet doit être découpé de telle sorte que la complexité soit minimale aux interfaces des modules. Lorsque cela est possible, on parle d'architecture modulaire. À l'opposé, lorsque qu'une fonction est accomplie à travers plusieurs composants la complexité est diffuse. Cette architecture est dite intégrale. Historiquement, l'architecture intégrale a dominé l'industrie automobile. Ce n'est que récemment que certains constructeurs ont repensé les véhicules comme des assemblages de modules (VW, Mercedes-SMART, Tata-Nano). Ces modules sont en général conçus avec l'aide des fournisseurs qui, bénéficiant d'un savoir faire capitalisé sur l'expérience de plusieurs clients-constructeurs, maîtrisent les technologies et la R et D, la conception et la production de ces modules. L'avantage pour les constructeurs est que ces modules sont livrés en juste-à-temps réduisant d'autant la complexité des opérations d'assemblage, donc de leurs coûts tout en augmentant la flexibilité de la chaîne. Le fournisseur lui-même peut décomposer le module en sous-modules pour ses besoins propres et organiser ses fournisseurs selon le même schéma d'organisation pour en tirer les mêmes avantages mais plus en aval.

En combinant ouverture et modularité trois types d'architectures sont remarquables (Tableau I) :

Tableau 1: Typologie des architectures

Modulaire	Intégrale
1.1. Expériences modules/plates-formes et industrialisation pour quelques constructeurs	1.2. Situation prévalant jusque les années 1980–1990
2.1. Existe à l'état de « concept car »	2.2. Non significatif

Typologie des architectures. Adapté de Fujimoto (2008)

1. Architecture intégrale fermée (1.2). C'est la situation qui prévaut historiquement chez les constructeurs. Chaque nouveau véhicule est repensé dans son intégralité et exclusivement par et pour le constructeur.
2. Architecture modulaire fermée (1.1). Quelques constructeurs se sont lancés dans cette voie en condensant dans des « plates-formes » les composants de la base roulante (Powertrain) rendus communs à plusieurs véhicules. Sur ces plates-formes sont développés des carrosseries et des intérieurs visuellement différents. Le découpage des véhicules est pensé en modules. La plate-forme permet (1) de profiter des économies dues aux effets de volume, (2) de minimiser simultanément les coûts induits par la variété, (3) de maximiser les avantages commerciaux par une offre à bas prix et plus ciblée de véhicules sophistiqués à identité distincte. La maîtrise d'architecture modulaire fermée est un avantage compétitif exclusif du constructeur qui, dans la logique de la gouvernance centralisée, ne se partage pas. On observera que ce type d'architecture implique l'existence, au sein de firmes où domine la gouvernance centralisée, d'espaces, au moins temporaires, de transversalité managériale et de gouvernance décentralisée (Navarre et Jolivet 2001).
3. Architecture modulaire ouverte (2.1). C'est évidemment l'architecture de la gouvernance décentralisée. En lançant son PC, IBM avait innové en créant le premier ordinateur conçu sur une architecture modulaire ouverte. Chaque ordinateur devient ainsi une sorte de Lego. Les fabricants ont la liberté en toute indépendance de développer leurs composants selon les contraintes logiques techno-industrielles qui leurs sont propres tant et aussi longtemps qu'ils respectent à la lettre les standards des interfaces

auxquelles ils attacheront leurs produits. La conception et la production de chaque composant fait l'objet d'une concurrence intense entre quelques producteurs qui assument le progrès technique tout en bénéficiant de volumes appréciables. Ils sont eux-mêmes les têtes de ponts de chaînes de valeur complexes centrées sur la conception « des composants des composants » qui eux-mêmes peuvent se décliner autour d'architectures ouvertes. L'adoption de ce type d'architecture a radicalement transformé l'industrie des ordinateurs. Pour l'instant, ce territoire est vierge de toute expérimentation ou projets de la part des constructeurs d'automobiles. Seul GM a approché, avec la voiture concept « Autonomy » (Borroni-Bird, 2002 ; Burns, McCormick et Borroni-Bird 2002) les principes d'une architecture modulaire ouverte. On notera que le remplacement d'organes mécaniques par des systèmes électro-électroniques déplacera l'espace des solutions à la « modularisation » des véhicules dans la sphère du génie logiciel.

La combinaison des innovations de types I, II et III, et la nécessaire réduction drastique du poids des véhicules sont autant d'opportunités stratégiques pour réinventer l'automobile selon le modèle d'une architecture modulaire ouverte. Tata, en a, d'ores et déjà, jeté les prémices avec son concept de « *Open Distribution* ».

Rebâtir la chaîne de valeur par le local et l'auto-organisation selon les modes de la gouvernance distribuée
Notre thèse est que dans l'avenir un véhicule électrique « *X-by-wire* » (innovations de type I) et communicant (innovations de type II et III combinées) à architecture modulaire ouverte s'imposera sur les marchés mondiaux. La production et l'assemblage de ces véhicules seront décentralisés (voir Tata) réduisant ainsi les coûts de transports tout en rapprochant des usagers les services de réparations, les sources de pièces et d'expertise.

L'intégration de ces véhicules dans des systèmes intelligents de transport, largement auto-organisés, aura pour effet d'importantes migrations de valeur des constructeurs vers les services, de l'amont vers l'aval, qui donnera prééminence absolue au local. Chaque grande agglomération est unique. Il faut y coordonner les flux routiers, les systèmes de transports collectifs (taxis, bus, métro, tramway, etc.), les services municipaux (pompiers, police, écoles, etc.), les données de trafic, gérer une signalisation réactive aux conditions de circulation et intelligente, le péage à la volée, etc. Ces investissements[12], pour l'essentiel, la création de vastes ensembles mêlant réseaux de télécommunications et centres de calcul (les véhicules devenus des agents y sont eux-mêmes des nœuds des réseaux et des centres de calcul mobiles), seront pilotés par les autorités locales parce qu'ils sont les plus proches du terrain.

Le véhicule deviendra le réceptacle potentiel de services de toutes sortes, ultraparticularisés. Il est impossible d'imaginer tous ces services. Encore moins d'en imaginer quels seraient les contenus spécifiques à Los Angeles, à Paris, à Ottawa, à Shanghai, etc. Encore moins d'en imaginer, pour une ville donnée, quels seraient les contenus spécifiques à certains quartiers tous distincts (par la langue, l'ethnicité, le niveau de sécurité, les infrastructures commerciales, les niveaux de revenus, etc.).

Il faudra s'en remettre à l'énergie et à l'imagination sans limite des entrepreneurs. L'histoire de DOCOMO (Rheingold, 2002) illustre parfaitement comment il est possible de créer en peu de temps (moins de trois ans) des milliers de serveurs de services marchands en investissant dans une infrastructure de télécommunication à architecture ouverte.

Au total, la chaîne de valeur se recomposera autour de la distribution de services extrêmement particularisés, distribués par des acteurs multiples (municipalités et régions pour les infrastructures, propriétaires de chaînes régionales d'assemblage de véhicules, entreprises de service d'entretien et de réparation, institutions financières, entreprises de services de transports intelligent et de distribution des données de trafic, etc.) se coordonnant autour d'architectures modulaires et ouvertes (produits et « *process* ») au bénéfice d'usager consommant des services de mobilité, socialement responsables et non plus consommateurs de transport automobile.

Pour conclure, il reste à identifier quelle pourrait être l'amorce de la réaction en chaîne vers ce modèle. Quatre scénarios sont imaginables :

1. Convaincu que la migration de valeur vers les services et l'aval est inéluctable, l'un des 11 constructeurs dominants décide, comme IBM le fit en son temps pour l'industrie des ordinateurs, de prendre l'initiative en considérant qu'il y a toujours un avantage stratégique à être le premier à ouvrir des nouveaux marchés. On peut imaginer, dans un premier temps, un scénario à la Microsoft de mise en marché d'un modèle d'architecture semi-ouverte qui permettrait à une telle entreprise

de n'ouvrir que les modules et interfaces qu'elle jugerait non stratégiques (Toyota a expérimenté avec la Scion une version faible de ce modèle d'architecture).
2. Convaincu qu'il faut sortir du rapport de force avec les constructeurs dominants qui le place dans une situation stratégiquement sans issue, un petit constructeur lance une architecture ouverte. Tata a déjà fait le premier mouvement avec son concept de distribution ouverte. Il pourrait rapidement pousser cette stratégie plus loin. Ou encore, la Chine et son hinterland si propice à l'expérimentation pourrait être la matrice de constructeurs audacieux.
3. Il y a toujours du capital-risque pour des innovations à forte création de valeur. Réinventer l'industrie automobile est tentant pour des « capital-risqueurs » audacieux. Par exemple, on trouve quelques bonnes fées autour de projets tels que Tesla (voiture électrique de sport en Californie) ou Project Better Place (mise en place d'un réseau de distribution de batteries rechargées par des sources renouvelables en Israël) ou encore la voiture électrique « Think » (développée en Norvège).
4. Enfin, une municipalité, une région rongée par les nuisances des modes de transports existants, menée par des hommes politiques audacieux décide de réinventer la ville (tout au moins les façons de s'y déplacer) autour de systèmes intelligents de transports avec au passage la réinvention de l'automobile (Paquet et Roy 2003; Paquet 2002).

Avec la perspective de faillites spectaculaires des grands constructeurs américains (au moins sur les marchés d'Amérique du Nord) provoquées par des ruptures radicales irréversibles des modes de consommation, ces divers scénarios sont de plus en plus réalistes.

Notes

[1] L'œuvre de Gilles Paquet est protéiforme et très abondante. On trouvera la liste exhaustive de ses publications à l'adresse suivante (consultée le 19 août 2008) : http://gouvernance.ca/index.php?page=cv&lang=cf. On trouvera aussi à l'adresse suivante (consultée le 19 août 2008) 163 publications prêtes au téléchargement en format pdf : http://gouvernance.ca/index.php?page=pubs&lang=cf.

[2] Constructeurs, fournisseurs de composants et de carburant, concessionnaires, institutions financières—banque, crédit, assurances—, entreprises de réparations,

de distribution de pièces et bientôt de récupération, firmes actives sur le marché du véhicule usagé, etc.

3   En gros, les pays du G8 moins la Russie.
4   Par exemple :
    1. Au Canada, en 2007, 70 % des 3000 franchises sont la propriété d'entrepreneurs qui ne possèdent qu'une seule concession. Dans ces conditions, il leur est difficile de ne pas se plier aux pressions des constructeurs.
    2. Le plus grand groupe de distribution aux États-Unis, Autonation, ne possède qu'un peu plus de 400 franchises sur un total de l'ordre de 20 000 pour l'ensemble du territoire, toutes marques confondues. Les constructeurs n'ont pas d'interlocuteurs suffisamment puissants pour remettre en cause leur contrôle de la distribution.
5   Le Car Internet Research Program (CIRP) basé à l'Université d'Ottawa, a développé une série d'enquêtes (Canada, États-Unis, France, Royaume-Uni) visant à vérifier l'ampleur des transformations qui affectent d'une part les consommateurs et le processus d'achat et d'autre part les concessionnaires et le processus de vente. Voir pour plus de détails http://www.cirp.uottawa.ca/.
6   Évidemment, ces véhicules devront être conformes aux réglementations des pays d'exportation protégeant pour un temps les oligopoles régionaux.
7   Aujourd'hui, les constructeurs chinois contrôlent, en gros, de l'ordre de 40 % de ce marché mondial. Ce résultat a été obtenu en 10 ans.
8   Par comparaison, GM dépose, bon an mal an, de l'ordre de 300 brevets et dépense plusieurs milliards de dollars US en R et D.
9   La notion d'agent est reprise des travaux sur l'intelligence artificielle selon laquelle un agent est une entité qui interagit avec son environnement selon ses propriétés/capacités, préférences et buts. Cet agent peut être une abstraction, un logiciel, un dispositif physique, un humain, une substance chimique.
10 Ces innovations sont développées dans le monde entier sous la dénomination générique des Systèmes de transports intelligents (STI)/Intelligent Transportation Systems (ITS).
11 Les projets ne manquent pas. Par exemple :
    - Sur le thème de la réinvention de la voiture électrique, y compris l'architecture du véhicule et la chaîne de valeur, voir http://www.think.no/.
    - Sur le thème de la batterie amovible distribuée sur le modèle de la distribution de l'essence, voir http://www.betterplace.com/.
    - Sur le thème de la voiture électrique performante, voir http://www.teslamotors.com/.
    - Sur le thème de la petite voiture de ville, voir http://www.zenncars.com/.
12 Le CIRP a organisé à Tokyo et à Ottawa respectivement en octobre 2003 et juin 2004 deux ateliers multidisciplinaires centrés sur ces questions.

Références

Akerlof, George A., « The Market for "Lemons": Quality Uncertainty and the Market Mechanism », *The Quarterly Journal of Economics*, vol. 84, n° 3 (août), 1970, 488-500.

Badot, O., Navarre, C., «L'attitude des concessionnaires de la distribution automobile à l'égard d'Internet: les résultats contrastés d'une étude exploratoire sur quatre pays européens» in Management et avenir, Paris, Numéro 7, 2006/1, 61–90.

Badot, O., N. Navarre, M. Jarvin et B. Morisse, « Ré-intermédiation et comportements expérientiels dans le e-commerce : le cas de l'achat de véhicules automobiles sur Internet », *Consommation et Société*, n° 4, 2004. Accessible électroniquement à l'adresse http://www.argonautes.fr/sections.php?op=printpage&artid=230 [consulté le 3 février 2009].

Bidault, Francis, *Le champ stratégique de l'entreprise*, Paris, Économica, 1989.

Böhm-Bawerk, Eugen von, *Théorie positive du capital*, Paris, Marcel Giard, 1929.

Borroni-Bird, Christopher E., « Designing AUTOnomy », *Scientific American Magazine*, http://www.sciam.com/article.cfm?id=designing-autonomy [consulté le 3 février 2009].

Burns, Lawrence D., J. Byron McCormick et Christopher E. Borroni-Bird, « Vehicle of Change », *Scientific American Magazine*, October 2002, Vol. 287, pp. 64–73.

Christensen, C., *The Innovator's Dilemma*, Boston, Harvard Business School Press, 1997.

Clark, Kim B. et Takahiro Fujimoto, *Product Development Performance: Strategy, Organization, and Management in the World Auto Industry*, Boston, Harvard Business School Press, 1991.

Coriat, Benjamin, *Penser à l'envers : Travail et organisation dans l'entreprise japonaise*, Paris, Christian Bourgois, 1991.

Ealey, Lance et Luis Troyano-Bermudez, « Are Automobiles the Next Commodity? », *McKinsey Quaterly* (novembre), 1996, 63-75.

Fujimoto, Takahiro, *Architecture, Capability, and Competitiveness of Firms and Industries*, Université de Tokyo, http://www.e.u-tokyo.ac.jp/cirje/research/dp/2002/2002cf182 [consulté le 20 août 2008].

Fujimoto, Takahiro et Ge Dongsheng. « The Architectural Attributes of Auto Parts and Transaction Patterns on Design Drawings », *International Journal of Automotive Technology and Management*, vol. 6, n° 4 (2006), 370-386.

Houssiaux, Jacques, *Le pouvoir de monopole : essai sur les structures industrielles du capitalisme contemporain*, Paris, Sirey, 1958.

Laurent, P. et Gilles Paquet, *Épistémologie de la relation – coordination et gouvernance distribuée*, Paris, Vrin, 1998.

Leblond, André et Gilles Paquet, « Stratégie et structure de l'entreprise de l'an 2000 », dans *Gestion stratégique internationale*, J. Jabes, (éd.), Économica, Paris, 1988.

MacKinsey. *HAWK 2015, Knowledge-based Changes in the Automotive Value Chain*, 2003, Rapport de recherche, Düsseldorf, McKinsey & Company, Inc.

Midler, Christophe et Christian Navarre, « Project Management in the Automotive Industry », dans Peter W.G. Morris et Jeffrey A. Pinto, (éd.), *The Resource Book On The Management Of Projects*, New York, Wiley, 2004, pp. 1368–1388.

Navarre, Christian et Jean-Louis Schaan, « De la bataille pour mieux produire… à la bataille pour mieux concevoir », *Gestion 2000: Management and Prospective*, Belgique, vol. 6, (décembre 1992), 13-30.

Navarre, Christian et F. Jolivet, « Automobile : du management par métiers au management par projets, objets et services », Innovation et Conception de projets – Congrès francophone du management du projet 2001, Actes des conférences, AFITEP, Paris, 6 et 7 novembre 2001.

Ostrom, E., *Governing the Commons: The Evolution of Institutions for Collective Actions*, Cambridge, University Press, 1990.

———., *Crafting Institutions for Self-governing Irrigation Systems*, San Francisco, ICS Press, Institute for Contemporary Studies, 1992.

Paquet, Gilles, *Smart Communities and the Geo-Governance of Social Learning*, Discussion Paper, 2001. http://gouvernance.ca/index.php?page=embed&lang=cf&embed=publications/01-02.pdf [consulted January 15, 2009]

———., *Pathologies de gouvernance : essais de technologie sociale*, Montréal, Éditions Liber, 2004.

———., *Gouvernance : une invitation à la subversion*, Montréal, Éditions Liber, 2005.

———., *Gouvernance mode d'emploi*, Montréal, Éditions Liber, 2008.

Paquet, Gilles et Jeffrey Roy, *Smarter Cities in Canada through E-Governance*, Ottawa, Centre on Governance, University of Ottawa, 2003. http://gouvernance.ca/index.php?page=embed&lang=cf&embed=publications/03-6.pdf [consulté le 5 février 2009].

Porter, Michael, E., *The Competitive Advantage: Creating and Sustaining Superior Performance*, New York, Free Press, 1985.

Rheingold H., *Smart Mobs, The Next Social Revolution*, Perseus Books Group, trad. fr. 2005, *Foules intelligentes, une révolution qui commence*, Paris, M2 Éditions, 2002.

Rosnay, Joël de. *Le macroscospe*, Paris, Seuil, 1975.

Womack, James P., Daniel T. Jones et Daniel Roos, *The Machine That Changed the World*, New York, Simon & Schuster, 1990.

Chapter 26

Gilles Paquet's Contributions to the Study of Higher Education

Michael L. Skolnik

About twenty years ago, I had the good fortune to come across the text of a presentation that Gilles Paquet (1988b) had given at a conference in Mississauga, Ontario. This presentation, which subsequently resulted in a publication (Paquet 1990), was on something called the Shadow Sector in higher education. The Shadow Sector is a term that has been used to refer to courses and programs that are similar to those provided by higher-education institutions but that are provided by other types of organizations than colleges or universities, particularly by private and public sector employers for their employees. The Shadow Sector was a rapidly emerging development in higher education in the 1980s. As a professor whose primary focus of study was the organization of higher education, I wanted to understand both why the Shadow Sector was expanding so rapidly and the implications of this expansion for traditional post-secondary institutions.

All of the literature that existed on this subject at that time was from the United States. I was thus delighted to discover a paper that looked at the Shadow Sector in a Canadian perspective and even offered estimates of the size of that sector in Canada. Not only that, but the paper also provided a theoretical framework for examining the Shadow Sector, something that was missing from the literature that existed on this subject. I was to learn subsequently that employing a theoretical framework as a foundation for analysis is a characteristic, and a considerable strength, of all of Paquet's writing about higher education.

I immediately wrote to Gilles after reading his paper, and after that we had what was for me a productive and enjoyable, if only occasional, correspondence.

I had the pleasure of engaging Gilles as external examiner for one of my PhD students, who did a very ambitious and sophisticated dissertation, ironically, on an aspect of the "non-shadow sector," the use that large corporations make of universities for developing the knowledge and skills of their managers. I had a very enjoyable interaction with Gilles at an extraordinary conference in the late 1980s on the state of liberal education in Canadian universities, sponsored by the Social Science Federation of Canada. In 2006, I was asked to write a "think-piece" for a review of post-secondary education in British Columbia that the government there was conducting. I was delighted when I discovered that Gilles was also one of the handful of people asked to produce a think-piece for this review. I consider Gilles's think-piece—which started off with a wonderful explanation of what a think-piece, ideally, should aim to accomplish—one of the outstanding essays that I have read in the field of higher education. It provides a beautiful example of the insights pertaining to a field of study that can be offered by a thoughtful and well-informed scholar who understands but is not immersed in that field of study.

In the commentary that follows, I view the two pieces of Gilles's writing about higher education that I have just described as the bookends. My objective here is to summarize briefly what I regard as his major contributions to the study of higher education, and to show how his contributions can deepen our understanding of important developments and problems in higher education, including some issues in higher education that his work does not address. I also want to place Gilles's contributions within the literature on, and current discourse about, higher education. Since most of his writing that I will be dealing with here dates back to the late 1980s or early 1990s, I will also be interested in how well it fits the circumstances of late in the first decade of the twenty-first century.

Theoretical Framework
The foundation of Paquet's analyses of various issues in higher education is a depiction of the major goals of education or human capital formation in the form of a triangle in which each apex refers to one of the goals: education, training, and personal development. Any higher-education program, institution, or even system may be characterized by locating it at a point within this triangle that corresponds to the relative prominence given to each of the three goals. In this framework, education is defined in terms of "the development of the mind and the ability to reason; Training as pertaining to the acquisition of skills and practical knowledge;

Development as broadly embracing components of both, but also development of character, self-awareness and interpersonal/communication capabilities and competence" (Paquet 1988b, 2). In his most recent exposition of this theoretical framework, Paquet (2006) uses the French-language terms *savoirs*, *savoir-faire*, and *savoir-être* for the three goals of post-secondary education. I found these terms to be even more evocative of the differences that Gilles is attempting to elucidate than education, training, and development. I also found the elaboration on these concepts in the 2006 paper to be particularly helpful in understanding the distinctions. There Gilles draws on "the Aristotelian triad of *episteme*, *techne*, and *phronesis*: knowledge that is universal, general, and non-contextual; knowledge that is practical, instrumental, product-oriented know-how; and knowledge that is experience-based, prudence, practical wisdom concerning how to exercise ethical and moral judgment in particular and concrete situations" (19).

An important part of the theoretical framework is the explanation of how the predominant understanding of the education apex of the triangle evolved through the late nineteenth and twentieth centuries particularly as a result of positivist influence. This part of human capital formation has come to be construed more and more in terms of the development of the capability to analyze and reason through content-neutral curricula, and emphasis on theory and especially methodology and a corresponding lessening or abandoning of interest in the local, particular, and contextual. A common thread in Gilles's writing about post-secondary education is his concern about the reductionist view of knowledge that lies at the heart of the university, as Gilles explained in the 2006 paper: "For years, I have been bemoaning the reductive turn that higher education in Canada has taken: a turn to content-free Methodism, based on a disembodied form of literacy and numeracy, and taking more and more distance from a broader approach that would allow for the full use of the whole range of types of perceptions and knowledge, the improvement of skills, and the personal development of the individual" (3).

In parallel with the decontextualization of education, there has been a tendency toward uncoupling the three major goals from one another. Gilles laments that trend and argues that the process of human capital formation is at its most vital, robust, and useful when it involves the presence of all three and ideally integration among them. Instead of integration, however, what has occurred is compartmentalization of the three goals into different institutional realms. Gilles's writing focuses mainly on two of these realms and describes the consequences of a situation in which universities concentrate on education, while colleges and technical institutes concentrate on training. Rereading his work for this chapter led me to reflect on what has happened to the personal development function. It used to be thought of as a major function of the university. For example, the institutional paradigm associated with Newman's idea of the university has been described as the personality development model (Gellert 1991, 34). It seems, however, that now personal development has ceased to be an explicit goal of the formal post-secondary system and is left to adult educators, or perhaps more often to purveyors of various psychological therapies, implying that there is something pathological about the quest for personal development.

As specialization has proceeded among the providers of programs that correspond to each of the three goals, the corresponding status hierarchy that has developed among the different providers has become sharper and more rigid. At the top of the hierarchy stands not just institutions called universities but also those institutions that subscribe to a particular idea of what a university should be. That idea of the university excludes institutions whose programs are judged to be more practical and training intensive regardless of the sophistication and complexity of their curricula. Institutions that focus substantially on knowledge that is more applied and experiential rather than abstract and general occupy a much lower place on the status hierarchy of post-secondary education. The difference in the social status of the institutions and organizations that serve the different goals of education and human capital formation have had important limiting implications for the types of opportunities available for learners.

Issues Addressed in Paquet's Writings on Higher Education

Paquet's writings on higher education examine six interrelated issues within the context of the theoretical framework described above: (1) problems of education and research in the professions; (2) lack of meaning and coherence in the undergraduate curriculum; (3) loss of purpose in the social sciences and humanities; (4) disarray in the state of technical education; (5) problems in the relationship between the university and the educational needs of the workplace; and (6) the crisis of confidence in higher education.

At the heart of Paquet's critique of professional education in the contemporary university is the idea that, for many professions, including that of management, immersion in that milieu has led to the adoption of an epistemology that is poorly suited to the needs of education and research in the professions (Paquet 1989a, 50). What Paquet refers to as "contagion and coercion" from the scientific disciplines are what in the literature on higher education are called the conformity-producing effects of normative, coercive, and mimetic isomorphisms (Bess and Dee 2008; Huisman 1998). Paquet describes how pressure on the field of management to conform to the same knowledge paradigm as the pure disciplines has thwarted attempts to develop a different epistemology, one similar to Schon's (1983) idea of reflection-in-action or what Paquet describes as delta knowledge (Gilles and Paquet 1989). Delta knowledge "depends on learning by doing, conversation with the situation that focuses on know-how more than know-that, and is produced according to rules that are largely implicit, overlapping, diverse, variously applied, contextually dependent, subject to exceptions and to critical modifications" (Paquet 2006, 17). In these alternative knowledge paradigms, which typically take as their starting point issues encountered in practice, theory is more a product than a precursor of learning from experience and problem solving in a particular context. Besides its similarities to Schon's more general critiques of the state of professional education, Paquet's analysis of the problems of management education is consistent also with what my colleague David Hunt (1987) argued to be the case in the fields of education and psychology and with what I wrote concerning the field of education (Skolnik 1989).

The problems of professional education in the contemporary university that Paquet described so well for management are also evident in another field that I have looked at, nursing education. The first university nursing education program in Canada was established in 1919. Yet until recently only a small proportion of nurses was trained in universities, mainly those destined for senior management and research positions. As of the mid-1960s in Ontario, universities accounted for only about five percent of nursing graduates and by the mid-1990s less than twenty percent. During this long period, the kind of split that Paquet described was striking: most new nurses came from college programs and were products of a training culture; the minority came from university programs with the limitations that Paquet argues were inherent in the education model when it was divorced from training (and development). It was not only cost considerations that prevented nursing education from shifting wholly to the university but perhaps even more so concerns about a possible weakening of the connection between education and practice.

With the recent decisions of most provincial governments to require a baccalaureate for entry into nursing, the universities have gained control over nursing education, with the consequences for the dominant knowledge paradigm within the nursing field being similar to what Paquet reported for management education. For example, a former doctoral student of mine, Vickie Greenslade, showed in her PhD dissertation (2003) how nursing practice is being squeezed out of the professional activity profile of nursing educators. It will be difficult for nursing educators, who are not themselves engaged in practice, to teach delta knowledge or develop in their students the skills and habits of reflection-in-action. Largely for economic reasons, but also in the hope of having a good blend of education and training in the preparation of nurses, governments have been promoting joint university-college programs for preparing new nurses. However, because of the control that universities have over curriculum and staffing arising from their degree-granting authority, the university knowledge paradigm is the dominant paradigm in the joint programs too. The nursing profession will have gained the status that comes with being a university-based profession—but at what cost in regard to the practical knowledge of nurses of the future?

In other writing, Paquet developed the implications of his critiques for the core arts and sciences division of the university. He observed that, when combined with the imperatives of professionalism, the paradigm of knowledge specialization resulted in an incoherent curriculum for undergraduates. The curriculum is made up of courses from various disciplines, each of which is designed to prepare students for the next course in a hierarchy of knowledge within the discipline, rather than to articulate horizontally with courses in other disciplines and thus enable the student to integrate knowledge from different areas. However, rather than moving from this analysis to calling for "a new classicism," as critics such as Bloom (1987) have done, Paquet (1989b) urged a rethinking of the purpose of undergraduate education and the laborious process of attempting to derive curriculum principles from goals.

In a related vein, another Paquet writing (1988a) voiced concern about the effects of overspecialization and scholasticism within disciplines on the nature of inquiry in the social sciences and humanities. Drawing upon literature on the sociology of knowledge and the history of the university, Gilles argues that, in parallel with "the displacement of content by process," these fields have lost touch with the questions that led to their founding. In rereading this essay recently, I was struck by how well it forewarned of a trend that has accelerated over the past two decades and how effectively it integrated a number of related criticisms of the academy. For example, the problem of unreadable prose coming off academic presses that so many have remarked about recently was described by Paquet in this way in 1988: "an increase in the volume of publications read by an ever-diminishing number of people, both because of general lack of interest in the issues discussed and because of the technical and opaque verbiage in which it is couched" (37). I am reminded of Robert Fulford's (1998a) description of such writing as reflecting "the new illiteracy." Paquet's own writing on this subject supports by example Stephen Klees's wonderful remark that the claim to expertise by social scientists rests not on their theories and empirical methodologies but on the fact that they "are *trained* to be articulate and thoughtful examiners of ideas and their implications" (1986, 607). In the context of this chapter, I think it appropriate to italicize the word *trained*.

From the late 1970s onward, many articles and books about higher education have alleged that the enterprise is gripped by some sort of crisis (Birnbaum and Shushok 1998; Jones 1990; Tight 1994). The problems that Paquet described in the social sciences and humanities and in the professional faculties, reflect some of what has been referred to as the crisis in higher education in this body of literature. However, in contrast to most of the "crisis in higher education" literature, which is characterized by vagueness, overgeneralization, and hyperbole, Paquet restricts his use of the term to a crisis of confidence, and he is very specific about the nature and causes of that crisis: higher education is failing to meet the needs of many learners and significant stakeholders. In the essay in which he talks about a general crisis of confidence, he considers possible remedies and raises the question of whether we need a national strategy for post-secondary education in Canada (Paquet 1987). This, of course, is an idea that keeps resurfacing and in fact has been advocated again recently by both the Canadian Council on Learning (2007) and former Ontario premier William Davis (2008). As for dealing with the problems that he describes, Paquet suggests two general approaches: greater intervention by the government in higher education, and freeing up the market for higher education so that competition can bring about needed change. He doesn't develop these ideas in much detail, though the 2006 think-piece contains some creative proposals for the transformation of higher education that no doubt would be considered outlandish by the higher-education establishment. For example, one suggestion is that the requirement to create, teach, and disseminate delta knowledge be integrated formally into the mandates of all post-secondary education institutions.

An Extrapolation of Paquet's Analysis: Indigenous Knowledge

Besides the facets of higher education that Paquet discusses in his writings, another area where his analysis fits quite well is in regard to the place and treatment of indigenous knowledge. Such knowledge seems to be a good example of an educational phenomenon in which all three types of human capital formation are highly integrated and in which personal development has an important place. It has in common with delta knowledge that it is strongly embedded in practice, and much of it is local, oral, and tacit. Because indigenous knowledge involves such a different paradigm than the dominant scientific paradigm in academe, universities don't know how to deal with it. The dominant academic community is torn between its desire to show respect for Aboriginal culture, and its inability to apply its normal criteria for assessing the validity of knowledge and the quality of teaching and research in this area of study. Many Aboriginal educators believe that their institutions and programs cannot be judged fairly by academics whose frame of reference involves such different assumptions and values concerning knowledge and scholarship. In reaction to similar concerns felt by Aboriginal educators in different countries, there now exists an international indigenous accreditation body under the auspices of the World Indigenous Nations Higher Education Consortium (Corbiere 2007). Although there are historical, cultural, and political issues that are unique to Aboriginal post-secondary education, there are also issues that Aboriginal education has in common with other sectors of post-secondary education that have to struggle against barriers of epistemological bias and social status to gain recognition of programs that value applied knowledge and personal development. Paquet's theoretical framework helps us to understand these commonalities.

The Problem of Technical or Polytechnical Education

In recent years, one of my main areas of academic interest has been the design of higher-education systems, particularly the relationship between different types of post-secondary institutions. I have found Gilles's theoretical framework particularly helpful in thinking about this issue. Because of the institutional separation of training from education and the lower social status of training that

Gilles describes, it has proven difficult to offer high-level programs that combine training and education in Canada. At the time of his first essays on this subject, Canada had two technical universities, Ryerson Polytechnical Institute in Toronto, and the Technical University of Nova Scotia (TUNS) in Halifax. During the 1990s, both institutions underwent significant changes. In Nova Scotia, TUNS was abolished and its resources transferred to Dalhousie University. Ryerson Polytechnical Institute was transformed into Ryerson University. Some advocates of technical education alleged that in this transformation Ryerson became a conventional university, although it continues to describe itself on its website as a place of "quality, career-ready learning that combines academic rigour with relevant practical experience." Still, with the kinds of pressure that Ryerson will likely face to conform to the mainstream university model, as described by Paquet and the institutional differentiation literature referred to earlier, the removal of the word *polytechnical* from its name is not an encouraging sign for those who believe that there is a need for a technical university in Ontario.

Another technical university, the Technical University of British Columbia, was started in 1999 and closed in 2002, the same year as the University of Ontario Institute of Technology (UOIT) came into being. The UOIT was established in response to the articulation of two quite different needs: to provide the same type of higher-education opportunities for the population of the Durham-Northumberland region of Ontario as existed in other regions, and to be a university-level institute of technology. These two distinct visions of the institution will likely be in conflict as it develops. Paquet's analysis of the dynamics of such conflict among the different goals of post-secondary education suggests that the more mainstream model of the university may prevail in this case.

Another noteworthy attempt to combine education and training within a single post-secondary institution was the establishment of five university colleges in British Columbia. These institutions were intended to combine the academic character of the university with the applied and open-access orientations of the college. This experiment with a new type of educational institution was brought to a halt when the Commission on Post-secondary Education in British Columbia for which both Gilles and I wrote think-pieces decided that there wasn't a place in the BC post-secondary landscape for hybrid institutions (Plant 2007). I don't like to think about what it says about our persuasive powers that both of us had touted the virtues of hybrid institutions in our think-pieces. The commission's conclusion, which was accepted by the government, was that post-secondary institutions had to be either universities or colleges, and since it was impractical to move back to being colleges these institutions should become universities. A few years earlier Canada's only other university college, University College of Cape Breton in Nova Scotia, had been converted into a university for the same reason. This reasoning reflects what my colleague Charles Pascal describes as "hardening of the categories."

In spite of these setbacks, the quest to create institutions that combine the academic characteristics of the university with the practical orientation of the college continues. In the same year as the BC commission reported, the Commission on Post-secondary Education in New Brunswick submitted a report with recommendations that were diametrically opposed to those of the BC commission. The New Brunswick commission recommended combining the St. John campus of New Brunswick Community College with the St. John campus of the University of New Brunswick to create a new polytechnical institution (Commission on Post-secondary Education in New Brunswick 2007). Apparently, the university faculty in New Brunswick have the same views about hybrid post-secondary institutions as the BC commission. The reaction of university faculty in New Brunswick has been so negative that this recommendation seems unlikely to be implemented.

While the polytechnical idea may have suffered setbacks in British Columbia and New Brunswick, there is still a national organization, made up of seven colleges and institutes in Alberta, Ontario, and British Columbia, that continues to advocate for the virtues of this model of post-secondary education. Moreover, Alberta, which usually seems to have the most sensible approach to post-secondary education of any province, recently decided to give polytechnical status to its two institutes of technology. Ontario continues to deliberate on whether to give polytechnical status to any of its colleges, and in what is perhaps the grandest validation of Paquet's critiques of education policy, British Columbia seems to have ignored the venerable and highly regarded British Columbia Institute of Technology while at the same time elevating five other institutions to university status.

Simultaneous to many of the developments pertaining to technical universities and polytechnicals that I have just been describing, colleges in Alberta, British Columbia, and Ontario were given the authority to award applied degrees in selected areas. I have described this development in a chapter of a book that examines similar developments in the United States (Floyd, Skolnik, and Walker 2005). It is not entirely clear where these applied degrees would fit in Paquet's triangle. Since the liberal education components of these degree programs are pretty modest, I would regard the degrees as still being close to the training apex of the triangle, though with a higher level of sophistication and complexity of the career education content than the sub-baccalaureate programs offered by the colleges.

The appearance of colleges awarding baccalaureates—even if in small numbers—and engaging in formal programs of research—even if exclusively of the applied variety—has led to the assertion that the traditional boundary between colleges and universities has been breached. Moreover, the increased emphasis in universities on commercialization of research and the introduction of several applied, career-focused, baccalaureate programs there, such as sports management, oenology and viticulture, advanced wood processing, and commercial aviation management, suggests that the breach is coming from both directions. Judging just from the program names, such programs seem to be more narrowly focused than older, university, career-oriented programs such as engineering and business. On the basis of such evidence, it has been alleged that a blurring of the boundary between sectors is occurring in Canadian higher education (Fisher and Rubenson 1998). These new university programs may constitute a significant departure from the university program model that Paquet described, but without more study of the actual curricula of the new programs it is not possible to tell how closely they resemble the kinds of programs offered in the colleges. As for the applied baccalaureate programs offered by the colleges, they seem to be an extension of their existing career education mandate with fairly limited liberal arts content, especially in the Alberta programs. Also, the enrolment in these programs is relatively small; for example, in Ontario college baccalaureate programs account for less than one percent of total enrolment in post-secondary programs. In short, during the past decade, there may have been a modest market-induced shift away from the institutional separation of education from training that Paquet describes, but more research is necessary to demonstrate how much of a shift has actually occurred.

I hope that in this brief chapter I have been able to give you some sense of the value and significance of Paquet's contributions to the study of higher education. Although this chapter may suggest otherwise, I do not find myself in agreement with all of his observations about higher education. For example, I have slightly different views than Gilles about the reasons for the expansion of the Shadow

Sector. Still, I find that, whether I agree or not with anything in his writing about higher education, his work enhances my understanding of my field in the ways that he describes a think-piece is meant to "provoke reflection, but also to generate positive and negative reactions from the readership with a view to breaking out of the box of conventional thinking, and to producing innovating avenues that might not have been explored otherwise" (Paquet 2006, 2).

References

Bess, J. L., and J. R. Dee. (2008). *Understanding College and University Organization*. Vol. 1. Sterling, VA: Stylus Publishing.

Birnbaum, R., and F. Shushok. (1998). "The Crisis in Higher Education: Is That a Wolf or a Pussycat at the Academy's Door?" Paper presented at the Twenty-Third Annual Conference of the Association for the Study of Higher Education, Miami, November 5–8.

Bloom, A. (1987). *The Closing of the American Mind*. New York: Simon and Schuster.

Canadian Council on Learning. (2007). *Report on Learning in Canada 2007*. Ottawa: Canadian Council on Learning.

Commission on Post-secondary Education in New Brunswick. (2007). *Advantage New Brunswick: A Province Reaches to Fulfill Its Destiny*. Fredericton: Commission on Post-secondary Education in New Brunswick.

Corbiere, M. (2007). "Accreditation and Aboriginal Higher Education: An Issue of Peoplehood." PhD diss., University of Toronto.

Davis, W. (2008). "National Strategy Vital for Advanced Education." *College Voice, January, 2008*, 2. www.collegesontario.ca.

Fisher, D., and K. Rubenson. (1998). "The Changing Political Economy: The Private and Public Lives of Canadian Universities." In *Universities and Globalization: Critical Perspectives*, ed. J. Currie and J. Newsom. London: Sage Publications, 77–98.

Floyd, D. L., M. L. Skolnik, and K. P. Walker. (2005). *The Community College Baccalaureate: Emerging Trends and Policy Issues*. Sterling, VA: Stylus Publishing.

Fulford, R. (1989). *Literature and Literacy: The Future of English Studies*. The 1989 Jackson Lecture. Ontario Institute for Studies in Education. Toronto: OISE Press.

Gellert, C. (1991). "Higher Education: Changing Tasks and Definitions." *Higher Education in Europe, 16.3*, 28–45.

Gilles, W., and G. Paquet. (1989). "On Delta Knowledge." In *Edging towards the Year 2000: Management Research and Education in Canada*, ed. G. Paquet and M. von Zur Muehlen. Ottawa: Canadian Federation of Deans of Management and Administrative Studies, 15–30.

Greenslade, M. V. (2003). "Faculty Practice as Scholarship in University Schools of Nursing." PhD diss., University of Toronto.

Huisman, J. (1998). "Differentiation and Diversity in Higher Education Systems." In *Higher Education Handbook of Theory and Research, Vol XIII*, ed. J. C. Smart. New York: Agathon Press 1998, 75-109.

Hunt, D. E. (1987). *Beginning with Ourselves: In Practice, Theory, and Human Affairs*. Brookline, MA: Brookline Books.

Jones, G. A. (1990). "Imminent Disaster Revisited, Again: The Crisis Literature of Canadian Higher Education." *Canadian Journal of Higher Education, 20.2*, 1–8.

Klees, S. J. (1986). "Planning and Policy Analysis in Education: What Can Economists Tell Us?" *Comparative Education Review, 30*, 574–607.

Paquet, G. (1987). "Post-Secondary Education: An Enterprise Less than Optimally Managed?" In *Education Canada? Higher Education on the Brink*, ed. G. Paquet and M. von Zur Muehlen. Ottawa: Canadian Higher Education Research Network, 1–10.

———. (1988a). "Two Tramps in Mud Time: Social Sciences and Humanities in Modern Society." In *The Human Sciences: Contributions to Society and Future Research Needs*, ed. B. Abu-Laban and B. G. Rule. Edmonton: University of Alberta Press, 29–57.

———. (1988b). "Training and Development: The Shadow Higher Education Sector in Canada." Paper prepared for the Canada–UK Colloquium on Post-secondary Education, Mississauga, November 21–22.

———. (1989a). "Management Education and Research beyond the Ivory Tower." In *Edging towards the Year 2000: Management Research and Education in Canada*, ed. G. Paquet and M. von Zur Muehlen. Ottawa: Canadian Federation of Deans of Management and Administrative Studies, 49–64.

———. (1989b). "Liberal Education as Synecdoche." In *Who's Afraid of Liberal Education?*, ed. C. Andrew and S. B. Esbensen. Ottawa: Social Science Federation of Canada, 1–20.

———. (1990). "Training and Development: The Shadow Higher Education Sector in Canada." In *Post-Secondary Education: Preparation for the World of Work*, ed. R. L. Watts and J. Greenberg. London, UK: Dartmouth Press, 189–202.

———. (2006). "Savoirs, savoir-faire, savoir-être: In Praise of Professional Wroughting and Wrighting." A think-piece prepared for Campus 2020, an inquiry into the future of British Columbia's post-secondary education system. http://www.aved.gov.bc.ca/campus220/think_pieces.htm [consulted January 18, 2009].

Plant, G. (2007). *Campus 2020, Thinking Ahead: The Report*. Victoria: Ministry of Advanced Education.

Schon, D. A. (1983). *The Reflective Practitioner*. New York: Basic Books.

Skolnik, M. L. (1989). "How Academic Program Review Can Foster Intellectual Conformity and Stifle Diversity of Thought and Method in the University." *Journal of Higher Education, 60.6*, 619–43.

Tight, M. (1994). "Crisis, What Crisis? Rhetoric and Reality in Higher Education." *British Journal of Educational Studies, 42.4*, 363–74.

Part Nine

Interpretations

Chapitre 27

Six observations sur la croissance québécoise à la manière de Gilles Paquet

Pierre Fortin

Les gens ont des raisons de faire ce qu'ils font.

—Herbert Simon

Le conformisme est la plaie de l'université.

—Maurice Bouchard

Ayant lu à un tout jeune âge l'*Histoire économique et sociale du Québec 1760-1850* de Fernand Ouellet, j'ai adhéré au départ à l'image que les littérateurs de son époque ont construit de la société canadienne-française d'autrefois : un peuple empêtré dans une irrationalité aveugle et un conservatisme indécrottable, qu'il fallait sortir au plus tôt de son état d'arriération économique et sociale. Cependant, dans les années 1970, les travaux de Paquet et Wallot, colligés dans leur livre récent *Un Québec moderne 1760-1840*, m'ont fait découvrir que les habitants canadiens-français n'étaient pas exactement la bande d'arriérés qu'on avait dit. Ces gens, comme disait Herbert Simon, avaient des raisons de faire ce qu'ils faisaient. Le devoir des chercheurs était de comprendre cette rationalité avant de juger.

Paquet, contestataire et inspirateur

Paquet et Wallot ont établi que les habitants maximisaient astucieusement le rendement économique sous les contraintes institutionnelles et géotechniques auxquelles ils étaient confrontés. De plus, ils ont démontré que les Canadiens français ont commencé à entrer dans la modernité dès la fin du XVIIIe siècle, passant de la trappe et de l'agriculture au capitalisme commercial, puis industriel, et luttant pour accéder au parlementarisme responsable. Paquet et Wallot ont aussi fait la preuve qu'en histoire, comme dans les autres sciences humaines, la minutie quantitative est payante, pourvu que la longue et pénible identification de chacun des arbres ne finisse pas par faire perdre de vue la forêt et sa trame événementielle.

J'ai ensuite appris à connaître plus personnellement cet admirable contestataire qu'est Gilles Paquet. Les chercheurs qui font avancer les choses ne sont pas les conformistes qui ajoutent des points-virgules aux paradigmes dominants, mais plutôt les contestataires qui, comme lui, mettent en question de grands pans de l'ordre intellectuel reçu. Ses analyses de l'arriération économique présumée des Canadiens français et des conséquences de la Révolution tranquille des années 1960 au Québec ressortent tout particulièrement. Non seulement elles rejettent la sagesse conventionnelle, mais elles proposent des interprétations alternatives cohérentes. Paquet n'a pas toujours raison. Mais même quand il se trompe, il le fait de la bonne manière, et jamais sur une insignifiance.

Paquet est l'un des premiers économistes canadiens à avoir promu l'analyse *behaviorale*, laquelle vise à intégrer en économie les découvertes de la psychologie et de la sociologie. Son insistance sur le rôle économique fondamental de l'identité, des institutions et du capital social a été précoce. Elle n'a attendu ni Akerlof ni Acemoglu ni Putnam ni Helliwell. Paquet a ardemment défendu l'insertion de l'intellectuel dans la vie publique. En ce domaine, il a montré la voie en s'impliquant plus que tout autre économiste canadien de sa génération dans les corps scientifiques et dans l'activité médiatique. Il est une inspiration pour ceux d'entre nous qui cherchons à débarrasser l'analyse économique de ses œillères disciplinaires et à communiquer ses intuitions de base à un public large.

C'est sur le sujet de la croissance économique du Québec au XXe siècle — plutôt qu'aux XVIIIe et XIXe — que mes intérêts scientifiques ont surtout croisé ceux de Paquet. J'ai donc pensé que la meilleure façon de lui rendre hommage est de proposer un programme de recherche structuré sur certaines grandes questions que pose la croissance québécoise contemporaine.

Paquet s'est surtout appliqué à comprendre la politique économique de Maurice Duplessis et de Jean Lesage, son successeur qui a lancé la Révolution tranquille en 1960. Son ouvrage *Oublier la Révolution tranquille* n'a pas été tendre pour les artisans et les profiteurs — citélibristes comme nationalistes — de cette révolution. La thèse qui s'y trouve avancée est qu'en pratiquant la coupe à blanc dans les institutions traditionnelles du Québec, ces gens ont saccagé sans discernement le capital communautaire accumulé depuis deux siècles, ils ont entraîné le Québec dans un étatisme et un corporatisme outranciers, et ils ont ainsi freiné son essor économique et social. Le Québec aurait ainsi sombré dans les travers appréhendés aussi bien par Putnam que par Olson.

Pour une estimation précise de la trajectoire de la croissance québécoise

Il n'y a aucun doute dans mon esprit que la thèse d'*Oublier la Révolution tranquille* contient plusieurs éléments de vérité. Le travail de Paquet sur la Révolution tranquille n'a cependant pas encore la solidité empirique de celui qu'il a accompli avec Wallot sur la période 1760-1840. Cela s'explique en partie par l'absence, dans la littérature contemporaine, d'une estimation précise de la trajectoire de la croissance québécoise au XXe siècle. J'ai pensé qu'une bonne façon de rendre hommage à la manière de Paquet est de présenter une telle estimation. Il va forcément en sortir un bouquet de questions à poser et d'hypothèses à vérifier sur l'histoire économique du Québec contemporain.

J'emprunte la voie comparative. La croissance économique du Québec réagit à certaines forces qui lui sont spécifiques, mais elle résulte également de nombreux facteurs d'origine extérieure — nationaux, continentaux, mondiaux. Afin d'isoler les aspects spécifiques, j'adopte la stratégie très simple qui consiste à étudier comment évolue dans le temps le *rapport* entre la trajectoire de la croissance québécoise et celle de la croissance ontarienne. Un tel rapport élimine en grande partie l'influence des facteurs d'origine extérieure et il fait porter l'attention sur les phénomènes propres aux deux provinces. Le choix de l'Ontario, province sœur du Québec, est naturel. L'Ontario est le cœur de l'économie canadienne par la taille, la profondeur et la diversité. Comparer le Québec à un ensemble incluant les provinces qui sont éloignées ou dont l'économie dépend en grande partie de l'exploitation des ressources naturelles n'aurait aucun sens.

L'observation de la croissance économique du Québec et de l'Ontario repose sur l'évolution estimée de leur *revenu réel par habitant d'âge actif*. Pour chaque province, on obtient cette mesure en divisant le produit intérieur brut (PIB) par l'indice des prix de la dépense intérieure, et le résultat par la population de 15 à 64 ans[1].

De la Confédération à 1929 : la double constatation de Raynauld

Pour commencer, le tableau 1 présente le rapport entre le revenu par habitant du Québec et celui de l'Ontario à intervalles de 20 ans en 1870, 1890, 1910 et 1929. Ce rapport n'affiche pas de fluctuations très fortes de 20 ans en 20 ans. Le Québec et l'Ontario semblent avoir suivi, depuis la Confédération jusqu'en 1929, des trajectoires de croissance à peu près parallèles. Cette constatation fut faite par Raynauld en 1961[2]. Elle comporte deux éléments. D'une part, le taux de croissance annuel moyen du revenu par habitant paraît avoir été à peu près le même dans les deux provinces. Mais, d'autre part, la trajectoire québécoise s'est maintenue continuellement sous la trajectoire ontarienne, accusant un retard de 16 % à 19 % selon les époques. L'observation importante est que, pendant ces 60 années, le revenu par habitant du Québec n'a pas manifesté de tendance ferme à rattraper celui de l'Ontario.

Tableau 1 : Revenu réel par habitant d'âge actif du Québec exprimé en pourcentage de celui de l'Ontario pour les années 1870, 1890, 1910 et 1929

Année	Québec en pourcentage de l'Ontario
1870	84 %
1890	82 %
1910	81 %
1929	84 %

Source : Calculs basés sur les données de Inwood et Irwin, de Green et des recensements du Canada[3]

De 1929 à aujourd'hui : un découpage en cinq épisodes

La figure 1 trace l'évolution du même rapport entre le revenu par habitant du Québec et celui de l'Ontario avec les données annuelles de la période de 82 ans allant de 1926 à 2007[4]. Il y a une différence majeure entre les résultats de la figure 1 et ceux du tableau 1. Faute de données probantes, les chercheurs qui ont construit les données conduisant aux pourcentages du tableau ont imposé l'hypothèse que les dollars dépensés avaient le même pouvoir d'achat au Québec qu'en Ontario en 1935-1939. Cette hypothèse est contraire à la réalité. La figure corrige le tir. Elle adopte le point de vue plus vraisemblable que le coût de la vie était plus élevé en

Ontario qu'au Québec en 1935-1939 comme en 2007[5]. La trajectoire comparative du revenu par habitant du Québec sur la figure s'en trouve ainsi relevée par rapport aux données du tableau 1. Cela explique que, pour l'année 1929, le rapport Québec-Ontario non corrigé soit de 84 % au tableau 1 et qu'il soit porté à 92 % une fois la correction introduite sur la figure 1. C'est évidemment ce dernier pourcentage qui est plus fidèle à la réalité.

Figure 1 : Revenu réel par habitant d'âge actif du Québec exprimé en pourcentage de celui de l'Ontario, 1926-2007

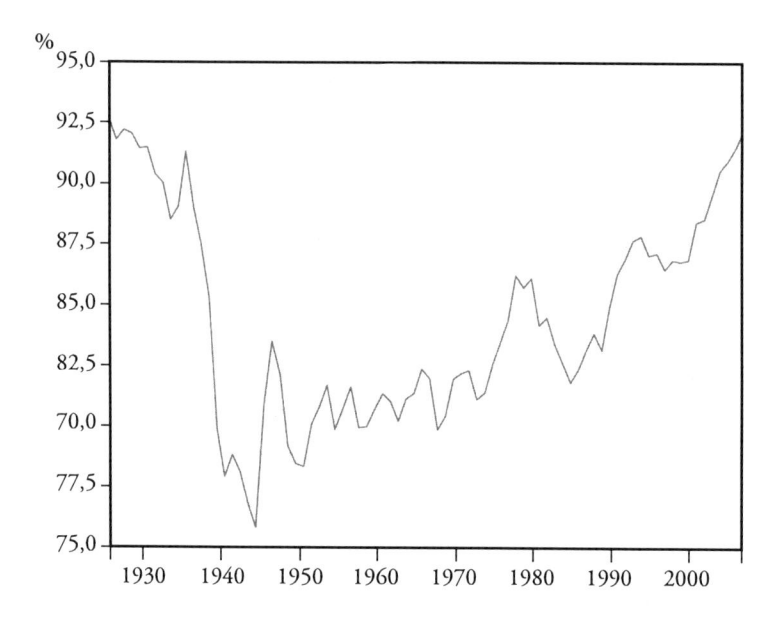

Source : Calculs basés sur les données de Statistique Canada

La trajectoire de la figure 1 évoque un découpage de la période 1929-2007 en cinq épisodes : la Grande Dépression des années 1930, la Guerre de 1939-1945, les Trente glorieuses (1945-1975), la « descente aux enfers » de 1975 à 1989 et la « résurrection » de 1989 à aujourd'hui. Le tableau 2 montre comment les changements dans le rapport Québec-Ontario dépendent précisément des différences observées dans la croissance cumulative du revenu par habitant de chacune des deux provinces prise séparément.

Tableau 2 : Croissance cumulative du revenu réel par habitant d'âge actif au Québec et en Ontario au cours de cinq épisodes de la période 1929-2007

Épisode	Québec	Ontario	Québec *moins* Ontario
Grande Dépression (1929-1939)	-12 %	-5 %	-7 %
Guerre de 1939-1945	47 %	66 %	-11 %
Trente glorieuses (1945-1975)	132 %	113 %	9 %
Descente aux enfers (1975-1989)	34 %	34 %	1 %
Résurrection (1989-2007)	33 %	19 %	11 %

Source : Données sous-jacentes de la figure 1

La Grande Dépression et la Guerre de 1939-1945 : la dégringolade du Québec

Au départ, la Grande Dépression n'a pas frappé l'économie du Québec beaucoup plus durement que celle de l'Ontario. Du sommet de 1929 au creux de 1933, le revenu par habitant a plongé de 26 % en Ontario et de 28 % au Québec. La croissance a récupéré assez rapidement au Québec en 1936, mais elle a ensuite eu grand peine à suivre la croissance ontarienne en 1937-1939.

La dégringolade relative du Québec a été encore pire pendant le deuxième épisode identifié par le tableau 2, soit celui de la Guerre de 1939-1945. Ce furent, comme on sait, des années de croissance rapide pour les deux provinces, mais, relativement parlant, la croissance cumulative de 66 % en Ontario pendant ces six années a laissé sur place celle de 47 % au Québec. Loin de se redresser, la position comparative du Québec a continué à se détériorer en 1940 et pendant le reste de la Guerre. De 92 % de celui de l'Ontario en 1929, le revenu par habitant du Québec a atterri à 76 % en 1945. Ce n'est que 62 ans plus tard, en 2007, que le Québec a pu regagner complètement le terrain perdu par rapport à l'Ontario pendant la Dépression et la Guerre.

Les causes de la sous-performance du Québec pendant la Guerre n'ont pas été bien étudiées. Une hypothèse intéressante à explorer est que le Québec a payé cher la réticence de sa population à appuyer l'effort de guerre. La solde militaire, qui atteignit 1,1 milliard de dollars ou 22 % de la rémunération civile totale au Canada en 1944, offre un bon exemple. Les parts respectives du Québec et de l'Ontario dans cette solde étaient de 100 et de 500 millions de dollars. Ces montants représentaient donc 9 % et 45 % du total canadien. Or, en 1944, les hommes de 18 à 64 ans du Québec et de l'Ontario formaient respectivement 27 % et 34 % de ce groupe d'âge au pays. La distorsion régionale de la solde militaire fut donc très prononcée. Il est possible qu'elle ait été également présente dans les autres dépenses de la défense nationale, qui dépassèrent 2,5 milliards en 1944, ainsi que dans les activités militaro-industrielles du secteur privé. Cela doit être vérifié.

Les Trente glorieuses (1945-1975) : la récupération incomplète
Le troisième épisode reconnu par le tableau 2 est celui des Trente glorieuses (1945-1975). Pendant ces trois décennies, l'économie a progressé à vive allure au Québec comme en Ontario. Cumulativement, le revenu par habitant du Québec a pu dégager un avantage de 9 % sur celui de l'Ontario. Toutefois, la figure 1 montre que cet avantage traduit principalement une récupération — très incomplète — qui a eu lieu dans l'après-guerre immédiat. À la fin de la Guerre de Corée, en 1953, le revenu par habitant du Québec avait réussi à remonter un peu au-dessus de 80 % de celui de l'Ontario. La croissance s'est bel et bien poursuivie pendant les 20 années qui ont suivi, y compris celles de la Révolution tranquille (1960-1966), mais la performance relative du Québec a alors connu un parcours en dents de scie sans tendance marquée. À la fin des Trente glorieuses, en 1975, le revenu par habitant du Québec faisait encore du sur-place autour de 82 % de celui de l'Ontario. On était encore loin du niveau de 92 % enregistré à l'orée de la Grande Dépression.

Qu'est-ce qui a empêché le revenu par habitant du Québec de remonter la côte relativement à celui de l'Ontario entre 1954 et 1975 ? Une façon d'y réfléchir est d'observer que la croissance du revenu par habitant a deux grandes sources possibles : une fraction plus grande de la population adulte au travail (hausse du taux d'emploi), ou plus de valeur produite par personne employée (hausse de la productivité). Ce qu'on observe à partir du milieu des années 1950, c'est une évolution de ces deux forces — taux d'emploi et productivité — dans des directions opposées. Elles se sont en quelque sorte annulées mutuellement dans leur impact sur la croissance québécoise.

La productivité québécoise a connu des hauts et des bas, mais dans l'ensemble elle a gagné du terrain, passant de 85 % de la productivité ontarienne en 1953 à 94 % en 1975. Par contre, le taux d'emploi de la population en âge de travailler a marqué le pas au Québec pendant qu'il faisait un bond remarquable en Ontario.

Cette dernière province a successivement bénéficié du progrès de l'éducation (notamment avec le *G.I. Bill* canadien), de la hausse du taux d'activité féminin, du boom des ressources naturelles et de l'avènement de la Voie maritime du Saint-Laurent et du Pacte de l'automobile. Ces développements n'ont pas favorisé le Québec au même degré. La province a été durement frappée par la récession et la stagnation de 1957 à 1961 et s'en est ensuite relevée péniblement.

Les figures 2 et 3 permettent de bien visualiser l'évolution du marché du travail depuis la fin de la Guerre de 1939-1945. La figure 2 indique que le taux d'emploi du Québec, qui atteignait 96 % de celui de l'Ontario en 1953, avait glissé à 90 % à la fin des Trente glorieuses, en 1975. La figure 3 montre que le taux de chômage du Québec, qui avait coutume de dépasser celui de l'Ontario d'un seul point de pourcentage jusqu'en 1953, est demeuré suspendu à 2,5 points au-dessus du taux ontarien en moyenne de 1955 à 1975.

Figure 2 : Taux d'emploi de la population en âge de travailler du Québec exprimé en pourcentage de celui de l'Ontario, 1948-2007

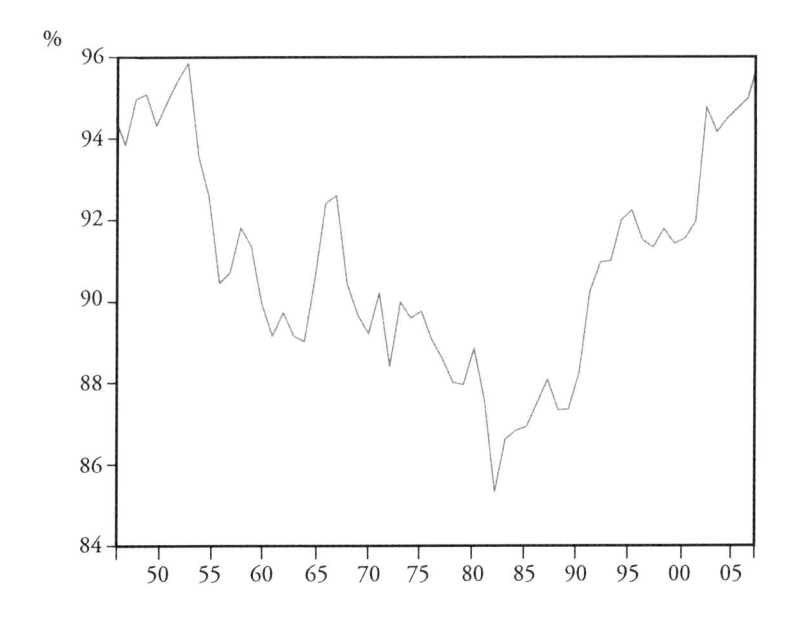

Source : Calculs basés sur les données de Statistique Canada

Figure 3 : Différence entre le taux de chômage de la population active du Québec et celui de l'Ontario, 1946-2007

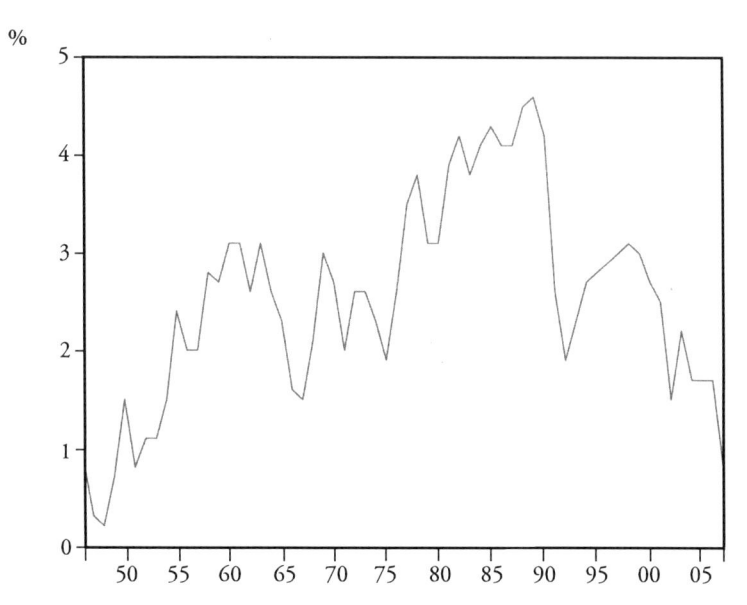

Source : Calculs basés sur les données de Statistique Canada

La descente aux enfers des années 1975-1989

L'épisode suivant est la « descente aux enfers » de 1975-1989. La descente, c'est celle du taux d'emploi du Québec, qui a atteint un creux de 85 % de celui de l'Ontario en 1982 — son plus bas niveau du XXe siècle (figure 2). L'enfer, c'est le taux de chômage de 14 % enregistré en 1982 et en 1983 — le plus haut niveau depuis la Grande Dépression — et un excédent moyen de plus de 4 points de pourcentage par rapport au taux de chômage ontarien dans l'ensemble de la décennie 1980 (figure 3). Pendant la période de 14 ans de 1975 à 1989, la croissance a considérablement ralenti par comparaison à la période précédente des Trente glorieuses, en Ontario comme au Québec (tableau 2). Le revenu par habitant ayant crû au même rythme moyen dans les deux provinces, la position relative du Québec était à peu près la même en 1989 qu'en 1975 (figure 1).

Le début de la période fut marqué par le boom de la Baie James, qui eut lieu de 1975 à 1983. La corrélation entre la trajectoire formée par la saillie remarquable sur la figure 1 et celle des investissements en immobilisations d'Hydro-Québec est très étroite (93 %), ce qui ne laisse subsister aucun doute sur l'interprétation. Ce fut un boom de productivité, et nullement un boom d'emploi. Au contraire, pendant l'exécution des travaux de construction de la centrale La Grande-2 (aujourd'hui Robert-Bourassa), le taux d'emploi a plongé et le taux de chômage a considérablement augmenté au Québec. Et malgré la reprise postérieure à 1983, les comparaisons de revenu par habitant, de taux d'emploi et de chômage avec l'Ontario ne s'étaient pratiquement pas améliorées à la fin de la décennie 1980, comme on peut le voir sur les figures 1 à 3.

Comment expliquer cette descente aux enfers de l'emploi au Québec au cours de la période 1975-1989 ? L'hypothèse qui paraît la plus vraisemblable est que le marché du travail a éprouvé de graves difficultés de fonctionnement au Québec à partir de la fin des années 1960. Les arrêts de travail dans les services essentiels (électricité, médecins, infirmières, policiers, pompiers, etc.) et la désobéissance civile furent monnaie courante. Des chefs syndicaux furent emprisonnés. Le chantier de la Baie James fut saccagé et mis à feu. Une commission d'enquête sur la violence et la corruption sur les chantiers de construction fut instituée. Le vol de matériel sur le chantier olympique fut endémique et les conflits de travail vinrent près d'entraîner l'annulation des Jeux de Montréal. Au cours de la période 1972-1983, deux fois plus de jours par emploi salarié furent perdus pour cause de grève ou lockout au Québec qu'en Ontario.

Ces difficultés sociales ont été accompagnées d'une importante explosion salariale. La figure 4 démontre que la rémunération hebdomadaire moyenne du Québec est passée de 93 % de la rémunération ontarienne en 1973 à 101 % en 1980-1983, avant de revenir au niveau de départ de 93 % à la fin des années 1980. La déconnexion entre les salaires et la productivité fondamentale au Québec pendant la période 1975-1989 ne fait pas de doute. La seule façon pour les employeurs d'amener la productivité du travail au niveau élevé des salaires ambiants fut de mettre à pied les travailleurs les moins qualifiés et d'éviter d'en embaucher de nouveaux. D'où la stagnation du taux d'emploi, le chômage élevé et persistant, et la faiblesse de l'investissement des entreprises.

Figure 4 : Salaire hebdomadaire moyen du Québec en pourcentage de celui de l'Ontario, 1961-2007

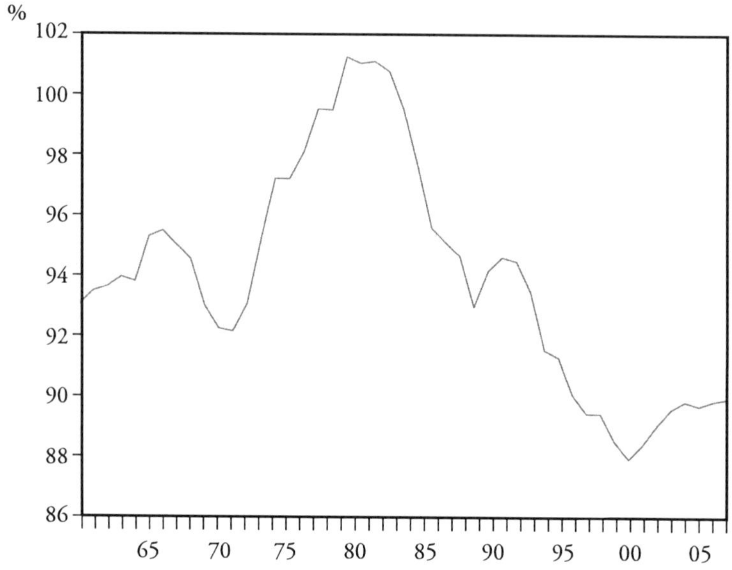

Source : Calculs basés sur les données de Statistique Canada

La résurrection des années 1989 à aujourd'hui

Un virage fut cependant opéré à partir de 1983. Les salaires publics furent gelés pour un temps, puis une loi sur le maintien des services essentiels fut conçue et adoptée. Les syndicats commencèrent à mettre l'accent sur la sécurité d'emploi plutôt que sur les augmentations de salaire. La paix sociale s'est installée. Depuis le milieu des années 1990, le nombre de jours perdus dans des conflits de travail a considérablement diminué et n'a pas été plus élevé au Québec qu'en Ontario. La figure 4 montre que la modération salariale a pris le dessus. Le salaire moyen du Québec est redescendu à 90 % de celui de l'Ontario. Ces évolutions ont sans doute appuyé la « résurrection » de 1989 à 2007. À partir du début des années 1990, le taux d'emploi relatif du Québec a commencé à remonter la côte (figure 2) et l'excédent de chômage par rapport à l'Ontario à diminuer (figure 3). Les deux provinces ont été durement éprouvées par la longue récession de 1990-1993 et ses séquelles, mais la figure 2 montre que, pendant ce pénible épisode, l'emploi a tenu le coup beaucoup mieux au Québec qu'en Ontario. Au cours des 18 années de 1989 à 2007, le revenu par habitant a augmenté de 33 % au Québec et de 19 % en Ontario (tableau 2). Le rapport entre les revenus par habitant des deux provinces est passé de 83 % en 1989 à 92 % en 2007 (figure 1)[6]. Le Québec a ainsi fini par retrouver la position relative qu'il occupait juste avant la Grande Dépression des années 1930[7].

L'amélioration des relations du travail n'est pas la seule évolution qui a favorisé la remontée du taux d'emploi du Québec de 87 % de celui de l'Ontario en 1989 à 96 % en 2007 (figure 2). Un phénomène important est la forte accélération de l'entrée des femmes québécoises dans la population active. Des années 1950 aux années 1980, un important écart s'était creusé entre le rapport de féminité du Québec et celui de l'Ontario. En 1989 il y avait 81 femmes pour 100 hommes en emploi en Ontario contre 75 au Québec. L'écart s'est presque entièrement refermé depuis. En 2007, l'Ontario comptait 92 femmes pour 100 hommes en emploi et le Québec, 91. En pure arithmétique, cette seule évolution « explique » la moitié de la remontée du taux d'emploi relatif du Québec depuis la fin des années 1980.

Enfin, la révolution éducative qui a marqué le Québec depuis les années 1950 a fini par porter fruit. Il y a 50 ans, la population québécoise était parmi les plus illettrées du continent nord-américain. En 1961, les jeunes hommes Québécois complétaient 10 années à l'école en moyenne. Cela se comparait à 11 années pour les jeunes noirs américains, à 12 années pour les jeunes Ontariens et à 13 années pour les jeunes blancs américains. Quarante ans plus tard, en 2001, le nombre médian d'années d'études des jeunes adultes âgés de 25 à 29 ans était de 15 au Québec et en Ontario et de 14 ou moins ailleurs au Canada et aux États-Unis. De plus, les jeunes Québécois se classent aux tout premiers rangs mondiaux dans les évaluations internationales des compétences en mathématiques, en lecture et en sciences telles que le Programme international de suivi des acquis (PISA) de l'OCDE. Étant donné l'étroite corrélation entre scolarité et emploi, l'ascension du taux d'emploi relatif du Québec était en quelque sorte inévitable.

Pourquoi mettre tant d'insistance sur l'essor comparatif de l'emploi au Québec depuis 1989 ? C'est que la « résurrection » du revenu par habitant vécue par le Québec au cours des deux dernières décennies est une résurrection de l'emploi, et nullement de la productivité. De 1989 à 2007, telle que mesurée par la production intérieure réelle par heure travaillée, la productivité a progressé à un rythme annuel moyen plutôt lent de 1,4 %, au Québec comme en Ontario. En productivité et en revenu par habitant, la performance des deux provinces centrales du Canada est l'une des dix plus médiocres parmi les 60 États d'Amérique du Nord. Compte tenu du vieillissement démographique qui va bientôt freiner l'essor de l'emploi, il ne fait aucun doute que le principal défi économique que les deux partenaires auront à relever va consister cette fois à ressusciter la croissance de leur productivité.

Résumé : six observations sur la croissance québécoise

Constatant l'absence d'une estimation précise de la croissance québécoise au XXe siècle, j'ai pensé qu'une bonne façon de rendre hommage à la manière de Paquet est de présenter une telle estimation. En observant les étapes de cette croissance depuis la Confédération, j'ai présenté plusieurs questions à élucider et quelques hypothèses à vérifier sur la croissance québécoise contemporaine.

Au départ, j'accorde une grande importance à la mesure de la croissance adoptée. J'ai fixé mon attention sur l'évolution d'une mesure du pouvoir d'achat de la population que j'ai appelé le *revenu intérieur réel par habitant d'âge actif*. Trois aspects de cette mesure ont requis un certain soin : l'usage de la population d'âge actif, soit celle de 15 à 64 ans, comme base afin d'éliminer les effets démographiques purs ; l'adoption d'un cadre de comparaison avec une région environnante (l'Ontario) afin d'atténuer les effets nationaux, continentaux et mondiaux ; la conversion des dollars mesurés en unités de pouvoir d'achat identiques d'une région à l'autre.

L'observation du rapport entre le revenu par habitant du Québec et celui de l'Ontario suggère un découpage de la période 1929-2007 en cinq épisodes : la Grande Dépression des années 1930, la Guerre de 1939-1945, les Trente glorieuses (1945-1975), la « descente aux enfers » de 1975 à 1989 et la « résurrection » de 1989 à aujourd'hui.

J'aboutis à six conclusions

Premièrement, la double constatation faite par Raynauld en 1961 se trouve confirmée. Pendant les 60 ans qui ont suivi la Confédération, le Québec et l'Ontario ont emprunté des sentiers de croissance parallèles, mais la trajectoire du revenu par habitant du Québec est restée constamment inférieure à celle de l'Ontario. Ce dernier fait — l'absence de convergence — reste mystérieux.

Deuxièmement, la Grande Dépression des années 1930 et la Guerre de 1939-1945 ont eu l'effet d'une bombe atomique sur la performance relative de l'économie du Québec. De 92 % de celui de l'Ontario en 1929, le revenu par habitant du Québec a atterri à 76 % en 1945. Ce n'est que 62 ans plus tard, en 2007, que le Québec a pu regagner complètement le terrain perdu par rapport à l'Ontario pendant la Dépression et la Guerre. J'ai soulevé la possibilité que le rejet politique massif de la participation à la Guerre par les Québécois ait eu des conséquences économiques majeures, et peut-être durables, liées au déplacement de la solde militaire et des activités de la défense nationale et du complexe militaro-industriel hors du Québec. Cela doit être vérifié.

Troisièmement, les années 1945-1975, qu'on appelle souvent les Trente glorieuses, ne furent pas glorieuses du tout pour la position économique relative du Québec. La province a participé à la croissance rapide qui a marqué l'économie nord-américaine dans l'après-guerre, mais n'a pas du tout réussi à se démarquer. La productivité québécoise a fait mieux que l'ontarienne, mais la situation comparative de l'emploi n'a pas cessé de se détériorer au Québec de 1954 à 1975. Cette détérioration a traversé les années Duplessis, Lesage, Johnson et Bourassa. Les saints hommes n'ont pu y faire grand-chose. Les explications définitives sont encore à venir.

Quatrièmement, j'avance l'hypothèse que la réforme du régime des relations du travail issue de la Révolution tranquille a pu être une cause importante de la grave détérioration du climat social et de l'explosion salariale qui ont marqué les années 1975 à 1989. Cette période fut témoin d'une « descente aux enfers » qui a vu le taux d'emploi relatif du Québec plonger et le chômage atteindre un sommet depuis la Grande Dépression, en niveau absolu comme en comparaison avec le reste du Canada. Fait remarquable, l'ascension du chômage s'est produite en plein boom de la Baie James.

Cinquièmement, un vigoureux revirement de tendance a eu lieu depuis 1989. Je l'attribue provisoirement à trois évolutions : le virage des années 1980 vers la paix sociale et la modération salariale, l'entrée accélérée des femmes dans la population active et la maturation de la révolution éducative amorcée dans les années 1950 et 1960. Le revenu par habitant du Québec a maintenant retrouvé la position relative qu'il occupait juste avant la Grande Dépression. Le taux d'emploi relatif du Québec est remonté au niveau du dernier sommet, de 96 %, enregistré dans les années 1950, et son taux de chômage ne dépasse plus celui de l'Ontario que d'environ 1 point de pourcentage.

Sixièmement, au Québec comme en Ontario, la productivité a avancé à pas de tortue depuis 1989, soit de 1,4 % par année en moyenne. Cela soulève une inquiétude, car au sein d'une population vieillissante où la progression de l'emploi sera beaucoup plus difficile, le défi de la croissance dans l'avenir sera incontestablement celui de la productivité.

Voilà, en résumé, mes six observations sur la croissance québécoise à la manière de Gilles Paquet : en contestataire, le nez collé sur les faits.

Notes

[1] Militaires inclus. Les enfants de moins de 15 ans et les adultes de 65 ans ou plus sont exclus du concept de population utilisé parce qu'on veut éliminer les variations de pouvoir d'achat qui seraient d'origine purement démographique. Un exemple est l'enrichissement artificiel qui a résulté mathématiquement de la baisse rapide du nombre d'enfants par famille à partir des années 1960. Dans la suite du texte, *revenu par habitant* est un raccourci qui désigne partout le revenu réel par habitant d'âge actif.

[2] A. Raynauld, *Croissance et structure économiques de la province de Québec*, ministère de l'Industrie et du Commerce, Québec, 1961.

[3] K. Inwood et J. Irwin. « Land, Income and Regional Inequality: New Estimates of Provincial Incomes and Growth in Canada, 1871-1891 », *Acadiensis*, vol. 31, n° 2, printemps 2002, tableau 1; A. G. Green, *Regional Aspects of Canada's Economic Growth*, Toronto, University of Toronto Press, 1971, appendice B.

[4] Une série complète du revenu intérieur pour la période 1926-2007 est construite en raccordant en 1961 la vieille série du revenu personnel provincial (amputé des transferts aux particuliers), qui est disponible depuis 1926, avec celle du PIB provincial, qui est publiée depuis 1961. Pour construire l'indice des prix de la dépense intérieure, il faut raccorder en 1971 le vieil indice des prix à la consommation de Montréal (ou de Toronto) avec l'indice des prix de la demande intérieure finale qui, lui, est publié depuis 1971.

[5] De combien ? Statistique Canada rapporte qu'en octobre 2007 les prix à la consommation étaient en moyenne 10 % plus élevés à Ottawa et 17 % plus élevés à Toronto qu'à Montréal. En plus de la consommation, la dépense intérieure comprend l'investissement des entreprises et les dépenses publiques. En supposant, de façon plutôt conservatrice, que les prix de ces deux dernières composantes étaient à peu près les mêmes dans les deux provinces, on en déduit que les prix de la dépense intérieure devaient être en moyenne 9 % plus élevés en Ontario qu'au Québec en 2007. En remontant jusqu'en 1935-1939 avec l'indice des prix de la dépense intérieure, on

trouve que les prix ontariens ont dû dépasser les prix québécois de 10 % en moyenne pendant cette période.

6 On peut être surpris d'observer sur la figure 1 que la croissance québécoise a été plus rapide que la croissance ontarienne depuis 1989. C'est que les données habituellement rapportées dans la presse sont celles de la croissance du PIB réel *total* plutôt que du PIB réel *par habitant*. De 1989 à 2007, par exemple, le PIB réel total a crû en moyenne de 2,1 % par année au Québec et de 2,5 % en Ontario ; le PIB réel par habitant, de 1,5 % par année au Québec et de 1,2 % en Ontario. Gare à la confusion démographique.

7 Un concept élargi de niveau de vie ajouterait au revenu monétaire la valeur du revenu auquel les citoyens d'un pays renoncent individuellement ou collectivement afin de disposer de plus de temps libre. Les Québécois travaillent moins d'heures par semaine, moins de semaines par année et moins d'années dans leur vie active que les Ontariens. Il est certainement permis de soutenir, dans cette optique, que les Québécois ont aujourd'hui atteint la parité de niveau de vie avec les Ontariens.

Chapter 28

The Dialectics of the Heart: Gilles Paquet on Moral Contracts and Social Learning

Ralph Heintzman

There was a new feature in Pierre's relations with . . . all the people he met now, which gained for him universal goodwill. This was his acknowledgement of the freedom of everybody to think, feel and see things in his own way. . . . This legitimate individuality of every man's views, which in the old days used to trouble and irritate Pierre, now formed the basis of the sympathy he felt for and the interest he took in other people.

—L. N. Tolstoy

Perhaps it is not surprising to find that the idea of conversation is one of the connecting threads in Gilles Paquet's writing and thought. Paquet is, after all, one of our best academic conversationalists. But the lens of conversation lends both an organic unity to his work and reveals him in ways somewhat different from those by which he sometimes presents himself.

The Paquet persona is that of a realist and a skeptic. He sometimes refers to himself (at least in the lively conversations at which he excels) as an Aristotelian or even an Epicurean. And maybe there is something in this. He is certainly more alert to the facts of the real world than many a self-declared, hard-headed empiricist.

But a close look at Paquet's own writing suggests that Gilles is also a distinguished latter-day representative of quite a different tradition, a tradition associated instead with names like those of Plato and Hegel. The Platonic and Hegelian flavour of Paquet's oeuvre is apparent in its literary élan (especially in French), its playful delight in language, its irony, its relishing of obscure terminology, its strong emotional and moral charge, and its subterranean but passionate idealism. But above all is Paquet's indelibly dialectical vision of the mind, of society, and of life itself.

Dialectics of Mind and Society

The fundamentally dialectical quality of Paquet's cast of mind can be detected in at least two forms: procedural and substantive.

By procedural, I mean the emphasis on discussion, deliberation, and dialogue that pervades almost everything that Gilles has written. For him, the give and take, question and answer, statement and response of dialogue or conversation are the basis of individual mental processes, organizational dynamics, political deliberation, and social well-being. And this dialogical imperative was, of course, the original meaning given to dialectic by Plato. In the Platonic canon, dialectic appears to have at least four meanings. But all of them derive from the root meaning of the "back-and-forth of discussion" that was at once Plato's basic philosophical procedure—reflected in the famous Platonic dialogues—and his vision of the good (Gadamer 1980, 1).

By substantive, I mean that, beyond procedure, the world as it emerges from Paquet's writing also displays a dialectical ontology or, at the least, a dialectical epistemology. We do not simply explore the world through the dialectical process of conversation: it *is* dialectical in the very marrow of its being. Or at least as the being of the world can be known to us. And this is the dialectical world—emerging from but going substantially beyond the ancient notion of dialectic—that Hegel above all others taught us to see (Gadamer 1976).

Dialectic in this modern Hegelian or neo-Hegelian sense might be defined as "a concrete unfolding of linked but opposed principles of change" or "the concrete unity of opposed principles" (Lonergan 1958, 217, 233). And this concrete, dynamic, evolving unity of opposed principles is also the defining characteristic of the world that Paquet's essays reveal to us. The world that they explore is shaped by a conflict of goods, by "the basic tensions with which humanity must live." It is a "world of paradoxes and essentially contested concepts." It is constituted—but also maintained and developed—by "creative dialectical relationships" (Paquet 1999, 243–45). For Paquet, institutions and societies are "social armistices" embodying a "workable tension" between opposed principles or dynamics such as coherence and flexibility, resilience and learning, freedom and order. These imperatives may point in "contradictory directions," but each must be respected and "balanced" with its opposite to achieve the good (Paquet 2005a, 151; 2005b, 17, 281, 7). Paquet's playful description of his own outlook as "chaordic" (chaos + order!) or "baroque" is intended to capture precisely this ideal of polyphonic balance and counterpoint of which the music of Bach is the consummate expression (Paquet 2005b, xii-xiii). Paquet might have been thinking of himself just as much as Canada when he chose one of the epigraphs that are such a striking feature of his essays—a charmingly old-fashioned practice that perhaps betrays both his pre-Quiet Revolution *cours classique* and the profoundly literary, humanistic, even artistic spirit of his enormous intellectual enterprise—an epigraph from the Canadian literary critic Malcolm Ross: "Our natural mode is therefore not compromise but irony, the inescapable response to the presence and pressure of opposites in tension. Irony is the key to our identity" (Paquet 2005b, 239).

There are obvious and important connections, of course, between the procedural and the substantive, which is perhaps why Hegel preserved the ancient terminology while giving it a new, substantive meaning. For Plato, the dialogical procedure—like the ideal state of *The Republic*—was an image of how the mind itself works when it is at its best: constantly questioning itself and responding to its own questions through new insights. And for Hegel our knowledge of the external world is always in some sense a manifestation of mind or spirit knowing itself. So the substantive dialectic of the external world and the internal procedure of dialogue are mirror images. And the best way to uncover the complex, contradictory, paradoxical, evolving reality of the external world is through the dialectical give-and-take of conversation: the internal conversation that begins in our own minds and hearts and continues in the external world, in our families, friendships, institutions, and communities. Charles Taylor has called this "the transcendental condition of interlocution" (1989, 39).

For Paquet, the world is far too complex, ambiguous, diverse, dynamic, and self-contradictory ever to be adequately captured by broad generalizations, universal principles, or general rules. He is on the side of Pascal's *esprit de finesse*, constantly warning (like Pascal himself) about the damage to be done by an excessive reliance on the modern, linear *esprit de géométrie* with its reductionist consequences (Pascal 1973, 307–09). Everything depends on context, and everything is in a constant process of change. In this kind of world, the only reliable way to know or to shape reality is through the alert, sensitive, pragmatic, ongoing procedure of question and answer. A dialogical procedure of this kind generates the feedback "loops"—even "double loops"—that are necessary to ensure accurate readings of complex, evolving realities and continually redefine our objectives in light of new learning (Paquet 2005b, 3; 1999, 238).

Because learning is where dialogue leads.

Social Learning

Learning is another fundamental theme of Paquet's thought. Learning is the lens through which Gilles normally interprets the world, and it is his metaphor for how that world should be governed, led, reformed, or managed.

This learning paradigm is the logical and necessary outcome of his dialectical metaphysics. If the human world is not stable but dynamically evolving, if it is not "logical" but self-contradictory, if it follows the logic of paradox rather than the law of the excluded middle, if it is not given to us and directly knowable but only revealed—or even created—through an unceasing process of question and answer, an unending human dialogue, if it is all of these things, then it can only be appropriated—or constructed—through something similar, through some kind of permanent learning process. Paquet could readily subscribe to Northrop Frye's observation that "nothing is really happening in the world except the education of the people in it" (1971, 47).

The striking features of Paquet's learning paradigm follow naturally from his dialectical presuppositions. One is that learning is a fundamentally public process: it is *social* learning. Although as far as I know Paquet does not mention it, even the critical internal dialogue that takes place in our own heads depends on social learning both for its first growth and for its later development. It is initiated by our first conversations with the external world, in our families, schools, and communities. And it continues to be developed by our engagement in the external conversations of our families, professions, and communities, conversations without which we could not know whether our perceptions and thoughts were actually connected to the real world.

But for Paquet even the public processes of our professions, organizations, communities, and governments are best conceived as forms of organizational and social learning: "*des espaces d'apprentissage collectif permettant aux intervenants de dialoguer efficacement*" (2004, 109). The modern paradigm of rational planning and top–down execution is a dangerous illusion that does not take adequate account of the complex, evolving, contradictory nature of social reality. The only way to cope with this kind of world is instead to feel your way forward, with experiments, pilot projects, and "feedback processes among interacting systems," relying on the give-and-take between intelligent, pragmatic citizens, stakeholders, professionals, and "decentralized and flexible teams," especially between those who know what they are talking about, on the front lines of execution (Paquet 2005a, 149; 2005b, 3, 6). This kind of organizational and social learning resembles nothing as much as a conversation.

Another feature of Paquet's learning paradigm that helps to explain the first is his recognition, following Michael Polanyi, of the importance of "tacit knowledge." One reason that a social-learning paradigm is so important is that we always "know more than we can tell" (Paquet 1999, 239). Rationalistic, technocratic, top–down solutions fail because they can only be based on what's already on the surface, on what we know we know. They cannot, by definition, take account of a deeper and often more important knowledge: what we know in a profound way but don't yet know we know or cannot say. We can often find this out only in the encounter with the concrete circumstances of the real world and in the condition of "interlocution" with other minds and other perceptions.

While I don't believe that Paquet makes such distinctions, it is possible to identify at least three kinds of "tacit knowledge" that need to be unearthed through the encounter with the concrete world and with other minds. One is the things that we simply take for granted because they are part of the culture and conversation by which we were formed. R. G. Collingwood (1940) called these tacit assumptions "absolute presuppositions," absolute because they are so difficult to see, let alone evaluate or criticize. They are simply part of the background, what we take to be reality, because it is the only reality that these presuppositions will allow us to see. This kind of tacit knowledge might more properly be called "tacit belief." In any event, social learning can help us to drag these absolute presuppositions out into the open and to see them more clearly for what they are.

Another kind of tacit knowledge that social learning can help us to excavate is the deep intuitions and perceptions of our own minds. These deep intuitions may also have come from the background, but, if so, they have somehow been validated by our own authentic experience and are in some way deeply ours, and deeply important, even though we can't normally see them. It is very important to uncover this kind of knowledge because it may contradict or confirm what our conscious minds and our surrounding environments—even our whole culture—are telling us. Yet another kind of tacit knowledge is what Paquet has sometimes called "delta knowledge," the unarticulated, practical knowledge of highly skilled craftspeople or professionals, based on practice and experience rather than conscious analysis (Paquet 1999, 239; Paquet and Gélinier 1991; Schon 1983). Both kinds of tacit knowledge require the confrontation with concrete realities to be mobilized or recognized for what they are.

In emphasizing the importance of tacit knowledge, Paquet again shows his Platonic and Hegelian filiation. Bringing tacit knowledge to the surface recalls Hegel's emphasis on mind or spirit knowing and realizing itself. And uncovering tacit knowledge is less like learning something new than like remembering something already known. It therefore brings to mind Plato's view that all learning is ultimately a form of remembering (1956, 42).

A third feature of social learning that follows from the first two is its pragmatic, tentative, and experimental character. Learning for Paquet is a "learning by doing" (Paquet 2005a, 149; Paquet and Gélinier 1991). We do not learn and then act. We act and then learn. We learn about the world by acting in it and adjusting to the consequences. And since we cannot know beforehand what we really think, or what the world is really like, but will know them only by acting in it, we have to be prepared for mistakes. That's the price of learning. We have to recognize "error as a fundamental building block in social learning" (Paquet 1999, 239).

And a fourth feature of social learning is that it, too, is dialectical. Like a pendulum, it swings in "contradictory directions," correcting itself when it swings too far. Social learning feels its way forward by "bouncing off the limits" (Paquet 1999, 237). From the point of view of social learning, Paquet would no doubt agree with William Blake's proverb that "You never know what is enough unless you know what is more than enough" (1975, xxix).

Although Paquet does not use the term, the social contract necessary to underpin this kind of vision of social learning can be called an "educational contract" (Frye 1976, 42; Heintzman 1979). The force of such an implicit educational contract derives from the recognition that, because of our necessarily limited vantage point and experience, each of us can perceive only a portion of reality, a portion of truth. It is a unique portion because it is the portion available only from our own perspective. No one else can have it. But if we want to complete it, or at least get a fuller purchase on the whole truth, then we must depend on the insights of others, on all the other unique perspectives that are now or have ever been. The more of them that we can bring together, and the more authoritative they are, the better our chance of getting closer to some kind of ultimate truth.

The educational contract is a contract because it is a two-way street. We "contribute to a common fund of knowledge but also receive from it" (Lonergan 1958, 703). We depend on the insights of others to enlarge our understanding, but they also depend on us to contribute the insights that are uniquely ours to the process of social learning. As Paquet puts it, "everyone must take part in the conversation, and bring forward each bit of knowledge and wisdom and those capabilities that he or she has that have a bearing on the issue" (2005b, 6).

Now at this point an important corollary emerges. An educational contract of this kind requires certain attitudes and behaviours from those who participate in it or benefit from it. It requires commitment, for example a commitment first of all to truth: truth to ourselves—because dishonesty starts by fooling ourselves—and then truth to other people. This basic requirement of honesty then inevitably calls upon a range of related attitudes and behaviours, beginning with trust and faithfulness. The educational contract cannot function without "a sense of mutual obligation" (Paquet 1999, 230).

In other words, the educational contract is necessarily and inescapably a moral contract.

Values in a Moral Universe

A close reading of Paquet's writing reveals the perhaps surprising degree to which the human world that Gilles describes is a fundamentally moral universe. The state, for example, is essentially a "moral agent," leadership is "first and foremost a moral issue," and in the contemporary world "the core of our difficulties" turns out to be a "moral vacuum" (1999, 190, 224).

In this kind of moral universe, values naturally assume high importance. They are the condition, the instrument, and the result of healthy organizations, communities, and societies. All of them depend on "shared values," on "a robust underlying ethos" (Paquet 1999, 219, 240). This is one of the places where Paquet proves to be a genuine Aristotelian. His use of the word *ethos* here is significant because it harks back to Aristotle's discussion of the distinction between intellectual and moral virtue in the *Nicomachean Ethics*. Aristotle pointed out that the word *ethics* is a slight variation of the Greek word *ethos*, meaning "habit." This derivation underlines the fact that we learn the virtues "by first exercising them.... [W]e learn by doing them." Intellectual virtue can be conveyed through teaching, Aristotle argued, but moral virtue is formed not by teaching but by habit, "by doing the acts that we do in our transactions with other[s]" (1947, 331–32).

An ethos is a set of behavioural habits shared by the members of some community. Values and habits are inseparable because values themselves are habits. Values are habits of feeling about the good that express themselves in habits of behaviour or virtues (Heintzman 2007b, 579, 594). If values do not express themselves in consistent behaviour or virtues, then they are not genuinely and habitually felt but are only espoused values, something residing in the mind perhaps but not in the gut. Habit or consistency is "the basis of all virtue": "The only person who is honest is the person who is consistently honest," as Frye remarks (1988, 94). Following Aristotle, James Q. Wilson also emphasizes the importance of habits as the foundation of moral life, contrary to the modern emphasis—inherited from Kant and the Enlightenment—on the observance of rationally derived rules: "A moral life is perfected by practice more than by precept," he remarks; "children are not taught so much as habituated" (1993, 249). Robert Bellah and his colleagues (1996) call these kinds of habits the "habits of the heart," a phrase borrowed from Tocqueville—"*les habitudes du cœur*" (1986, 426)—that goes back to Pascal, Saint Paul, and the Old Testament. In this sense, "heart" encompasses all the vital dimensions of what it means to be a human being, not just the mind or intellect but also will, intention, and feeling. We cannot even know who we are, Bellah and his colleagues remark, without some kind of "ritual and moral 'structure' that orders our freedom and binds our choices into something like habits of the heart" (1996, 312, 137).

These kinds of habits of the heart are what Paquet seems to have in mind when he talks about the importance of context for human action, especially a "context of habits" (1999, 236, 238). It is in this kind of context that one really learns what is genuinely important in life, the habits of the heart. Or not just *in* a context but also *from* it. One learns by watching, observing, and imitating. The habits of the heart are learned from "example as much as training" (Paquet 1999, 242). Like Aristotle, Paquet believes that learning values is a kind of doing. It is not like following a recipe or a book of rules. It is "like learning to swim." Under the watchful eyes of those more skilled in the craft, you practise over and over until the skill or competence becomes second nature, and you can do it on your own. Until it becomes "part of the fabric of the trainee" (Paquet 1999, 239).

Paquet's playful enjoyment of language sometimes indulges itself, as already mentioned, in a zestful employment of obscure or puzzling terminology. But it can also be expressed in the renovation and re-employment of familiar or even somewhat antiquated language, often with a new twist. One word that Gilles enjoys "rehabilitating," for example, is *casuistry*. For Paquet, it means the practical resolution of particular moral perplexities in a way that avoids both rigid moral absolutes and total moral relativism. Another word that he reclaims for new uses in this learning context is *connoisseurship*. In his usage, it describes the kind of knowledge or expertise that comes from concrete experience of many specific cases, just like wine-tasting or the common law. Connoisseurship can rarely be articulated or captured in general rules. It reveals itself only or mainly in its application or use. It is demonstrated in an instinctive response to specific circumstances, an intuitive awareness of the many different factors or elements in each of them, and a reliable judgment about how they should be assessed or balanced and about the appropriate response or course of action. In line with this notion of connoisseurship, Wilson suggests that getting the balance right is "more an aesthetic than a philosophical matter" (1993, 243). Connoisseurship is not so much a tacit knowledge as a "tacit '*savoir-faire*' and '*savoir-être*'" (Paquet 1999, 238–39). Connoisseurship is what the most valuable learning aims at. It is Pascal's (1993) *esprit de finesse* in action. It is the practical outcome of sound and well-developed habits of the heart.

Of course, this raises the inevitable and endemic modern problem of "inappropriate connoisseurship" and what can be done about it (Paquet 1999, 244). One of Paquet's answers is the concept of "professionalism." Since social learning and connoisseurship require a supportive culture and ethos to flourish, one place to start is within specific professional cultures or "*communautés de pratique*," such as the public service, where it is possible to develop the necessary dialogue—or "multilogue"—and the habits and culture of professionalism (2005a, 149). For Paquet, genuine professionalism and connoisseurship are closely connected concepts, perhaps even two sides of the same coin. Professionalism is more than just practical knowledge and social skills. Becoming a professional means committing oneself to a common professional culture, "the ensemble of values underpinning this culture and the unwritten agreement in which the mutual obligations these entail are recorded" (1999, 211). Unwritten agreements entailing mutual obligations are *moral contracts*. But professions are simply more manageable microcosms of a wider social challenge. So in the wider society as in a public service, social learning and progress depend on developing a "robust ethos" embodied in a number of implicit or explicit "moral contracts" (1999, 240). And the connoisseurship necessary to participate in such a learning process—and, even more, to develop or lead it—depends on cultivating a lively awareness of the existence, role, and importance of these moral contracts.

Moral Contracts as Social and Organizational Glue

One of the striking features of the "world according to Gilles Paquet" is the degree to which it is a world positively saturated with moral contracts. For Paquet, moral contracts are "informal arrangements and conventions that embody values and norms on which people agree. They define mutual expectations, legitimate entitlements and obligations, and the corridor or boundary limits within which people have agreed to live" (2005b, 267). Modern organizations and societies are best thought of not so much as technocratic hierarchies but as complex moral networks, a "nexus of moral contracts" (259). They are "networks of mutual trust," "informal networks based on shared values" (1999, 211, 219).

That is true enough of self-contained or self-governing organizations. But it is even more the case for the new, informal modes of public governance that spring up in the contemporary world. One of Paquet's important contributions to contemporary debate is the attention that Gilles has drawn to the way in which organizational and state boundaries are dissolving and how much critical interaction now takes place in the white space between organizations, between sectors, between and across governments: "*nos systèmes sociaux sont construits de plus en plus sur la collaboration et l'interdépendance*" (2004, 38). In this kind of world, moral contracts are more important than ever and are a key element of the "soft laws" through which such a world is governed. When power is diffuse and conditions are fluid, social learning takes place best "through decentralized and flexible teams woven by moral contracts and reciprocal obligations, negotiated in the context of evolving partnerships" (Paquet 2005b, 5–6).

Paquet pays particular attention to three types of moral contract: contracts between citizens, between citizens and governments (especially as represented by their public servants), and between senior and junior public servants or between headquarters and regions. The first type of moral contract is especially important because of the contemporary "shift from government to governance." Resources, information, and power are now much more widely distributed and "horizontal (community) relationships are as important (perhaps more important) as the vertical ones" with governments. In this new context, citizenship properly understood now means "the ensemble of values, principles, privileges and responsibilities that define the moral contracts. These contracts constitute the necessary social technologies of coordination, capable of bringing forth the good life in all its various senses for the different agents" (Paquet 2005b, 262). They are an important part of the new "social glue," holding societies and institutions together in a pluralist and fragmented world (264, 276, 278). For Paquet, the "task is clear" as far as these first moral contracts between citizens are concerned: "what is needed is a nexus of moral contracts (1) that ensures the requisite degree of rights, obligations, participation, *appartenance*, and identity . . . ; (2) that ensures that all the stakeholders retain their basic freedoms . . . in order to increase their capabilities; and (3) that the appropriate trade-offs are defined between these two sets of priorities" (279).

But, with only slight alteration, the same objective could also hold for the other two contracts. The new moral contract between citizens and governments, Paquet argues (1999, 211–12), should be "based on the citizens' right to know, but also on [the] client publics' right to be involved in the evaluation of the public service." It should establish "both the entitlements of citizens (within limits) and the obligations of public servants (but also the limitations that might apply) *and* . . . a transparent evaluation process for the public service based on the participation of citizens." The moral contract between senior and junior public servants (or between headquarters and the "field") should be "based not only on a sense of respected identity, but also on rules of mutual obligation and a sense of *quid pro quo*." This kind of moral contract would help to create "a milieu in which openness, candour, and deliberation (i.e., a true, open, internal forum) exist and there is respect for responsibility."

Paquet is somewhat skeptical about the degree to which improvements in government service delivery can contribute to strengthening the first contract, between citizens and governments. He is certainly right to highlight both the limits and the ambiguities of an exclusive focus on the quality of government service delivery (1999, 211–12). Passive receipt of a government service is certainly not the same as exercising all the rights and responsibilities of citizenship (Canada

2000, 31–33). Citizenship cannot be built on an "entitlement mentality" but must rest instead on a "sense of mutual obligation" (Paquet 1999, 230). But Paquet may also have underestimated the degree to which a self-consciously "citizen-centred" service can and should contribute to strengthening citizenship and the wider civic culture. Citizens' satisfaction with the service experience—satisfaction with the "moments of truth" of their daily interactions with government—can and should contribute to their sense of the value of their own democratic citizenship, and to the trust and confidence in public institutions on which democratic citizenship depends (Heintzman 2001b, 2007a; Heintzman and Marson 2005). As long ago as 1822, Hegel himself observed that the "conduct and culture" of front-line government officials, in their "direct and personal" contacts with citizens, have a major influence on "the contentment of citizens and their confidence in the government." In language remarkably consistent with the most sophisticated insights of today's advocates of citizen-centred service, he even noted that "feeling and sentiment may easily rate the manner of execution as highly as the very content of the command to be executed, even though the content may in fact be the imposition of a tax" (1967, 192).

Given the similarity between Paquet's third contract and the *diagnostique* of the Tait report, it is interesting that Gilles nowhere mentions a fourth potential moral contract, one that may well be essential for the last two to work. The Tait task force heartily agreed with Paquet's view that "the *métier* of public servants must be refurbished and repromoted to the rank of 'honourable profession'" (Paquet 1999, 211). In fact, Paquet's words echo its celebrated conclusion about public service as a "special calling" (Canada 2000, 63). The Tait report's analysis and recommendations all pointed in the same direction as Paquet's discussion of moral contracts, especially the relationship between senior public servants and the rest. But one of the essential conditions for rebuilding the professionalism of the public service as a "special calling," it argued, is another moral contract not mentioned by Paquet, one between the elected and the non-elected, a three-way contract between ministers, Parliament, and the public service. This fourth moral contract is essential because a public service cannot give itself its own values. A public service does not exist for its own sake: it exists to support legitimate, democratic governance. The values of public service must therefore be rooted in a "moral contract" with legitimate constitutional authority (Heintzman 2007b, 581–82). So the Tait task force recommended that the "Government and Parliament of Canada should adopt a statement of principles for public service, or a public service code . . . to provide not only a new foundation for public service values, but [also to] establish a new moral contract between the public service, the Government and Parliament of Canada" (Canada 2000, 60–61).

The Tait report's recommended "statement of principles or code" embodying this three-way moral contract subsequently came to be referred to as a "Charter of Public Service" (Heintzman 2001a). This concept was again recommended by the external Working Group on the Disclosure of Wrongdoing in 2004, endorsed by Donald Savoie and Kenneth Kernaghan, and subsequently recommended by the Gomery Commission (Canada 2004, 28–30; 2006, 67; Kernaghan 2006; Savoie 2003, 274–75). By that time, a commitment to establish such a charter had already been included in the *Public Servants Disclosure Protection Act*, unanimously approved by Parliament in 2005 (Canada 2005). The Harper government shows no current interest in following through on this legislative commitment, but a Charter of Public Service to articulate this fourth moral contract is a critical step toward implementing the three other moral contracts highlighted by Paquet, especially the two involving the public service.

It is not the only one, however. There is also the critical lever of leadership.

The Lever of Leadership

To foster social learning and the moral contracts that it both requires and constructs, Paquet suggests that "leadership is the lever" (1999, 240). But this modern challenge requires a specific kind of leadership. Modern life and organizations do not call for Weberian charismatic leadership but rather for the "leader as servant." Values are at the "heart" of this kind of leadership. In fact, it must become a "values-based leadership" because leadership in the contemporary world is "first and foremost a moral issue" (218, 199, 222, 224).

Leadership is a moral issue because of the tasks that modern leaders must perform. Since organizational success depends less on top-down direction than on a successful process of organizational and social learning, top leaders must henceforth be conceived primarily as facilitators of the learning process. The primary leadership skills now include the abilities to listen and to dialogue (Paquet 1999, 218). But successful listening and dialogue, as we already saw, have moral conditions. The ability to lead and foster organizational and social learning is essentially a "by-product" of something else, a by-product of "trust" earned by "serving" followers (240). Trust is built through actions, not words, actions that express respect, concern, fairness, consistency, reliability, and a commitment to truth-telling. Organizational learning is essentially the pursuit and cultivation of truth in organizations (Heintzman 1994). Successful leaders are those who know how to "engage" employees and stakeholders and to build the vital "social capital of trust, reasonableness and mutual understanding" (Heintzman 2007a; Heintzman and Marson 2005; Paquet 1999, 224). They do this not by talk but by walk: by example and role modelling. By embodying these values. "*Le savoir-faire et le savoir-être doivent s'incarner*" (Paquet 2005a, 154).

Paquet's emphasis on leadership as a key to fostering moral contracts and social learning raises a critical, even disturbing, question about the probabilities that this kind of leadership can or will emerge. Most of his comments on leadership seem to be related to the public service, and he is categorical that senior public servants have not so far been able to perform the task of designing moral contracts "to the necessary degree." In fact, following Michel Crozier, he believes that the public service lacks appropriate "leaders and models" (Paquet 1999, 210, 212). Why should this be so? Although Paquet does not suggest it, part of the problem may lie in a profound paradox pointed out by Alasdair MacIntyre (1984). The virtues of truthfulness, courage, respect, and fairness are habits of the heart that are essential to an institution such as the public service: they are what makes a public service a public service (Heintzman 2007b, 595–96). And the institution is essential to them. It is always within "some particular community" such as a public service that "we learn or fail to learn to exercise" such virtues. Without the institution, the values and their corresponding virtues would not exist. Nor, without the values, would the institution exist in a form worthy of the name. But while these values are necessary to *sustain* an institution such as the public service, they may actually be an obstacle to individual success or power *within* such an institution. "The possession of the virtues—and not only of their semblance and simulacra—is necessary to achieve [those goods that are internal to the practices themselves]; yet the possession of the virtues may perfectly well hinder us in achieving [power and status within the institution]. . . . [N]otoriously the cultivation of truthfulness, justice and courage will often, the world being what it contingently is, bar us from being rich or famous or powerful. . . . [T]he virtues are always a stumbling block to this comfortable ambition" (MacIntyre 1984, 196). Paradoxically, then, the least likely place to find the values of an institution such as the public service, according to MacIntyre's paradox, is at the top.

If so, then what, if anything, can be done to mitigate this institutional contradiction or paradox? What practices can help to increase the probability that the leaders of an institution such as the public service authentically reflect its values—and are thus equipped to provide "servant leadership," to lead processes of organizational and social learning, and to build the social capital of trust and mutual understanding? What will increase the chances that public service leaders will have the connoisseurship needed to establish the kind of moral contract between senior and junior public servants that Paquet hopes for—a moral contract based on mutual respect and obligation—and to nourish a culture of openness, candour, and deliberation that he rightly sees as critical for the future? How can they develop the necessary habits of the heart?

Like the Tait report, Paquet points to the practices of accountability, especially the potential of a new emphasis on 360-degree accountability (1999, 236, 243). He does not provide much detail on how this could work. But the Tait report was more explicit on at least one dimension of this challenge. Recognizing that the traditional strengths of the public service in "managing up" now need to be balanced by forms of downward accountability, the report recommended that "360 degree feedback instruments, upward feedback, and organizational climate surveys should now be used routinely at the highest levels to ensure adequate measures of leadership and people skills are included in future accountability regimes for the top level of the public service." Such measures cannot be window-dressing, however, but must be widely perceived "to have an effect on decisions about appointments, promotions and reward" (Canada 2000, 50).

In the decade since the Tait report, the Canadian public sector has learned a great deal about how to measure "employee engagement," and some provincial and municipal governments have begun to build these measures into their accountability regimes, even into the calculation of performance pay for senior executives. These practices offer significant promise for mitigating MacIntyre's (1984) institutional paradox, and it is devoutly to be wished that they will soon be generalized across the Canadian public sector, including the federal public service. They can help to build not only the internal moral contract between senior leaders and the wider body of public servants but also the external moral contract between citizens and government (Heintzman and Marson 2005). But even these practices may not be fully effective without still other reforms to the institutional boundaries of the public service, including changes to the procedures and location of responsibility for deputy minister appointments (Aucoin 2006; Canada 2006, 148–51)—in other words, without a renewal of the fourth moral contract, between the elected and non-elected leaders of government (Heintzman 2007a).

Conclusion: Friendship and the Dialectics of the Heart

His dialectical metaphysics lead Paquet naturally to a paradigm of conversation between different and even conflicting points of view, a paradigm of social learning. But this leads him, in turn, to an awareness of the moral and ethical values required for such a paradigm to work. Learning in a dialectical world entails mutual obligations between the participants in the conversation—between question and answer, between the statement and the response—or no such exchange can occur, even within the mind of the questioner, let alone between different individuals and groups. It entails shared habits of the heart, shared values of commitment, honesty, trust, and faithfulness, among others. Taken as a whole, such shared values constitute a moral contract. The "educational contract" is necessarily and inescapably a moral contract.

Paquet often writes as if these contracts needed to be created or negotiated, and there is certainly much truth in this. But they can also be viewed from another lens. In identifying three dimensions of citizenship—legal status, participation in governance, and the sense of belonging—Paquet notes that "belonging," for example, can be viewed in two ways. It can be viewed as something needing to be constructed "by activism," or it can be viewed, alternatively, as something "already there," needing only to be discovered and "*mise en visibilité*" (2005b, 268).

Perhaps something similar can be said about moral contracts. From one angle, they need to be actively negotiated and agreed upon. From another, they are *already there*, and all we need to do is discover them. But this discovery changes everything. A world in which every human relationship already bears with it an implicit moral contract is a world transformed. It is a different world. And it calls upon us in different ways.

For Paquet, as we saw, moral contracts define "mutual expectations, legitimate entitlements and obligations, and the corridor or boundary limits within which people have agreed to live" (2005b, 267). In other words, they are based on a rational calculation of mutual benefit, on what has been called an "ethic of freedom and mutual benefit." But it may be legitimately asked whether such an ethic adequately reflects the morally charged world that Paquet himself takes for granted or whether it can really sustain the nexus of moral contracts that for him is both an empirical reality and a normative ideal. Does this kind of world presuppose certain moral goods that it cannot furnish by itself? Can such a world really exist without support from another kind of human impulse, one that "goes way beyond any possible mutuality, a self-giving not bounded by some measure of fairness" (Taylor 2007, 171, 430)?

A traditional name for this kind of ethos is the word *friendship*. Thomas Aquinas suggested that we find what is most important for human beings "working through friendship" (1955, 154). And there are important connections between friendship and conversation. Friendship often takes the form of conversation, and conversation, to be its best, must become a kind of friendship.

R. G. Collingwood and Hans-Georg Gadamer, the father of modern philosophical hermeneutics, are two of the greatest modern thinkers about the moral implications of conversation. Gadamer (2002, 377–79), like Paquet, believed that human understanding can only advance through "a dialectic of question and answer," and this kind of dialectic "makes understanding appear to be a reciprocal relationship of the same kind as conversation." The "conversation that we ourselves are" involves a "fusion of horizons." In a successful conversation, Gadamer argued, the partners in dialogue "come under the influence of the truth of the object and are thus bound to each other in a new community. To reach an understanding in a dialogue is not merely a matter of putting oneself forward and successfully asserting one's point of view, but being transformed into a communion in which we do not remain what we were."

In developing his view of human understanding as conversation and communion, Gadamer was strongly influenced by Collingwood—"almost the only person I could find a link with here"—especially the "logic of question and answer" developed in Collingwood's brief intellectual *Autobiography* (Collingwood 1939, 29–43; Gadamer 2002, 370). Gadamer was apparently unaware that the same dialectical perspective had been richly developed in Collingwood's unfinished masterpiece, "The New Leviathan," a profound meditation on the meaning of civilization. Collingwood defined civilization not as a state but as a process, a process in which humankind moves closer to—or farther away from—an ideal of civility. He defined civility by reference to Plato's distinction between *dialectic* and *eristic*

(Plato 1956, 34). For Plato, an eristic discussion is one in which the participants aim not for agreement but for victory. In a dialectical discussion, in contrast, "you aim at showing your own view is one with which your opponent agrees, even if at one time he denied it; or conversely that it was yourself and not your opponent who began by denying a view with which you really agree." For Collingwood, the ideal of civility is one in which human relations and human politics are dialectical, in which human beings are transformed into a moral communion, bound to each other by the moral contract of conversation, the search for agreement. "We can think which we will do," said Collingwood, "live eristically, or live dialectically. Here . . . begins the process of civilization" (1942, 181, 306).

Collingwood's deep reflections on the meaning of civilization have been carried forward into our time by Iain Pears's remarkable novel *The Dream of Scipio* (2002). Interweaving three separate stories, each separated by a thousand years — the last of which is set in the dark years of the early 1940s that inspired Collingwood's own meditation—Pears's narrative explores the different potential meanings of civilization: what is lost when it is threatened, and what can be done to protect it. Is civilization a heritage of thought, or of art or literature, or of cultivated refinement? The novel's implicit answer is that it is none of them. It is not great ideas, or great buildings, or great technical achievements, or great luxuries. It is not in science, or industry, or public administration. Indeed, all of these can be instruments of barbarism if they are not animated by something else. It is not an abstract otherness "lying outside the individual." It is not in the external world and not even in the mind or the understanding. There is a "difference between clever patterns of words, and the answers of the soul." Indeed, it may sometimes be necessary to "protest against great ideas for the sake of a small humanity." Because the true source of civility is really detected in "the impulsions of the heart." What gives the human spirit its nobility may well be an otherness, but it is an otherness discovered deep in the human heart. This kind of otherness is encountered in simple "kindheartedness" and selflessness. Civilization may indeed be the "exercise of friendship manifested through conversation," as one of Pears's characters affirms. But, if so, such friendship and conversation have imperatives that go way beyond mutuality. A commitment to the truth. A faithfulness to obligation. A loving kindness and mercy. A reverence for others. A refusal to do wrong or to do harm or to betray. And a willingness to pay the price of such a refusal. A willingness even to the point, if necessary, of laying down one's life for one's friends (Pears 2002, 370–71, 124, 89, 367, 381, 140).

The essence of civilization may be a way of living dialectically, as Collingwood suggested. But precisely because it is a way of *living*, it cannot be just a dialectics of thought or of the mind. It is also—and before anything else—what Pascal might have called a dialectics of the heart.

In their own unique way, Gilles Paquet's thought and work help to remind us of these simple but decisive truths. These few pages are intended as a friendly expression of admiration and appreciation for that achievement. May they also be a small contribution to an ideal of civility based on friendship, conversation, and the dialectics of the heart.

References

Aquinas, T. (1955). *Summa Theologica*. In *Theological Texts*, by Thomas Aquinas, selected and translated by Thomas Gilby. London: Oxford University Press.

Aristotle. (1947). *Nicomachean Ethics*. In *Introduction to Aristotle*, ed. Richard McKeon. New York: Modern Library, 300–543.

Aucoin, P. (2006.) "The Staffing and Evaluation of Canadian Deputy Ministers in Comparative Westminster Perspective: A Proposal for Reform." In *Parliament, Ministers, and Deputy Ministers*, vol. 1 of *Restoring Accountability: Research Studies*, by the Commission of Inquiry into the Sponsorship Program and Advertising Activities (Gomery Commission). Ottawa: Public Works and Government Services Canada, 297–336.

Bellah, R. N., R. Madsen, W. M. Sullivan, A. Swidler, and S. M. Tipton. (1996). *Habits of the Heart: Individualism and Commitment in American Life*. Updated edition with a new introduction. Berkeley: University of California Press.

Blake, W. (1975). *The Marriage of Heaven and Hell*. London: Oxford University Press, in association with Trianon Press, Paris.

Canada. 2006. Commission of Inquiry into the Sponsorship Program and Advertising Activities (Gomery Commission), *Restoring Accountability: Recommendations [Phase 2 Report]*. Ottawa: Public Works and Government Services Canada.

———. 2005. Public Servants Disclosure Protection Act. C.S.R. 2005, c. 46.

———. 2004. Public Service Human Resources Management Agency, Working Group on the Disclosure of Wrongdoing. *Report*. Ottawa: Public Works and Government Services Canada.

———. 1996, 2000. Task Force on Public Service Values and Ethics. *A Strong Foundation*. Ottawa: Canadian Centre for Management Development."

Collingwood, R. G. (1939). *An Autobiography*. London: Oxford University Press.

———. (1940). *An Essay on Metaphysics.* London: Oxford University Press.
———. (1942). *The New Leviathan.* London: Oxford University Press.
Frye, N. (1971). "The Quality of Life in the Seventies." *University of Toronto Graduate, 3.5,* 38–48.
———. (1976). "The University and Personal Life." In *Spiritus Mundi: Essays on Literature, Myth, and Society.* Bloomington: Indiana University Press, 27–48.
———. (1988). "Education and the Rejection of Reality." *On Education,* by N. Frye. Toronto: Fitzhenry and Whiteside, 93–100.
Gadamer, H.-G. (1976). *Hegel's Dialectic: Five Hermeneutical Studies.* Trans. P. C. Smith. New Haven: Yale University Press.
———. (1980). *Dialogue and Dialectic: Eight Hermeneutical Studies on Plato.* Trans. P. C. Smith. New Haven: Yale University Press.
———. (2002). *Truth and Method.* 2nd ed. Trans. J. Weinsheimer and D. G. Marshall. New York: Continuum.
Hegel, G. W. F. (1967). *Philosophy of Right.* In *Hegel's Philosophy of Right,* trans. T. M. Knox. London: Oxford University Press.
Heintzman, R. (1979). "The Educational Contract." *Journal of Canadian Studies, 14.2,* 1–2, 142–45.
———. (1994). *Continuous Learning: A CCMD Report.* Ottawa: Canadian Centre for Management Development.
———. (2001a). "A Strong Foundation: Values and Ethics for the Public Service of the Future." *Isuma: Canadian Journal of Policy Research, 2.1,* 121–26.
———. (2001b). "Toward Citizen-Centred Service: The Government of Canada's Service Improvement Strategy." *Canadian Government Executive, 4,* 26–30.
———. (2007a). "Toward a New Moral Contract: Reclaiming Trust in Public Service." *Optimum Online, 37.3,* 33–48. www.optimumonline.ca [consulted January 18, 2009]
———. (2007b). "Public Service Values and Ethics: Dead End or Strong Foundation?" *Canadian Public Administration, 50.4,* 573–602.
Heintzman, R., and B. Marson. (2005). "People, Service, and Trust: Is There a Public Sector Service Value Chain?" *International Review of Administrative Sciences, 71.4,* 549–75.
Kernaghan, K. (2006). "Encouraging 'Rightdoing' and Discouraging Wrongdoing: A Public Service Charter and Disclosure Legislation." In *The Public Service and Transparency,* vol. 2 of *Restoring Accountability: Research Studies,* by the Commission of Inquiry into the Sponsorship Program and Advertising Activities (Gomery Commission). Ottawa: Public Works and Government Services Canada, 73–114.
Lonergan, B. J. F. (1958). *Insight: A Study of Human Understanding.* London: Darton, Longman, and Todd and Philosophical Library.
MacIntyre, A. (1984). *After Virtue.* 2nd ed. Notre Dame: University of Notre Dame Press.
Paquet, G. (1999). *Governance through Social Learning.* Ottawa: University of Ottawa Press.
———. (2004). *Pathologies de gouvernance: Essais de technologie sociale.* Montreal : Éditions Liber.

———. (2005a). *Gouvernance: Une invitation à la subversion*. Montreal: Éditions Liber.

———. (2005b). *The New Geo-Governance: A Baroque Approach*. Ottawa: University of Ottawa Press.

Paquet, G., and O. Gélinier, eds. (1991). *Le management en crise: Pour une formation proche de l'action*. Paris: Economica.

Pascal. (1973). *Pensées*. Paris: Garnier-Flammarion.

Pears, I. (2002). *The Dream of Scipio*. Toronto: Alfred A. Knopf.

Plato. (1956). *Meno*. In *Great Dialogues of Plato*, ed. W. H. D. Rouse. New York: Mentor Books, 28–68.

Savoie, D. (2003). *Breaking the Bargain: Public Servants, Ministers, and Parliament*. Toronto: University of Toronto Press.

Schon, D. A. (1983). *The Reflective Practitioner: How Professionals Think in Action*. New York: Basic Books.

Taylor, C. (1989). *Sources of the Self: The Making of the Modern Identity*. Cambridge, MA: Harvard University Press.

———. (2007). *A Secular Age*. Cambridge, MA: Belknap Press.

Tocqueville, A. de. (1986). *De la démocratie en Amérique*. Vol. 1. Paris: Gallimard/Folio.

Wilson, J. Q. (1993). *The Moral Sense*. New York: Free Press.

Chapter 29

Skills: Banal Creativity and Spontaneity in a Learning Intensive Society

Riel Miller

A Harbinger Encounter, Carleton University, 1976
I opened the door. Gilles was sitting at the head of the table. The room was small, painted white, and, to my recollection, windowless. He did not turn as we walked in. He sat and waited. Our delegation of four sat down. It felt very formal. Electricity was in the air. The stakes were high.

After three nights of excited and uncomfortable sleep on the floor of the president's office, we were ready to negotiate. Only we were unsure about the "establishment's" chief negotiator. Who was this guy? We knew the president, Michael Oliver, who happened to be away in Africa at the time. We knew John Porter, the vice president of the university, as students in his classes. But who was this dean?

It didn't take long to find out. No nonsense, to the point, and fair. He kindly guided us through the discussion. Laid out the political realities and listened carefully. In ten minutes, it was over. The occupation was terminated. The university senate would be asked to provide official permission for students to attend a protest rally in Toronto and to consider a motion objecting to the government's policies of the time. No guarantee of the outcome of the votes. In turn, we, the brave student protesters, would vacate the president's office immediately. Occupation over.

Quintessential Gilles, an elegant and respectful teacher practising what he preaches as a decision maker and thinker. When Gilles and I crossed paths next,

I was working for the OECD in Paris, and Gilles was running the Centre on Governance at the University of Ottawa. By then, having read his writings and seen him in action at a podium, I also appreciated the deeply inquisitive and subversive nature of his thought. Today the word *innovation* is overused to the point of becoming meaningless, but applied to Gilles it is fitting. He embodies in thought and deed that rare combination of creativity and problem solving that generates insights that go beyond existing theories, systems, and practices. He is an explorer who seeks the emergent with gusto and style.

Finally, most recently, I would be remiss to my own inner voice if I didn't also mention that Gilles offered honest and comforting words at the funeral commemoration for my father, Morris Miller, in February 2008. For this and all the rest, I am grateful to Gilles.

Beyond Skills: A Short Essay in a Paquetian Key[1]

The "Paquetian key" is non-ergodic, which means that it is a way of thinking that tries to imagine a "change in the conditions of change." The Paquetian key helps policy makers to hear (make sense of) emerging systemic patterns and to explore new ways of making sense of phenomena observed in the present by imagining what a discontinuous future might be like. The point is not to offer an alternative model that serves as planning target for policies meant to chart a path or control the future. The aim is at once more modest and more ambitious. It is more modest because it makes no case for any particular future outcome. It is more ambitious because the hope is to tell a story in terms that help decision makers to understand the anticipatory assumptions that underpin their choices.

This short essay offers a quick sketch of an imaginary "learning intensive society" as an example of non-ergodic, thinking–sense making in a Paquetian key. The imagined discontinuity at the core of this essay is in the relationship between knowledge and wealth. For a long time, this relationship has been considered equivalent to the relationship between certified skills and paid employment in the form of a "job."[2] As everyone knows, this is a limited way of defining both what people know how to do and the value added by people's efforts. Considerable attention has been paid to different ways of accounting for broader conceptualizations of work and wealth, but it has been difficult to get beyond the categories defined by the existing rules and norms of the industrial system.[3]

One way of moving outside the existing accounting frameworks is to imagine an alternative wealth creation system. This does not mean that existing industrial systems, including the services subject to the organizational logic of hierarchical specialization (e.g., division of conception and execution) and scale economies (e.g., mass standardization), are not changing. But these changes are perceptible and make sense within a framework of variables, relationships—and historical observations that are ergodic—the parameters of the model stay the same. The attempt at non-ergodic thinking, in a Paquetian key, tries to imagine a change in the parameters of the model.

Section 1: Imagining a Changed Context—A Sketch of the Learning Intensive Society (LIS)

The imaginary subject used for this exercise can be described in terms of two overarching attributes. The first attribute, depicted in Diagram 1, is about the composition of wealth-creating activity. The second attribute, depicted in Diagram 2, is related to the "intensity" of learning in everyday life. Taken together these descriptive frames allow for a picture to be sketched, at a general level, of a socioeconomic system: a learning intensive society that is distinctly different from the present.

Diagram 1 depicts an imaginary change in the composition or different shares of different types of production activity[4] in total wealth creation (at each point in time, the shares add up to 100% of wealth created). The decline of the share of activity devoted to producing agricultural products[5] is a familiar story. A similarly recognizable pattern, although now considered with much more anxiety, is the "hollowing out" of industrial activity. I include all types of industrial activity, from hospitals and schools to factories and banking, since from a workflow organizational perspective all these activities share the same basic logic: specialization (division of labour, in particular the distinction between conception and execution) and economies of scale (standardization).[6] Diagram 1 offers an illustration of an imaginary reallocation of wealth-creating activities such that industry becomes relatively marginal, while "household" and "craft" become more important as a share of total production activity.

The terms used in Diagram 1—household and craft—are not meant to be definitive or, I reiterate for emphasis, predictive. The language of the future—the words that we will use to describe the world—has yet to be invented, and the

Diagram 1: Imagining the Learning Intensive Society: Compositional Dimension

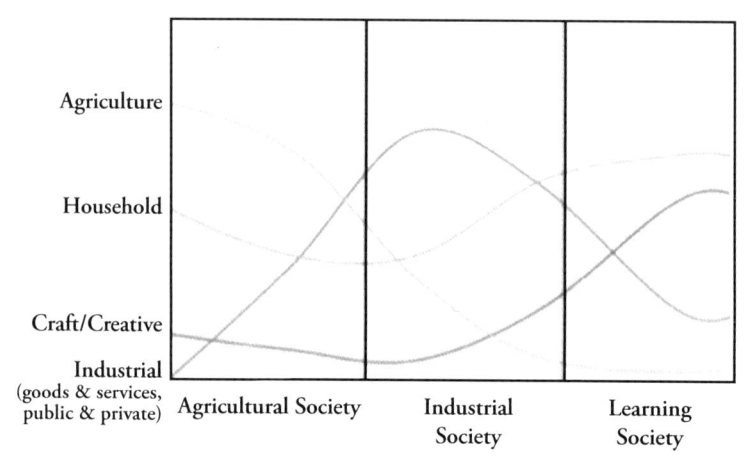

Compositional Transformation
Share of total wealth creation by source

Agriculture

Household

Craft/Creative

Industrial
(goods & services,
public & private)   Agricultural Society   Industrial Society   Learning Society

forms suggested by the terms used here may never become manifest. Either way it is not possible to use what does not yet exist. The point is that in this story humans continue to find things to do—ways to add value or create utility (even if what is deemed useful to one person is considered a waste to another and what is "value" changes over time). The category "household" activity, largely unaccounted for by industrial-era bookkeeping, involves the many activities that are not only essential for everyday life but also a fundamental component of the everyday life.

Diagram 2 illustrates this idea of a growing average learning intensity of everyday life, over an entire lifetime and across an entire society, using the four knowledge variables: know-what, know-how, know-who, and know-why. The deskilling/reskilling of know-how reflects the rise and fall of the extreme division of conception and execution achieved by the industrial creative society, with its thin layer of cream on the top, giving way to a much broader diffusion of DIY (do-it-yourself) and integrated pro/am (professional/amateur). Know-what explodes in the industrial era with the diffusion of basic literacy and the mediums of mass communication, reaching the point of information overload—not enough control to filter the raw data of information and to pay attention only to relevant sources.

Diagram 2: Imagining the Learning Intensive Society: Learning Dimension

Average Learning Intensity of Daily Life

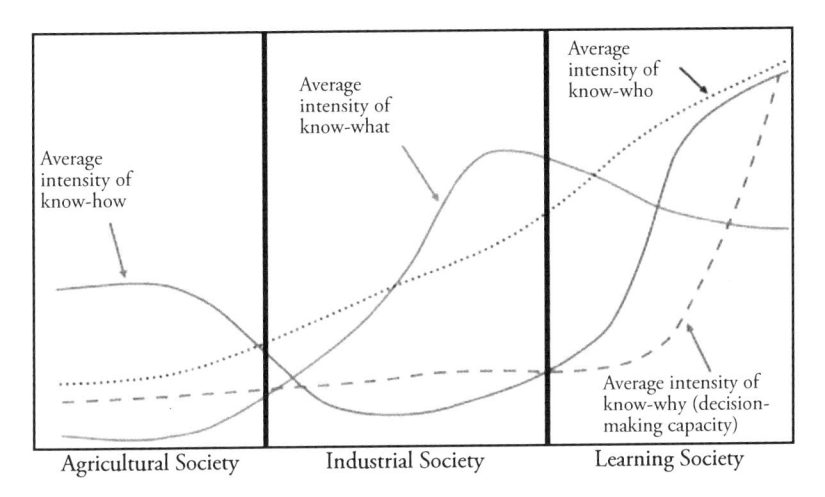

[Graph showing curves across three eras—Agricultural Society, Industrial Society, Learning Society—with labels: Average intensity of know-how, Average intensity of know-what, Average intensity of know-who, Average intensity of know-why (decision-making capacity).]

Source: Riel Miller, XperidoX Futures Consulting (rielm@yahoo.com).

Know-who increases across all "eras" as the permissions and means for connecting beyond the perimeter of the already familiar grow. The boundaries of the village, or schoolyard, or water cooler, or cafeteria all begin to fade as the connections of daily life bring a wider range of contacts. Finally, the last and potentially most influential variable for changing the overall average, since it starts from a relatively low base and grows quite quickly, is know-why. Again, not in a cosmic or "rocket science" sense of the term, but in a way that is meaningful for what people do in their everyday lives, and how they construct the "unique creations" and identities that are their world. It is this attribute, the search at a mundane and personal level for know-why, that gives the term "LIS" its meaning.

On the basis of these two frames—one related to sectoral composition and the other to learning activity—four other general attributes of the LIS can be described. Diagram 3 presents, in highly reduced form, some of the other key dimensions of a learning intensive society. Each of the possibility spaces focuses on a key dimension: technological, economic, social, and governance.

Diagram 3: Possibility Space Diagrams of Transition Scale Changes in Key Technological, Economic, Social, and Governance Variables

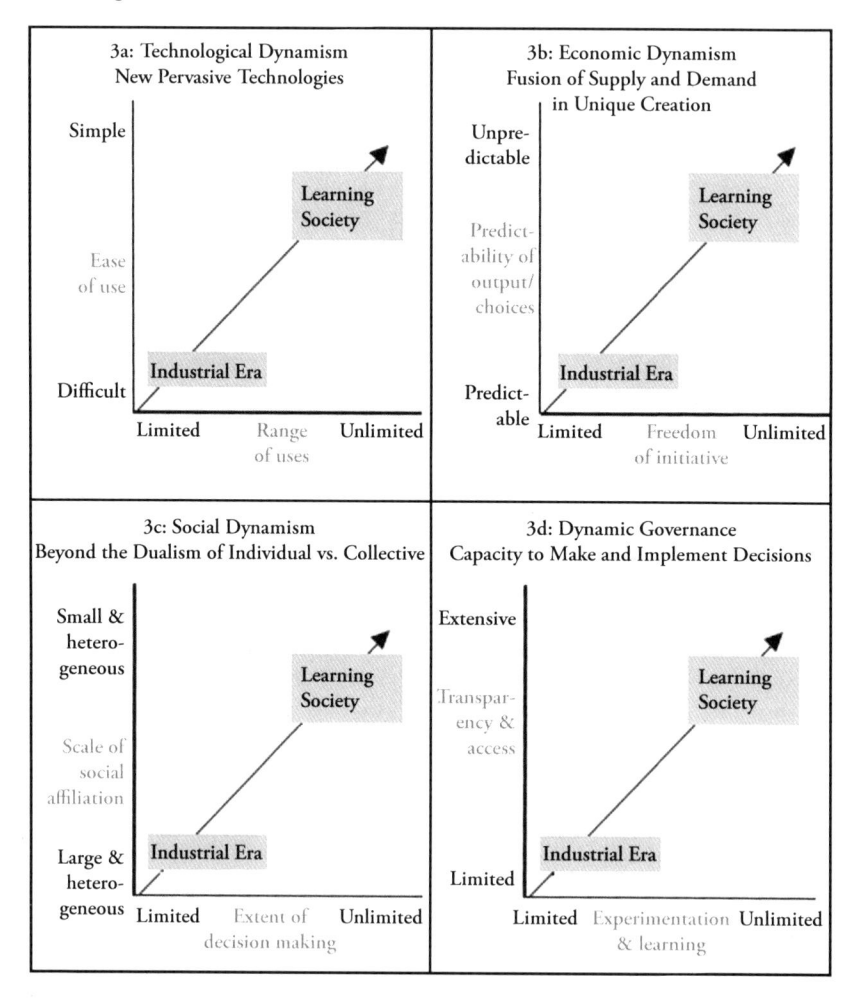

3a: Technological Dynamism New Pervasive Technologies (Simple → Difficult, Ease of use; Limited → Unlimited, Range of uses) Industrial Era → Learning Society	3b: Economic Dynamism Fusion of Supply and Demand in Unique Creation (Unpredictable → Predictable, Predictability of output/choices; Limited → Unlimited, Freedom of initiative) Industrial Era → Learning Society
3c: Social Dynamism Beyond the Dualism of Individual vs. Collective (Small & heterogeneous → Large & heterogeneous, Scale of social affiliation; Limited → Unlimited, Extent of decision making) Industrial Era → Learning Society	3d: Dynamic Governance Capacity to Make and Implement Decisions (Extensive → Limited, Transparency & access; Limited → Unlimited, Experimentation & learning) Industrial Era → Learning Society

In quadrant 3a, "technological dynamism" depicts the extent to which a new technology (or set of technologies—e.g., info-, nano- or biotechs) might become pervasive. In quadrant 3b, "economic dynamism" is described by variables that relate to changes in the basic conditions of production and consumption. In quadrant

3c, "social dynamism" is described by variables that track change in the nature of social identity—the "Who am I?" question. And in quadrant 3d, the "governance dynamism" variables capture ways in which changes in decision-making capacity can be described.

In all of these possibility spaces, the arrow of change goes from the lower left (mass era) to the upper right (learning society). Once again this is not because such a movement is considered likely or desirable. That is not the point here. The aim is solely to specify variables that can help to describe an imaginary and different social order. The LIS is meant to be a society that exhibits transition scale transformation, where transition scale is equivalent to the kinds of changes in the conduct of daily life that characterized the shift from agricultural to industrial society.

A brief elaboration of the attributes of the LIS in three of the dimensions (economic, social, and governance) may help to clarify why the LIS is discontinuous: that is, in what way there has been a change in the conditions of change (a new model, one that is not ergodic with the present model—that is, does not share the same parameters).

Economic Dynamism

This descriptive area considers discontinuity in the way that production and consumption are organized. The activity at the core of this change is "unique creation" (UC). It is what the terms imply. It is creative, something dreamt up—an "ah ha" moment—by the unique person or team that had the idea.[7] Quadrant 3b offers a partial description of the unique creator, the "artist," in the upper right of the possibility space. This diagram evokes the main organizational attributes of production: how it is coordinated and where the value added comes from. Unique creation overthrows the centrality of the two profound dualisms of industrial society, between demand and supply, conception and execution. Not quite a change in the "mode of production"—markets and private property still reign—but certainly a change in the ownership of the means of production and a decisive break with the image of the pyramidal hierarchy of creativity and talent that is used to legitimate meritocracy.

There is also a craft dimension to unique creation, highly specialized skills that are networked with both household and industrial production through co-production. This is "personalization," the self or local bespoke value added—intangible or tangible—that entails the refinement of specific skills. The artisan and expert do not disappear, but the cost of integrating their knowledge into UC through highly fluid, transparent, and dense networks is much lower. The "banal creativity" of every person as artist does not negate the role of craft but integrates and extends it in new ways.

Imagining this kind of transformation extrapolates or generalizes phenomena that are currently peripheral or only beginning to hint at the emergence of other systems, such as the growing importance of DIY and the social networks of Web 2.0 as platforms for collaborative unique creation. Such experiences and infrastructure are essential for building up the capacity, so at odds with the passivity of mass consumption and mass production, to discover and refine what matters in a unique creation economy. This investment and pursuit of meaning in unique creation, which on the surface looks like the branding and individualism of today's hyperactive conspicuous consumption, connects to another critical attribute of the LIS, the "personalization of community."

Social Dynamism

What distinguishes the present from the LIS in the "social" sphere is the basic way that identity evolves. The LIS breaks away from the dualism so dominant and powerful up until now between the individual and the state, the private and the public. Quadrant 3c describes the personalization of community through the creation of identity. In the LIS, the frenzy of efforts to fill the vacuum left by the insufficiency of yesterday's mass identities, be it nation, religion, or class, has opened up by creating space for a more engaged and collective construction of personal identity. In the LIS, learning-by-doing occurs in a highly interdependent and densely networked context. People are engaged in constant and diversified experiments in their search for an answer to the question of "Who am I?" In the LIS, there can be no mistaking that meaning is socially, interactively constructed. In the LIS, identity is personal and collective at the same time. Responsibility is internalized, not socialized.

Both the economic and the social dimensions of this imaginary LIS require an underlying capacity to be constantly engaged in decision making. It is a decision intensive social order. And since all decisions are about the future, it is also a society where anticipatory systems are called into play constantly. Relative to the industrial era, people in this imaginary LIS have an enhanced capacity to make choices. I call this "futures literacy" (FL), and it is similar to an important attribute of the functioning of industrial society, the capacity to read and write. In a similar fashion, FL plays an important role in facilitating the functioning of the economic and social organization of the LIS.

However, this enhanced capacity to make decisions does not at all imply—as might be thought on the basis of industrial-era notions of leadership, artistic genius, and entrepreneurial exceptionalism—that everyone becomes a visionary. The kind of creativity implied by the model of the LIS can be described in much more mundane terms related to the unique creations and identity development of each person, on his or her own terms and relative to his or her own path of discovery. This is the "banal creativity" that makes a learning intensive society practical, not some illusory world of hypereducated geniuses. Instead, meaning and wealth arise from the conduct of everyday activity: the day-in and day-out decisions about what to do, how to tell the story of one's self, whom to link up with and in what ways, what information is needed right now in order to act now, and so on.

Governance Dynamism
Quadrant 3d depicts this enhanced decision-making and anticipatory capacity. All other things held constant, it is reasonable to consider that, if people have more and better information, if they have more experience with making choices, and if they live in a context where value is put on developing the capacity to discover the potential of the present, then their capacity to make decisions should be better than if they lived in a context where they faced little choice, less information, fewer opportunities to experiment, and an authoritarian or fatalistic view of social well-being.

Section 2: Beyond Skills—Spontaneity, Futures Literacy, and Ambient Learning

In the LIS, the industrial-era mechanisms that create a link between skills and jobs are broken. Production activities with a one-way flow from conception to execution are no longer predominant in the LIS. Diagram 4 outlines the typical industrial-era production process that moves from an entrepreneur who has a brilliant (innovative) idea, to the design of a production process that requires specific skills, to hiring people with those skills from a pool of people trained to have those skills. Then come the test of the market and the reallocation decisions—to abandon the production process because it is not profitable or to redesign it, with implications for the skill mix.

Diagram 4: Determining Skill Needs in the Industrial Era: A Division of Conception and Execution

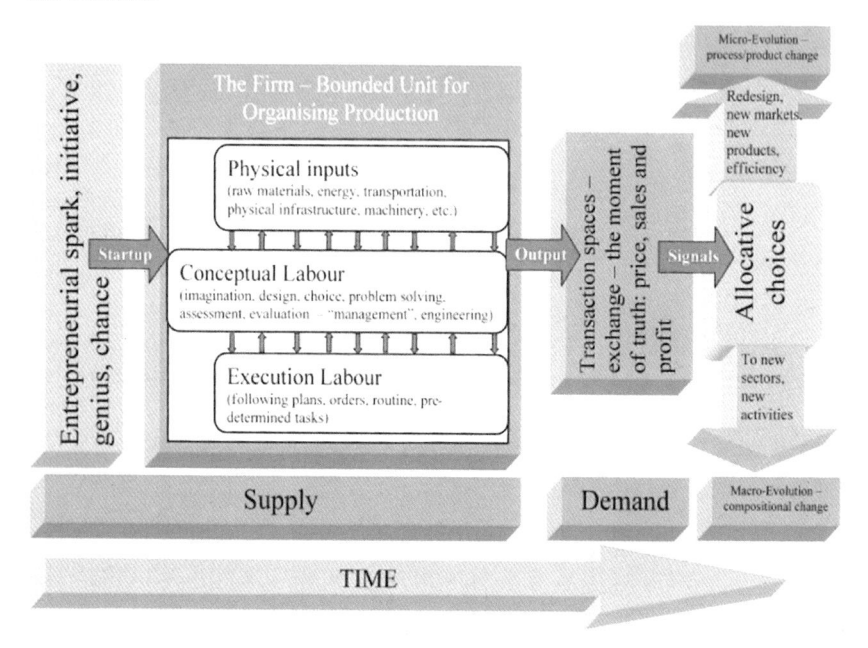

```
                    The Firm – Bounded Unit for
                    Organising Production
                ┌────────────────────────────────────┐
                │  Physical inputs                   │
 Entrepreneurial│  (raw materials, energy,           │                                    Micro-Evolution –
 spark,         │  transportation, physical          │                                    process/product change
 initiative,    │  infrastructure, machinery, etc.)  │                                    Redesign,
 genius,        │  ↑↑↑↑↑↑↑↑↑                         │   Transaction spaces –             new markets,
 chance         │  Conceptual Labour                 │   exchange – the moment            new products,
         Startup│  (imagination, design, choice,     │   of truth: price, sales    Signals efficiency
                │  problem solving, assessment,      │   and profit                        Allocative
                │  evaluation, "management",         │                                     choices
                │  engineering)                      │   Output →                          To new sectors,
                │  ↑↑↑↑↑↑↑↑↑                         │                                     new activities
                │  Execution Labour                  │
                │  (following plans, orders,         │
                │  routine, pre-determined tasks)    │
                └────────────────────────────────────┘

        Supply                                      Demand          Macro-Evolution –
                                                                    compositional change

                              TIME →
```

The process described in Diagram 4 applies to even the most "white-collar" creative work of the industrial era. The "creative class," even though they do invent things and are often the genius breakthrough innovators, like Steve Jobs or Google founders such as Page and Brin, still fit firmly within the flow of industrial production. These innovators are at the top of a pyramid and are the initiators, the decision makers who launch and control the production process and the skills that are specified and engaged in the production process. In the industrial era, production is organized for many reasons—including the way that value is accounted for (meaning what is feasible from a business model point of view)—in firms that however restructured and "modernized" remain administrative organizations.[8]

In the LIS, both the objective of the production process and the way of organizing production change profoundly.[9] First, the relationship between conception and

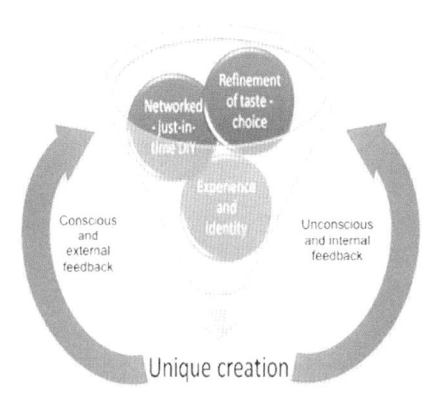

Diagram 5: Learning: The Organization of Unique Creation

![Diagram 5 showing three overlapping circles labeled "Networked - just-in-time DIY", "Refinement of taste - choice", and "Experience and Identity", with arrows connecting "Conscious and external feedback" and "Unconscious and internal feedback" leading to "Unique creation"]

execution is different since the key steps are personal and involve a fusion of what were formerly two sides of a clearly demarcated division between supply and demand. Second, given the spontaneous nature of the banal creative insights that drive personalized unique creation (material and immaterial, including identity), these "innovations" arise as people question, encounter, collaborate, discuss, reflect, and so on. This means that the skills needed to engage in these activities are largely internal to the personalization process: that is, they cannot be contracted out to someone with the skills and cannot be specified in advance because what is being produced is only discovered at the moment of its production. The more that process becomes product, the less amenable the production process to industrial-era forms of organization.

The contrast between Diagrams 4 and 5 is one way of illustrating the difference between the organization of wealth creation in the industrial era as opposed to the LIS. In Diagram 5, it is the internal process of reflection that is the fundamental moment of "production" (a term that undoubtedly is redolent of industrial-era ways of thinking). Certainly, there are feedback loops that then alter allocative choices. And there is also collaboration, in a wide variety of ways, some of which are still industrial in nature, such as outsourcing tasks or simply purchasing off-the-shelf inputs. But from a value-added point of view, largely because of the immense success of the productivity-enhancing evolution of industrial production, these outsourced activities are not the predominant source of society-wide value creation. As already suggested by the imaginary reallocation illustrated in Diagram 1, the shares of different sources of value creation have shifted. The efforts to become more competitive industrially have been successful and just like productivity enhancements in agriculture allowed resources to be devoted elsewhere.

What Diagram 5 shows is how the organization of the use of resources in the LIS is primarily devoted/created in learning: namely, learning intensive society. The preponderant share of value both used and created (input and output, stock and flow) in unique creation and the personalization of identity is not embodied in an artifact or even an experience; it arises from the learning that occurs by doing and experimenting. In other words, the radically different nature of the relationship between the socioeconomic system and skill is defined at its root by the specific nature of learning as simultaneous and inextricabe consumption (time, mental and physical energy, pleasure) and production (output of new insights, pleasure of realization, problem solved).

Of course, this does not at all imply that there is no in-depth knowledge. Quite the contrary because as people learn they deepen their knowledge of themselves in their lives, in their communities. They become wiser relative to their own aspirations and life (to be judged on heterarchical not hierarchical grounds). And, as already pointed out, there is still access to, and use of, the old industrial forms of expertise, but fortunately this is an inexpensive input. The sharing that is critical for learning is, however, central. Perhaps the easiest way to describe how value creation is organized in the LIS is with the image of a cloud.

Diagram 6 unfortunately is static in the media used here, but it should be swirling and reconnecting, with a continuous process of new hubs, new networks, new loners. It is a cloud of communities within which communities are born, and die, and change membership on a permanent basis in ways that are consistent with the unpredictability and spontaneity of complex evolutionary processes.

Imagining the LIS in this way—and it is only one way, for there is an infinite variety of other ways of describing this kind of society—puts high requirements on the achievement of transparency, access, and trust. For the LIS to be as fluid and spontaneous as the patterns within a cloud, it needs an operational infrastructure that corresponds. Such infrastructure, as Paquet underscored throughout his work on the emerging forms of governance and the limitations of current policy-making systems, still needs to be invented. The collective resources (technologies, norms,

SKILLS: BANAL CREATIVITY AND SPONTANEITY

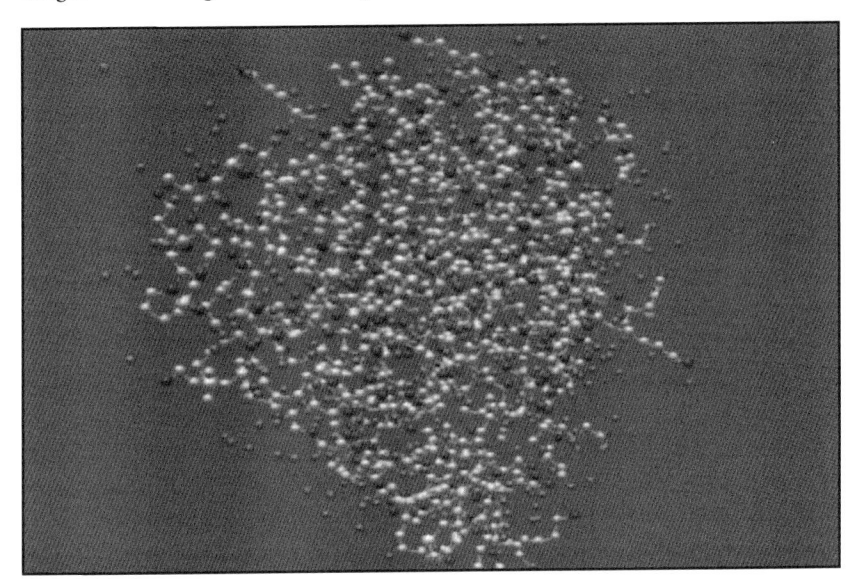

Diagram 6: Learning: Clouds of Unique Creation

institutions) such as the semantic web and ambient computing are the underlying conditions for this descriptive specification of the LIS—the environment, like the Earth's atmosphere and water that make cloud formation possible.

Similarly, the fluidity requirements for the functioning of an LIS community depend on new forms of governing networks, inventing the standards on the fly that enable asynchronous and synchronous connections with differing degrees of bandwidth (from text messages to face-to-face) combined with a high degree of interdependency. In this way, life adapts to the needs of learning as it happens, when it happens, with whom it happens, and where it happens. This is not the industrial era's organization of life to suit the needs of the place where they are willing to hire your skill set. The person is not a tool or input into a production process where the specification of the role of the tool is what defines the skill and ties the person to the job. The LIS is "beyond skills" because it is a way of imagining a community where people are not instrumentalized.

As Paquet notes, "**What is needed for a real change in the social system of knowledge production is a change in its theory. Such a change is more difficult** to neutralize, and it often turns out to be rather subversive: it triggers creative disequilibrium and cumulative causation of change" (Gilles and Paquet 1989, 11). Moreover, as Paquet mentions elsewhere, "It is difficult however to underestimate the toxic effect of positivism and scientism on the social sciences (including management). These forces denounced by Hayek (1952) have proved even more toxic than he had anticipated. Much of the research in management and governance has been vitiated by this virus, and most importantly alternative ways to strengthen the governance education have been grossly neglected" (2007, 15).

The description in this essay of a snapshot of an imaginary social order where skills are a defunct category of times gone by is meant to offer one alternative to the positivist approach to policy that Gilles so rightly exposes as a deception. What this essay in a Paquetian key attempts to do is follow his admonition to seek real change in a social system's production of knowledge by trying to change its theory. Imagining a world without skills is a practical way to reconsider the potential of the present because it helps us to challenge both implicit and explicit policy assumptions. As a practical approach to changing the theory that knowledge could fulfill, Gilles hopes that such change can trigger creative disequilibrium and cumulative causation.

Notes

[1] This short summary is based on a series of articles and presentations over the past decade, and picks up the theme of a presentation prepared for CEDEFOP. For more details and references, see www.rielmiller.com.

[2] See Goldin and Katz (2008) for a recent analysis of education and wages.

[3] See, for instance, the Canadian Index of Well-Being at www.atkinsonfoundation.ca/ciw and the "Alternative Measures of Well-Being," OECD Statistics Brief 11, May 2006.

[4] The term "production activity" is intentionally generic and could be measured in a variety of ways, including time, inputs or outputs, using monetary or non-monetary metrics. For the purposes of this story, the diagram simply illustrates a change in the shares of this type of activity.

[5] Resources devoted to the production of agriculture are not the same as the total resources devoted to what we eat, which include, among other activities, those of restaurants, home preparation of food, time spent shopping for food, learning how to cook, etc.

[6] This is not meant to imply that the different sectors are characterized by the same evolutionary processes: there are clearly distinctive dynamics in different activities, different ownership structures, etc. There are also parts of these sectors that resist

7. industrial productivity and competitiveness-enhancing changes such as the division of conception from execution, usually due to some mechanism that protects these activities from choice ,or profit, or reallocation imperatives, such as doctors and schools. Note as well that there are sectors where industrial forms of organization are finally penetrating, such as in agriculture and education.

7. Most of the discussions of the transformation of production along the lines of mass customization, unique creation, and co-design remain within the context of the overarching organizational forms of the industrial era—the firm and the administrative system. This is fair enough; the emergence of new systems happens from both within and outside existing ones—and certainly in relation to existing systems (one way or another—opposition, support, ignorance).

8. Obviously, it is possible to argue that the firm can evolve to the point where it no longer uses the administrative methods of command and control, hierarchical conception and execution, etc., but at some point in the evolutionary process resilience gives way to transformation, and there is a discontinuity of forms. The genetic origins of the human hand have been traced to the fins of fish, there is resilience or continuity of a fragment of genetic code, but it would be absurd to say that, therefore, a human is a fish.

9. The question of the business models, or how people generate income and engage in market exchange, is important, and the belief (anticipatory assumption) that firms, jobs, stores, and marketing are the only ways to make the economy go around is deeply entrenched. This is not the place to go into these how-to questions, but it is of course both historically true and within the range of our imaginations to think of a different way of realizing the advantages of market exchange and cash income.

References

Gilles, W., and G. Paquet. (1989). "On Delta Knowledge." In *Edging toward the Year 2000*, ed. G. Paquet and M. von Zur Muehlen. Ottawa: Canadian Federation of Deans of Management and Administrative Studies, 15–30.

Golding, C., and L. Katz. (2008). *The Race between Education and Technology*. Cambridge, MA: Harvard University Press.

Paquet, G. (2007). *The New Geo-Governance*. Ottawa: University of Ottawa Press.

Part Ten

A Tip of the Hat

Chapter 30

Carbon Pricing as a Wicked Problem

Thomas J. Courchene

Thank You, Gilles!

Every society needs a Gilles Paquet. He is a supradisciplinarian, a prodigious scholar who draws on the corpus of the social sciences and governance literatures to rethink and rework the complex interrelationships among and between traditional research areas. We also know him as a superb communicator and interpreter of Canadian policy and practice, not only through his many published books and articles but also bilingually via the electronic media (TVO, Radio-Canada). Indeed, one of the delights awaiting his readers or auditors is his creative wordsmithing, which has arguably now advanced to the point where a (Gillespeak?/Paquetois?) lexicon may well be in order. Moreover, Gilles has always been most generous with his time and talents. His public service ranges from his long-standing role as secretary of, and designated abstract translator of all journal articles for, the Canadian Economics Association through to his overseeing the intellectual endeavours of the Canadian academy as president of the Royal Society of Canada. On a more personal note, Gilles was always available as a presenter and/or a discussant for Queen's annual John Deutsch conferences, and I am pleased to see that these contributions have made their way into his recent edited volumes. Beyond all this, Gilles is a genuinely likable fellow: one always feels welcomed and important in his company and, of course, intellectually entertained.

Introduction and Overview[1]

Carbon pricing, whether via carbon taxes or emissions-trading systems, constitutes what Paquet (1999, 113) refers to as a "wicked problem": "These energy and environment dossiers raise complex questions; uncertainty and potential surprises become possible. The issues are not dealt with adequately by economic theory, for they include the complexity of economy-society-environment interactions where resources are not divisible, property rights are non-existent, market failures are prevalent, and other problems such as uncertainty, public goods, external effects, and irreversibility are omnipresent." The challenges at the policy level as distinct from the analytical level are equally formidable: we are unsure about the underlying science; action now will make a difference only in the distant future; vested interests are everywhere and powerful, and they include private firms as well as governments; huge amounts of money are at stake (profits for corporations, revenues for governments, prices/taxes for consumers and voters); and, perhaps most difficult of all, the interprovincial and federal–provincial politics are such that we may be headed for a rerun of the NEP-type intergovernmental conflict.

Notwithstanding these challenges, carbon-pricing policies, whether via carbon taxes or cap-and-trade systems, are clearly the flavour of the season in Canada and elsewhere. With its 2007 *Turning the Corner* regulatory framework, the federal government has committed itself to a twenty percent cut in 2006 GHG[2] emissions by 2020, in part by promising to introduce a carbon intensity (i.e., emissions per unit) cap and a permit-trading system in 2010. Ottawa's 2008 policy update promises carbon capture and storage requirements for the oil sands as well as several command-and-control measures (no dirty-coal electricity plants after 2012, vehicle emission standards, etc.). At the provincial level, Alberta became the first jurisdiction in North America to implement a soft (intensity-based) cap-and-trade regime in 2007. However, the geographical permit-trading area is limited to Alberta, and the price of the permit is effectively capped at fifteen dollars per tonne since emitters can purchase carbon offset credits at this price from an accredited R&D fund for the development of low-carbon technologies. Beyond this, both Alberta and Ottawa intend to grandfather existing industry players by distributing free of charge the initial allocation of permits (presumably in line with current activity) rather than auctioning them. This leaves the emissions market to apply, initially at least, only to "additional" permits. While this tends to be standard practice thus far in cap-and-trade systems, the preference of most environmental groups is to "auction" the initial permits (see Table 1 for information relating to cap-and-trade systems). Some or all of these features led Jeffrey Simpson (2008) to declare Alberta's approach to be "utterly untenable."

With its 2007 levy of 0.8 cent on every litre of gas and 0.9 cent on each litre of diesel fuel, Quebec became the first jurisdiction in Canada (indeed in North America) to impose a carbon tax. This is an origin-based carbon tax, and it is levied on roughly fifty large emitters and distributors.

However, Canada's carbon-pricing star is surely British Columbia. The province has introduced a consumption-based carbon tax of ten dollars per tonne to apply to all fuels (e.g., the tax on gasoline will be 2.4 cents per litre and 2.76 cents for diesel fuel). This price will rise to thirty dollars per tonne by 2010. The further innovation in British Columbia is to make this tax *revenue neutral*: namely, to use the carbon tax revenue to reduce personal and corporate taxes, and to provide low-income tax credits to help offset the rise in fuel prices. British Columbia and Manitoba also stand out as the first two Canadian members of a California-led

Table 1: Comparison of Greenhouse Gas Emission Trends

Country	Emissions Growth (without LULUCF) 1990 to 2004	Population Growth 1990 to 2004	Increase in Emissions (without LULUCF) per capita, 1990 to 2004
Australia	+24.3%	+17.0%	+6.3%
Canada	+26.6%	+17.0%	+8.2%
Japan	+ 6.5%	+ 3.1%	+3.4%
Russia	-33.1%	- 3.0%	-31%
United States	+15.8%	+17.1%	-1.2%
EU 15	-1.0%	+ 4.5%	-5.3%
Germany	-17.4%	+ 3.8%	-20.3%
UK	-14.3%	+ 4.8%	-18.2%
Rest of EU	+12.8%	+ 4.7%	+ 7.8%

Sources: Emissions data from UN FCCC emissions profiles (http://unfccc.int/ghg_ emissions_ data/ items/38954.php). Population data from US Census Bureau (http://www.census.gov/ipc/ www/idbrank.html).
Note: LULUCF is *Land-Use, Land-Use Change and Forestry.*
Reproduced from Harrison and Sundstrom (2007, Table 4).

Table 2: Cap–and–Trade Basics

Under a cap-and-trade system the authorities will determine the limit (cap) on the pollution allowed, and will issue "pollution permits" for this amount. If a company wants to produce more than it has permits for, it has to acquire additional permits from other companies, from approved "carbon offset" sources, or from the government itself in the form of, say, "price caps." This is the "trade" component of cap-and-trade and it will set the price of the permit.

Selected Features:
- Cap-and-trade systems are usually limited to large emitters.
- The cap will presumably be set in line with overall climate-change goals. The cap can be an "absolute" cap or an "intensity" cap (i.e., a cap on the emissions per unit of output). While as intensity cap may not reduce absolute emissions, it does facilitate new entrants, especially new entrants with lower-carbon technologies.
- The allocated permits are almost always distributed free of charge. However, most environmental NGOs, among others, would recommend that the permits be auctioned. This could be introduced at the outset, or the price of the permits distributed to the existing firms could be escalated gradually over time. This will yield revenues that can be used for other purposes, e.g., to provide low-income relief from rising energy prices, to reduce other taxes, to invest in low-carbon research. In this case, a cap-and-traded system takes on some of the characteristics of a carbon tax.
- In order to increase efficiency as well as to avoid price "spikes," the geographical trading area should be as large as is feasible.
  1. Some systems include a "price cap," i.e., a limit on how high the permit price can rise. This can undermine the integrity of the system. So can a guarantee that carbon offsets are available at a fixed price, since this is in effect a price cap. For example, in Alberta's cap-and-trade system, there is a widely available offset set at $15/tonne if the payment goes to a low-carbon-technology fund. If this price cap is effective, them the cap-and-trade system effectively becomes a variant of a carbon tax system.
  2. Cap-and-trade systems can be complex to implement and manage since, at a minimum, the trading component needs to include brokers, bankers, insurers, lawyers, carbon auditors, etc., as well as a host of regulations (replete with regulators).

This table draws in part from Matt Horne's "Cap-and-Trade" Fact Sheet (Pembina Institute, 2008).

group of seven western states (known as the Western Climate Initiative or WCI) that has embraced a cap-and-trade system to reduce members' GHG emissions by fifteen percent of 2005 levels by 2020.

Perhaps the most surprising recent development is the agreement between Ontario and Quebec announced at their joint cabinet meeting (June 2, 2008) to launch a cap-and-trade system anchored to the original Kyoto 1990 benchmark. The remarks by Premier Jean Charest indicate that the intention is to establish a market-based trading system to cut GHG emissions that will hopefully lay the groundwork for a national cap-and-trade system with more teeth than the current federal proposal. Earlier in 2008, Quebec also became a member of the WCI (followed by Ontario in July 2008). One might also note that, thanks to Quebec's hydroelectric power, among other factors, this province has already met the 2008–12 Kyoto targets and, therefore, is in a strong position to take a hard line on the climate-change front.

As I was writing this paper, the federal Liberals made public their Green Shift: namely, their revenue-neutral carbon tax on fossil fuels (modelled along the lines of the Mintz–Olewiler proposal, elaborated later in this paper), the Green Party made public its carbon tax, and the NDP has promised to introduce a cap-and-trade proposal in the near future.

With this brief overview of the wicked problem of climate change as well as the current state of play in terms of the equally complex range of carbon-pricing proposals as backdrop, this paper will focus on alternative approaches to carbon pricing as they relate to a series of contentious policy challenges: the ongoing Kyoto reality that developing countries should be exempt from formal climate change requirements; the related free-rider problems and international competitiveness; alternative versions of carbon taxation; cap-and-trade systems; environmental federalism; and the role of carbon pricing and taxing in the context of $140/barrel oil.

Canada and Kyoto

GHG Measurement Issues
My launching point into this broad-ranging set of issues is hardly original: namely, to argue that Canada's approach to Kyoto was a triumph of moral voluntarism over rational analysis. "Canada made a commitment at Kyoto that was the most difficult and expensive in the world. It took no account of our economic growth, population growth, cold temperature, vast distances and fossil fuel production; it contravened our federal system, because Ottawa broke a fragile federal-provincial consensus on the eve of the negotiations. So the first lesson must be to remember

these factors—and therefore undertake commitments and implement serious domestic policies that take these distinctly Canadian factors into account, because no other country has all of these characteristics" (Simpson, Jaccard, and Rivers 2007, 249–50). By way of some elaboration, and again drawing from Simpson, Jaccard, and Rivers (2007), over the 1990–2005 period Canada's average annual population growth rate was just over one percent, about two and a half times that of France, four times that of Germany, and five times that of Italy. Given that the Kyoto targets are *absolute targets*, this effectively sets the bar significantly higher for Canada than for the slower-growing European countries: that is, Canada will have to make greater per capita cuts in emissions than slower-growing countries to meet these absolute targets. Moreover, the selection of 1990 as the Kyoto benchmark year was very beneficial to Germany. When the two Germanys were reunited, the newly merged country inherited the East German-era plants that generated pollution levels that were extraordinary by Western standards. By simply closing these plants or by upgrading them to Western norms, Germany achieved its 2008–12 Kyoto targets by 1992!

Harrison and Sundstrom (2007) elaborate, noting that Germany's "windfall reduction" also applied to the United Kingdom (because of the ongoing conversion of its electricity generation plants from coal to offshore gas) and to Russia (because of economic collapse and the unwinding of heavy-polluting industries). To present a more realistic assessment of what has transpired under Kyoto, Harrison and Sundstrom rework GHG comparisons on a per capita basis (see Table 1), on which they comment as follows:

> While there is tremendous variation in performance, from a 33% decline in emissions in Russia to a 27% increase in Canada [column 1], the variation in population growth evident in the next column suggests that emissions trends reflect more than just policy efficacy. Canada, the US, and Australia have experienced much greater increases in emissions in large part because they have experienced much greater population growth than other jurisdictions. Indeed, when one compares trends in *per capita* emissions [column 3], it is striking that the only country to see a decline other than the three that experienced "windfall" reductions (Germany, the UK, and Russia) is the US, which has been vilified for its decision not to ratify the Kyoto Protocol. In fact, with the exception of Germany and the UK, the rest of the EU has experienced per capita emissions

comparable to Canada and Australia [compare the last row of column 3 with the first two rows] (14).

This is not the only area where Canada's Kyoto negotiators settled for arrangements that clearly disadvantaged Canada relative to other nations. Assigning emissions is another problem area.

Assigning Resource Emissions
The following is from a recent *Globe and Mail* op ed:

> At the recent World Petroleum Congress in Madrid, the head of India's state oil company stated that his company could invest up to $10 billion in Canada's oil sands. Let's assume that India does this and that, in return, it ends up importing $1 billion per year of oil-sands fossil fuel. Who should be assigned the carbon footprint of producing this oil? The Kyoto Protocol would say Canada, and so too would virtually all nations including Canada itself. But this is the wrong answer: the carbon footprint should be assigned to India! Moreover, while the focus is on the oil sands in this example, the principle should apply to the carbon footprint of all of our resource exports. Unless addressed, this fundamental error will wreak havoc with any and all Canadian approaches to climate change.
>
> Consider the following example: Canada produces 100 barrels of oil and exports 60 barrels, say to China. The carbon footprint of using (consuming) the 60 barrels will be assigned to the importing country and the footprint of consuming domestically the remaining 40 barrels will be assigned to Canada. So far, so good. The problem, however, is with the allocation of the carbon footprint of *producing* these 100 barrels.
>
> Under existing practice, this will be assigned to Canada and, given the resource intensity of the Canadian economy, contributes to our very high per capita greenhouse gas (GHG) emissions. In contrast, a country such as Japan, which imports virtually all of the vast resources that it consumes each year, is charged only with the GHG emissions attributable to their *consumption*; the very substantial carbon footprint ascribed to the *production* of these resources is charged to its trading partners. The net result of this practice is that countries such as Japan and many members of the European Union appear to be much better environmental citizens

than they really are, while the resource-producing countries such as Canada, Australia and Russia, appear much worse (Courchene and Allan 2008b).

To anticipate the ensuing analysis, the preferred analytical solution to this assignment problem is a "carbon-added" tax, along the European value-added-tax model or Canada's GST model. Under this approach, elaborated later, the full carbon footprint of a product (measured along the entire production chain) will be taxed at the consumer level. This will address the above assignment problem since the emissions arising from producing fossil fuels will be taxed based on where the ultimate products are consumed. Intriguingly, this is fully in line with California's approach to Canada's oil sands. Specifically, California intends to calculate the carbon footprint by looking through to the source of any imported fossil energy. If the resulting GHG emissions exceed the state's internal standard, then the energy cannot enter California. Recently, America's mayors have adopted a similar stance with respect to the oil sands, following on earlier US federal legislation along similar lines relating to the carbon footprint acceptability for gasoline for use in its various motor vehicle fleets. Ideally, one would prefer that California impose a tariff based on an appropriate per-tonne dollar value of GHG emissions so that it will be easier for Alberta to put in place the requisite technology to allow its oil sands energy to enter California. An outright ban can be modelled as an import tax of zero up to the trigger value of emissions, at which point the import tax becomes infinite. Why only these two extreme points? Admittedly, the answer might be that California does not have the constitutional ability to impose tariffs, whereas it can apply these "command-and-control" measures. In any event, the state's approach to the oil sands may have as much impact on Alberta's environmental policies as anything that Ottawa is likely to adopt over the near term.

I will return to this assignment problem and implications therefrom later in the analysis. I now direct attention toward the implications arising from exempting the developing nations from binding Kyoto commitments.

Exempting Developing Countries

Climate Change Issues
The final bit of Kyoto backdrop relates to the decision to put binding constraints only on the developed countries. The developing countries' mantra was, in effect,

that "We were not a major part of the cause of any climate change problem, so why should we be a major part of the solution?" Along these lines, the 1991 Beijing Ministerial Declaration on Environment and Development asserted that responsibility for the emissions of greenhouse gases should be viewed both in historical and cumulative terms, and in terms of current emissions. Specifically, the view was that equity considerations would dictate that those developed countries that have contaminated most in terms of the problem should contribute most in terms of the solution. Similarly, the 1997 Brazilian Protocol proposed to link each country's responsibilities to its current and earlier emissions. In the event, the Kyoto Protocol reflected these historical moral obligations. As of the end of 2007, 175 countries ratified Kyoto. Of these 175, only 37 developed countries (plus the European Union as a party in its own right) were required to reduce greenhouse gas emissions to the levels specified for each of them in the treaty. As for the remaining 137 developing countries that also ratified the protocol (including Brazil, China, and India), they have *no obligations* beyond monitoring and reporting emissions.

Even if one were to hold the view that, on moral and equity grounds, the developed nations must bear the lion's share in terms of combatting climate change, there are two fundamental difficulties with this aspect of Kyoto. The first, and most important of the two, is that, if addressing climate change is left only to the developed or industrial countries, then the world will not be able to avoid the environmental "tipping point." By way of elaboration, again consider China. In 2004, annual CO_2 emissions (in millions of metric tonnes) were 6,049 and 5,010 for the United States and China respectively. However, by 2006, the Netherlands Environmental Assessment Agency ranked China as number one in CO_2 emissions. Moreover, China is already the largest user of coal and is planning to open at least one new coal-fired power plant every week for the foreseeable future.

In more aggregate terms, in 2004, non-OECD emissions of carbon dioxide exceeded OECD emissions for the first time (*International Energy Outlook* 2007). And by 2030, CO_2 emissions from the non-OECD countries are projected to be half again as large as those from OECD countries (i.e., fifty-seven percent larger). Writing in the *New York Times*, Andrew Revkin (2007) cites yet another perspective on the developing/developed nations' role in addressing climate change: "Even if the established industrial powers turned off every power plant and car right now, unless there are changes in policy in poorer countries the concentration of carbon dioxide in the atmosphere could still reach 450 parts per million—a level deemed unacceptably dangerous by many scientists—by 2070. If no one does anything, that threshold is reached in 2040." John Allan and I (2008, FP15) concluded our recent *Financial Post* op ed with the following stark contrast: "In Ontario we lament the delay in closing a few coal-fired generating plants, while China's development plan calls for opening 560 such plants between now and 2012." China could counter with the argument that its "one-child policy" represents (indirectly) one of the most effective climate change initiatives anywhere, but the tipping-point reality implies that Kyoto needs to be rethought.

International Competitiveness Issues

The second reason why full exemption of the developing nations is problematic relates to "free-riding." As outlined elsewhere, there are two sorts of free-riding: "The first is that firms in non-signatory countries, or non-complying countries, will have an advantage in terms of exporting to complying countries, and to international markets generally. The second is that firms in complying countries will have enhanced incentives to outsource from, or offshore to, non-complying countries, and then re-export back to their home countries, thereby avoiding the domestic environmental regime. Moreover, as China, Brazil, India and the others continue their economic ascent, these free-riding concerns of complying countries will be correspondingly magnified and will surely test the resolve of those countries to hold to their commitments" (Courchene and Allan 2008a, 60).

It is not obvious that challenging Kyoto on this issue should be viewed, as some have argued, as the developed world turning its back on the developing world by using climate change as the new protectionist instrument. After all, China has, via export surpluses with the developed world, accumulated over a trillion US dollars in foreign exchange reserves, much of it earned from the exports of foreign multinationals operating in China. Phrased differently, the United States and the European Union have opened their domestic markets to Chinese exports (and much of this at a value for the Chinese Renminbi that was and remains hugely undervalued), so that any general charge of economic discrimination against the developing regions seems hard to sustain. In any event, the reality is that, if addressing climate change requires the developed countries to put their global economic competitiveness at risk, then many more countries than the United States will opt to remain off-side.

However, while the moral voluntarism underpinning Kyoto appears dead, as does free-riding, climate change policies are alive and well. The Europeans, after an initial cap-and-trade failure where the price of carbon-trading permits fell to zero, are operating a reworked cap-and-trade system. In the United States, Congress is currently debating a cap-and-trade bill, while the individual states are actively pursuing the establishment of emissions-trading systems. And as already noted, Ottawa and the provinces have mounted (or proposed) a wide range of carbon tax or trading systems. It is not clear what all of this means for the future of Kyoto. It may well be that the superpowers (developed and developing) will agree on a system that will then be applied more generally. In any event, the remainder of the analysis will focus on the domestic and international implications of alternative approaches to carbon pricing for Canada.

Carbon Pricing I: Carbon Taxes

A Carbon-Added Tax Model
It was this constellation of challenges (as well as interprovincial and federal provincial challenges elaborated later) that led John Allan and I (Courchene and Allan 2008a) to propose a two-tier approach to climate change. The first tier is what might be called the "tradeables tier," and the second tier can be referred to (with some degree of misrepresentation) as the "non-tradeables tier." I will deal with each in turn.

The Tradeables Tier
The tradeables tier would consist of a destination-based (consumption-based) tax on the carbon footprint of all goods and services, domestic and foreign. One variant of this could be along the lines of the Mintz-Olewiler model addressed below. However, our (analytically) preferred option would be what we call a "carbon-added tax": that is, the carbon equivalent of a traditional value-added tax (a European VAT or a Canadian GST). Under such a system, there will be a tax on the carbon emissions added at each stage. As the product moves through the various stages, the taxes levied in previous stages are rebated, so only the carbon added in a particular stage is taxed at that stage. Hence, when the product reaches the final stage, the tax is on the cumulative value of carbon emissions: that is, on the sum of the amounts of carbon emissions added at each stage. As with the GST, the tax accumulated to the stage where the product is exported will be rebated, so that the

carbon tax does not impact our international competitiveness. Relatedly, a carbon tax will be assigned on all imports in line with the aggregate amount of carbon emissions (including those arising from transporting the product to Canada).

Thus, *the carbon-added tax is export-import neutral* (it does not affect the international competitiveness of Canadian production in either domestic or external markets). The carbon tax on imports will be identical across countries (e.g., forty-two dollars per tonne) and be the same as the domestic tax rate. However, similar imports from different countries may carry different tax levies depending on their carbon emissions prior to landing in Canada. Given that value-added taxes are fully acceptable under WTO rules (indeed, they are not even considered as "border adjustments" since they are effectively regulated/imposed in the domestic production/consumption process), the presumption is that a carbon-added tax should, in principle, fall well within WTO guidelines. Measurement problems will likely be severe (depending on how detailed the classification is) so that international agreement here may be more difficult. However, the increasing concern about carbon has already launched a "carbon auditors" industry that may well make the measurement issues less severe than they might at first appear. Moreover, some recent papers provide a less information-intensive approach to assigning carbon-added taxes to imports (e.g., Ismer and Neuhoff 2007).

There is another way of viewing the carbon-added tax. Since most exports come from global multinationals, the international component of the carbon tax is in the first instance a tax on the carbon footprint created by the exports of these global multinationals rather than on the exporting countries themselves. That is, Wal-Mart's imports from its suppliers in China will be subject to the carbon tax whether or not China itself is a "signatory" to the carbon tax regime. One assumes that, other things equal, these multinationals will select production locations in order to minimize carbon footprints (including shipping). Similarly, one also assumes that all nations will recognize that introducing low-carbon-emitting fuels and production processes will make them more attractive places for production and export.

The revenues arising from a carbon tax can be made "revenue neutral" (as in the BC model) in a variety of ways: providing equivalent income tax cuts, providing income support to those most vulnerable to the carbon tax, allocating some of the revenues to transferring state-of-the-art-low-carbon technologies to the developing world, etc. More on revenues later.

Finally, while the carbon tax is offered as a global approach to climate change, its advantages (e.g., export–import neutrality) would also apply at a regional level (EU or NAFTA) or even at a national level.

The Non-Tradeables Tier
While the first tier deals with tax measures relating to the tradeables sector domestically and internationally, the second tier would focus on environmental policy relating to the non-tradeables economy and to domestic infrastructure more generally. The emphasis here could be on command-and-control measures (emissions caps, automobile emissions standards, energy-efficient appliances) as well as on policies that reduce emissions related to the provision of electricity and transportation. Since tier one largely eliminates international free-riding, a Kyoto-type approach may be suitable for this second tier. Specifically, while it would be important to try to strive for commitments from all countries, the developing countries could be accorded some second-tier flexibility. Beyond this, there should be commitments by developed nations to provide funding for the transfer of state-of-the-art-carbon-reducing technologies to developing countries. In addition, and as earlier alluded to, there will presumably be interest in the developing countries to reduce the carbon content of their particular infrastructure and economic system, since this will make their economies more attractive to global capital for exporting, outsourcing, and offshoring tradeables.

Prior to focusing on cap-and-trade systems for pricing carbon, it is appropriate to direct some attention to an alternative carbon tax model, namely that proposed by Jack Mintz and Nancy Olewiler (2008)—a model that has attracted considerable media attention and one that underpins the Liberal Party's Green Shift proposal.

The Mintz–Olewiler Carbon Tax
The Mintz–Olewiler carbon tax model would convert the existing ten cents per gallon federal tax on gasoline to a carbon tax equivalent (roughly forty-two dollars per tonne of CO_2). This carbon tax of forty-two dollars per tonne would then be extended to include heating oil, natural gas, coal, and so on, which in turn would ensure a level playing field across alternative fuels. Over time, this carbon tax could increase in line with the dictates of the climate change policy. Mintz and Olewiler (2008) follow the BC model by proposing that the resulting significant increase in revenues (potentially in the $15 billion range) be returned in the form of income

tax reductions or tax relief for low-income Canadians so that, overall, the carbon tax becomes revenue neutral. As already noted, this model underpins the Liberal Party's carbon tax policy.

Given that this carbon tax of forty-two dollars per tonne relates to the carbon emissions that will result from utilizing these fossil fuels for motive transportation (gasoline, propane), for generating electricity (coal, natural gas), for heating (coal, natural gas, heating oil), etc., there is also a need for an *upstream tax* to take account of carbon emissions that result from the *production* of these fossil fuels in the first place (refineries for oil and gas, etc.). Mintz and Olewiler (2008) are silent on this particular issue, but since their underlying principles include broad-based taxation and export-import neutrality one presumes that these carbon emissions would also be taxed at forty-two dollars per tonne and then become incorporated into the prices of the fossil fuels. However, because these upstream and downstream taxes would not be integrated along the lines of the above carbon-added tax, some specific import tariff will be necessary for imported fuels that have not been subject to the tax of forty-two dollars per tonne at the production end in the exporting country (and one needs to find some way to incorporate the shipping footprint). It may be more difficult to obtain WTO agreement for this sort of import tariff than would be the case under a carbon-added tax because the import tariff may have to differ across countries. Ideally, the solution would be harmonization internationally of environmental taxes.

While the carbon-added tax model is, arguably, a preferred model analytically, the Mintz–Olewiler model may be more amenable politically and practically since it is limited at its core to primarily taxing the carbon arising from consuming fossil energy. The explicit recommendation for the tax to be revenue neutral may also be an attractive feature in terms of public acceptability. Note that one could also apply revenue neutrality to the earlier carbon-added tax model.

Carbon Pricing II: Cap-and-Trade (C&T) Systems

Why would Canada opt for a carbon tax or a carbon-added tax when there seems to be a growing consensus internationally in favour of a C&T system? This is especially true in the United States, where an earlier C&T system successfully addressed the acid rain problem caused in part by SO_2 emissions. While there is some evidence that a carbon tax is drawing increasing attention at the analytical/conceptual level in the United States, cap-and-trade systems still dominate the policy agenda. The recent Quebec–Ontario proposal, which conceives of its C&T approach as the catalyst for the development of an integrated system domestically and internationally, may add to the likelihood that C&T will carry the policy day, even in Canada.

This being the case, it is instructive to highlight some of the strengths and weaknesses of cap-and-trade systems. Table 1 provides some relevant backdrop. One attractive feature of this approach is, of course, the existence of a "cap" on emissions, with strict penalties for non-compliance. Over time, this cap can be lowered by reducing the number of available permits. Many citizens and stakeholders favour a C&T system because it tackles carbon emissions *directly* rather than via the price (or tax) system that characterizes the carbon tax approach. Indeed, Environment Minister John Baird (2008) refers to the carbon tax as a "pay and pollute" system in contrast to a C&T system, which mandates cuts in emissions. However, and beyond the reality that both Alberta and Ottawa have embraced intensity rather than absolute caps in their C&T systems, the presence of "soft" price caps on tradeable permit prices in both of these C&T proposals (e.g., Alberta has a price of fifteen dollars per tonne on emissions provided that the payment is directed to a low-carbon-technology fund) means that these C&T systems effectively revert to carbon tax systems when the price caps are in play.

A second desirable feature is that permit trading will be efficiency enhancing: that is, it will serve to increase output for a given level of carbon emissions. Phrased differently, permit trading will serve to equalize the marginal cost of carbon abatement across all companies. However, the efficiency gains will be larger where the geographical trading area is larger. This is of special concern with respect to the Alberta C&T scheme, which limits trading and offsets to Alberta, with the consequent dual likelihood that permit prices will be highly volatile and that the price cap of fifteen dollars per tonne will come into play.

As the third item of Table 1 indicates, most of the time the bulk of the permits is distributed free of charge to the existing players. The alternative approach would be to auction these initial permits or at least to begin to assign a price to them over time. In turn, this will generate revenues that can be used for a variety of purposes, including sheltering lower-income Canadians from rapidly increasing carbon prices. Obviously, industry would favour the free initial distribution of permits since they are potentially very valuable assets (depending on the carbon-trading price) and since this puts new entrants at a distinct disadvantage. It is interesting to speculate whether the tendency for industry to favour a C&T system (rather than a carbon tax) would alter if all permits were to be auctioned.

By way of a few further observations relating to C&T systems, the scope of the coverage normally applies only to large emitters; that, in turn, requires that some complementary or supplementary system be in place for smaller emitters. Moreover, whereas the implementation challenge with a carbon-added version of a carbon tax is likely to be the information overload required for calculating carbon footprints, the implementation issue with C&T will be the creation of a trading network (bureaucracy) of traders, financial institutions, lawyers, auditors, insurers, etc., that will be required to run the trading component of C&T. Relatedly, the lead time required to mount a C&T system will be much longer than that for a carbon tax. Finally, and more positively, a carbon tax should be able to be married to a C&T system. One approach would be to combine a destination-based carbon tax with a cap-on-trade system for large emitters. Indeed, British Columbia seems committed to doing just this, so that we may have a real experiment from which to learn. The bottom line here, however, is that we need more analytical research and policy thinking on how these two systems can be integrated so that the resulting harmonization is effectively threefold: federal–provincial, interprovincial, and international.

Carbon Taxes and Environmental Federalism

This reference to the intergovernmental linkages leads rather directly into an analysis of the federal–provincial and interprovincial implications of alternative policy approaches to climate change. The appropriate initial comment is to congratulate and thank the provinces for their creative proposals for reducing GHGs. Intriguingly, in both the United States and Canada, it is the *subnational governments* that are driving the climate change agenda, while their respective federal governments are either politically or ideologically unable/unwilling to assume leadership on this file.

However, there is a potential downside to all of this: namely, that the proliferation of uncoordinated policies at the provincial level may well be hurtling us toward another NEP-style scenario. Indeed, Peter Lougheed has duly alerted Canadians to this as a distinct possibility. The emerging status quo is already showing signs of dissonance on both the economic and the political (intergovernmental) fronts. With Alberta imposing an origin-based emissions charge (essentially a tax on production) and with British Columbia, among others, imposing a destination-based carbon tax (essentially a tax on consumption), the stage is set for an interprovincial and a federal–provincial donnybrook. From past experience, the issues in play here are highly explosive.

- *Political/constitutional*: Who has the right to tax/regulate carbon emissions?
- *Fiscal/financial*: Who gets the revenues from carbon abatement?
- *Competitiveness*: How can we level the playing field for Canadian industry both interprovincially and internationally?

Unfortunately for the provinces, and in spite of their creative and most welcome climate change initiatives, they probably have to reconcile themselves to living with three inconvenient truths. First, while Section 92A gives the provinces substantial control over their resources, pricing carbon may not be viewed by the courts as equivalent to taxing or pricing resources. In other words, a carbon tax is an indirect tax, and indirect taxes fall within federal powers or at least are subject to federal paramountcy. Second, and relatedly, according to two recent analyses (Elgie 2007; Hogg 2008), Ottawa has the constitutional right to introduce a C&T system via one or more of the criminal power; the peace, order, and good government (POGG) power; the trade and commerce power; and perhaps the treaty-cum-executive power. However, it is not clear that this means that the provinces would necessarily have to vacate the field. Third, the provinces individually are not able to level the playing field for their industries because it is not within their constitutional powers to generate either interprovincial or international export–import neutrality (via interprovincial export rebates and import tariffs respectively). In the final analysis, therefore, we may well end up with dual tandems—a combination of C&T and carbon tax regimes, on the one hand, and federal and provincial carbon-pricing oversight, on the other.

By way of a final (and again highly controversial) comment relating to the fiscal or financial aspects of environmental federalism, I want to advance the argument that a destination-based carbon tax is an appropriate way to geographically allocate the revenues arising from carbon abatement policies. First, the impacts of carbon emissions and climate change are borne rather equally by *all Canadians no matter where they live* and not only by the residents of fossil fuel-producing provinces.

Indeed, if there is an area of Canada that suffers most from the effects of climate change, it is surely the North. Second, the export–import neutrality of a carbon-added tax serves to level the domestic and international competitive playing fields for Canada's industries since the tax is effectively paid by consumers. Third, it therefore seems appropriate that any revenues arising from carbon abatement ought to be distributed in a manner that relates to *the location of consumption rather than to the location of production*. Suppose the opposite was the case, that revenues from pollution abatement went, via origin-based emission taxes, to the energy provinces. This would mean that, not only would the energy provinces be receiving the huge rents/royalties from fossil energy, but they would also be receiving the revenues from carbon abatement taxes. Given the long-standing fiscal equity issue relating to the funding of energy royalties in the equalization program, an origin-based emissions tax the proceeds of which would accrue to the energy provinces would dramatically exacerbate an already acute interprovincial fiscal imbalance. Arguably, therefore, a nationally run, destination-based carbon tax regime seems to be the preferred policy option on this score because the revenues from carbon abatement policies will be distributed across the provinces in line with the carbon footprints of the consumed products. And fourth, this is not intended to be a federal revenue grab. Indeed, there is no reason for Ottawa not to seriously consider sharing these carbon-tax revenues with the provinces (just as it shares the HST in Atlantic Canada). Moreover, both Ottawa and the provinces may also want to pursue revenue-neutral strategies for their respective shares of the carbon tax.

By way of a concluding comment on why environmental federalism is so challenging, there is no equivalent on the environmental front to the roughly fifty-year history of federal–provincial fiscal relations dating from the inauguration of the equalization program in 1957. This includes scores of annual meetings of federal and provincial bureaucrats. The processes of fiscal federalism also include a host of federal–provincial agreements on equalization, tax-collection harmonization, and even securing the internal social and economic fiscal unions. However, over the foreseeable future, environmental federalism will likely become every bit as important as fiscal federalism. Indeed, it may embrace key aspects of fiscal federalism. Given this and the reality that the political and institutional machinery in the area of environmental federalism ranges from weak to non-existent in comparison with the fiscal federalism infrastructure, both Ottawa and the provinces (individually and/or via the Council of the Federation) need to take immediate steps to deepen the intergovernmental infrastructure relating to the substance and the processes of environmental federalism. As matters now stand, were one to call a federal–provincial meeting on climate change, it is not clear to whom one would send the invitations—to the environment ministers, to the finance ministers, to the industry ministers, to the intergovernmental ministers, or perhaps even to the first ministers? Of and by itself, this is probably a good reflection of the degree of disarray that pervades our climate change policies.

Carbon Pricing and $130 per Barrel Oil

It is appropriate to conclude with a few comments on carbon pricing in the face of $130 per barrel oil (at the time of writing). Specifically, should the timing and implementation of a carbon tax proceed without consideration of the level and recent history of energy prices? The theoretical answer may well be yes. After all, the oil price is set internationally by market forces, presumably with little reference at any point in time to global warming. Therefore, there is still a rationale for a carbon tax to offset the social or societal cost attributable to the carbon footprint of fossil energy production and consumption. Moreover, the mushrooming energy prices for oil and natural gas will serve to unlevel the playing field across all fossil fuels. For example, a rational response to skyrocketing oil and natural gas prices could well lead to a shift toward (now very much) lower-priced coal and, therefore, lead to a compounding of the GHG problem. Phrased differently, from a purist's vantage point, carbon abatement policy ought to ensure that the prices of alternative fuels reflect their environmental as well as their economic costs.

However, the political and policy implementation perspectives, in contrast to the analytical perspectives, may well work in the other direction. First, an increase in the price of natural gas or in the price of gas at the pump is, from a consumer's standpoint, identical to an equivalent increase in a carbon tax on these fuels (abstracting from a provision for revenue neutrality). Second, the actual carbon-equivalent tax corresponding to the recent energy price hikes is substantially higher than the proposed carbon tax in any of the recent climate change proposals. For example, the Liberals' Green Shift does not even propose an immediate hike in the existing ten-cent federal tax at the pump. Third, the already evident market responses to these higher energy prices are exactly the responses that one would expect from a carbon tax on gasoline and natural gas. For example, consumers are acting rationally and rapidly to these price hikes, so much so that the auto industry is mothballing production of trucks and SUVs in favour of developing electric cars. More generally, importers of a wide range of products are rethinking sourcing offshore because shipping costs are too high. Therefore, if energy prices remain at current levels, let alone move toward the $200 per barrel price that some are predicting, it is likely that market forces will be sufficient to modify societal behaviour in line with what was expected to be achieved by rigorous climate change policies. Hence, mounting a carbon tax in the context of $130 per barrel oil could be viewed as policy overkill (and possibly political overkill). Indeed, one alternative strategy that might be considered is to have a policy "on the shelf," as it were, that would gradually implement a carbon tax if and when global oil prices fall back to more traditional levels. In the interim, however, the responses of consumers and producers alike to these high energy prices are providing us with valuable information that should be brought to bear in terms of the design and magnitude of any eventual carbon-pricing regime.

Conclusion

In this paper, I attempted to spell out the various scientific, measurement, verification, fiscal, intergovernmental (domestic and international), constitutional, sectoral/industrial, and competitiveness issues—many of them zero sum in nature—that are conspiring to ensure that climate change qualifies as one of Paquet's "wicked problems." I then attempted to make some progress in coming to grips with climate change policies. My chosen solution is a VAT-style, carbon-added tax (developed in collaboration with my Queen's colleague John Allan) that addresses climate change in a comprehensive way by levelling the playing field across all products and integrating the tax regime across all jurisdictions. Thus far, however, it appears that the cap-and-trade model has the upper hand. This being the case, I have articulated the features that ought to be included in an effective cap-and-trade system.

The other theme of the above analysis is that implementing climate change policy in a decentralized federation such as ours is much more challenging than it is in a unitary state or even in a centralized federation. Beyond recommending that Gilles Paquet be designated to turn his prodigious analytical and wordsmithing talents toward taming the climate change policy dragon, my concluding comment and my own attempt at wordsmithing is that "environmental federalism" is about to enter our policy vocabulary, and it will surely enjoy a long and complex policy life.

Notes

[1] It is a pleasure to thank my Queen's colleague John Allan for valuable comments and suggestions in preparing this paper. In parts, the analysis draws heavily from our joint work (Allan and Courchene 2008; Courchene and Allan 2008a, 2008b). I have also borrowed freely from two recent presentations (Courchene 2008a, 2008b). The usual caveats apply.

[2] The terms "carbon" and "greenhouse gases" (GHGs) are used interchangeably in this paper.

References

Allan, J. R., and T. J. Courchene. (2008). "Level the Greenhouse." *National Post*, May 15, FP15.

Courchene, T. J. (2008a). "Climate Change, Competitiveness, and Environmental Federalism: The Case for a Carbon Tax." Background paper for Canada 2020 Address, June 3. Available as a working paper at www.irpp.org.

———. (2008b). "Thinking through Carbon Pricing: Competitiveness and Federalism Challenges." Background paper for a presentation for an IRPP Working Lunch, Fairmont Royal York Hotel, June 18, mimeo.

Courchene, T. J., and J. R. Allan. (2008a). "Climate Change: The Case for a Carbon Tariff Tax." *Policy Options*, (March), 59–64.

———. (2008b). "Kyoto Walks All over Canada: The Carbon Footprint Belongs to the Nations that Produce the Fossil Fuels or the Nations that Consume Them?" *Globe and Mail*, July 17, A13.

Elgie, S. (2007). "Kyoto, the Constitution, and Carbon Trading: Waking a Sleeping Bear (or Two)." *Review of Constitutional Studies/Revue d'études constitutionelle*, 13.1, 1–63.

Harrison, K., and L. M. Sundstrom. (2007). "The Comparative Politics of Climate Change." *Global Environmental Politics*, 7.4, 1–18.

Hogg, P. (2008). "Constitutional Authority over Greenhouse Gas Emissions." Presentation to the Canadian Petroleum Law Foundation, Jasper Research Seminar, June 28.

Horne, M. (2008). "Cap-and-Trade Fact Sheet." Pembina Institute, March.

International Energy Outlook 2007. (2007). Washington: Energy Information Administration.

Ismer, R., and K. Neuhoff. (2007). "Border Tax Adjustments: A Feasible Way to Support Stringent Emission Trading." Cambridge Working Papers in Economics 0409. Cambridge, UK: Department of Applied Economics, Cambridge University.

Mintz, J., and N. Olewiler. (2008). *A Simple Approach for Bettering the Environment and the Economy: Restructuring the Federal Fuel Excise Tax.* Prepared for the Sustainable Prosperity Initiative. Ottawa: Institute of the Environment, University of Ottawa.

Paquet, G. (1999). "The Environment-Energy Interface: Social Learning versus the Invisible Foot." In *Governance through Social Learning*, by G. Paquet. Ottawa: University of Ottawa Press, 109–26.

Revkin, A. C. (2007). "As China Goes, So Goes Global Warming." *New York Times*, December 16.

Simpson, J. (2008). "The Bell Tolls for Alberta's Climate Change Policy." *Globe and Mail*, May 27, A17.

Simpson, J., M. Jaccard, and N. Rivers. (2007). *Hot Air: Meeting Canada's Climate Change Challenge*. Toronto: McClelland and Stewart.

Chapter 31

Working Past Age Sixty-Five Will Soon Get More Respect in Canada

*Leroy O. Stone,
with special assistance from Jo Anne de Lepper*

Introduction

By dint of sustained attention to his intellectual development and related performance across a wide field of topics, Gilles Paquet has established himself as one of Canada's, if not the world's, quintessential renaissance men. My association with him began when I contributed to his book with Harvey Lithwick on urban development in Canada. Later on, Gilles was helpful with the production of my paper on retirement, which became the Statistics Canada submission to then Senator Croll's committee on retirement age policies. More recently, he helped to guide the development and wrote the opening chapter of the first of four major sections of my latest book, *New Frontiers of Research on Retirement* (Stone and Nouroz 2006). He was a major supporter in facilitating the eventually successful dissemination of this book among various stakeholder groups in Canada.

By continuing his productive output into what many will consider to be an advanced age, relative to the average age of workers, he has become one of the pioneers of a vast new movement that will be visited upon Canada in the decades ahead. This movement will comprise a large number of highly educated baby boomers (at least in comparison with earlier cohorts) who will be actively carrying on various kinds of productive work in the labour market and in the voluntary sector well past the age of sixty-five. The media are now calling this movement the "Silver Tsunami."

Analysis

What sorts of people are working past age sixty-five? This is the question to which this short piece is devoted. Although the people doing so now are by no means baby boomers, aspects of the composition of this group seem to be helpful as a partial foundation for forecasting what will happen when the people working past age sixty-five are primarily baby boomers.

In the 1980s and for most of the 1990s, baby boomers were invading the entry and higher levels of the labour market. At the same time, new computer-oriented production technologies were being developed and soon became a dominant force in corporate and other organizational output. Younger workers were the primary beneficiaries of the educational processes that brought command over the new technologies into the labour force. Furthermore, the early 1990s were a period of substantial downturn in the economy. Labour demand dropped markedly as governments had to trim their budgets and corporations had to become more "lean and mean" to survive. Under these conditions, it is hardly surprising that older workers became the Rodney Dangerfields[1] of the labour force. Indeed, their situation was worse than that of Dangerfield, who was tolerated as a rather genial, self-deprecating buffoon, because various schemes were devised to help show older workers the door (offer them a "golden handshake") in companies and other organizations.

At least three major developments have changed that setting by 2008. The first is the maturation of the baby boomer generation and the growing presence in the labour market of the much smaller Generation X, creating a potential for reduction in the labour supply that might hurt overall economic output and the flow of tax revenues. The second is that computer-oriented technologies have largely matured, and the productive systems using them have become sufficiently routine, by and large, that workers of all ages can, with some modest amount of education, adapt to their use. The third is that, as the knowledge economy has grown in the wake of globalization and with the shifting of a good deal of manufacturing activity offshore, emphasis has grown on the functions of experienced and mature workers in promoting key aspects of corporate performance. They include the development and maintenance of complex managerial systems, the preservation of complex client and intercorporate relations, the execution of production operations that involve complex judgments whose value depends on experience, and the protection and transfer among generations of employees of corporate intellectual capital, a matter that goes far beyond the maintenance of computer programs.

And so, as we approach the end of the first decade of the twenty-first century, a situation has developed in which leaders of corporate and other organizational production systems have begun to roll out the red carpet for the former Dangerfields of the labour market. Governments across the OECD countries are actively interested in protecting and promoting labour supply from older workers, and although the primary focus is on those in the fifty-five to sixty-four age range, there seems to be much interest in the productive activities of those who are even older. This interest is stimulated by the wave of baby boomer retirements.

One projection of the flow of these retirements in Canada is given in Chart 1. This projection suggests that the annual volume of retirements will rise to close to 200,000 per year by 2016, whereas it was about 140,000 in 2004. This projection is based on a piece of rather simple-minded arithmetic. First we estimated the ratio of annual retirees to the older labour force (fifty-five and over) in 2004. This ratio was simply applied to a projection of the size of the older labour force. While this is by no means a serious forecast, it provides a hint of an order-of-magnitude increase in the annual number of people taking retirement throughout most of the next ten years, compared with the numbers that were taking retirement around the year 2000.

For the purposes of this chapter, it is helpful to bring out one of the stories in retirement statistics that tends to get buried in the focus of articles and media coverage on the mean age of retirement. Many people are retiring at ages above and below the mean age. Moreover, it is helpful to think that a substantial percentage of these people have two phases of retirement. The first phase comprises departure from a career job or, if there is no such job, a very long-term pattern of labour market activity. Many people taking this kind of retirement can be expected to be found in, or to return to, the labour market at some future date. We call that "Phase-One retirement." "Phase-Two retirement" is a probable final departure from the labour force; at least there is a high probability of never returning.

Chart 2 illustrates the age patterns of these two types of retirement. The curve for Phase-One retirement is based on the Labour Force Survey (LFS) definition of retirement. Essentially, people who have left the labour force for several months are asked why they left it, and the survey accepts as one possible answer that persons left it to retire. The LFS definition implicitly focuses on retirement in terms of departing recently from the main pattern of labour market attachment over the life course.

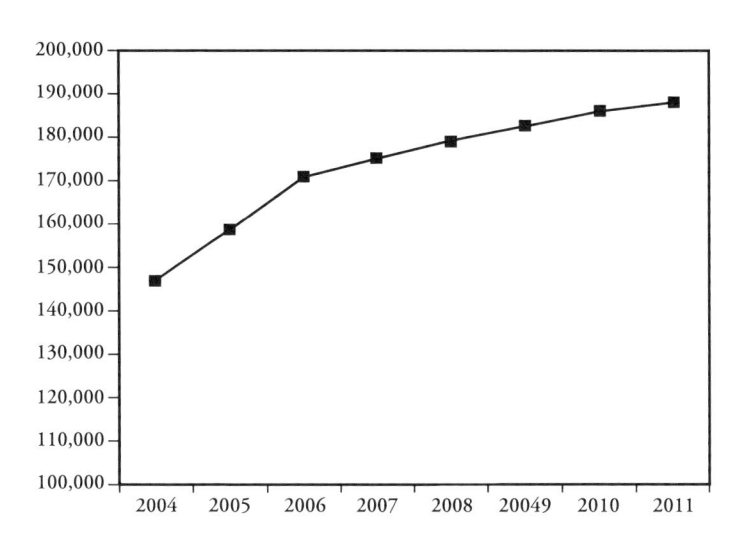

Chart 1: Projected Number of Retirees, Canada, 2004–2011

[Line chart showing values rising from about 147,000 in 2004 to about 188,000 in 2011, with data points at 2004, 2005, 2006, 2007, 2008, 2009, 2010, 2011]

Source: Statistics Canada, Labour Force Survey (LFS) historical data from CANSIM, un-published LFS data on number of retirements taken from 2000 to 2004, population projections and assumptions specified by the author.

The notion of Phase-Two retirement focuses more on probable permanent departure from the labour market. It is based on data from the Survey of Labour and Income Dynamics (SLID) and uses concepts exposited in Stone and Nouroz (2006). This approach focuses on continuous absence from the labour market by the time the observation of a SLID panel ends (with a minimum of six months) while receiving some form of retirement-related income. Each SLID panel is followed for six years.

Chart 2 shows that Phase-Two retirement has an older mean age and a substantial percentage of persons retiring after the age of sixty-five. Both curves on this chart indicate clearly that it is a mistake to believe that almost all retirements happen at the mean age of retirement. The curve for Phase-Two retirement, for example, has three local modes: ages 62, 65, and 69, whereas that for Phase-One has local nodes at 55, 61, and 65.

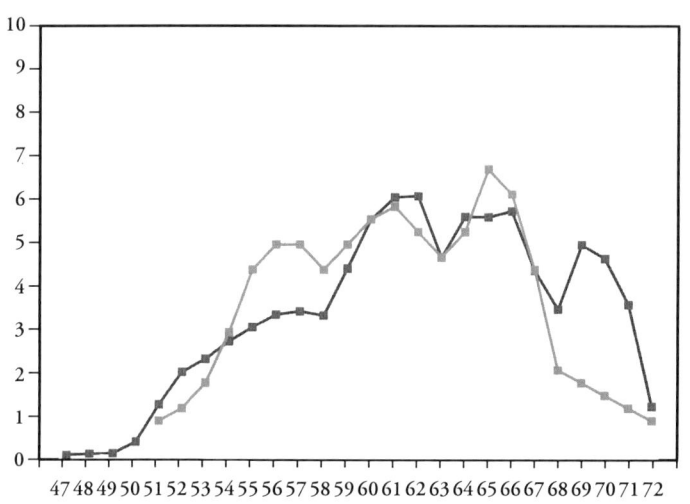

Chart 2: Estimated Age Distribution of Retirements Contrasting Phase-One and Phase-Two Types[1], Canada, late 1990s

1. Phase-One retirement is primarily departing from a career job. Phase-Two retirement is primarily final departure from the labour force. The indicator for this departure is at least six months of continuous absence from the labour market while receiving some form of retirement-related income. There must be no break of continuous absence throughout the duration of the pertinent SLID panel (See Stone and Nouroz 2006).
2. Phase-One type uses the LFS definition and Phase-Two type uses SLID data and the Stone-Nouroz definition.)
Source: Based on Labour Force Survey special tabulation provided by Henry Pold, covering years 2000 to 2004 and special estimates based on Panel Two of the Statistics Canada Survey of Labour and Income Dynamics (Panel Two was followed for six years [1996 to 2001]).

In addition to the fact that a large percentage of retirements take place before and after the mean age of retirement, and a substantial amount after sixty-five as regards Phase-Two retirement, a surge of labour force participation rates (henceforth called LFPR) at the older ages seems to be under way.

Chart 3 shows that the LFPR for the sixty-five-and-over group was more than twice as high in the immediate postwar era than it is now—near to twenty-five percent then, whereas we are now below ten percent. Among men aged sixty-five or more, the LFPR of the late 1940s was more than three times higher than it is today. Although there are good reasons for arguing that we will never go back to such lofty levels, unless there is a total breakdown of the first two pillars of our retirement income system, it seems reasonable to argue that the LFPR for the sixty-five-and-over population could go back to over fifteen percent and perhaps even close to twenty percent (one in five of the population). Whether this will happen over the next decade is unclear, but here's why those figures should be expected not long after 2016 in Canada.

Men aged sixty-five or more already had an LFPR of thirteen percent in 2007. While the curve for women has been more or less flat near five percent for over fifty years, we have still ahead of us the baby boomer cohorts. There has been a recent mini-explosion of the LFPR in the fifty-five to sixty-four age group of women. It could be an early warning signal of what will happen when these highly educated

Chart 3: Historical Labour Force Participation Rates[1] in the Older Population, Age 65 and Over, by Sex, Canada, 1946–2007

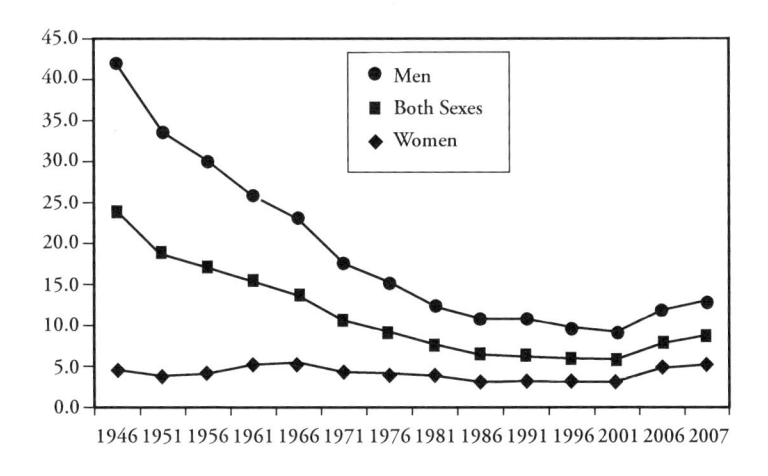

1. LFPR = 100 x labour force/population.
Source: Statistics Canada Labour Force Survey estimates, with special adjustments by the author for years before 1976.

baby boomer women, rich with lifelong labour-market experience, become the numerically dominant female cohorts in the sixty-five-and-over age groups. With the baby boomer men pushing the male LFPR in this age group well above its current level of thirteen percent, and their female counterparts playing catch-up, forecasting an overall rate well above fifteen percent seems reasonable.

We can find some support for this suggestion by looking at some recent provincial variations in older-population LFPRs. Chart 4 shows some relevant patterns. Alberta has always, it seems, been well ahead of the national average regarding the LFPRs in the older population. And in the recent surge of these

Chart 4: Historical Labour Force Participation Rates[1] in the Older Population, Age 65 and Over, Alberta and Canada, 1968 to 2007, USA 1980 to 2007

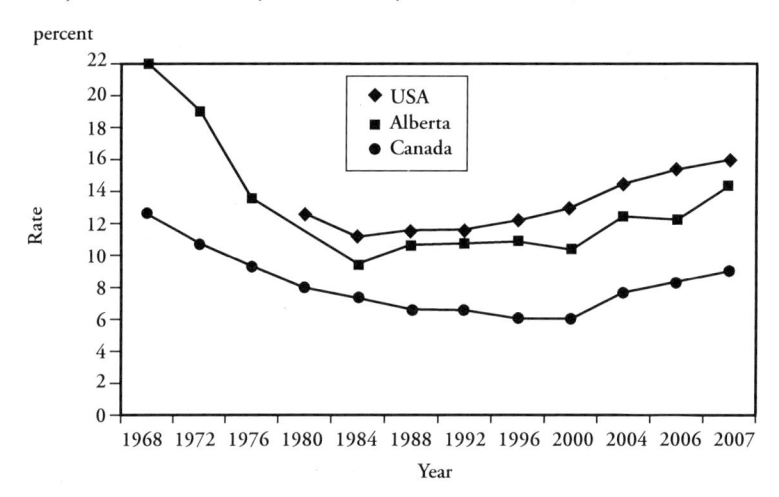

1. LFPR = 100 x labour force/population.
2. Data for 1976 and later years are from the latest revision published by Statistics Canada, Labour Statistics Division. For earlier years, the original figures were multiplied by the ratio of two estimates we had for 1976: 1) the latest revised number and 2) the number before revision. The latter number and the original values for years prior to 1976 were based on a 1976 revision published by Statistics Canada.
3. The figure for 2007 is a rough approximation, being the average of the published ratio for March, June and September.

Source: Statistics Canada Labour Force Survey estimates, with special adjustments by the author for years before 1976.

LFPRs, Alberta has stood out like a beacon. In 2007, its LFPR in the sixty-five-and-over age group (men and women aggregated) was already approaching fifteen percent, again far above the national average.

Although we still have to probe into the reasons why, Alberta is suggesting that in future years it will be feasible to achieve much higher labour input rates from the sixty-five-and-over group than what we see now in the national average, if the pull from the demand side of the labour market is there to support it.

Finally, let us look at the US patterns of LFPRs in the older population. That country's levels have traditionally been above ours, as Chart 4 shows. Notable in a recent publication is the fact that the US Bureau of Labour Statistics (BLS) projects only a modest rise in the rate for the fifty-five to sixty-four age group but a mini-explosion for the sixty-five-and-over group (Toossi 2005). In 2006, the US rate for those aged sixty-five or more was almost twice as high as that of Canada, and the BLS projects a rate of twenty percent by 2014.

Whether Canada can also go to such a high level some time later is a moot point. For one thing, the national policy environments concerning transfer income and health care supports for the elderly may differ enough between the two countries to be a factor in the pattern of differences. Nevertheless, if we assume support from the demand side (which is a key factor in Alberta, according to anecdotal evidence) and suitable improvements in the family friendliness and flexibility of work places, we should not be afraid to forecast that baby boomers will break the established mould and take us back toward the lofty older-population LFPRs of the postwar years, including the rates for those aged sixty-five or more.

An important point for the purposes of an article written in honour of the contributions of Gilles Paquet is the fact that, contrary to what one might initially think, the surge of labour force participation among older workers is not being dominated by persons who were at the lower end of the income and educational scales when they were young workers. Initial thinking leads one to expect that these would be largely lower-income individuals who must remain at work simply to survive. However, a large element of the said surge comprises workers with relatively high levels of education.

The invasion of the sixty-five-and-over group by baby boomers with their unprecedented levels of higher education has not yet started—the leading edge of the baby boomers turned sixty in 2006. Thus, we can expect a revolution in work performance and interest in continued productive activity by persons of advanced age, as these relatively highly educated baby boomers reach those ages.

By observing some of the distinctive features of the earlier (pre-baby boomer) cohorts who have remained active in the labour market at ages well beyond the current mean age of retirement, we can provide some part of the foundation for forecasting the pattern of the economic activity of workers of relatively advanced age in the years ahead.

According to the latest census, close to half a million Canadians aged sixty-five or more were employed or seeking employment in 2006. Of this number, just above one-third were women. A similar proportion comprised persons aged seventy or more.

The census labour force total of just above 470,000 aged sixty-five or more represents a participation rate close to eleven percent in 2006. The labour force participation rate for men aged sixty-five to sixty-nine is above twenty percent, and the rate is less than ten percent for their counterparts aged seventy and more. At the present time, the rates are much lower for women.

Persons over sixty-five in the labour force are generally better educated than those who are outside the labour force (see Chart 5, based on Labour Force Survey data). The percentage of men in the labour force aged sixty-five or more with a university degree is twice as large as that of their counterparts not in the labour force (twenty-five percent versus thirteen percent). The corresponding figures for women are seventeen percent for women over sixty-five in the labour force compared with seven percent for those not in the labour force. Since educational attainment in the baby boom generation is vastly better than in earlier cohorts, education may be a factor placing upward pressure on labour force participation rates for persons sixty-five and older in the future.

However, the evidence provided by earlier cohorts does not support the hypothesis that education alone is a major factor in predicting who will work past sixty-five. Our analysis (Stone 2007) does not show the university-educated group to have the highest probability of remaining at work past sixty-five (among a group whose attributes were measured prior to reaching that age). However, in that analysis, there is a proxy variable for wealth, and a high level on this proxy is a strong predictor of work past sixty-five. This factor is partly dependent on education.

Another key factor in predicting work past age sixty-five is whether or not one is self-employed. Our analysis (Stone and Nouroz 2008) indicates that those with a university degree are substantially more likely than those in the other levels of education to have moved into self-employment from the status of being a wage-and-salary worker.

Conclusion

What then can we expect of the baby boomers when they reach the age of sixty-five or more? They will boost the LFPR in this age range so that it is close to the current US value of twenty percent. There will be much interest and activity involving movement into and out of self-employment, and this will be especially marked among those with university education.

In the coming decade, the highly educated baby boomers aged sixty-five or more will escape Dangerfield's fate of getting no respect. On the contrary, they will be found across a wide swath of organizations holding positions that are key to corporate success. In particular, they will be mentoring and overseeing and participating in the intergenerational transfer of increasingly valued corporate intellectual capital. Already there are laudatory media reports about people of advanced age staying on at work and making key contributions to their organizations.

For example, Randi Chapnik Myers (2008), writing in the *Globe and Mail* of April 9, 2008, says that a surprising number of people over the age of eighty are still at work, and more are expected to make the same choice. She describes the typical work day of Angus McKenzie, who at age eighty-two specializes in estate law at McKenzie Lake Lawyers LLP in London, Ontario. His schedule would tire many workers of any age. Not all workers over the age of eighty are men. She also tells us about eighty-six-year-old Sheila Street, a Marpole, BC, office manager and about Mississauga mayor Hazel McCallion, aged eighty-seven, who is serving her eleventh consecutive term.

Note

[1] For those who are too young to know, or who are unaware of famous comedians, Dangerfield was an American comedian who became famous with routines based on the notion that no one respected him.

References

Chapnik Myers, R. (2008). "Past 80 and Still Going Strong." *Globe and Mail*, April 9.

Stone, L. O. (2007). "Possible Future Increases in Labour Force Participation Rates among the Older Population." Paper presented at the Third Annual Symposium of the Population, Ottawa, December 13–14.

Stone, L. O., and H. Nouroz, eds. (2006). *New Frontiers of Research on Retirement: Technical Annex*. Catalogue 75-512-XPE. Ottawa: Minister of Industry.

———. (2008). "Entry to Self-Employment during the Transition to Phase-Two Retirement." Paper presented at the 2008 meetings of the Canadian Economics Association, Vancouver, June 6.

Toossi, M. (2005). "Labour force projections to 2014: Retiring boomers." *Monthly Labour Review*, November, 25–44.

Conclusion

Caroline Andrew, Ruth Hubbard, and Jeffrey Roy

Oscar Wilde was once quoted as saying, "What is mind but motion in the intellectual sphere?" Without question, this volume demonstrates the degree to which Gilles Paquet is truly a man in motion, with a set of interests and accomplishments perhaps unrivalled in the history of Canadian academe. The breadth of those providing testament to, and insight into, his presence, personally and professionally, underscores a dedication and commitment to being not only a free thinker but also an active participant in, and contributor to, Canadian society.

While many scholars view academe as an opportunity for quiet reflection and specialization, Gilles has leveraged the university as a platform to constantly probe and dissect ideas, and to transform information into knowledge across the widest possible spectrum of subject matters. The resulting knowledge has been widely disseminated through formal academic publications (with a remarkably productive set of outputs), via media channels both new and old, as well as the classroom, where Gilles's deliberative spark and human spirit shine so bright.

As compelling as the various vignettes of this volume are, it is a holistic portrait of multichannel learning and engagement that emerges from their sum. As professor emeritus and as president of the Royal Society of Canada, Gilles refashioned that organization as an intellectual catalyst in the most complex of terrains. As a media commentator and policy analyst, he regularly challenges elected officials and policy makers on the pressing issues of the day. And as a teacher, Gilles entices students both young and not so young to view the world in new ways, to navigate uncertainty, and to grapple with shades of grey when the simplicity of black and white falls short.

Indeed, a seemingly elusive but critical common thread across such a diverse range of contributors and subjects is a willingness to embrace complexity rather than shy away from it. Gilles's interest in learning and education, and adaptive governance capacities speak to this profound desire to provoke in leaders and students alike a sense of self and societal reflection. Much as there is little about his career path that is linear and predictable, so too must individuals, organizations, and institutions constantly adapt to turbulence. In such a world, certainty matters a good deal less than humility and an openness to new ways of thinking, a philosophy both practised and preached by Gilles, accompanied by a fierce determination to challenge old assumptions and expose otherwise elusive cognitive blockages.

Gilles himself has at times fashioned his role as that of a "public intellectual" with a moral contract between the freedom and privilege offered by academe, and a broader set of obligations to society at large. To debate an issue is therefore both opportunity and duty, reflective of what Gilles has himself described as a blessed career where one is fortunate enough to be in a profession driven and sustained by learning. Accordingly, the boundaries between the university, the community, the media, and other segments of society are best viewed as fluid and open to constant negotiation and realignment.

Emerging from so many of the contributions in this volume, however, is also a personalization of Gilles's commitment to learning and engagement from the broadest levels of societal performance and institutional mechanisms to the tribulations and endeavours of individuals. Never has the phrase "my door is always open" been deployed with such sincerity as a lifetime commitment to assisting, mentoring, and collaborating with others in order to make a small (and at times large) difference whenever and wherever possible.

The stature and reach of Gilles Paquet are of no surprise to those of us fortunate enough to have edited this volume, and we thank all of the contributors for sharing their own connection to a remarkable career that remains—as Gilles himself would readily acknowledge—a work in progress. It is our hope that this collection will both enjoin many of those whose lives have been enriched by Gilles over the course of his career and serve as a testament to the remarkable potential that each individual carries to touch the lives of others and shape the world around them.

Bio-bibliographie de Gilles Paquet

L'homme

Né à Québec le 19 juillet 1936, Gilles Paquet a obtenu un B.A. et un B.Phil. de l'Université Laval en 1956, un B.Sc. économie de l'Université Laval en 1958 et un M.A. de l'Université Laval en 1960. Il a poursuivi ses études supérieures en sciences économiques à l'Université Queen's de 1960 à 1962 et des études postdoctorales en sciences économiques à l'Université de Californie.

Il a débuté sa carrière universitaire en sciences économiques à l'Université Carleton en 1963 où il devient éventuellement professeur titulaire. En 1973, il est nommé doyen des études supérieures et de la recherche à l'Université Carleton. En 1981, il devient Doyen de la Faculté d'administration à l'Université d'Ottawa et professeur titulaire, poste qu'il détient jusqu'à sa retraite en 2002.

Il est présentement professeur émérite à l'École de gestion Telfer de l'Université d'Ottawa et associé au Centre d'études en gouvernance (dont il était le Directeur fondateur en 1997) et à l'École supérieure d'affaires publiques et internationales.

Gilles Paquet a été Président de la Société royale du Canada (SRC : Les Académies des arts, des lettres et des sciences du Canada) de 2003 à 2005. Il a reçu des doctorats honorifiques de l'Université Laval, de l'Université Queen's et de l'Université Thompson Rivers. En 2006, il a reçu la Mention Service Public de l'Association professionnelle des cadres supérieurs de la fonction publique du Canada et il a été nommé Membre à vie de l'Association canadienne d'économique pour sa contribution remarquable à cette association et Membre honoraire de l'Association des économistes québécois, un honneur décerné à une demi-douzaine de personnes au cours des trente dernières années.

Il a écrit ou a édité une quarantaine d'ouvrages et a publié plus de 400 articles ou chapitres dans des revues scientifiques ou divers ouvrages sur des sujets allant de l'histoire économique du Canada, aux études urbaines et régionales, à l'organisation industrielle, à la gestion publique, à la gestion du savoir, et à la gouvernance ; il a publié aussi, un nombre comparable d'articles dans divers magazines et journaux.

Il a été Président de la Fédération des sciences sociales du Canada ainsi que de nombreuses associations canadiennes et québécoises. Il a été Secrétaire-Trésorier de l'Association canadienne d'économique de 1967 à 1981. En 1982, il a reçu la médaille Jacques-Rousseau pour ses contributions à la recherche multidisciplinaire et, en 1989, la médaille Esdras-Minville pour le corpus de ses travaux en sciences humaines. Il a été fait membre de la Royal Society of Arts (Londres) en 1989 et de l'Ordre du Canada en 1992.

Il a été actif comme journaliste dans les réseaux de radio et télévision de Radio-Canada, a écrit des éditoriaux pendant cinq ans pour le quotidien *Le Droit*, et a été un commentateur régulier sur les questions d'importance nationale à TVO. Il est le rédacteur en chef de www.optimumonline.ca — une revue de gestion publique et de gouvernance qui rejoint plus de 10 000 souscripteurs — depuis 1994.

Sélection des œuvres

Une liste complète de ses publications et communications est disponible sur son site Web www.gouvernance.ca. Ce qui suit est une sélection de ses livres (écrits et édités — seul ou en collboration) et ses principaux rapports dont il est l'auteur.

Livres

Paquet, G. et J.-P. Wallot. *Patronage et pouvoir dans le Bas Canada au tournant du 19ième siècle*, Montréal, Presses de l'Université du Québec, 1973, 188 p.

Laurent, P. et G. Paquet. *Épistémologie et économie de la relation – coordination et gouvernance distribuée*, Lyon/Paris, Vrin, 1998, 284 p.

Paquet, G., *Governance Through Social Learning*, Ottawa, University of Ottawa Press, 1999, 276 p.

Paquet, G. *Oublier la révolution tranquille – Pour une nouvelle socialité*, Montréal, Liber, 1999, 160 p.

Paquet, G. *Pathologies de gouvernance : essais de technologie sociale*, Montréal, Liber, 2004, 244 p.

Paquet, G. *The New Geo-Governance: A Baroque Approach*, Ottawa, University of Ottawa Press, 2005, 362 p.

Paquet, G. *Gouvernance : une invitation à la subversion,* Montréal, Liber, 2005, 400 p.

Paquet, G. et J.-P. Wallot. *Un Québec moderne 1760-1840 : Essai d'histoire économique et sociale*, Montréal, HMH, 2007, 750 p.

Hubbard, R., and G. Paquet. *Gomery's Blinders and Canadian Federalism*, Ottawa, University of Ottawa Press, 2007, 128 p.

Paquet, G. *Tableau d'avancement – Petite ethnographie interprétative d'un certain Canada français*, Ottawa, Les Presses de l'Université d'Ottawa, 2008, 232 p.

Paquet, G. *Deep Cultural Diversity: A Governance Challenge*, Ottawa, University of Ottawa Press, 2008, 226 p.

Paquet, G. *Gouvernance : mode d'emploi*, Montréal, Liber, 2008, 364 p.

Paquet, G. *Scheming Virtuously : The Road to Collaborative Governance*, Ottawa, Invenire Books, 2009, 280 p.

Paquet, G. *Crippling Epistomologies and Governance Failures: A Plea for Experimentalism*, Ottawa, University of Ottawa Press, 2009, 281 p.

Livres édités

Lithwick, N.H., and G. Paquet (Eds.). *Urban Studies: A Canadian Pespective*, Toronto, Methuen Publications, 1968, 290 p.

Paquet, G. (Ed.). *The Multinational Firm, and the Nation State*, Don Mills, Collier-Macmillan, 1972, 182 p.

Bazoge, B. et G. Paquet (Eds.). *Administration : unité et diversité*, Ottawa, Presses de l'Université d'Ottawa, 1986, 350 p.

Paquet, G., and M. von Zur Muehlen (Eds.). *Education Canada? Higher Education on the Brink*, Ottawa, Canadian Higher Education Research Network, 1987, 300 p.

Paquet, G., and M. von Zur Muehlen (Eds.). *Edging Towards the Year 2000: Management Research and Education in Canada*, Ottawa, Canadian Federation of Deans of Management and Administrative Studies, 1989, 130 p.

Paquet, G. (Ed.). *La pensée économique au Québec français : témoginages et perspectives*, Montréal, Association canadienne-française pour l'avancement des sciences, 1989, 364 p.

Demers, J., C. Moisan et G. Paquet (Eds.). *La pratique humaniste*, CEFAN, Québec, Société royale du Canada, 1991, 100 p.

Paquet., G. et O. Gélinier (Eds.). *Management en crise : pour une formation proche de l'action*, Paris, Economica, 1992, 162 p.

Boulet, J.A., C.E. Forget, J.P. Langlois et G. Paquet (Eds.). *Les grands défis économiques de la fin du siècle*, Montréal, Association des économistes québécois, 1992, 340 p.

Andrew, C., L. Cardinal, F. Houle, G. Paquet (Eds.). *L'ethnicité à l'heure de la mondalisation*, Ottawa, Association canadienne-française pour l'avancement des sciences, 1992, 114 p.

de la Mothe, J., and G. Paquet (Eds.). *Corporate Governance and the New Competition*, Ottawa, PRIME, 1996, 117 p.

de la Mothe, J., and G. Paquet (Eds.). *Evolutionary Economics and the New International Political Economy*, London, Pinter, 1996, 319 p.

Coulombe, S. et G. Paquet (Eds.). *La ré-invention des institutions et le rôle de l'État*, Montréal, Association des économistes québécois, 1996, 480 p.
de la Mothe, J., and G. Paquet (Eds.). *Local and Regional Systems of Innvoation*, Boston, Kluwer Academic Publishers, 1998, 341 p.
de la Mothe, J., and G. Paquet (Eds.). *Information, Innovation and Impacts*, Boston, Kluwer Academic Publishers, 1999, 339 p.
Downs, A. et G. Paquet (Eds.). *Les défis de la gouvernance à l'aube du 21e siè*cle, Montréal, Association des économistes québécois, 2000, 325 p.
Paquet, G. (Ed.). *Governance in the 21st Century*, Ottawa, The Royal Soceity of Canada, 2000, 224 p.

Rapports techniques

Paquet, G. "Economic Security in Old Age," Ottawa, Final Report of the Special Committee of the Senate on Aging, February 1966, pp. 69–84.
Paquet, G. "Critères de choix," Québec, Comité de recherches sur l'Assurance-santé, 1er rapport, janvier 1966, vol. 7, 49 p.
Paquet, G. "Report of the Study for Updating the Unemployment Insurance Program," Ottawa, 1969, vol. 1, ch. 2–5, 123 p. ; vol. 2, ch 7–8, 120 p.
Paquet, G. "Confluence énergétique : A Social Learning Franmework for a Wicked Problem," Ottawa, Energy Options, Summer 1987, 47 p.
Paquet, G., et al. "State of the Art Review of Research on Canada's Multicultural Policy," Ottawa : Social Sciences and Humanities Research Council/Multiculturalism Canada, 1992, 23 p. + appendices (7 p. + 638 p.).
Paquet, G., and J.A. Van Duzer. "Anticompetitive Pricing pratices and the Competition Act: Theory, Law and Practice," Competition Bureau, August 1999, 110 p. + appendices 34 p.
Paquet, G. et al. "Governance of the Ethical Process for Research Involving Human Subjects," Three Councils (MRC, SSHRC, NSERC), 2000, 63 p.
Paquet, G. et al. "Governance of the Red Cross Society: A Volunteer's Perspective," report to the Canadian Red Cross Society, August 2000, 50 p. + appendices.
Juillet, L., G. Paquet. "Information Policy and Governance," Access to Information Review Task Force, June 2001, 18 p.
Paquet, G. (en collaboration). "Reaching the World of SMEs: CIPO as Innovation Cartalyst," Industry Canada, March 2004, 62 p.
Paquet, G. "The Governance of Medical Journals," The *Canadian Medical Association Journal* Governance Review Panel, 2006, 19 p.
Paquet, G. "Savoirs, Savoir-faire, Savoir-être : In Praise of Professional Wroughting and Wrighting," Report prepared for Campus 20/20–An Inquiry into the Future of British Columbia's Post-Secondary Education System, July 31 2006, 25 p.
Paquet, G. (en collaboration). "The National Capital Commission: Charting new Course," Report of the NCC Mandate Review Panel, December 2006, 59 p.
Paquet, G. Background paper prepared for the Task Force on Governance and Cultural Change in the RCMP, 2007, 22 p.

Contributors

Andrew, Caroline
Caroline Andrew is a professor at the School of Political Studies and the director of the Centre on Governance at the University of Ottawa. Her research interests comprise intergovernmental relations in Canada, management of diversity, municipal politics, social policy (municipal), urban development, urban politics-planning and the process of public participation, voluntary sector, women (access to public services), and women and politics.

Arroja, Pedro
Pedro Arroja is the president of Pedro Arroja SGPS, SA (a holding company) and the editor of the online governance review www.governancia.com, which specializes in four areas: the public sector, the private sector, the civic sector, and citizenship. He is the author of a number of books and articles and has participated weekly in *National Jornal Vida Económica* since 2005.

Bégin, Monique
Monique Bégin, a sociologist, twice appointed as minister of national welfare, professor emeritus, is the visiting professor in health administration at the Telfer School of Management of the University of Ottawa.

Monique Bégin, sociologue, deux fois ministre de la Santé nationale et du Bien-être social, professeure émérite, est professeure invitée en Gestion des services de santé à l'École de gestion Telfer de l'Université d'Ottawa.

Bergeron, Pierre
Pierre Bergeron œuvre dans le milieu du journalisme et de l'information depuis plus de 30 ans. Il a été éditeur du *Droit* à Ottawa-Gatineau et du *Quotidien* du Saguenay-Lac-St-Jean. Il collabore régulièrement à la page éditoriale du *Droit* et publie une chronique hebdomadaire sur les affaires municipales de Gatineau.

Bonin, Bernard
Élu à la Société royale du Canada en 1985, il a été le secrétaire honoraire de la Société durant les présidences de Gilles Paquet et de Patricia Demers. Au moment de prendre sa retraite de la Banque du Canada en 1999, il était le premier sous-gouverneur, poste qu'il a occupé de 1994 à 1999.

Boulet, Jac-André
Jac-André Boulet est secrétaire de l'Association des économistes québécois de l'Outaouais (ASDEQ-Outaouais). Il a œuvré à divers titres au sein de l'Association depuis sa fondation en 1976. Au niveau national, il y a été vice-président et directeur ; à Montréal, directeur ; et en Outaouais, président, directeur, puis secrétaire. Ses premiers contacts avec le professeur Paquet remontent à l'époque où il était chercheur au Conseil économique du Canada. Depuis, il a collaboré à plusieurs reprises avec ce dernier à l'organisation d'activités de l'ASDEQ et la publication des Actes de Congrès.

Brzustowski, Tom
Tom Brzustowski is the RBC professor in the Telfer School of Management at Ottawa. Earlier he served as the president of NSERC (1995–2005), as a deputy minister in Ontario (1987–2005), as a professor of mechanical engineering (1962–87), and as the academic vice president at Waterloo (1975–87).

Burstein, Meyer
Meyer Burstein is an international consultant working in the field of social and economic policy. He is the former director general responsible for strategic planning, research, and analysis at the Department of Citizenship and Immigration Canada and the co-founder of Metropolis, a pre-eminent, international policy research project focusing on migration and diversity.

Courchene, Thomas J.
Thomas Courchene, born in Wakaw, Saskatchewan, is the Jarislowsky-Deutsch professor of economic and financial policy and the director of the Institute of Intergovernmental Relations at Queen's University, and he is a senior scholar at IRPP in Montreal. He is a fellow of the Royal Society of Canada, holds LLDs from Western, Saskatchewan, and Regina, and is an officer in the Order of Canada. His research focus is on federalism and public policy.

Fortin, Pierre
Pierre Fortin est professeur de sciences économiques à l'Université du Québec à Montréal (UQAM). Il est membre de la Société royale du Canada, membre du conseil scientifique de l'Institut canadien de recherches avancées, chroniqueur économique attitré du magazine *L'actualité*, et ancien président de la Canadian Economics Association.

Pierre Fortin is a professor of economics at the Université du Québec à Montréal (UQAM). He is a fellow of the Royal Society of Canada, a member of the Research Council of the Canadian Institute for Advanced Research, an economic columnist at *L'actualité*, and a past president of the Canadian Economics Association.

Frederickson, H. George
George Frederickson, the Edwin O. Stone distinguished professor of public administration at the University of Kansas and the president emeritus of Eastern Washington University, is a generalist in public administration with particular interest in public administration ethics, theories of public administration, systems of multilevel governance, and American local government.

Galbreath, McEvoy
McEvoy Galbreath is the president of The Summit Group, a contract publishing company in Ottawa, and the publisher of *Optimum: The Journal of Public Sector Management*, now known as *Optimum Online*. She has worked with Gilles Paquet for close to fifteen years on *Optimum*, providing the production arm for the journal in print and more recently online.

Gattinger, Monica
Monica Gattinger is an associate professor at the School of Political Studies, University of Ottawa, and an adjunct professor at the Institut national de la

recherche scientifique–Urbanisation, culture, et société (INRS-UCS). Her research examines public policy, public management, and governance issues in the energy and cultural sectors and in Canada–US relations.

Going, Tony
Tony Going is a graduate of Carleton University, having earned an honours bachelor of arts degree and a master's degree in economics. After working in various management positions in the federal government, Tony entered the field of management consulting, becoming an associate partner at Accenture and a partner at Ernst & Young. Currently, he is working for TerreStar Canada, a next generation satellite company, and is responsible for marketing and sales in Canada.

Heintzman, Ralph
Ralph Heintzman is an adjunct research professor in the Graduate School of Public and International Affairs, University of Ottawa. His career has spanned the university, research, and government worlds, and he has worked with Gilles Paquet in all three. He is a recipient of the Vanier Medal, Canada's highest honour in public administration.

Higham, Robin
Robin Higham is a retired Canadian career diplomat and a senior fellow at the University of Ottawa's Graduate School of Public and International Affairs. In addition to supporting the university's outreach objectives, his research work is mostly related to Canada's debates regarding the reasonable accommodation of newcomers and to the pursuit of foreign policy through international public diplomacy.

Hubbard, Ruth
Ruth Hubbard is a senior fellow at the School of Public and International Affairs as well as the Centre on Governance at the University of Ottawa and a senior partner in INVENIRE, a firm specializing in governance and stewardship. She spent more than a decade as a federal deputy minister. She is a teacher, writer, and adviser to senior executives.

CONTRIBUTORS

Laurent, Paul
Paul Laurent est maître de conférences à la Faculté des sciences économiques et de gestion de l'Université Lumière Lyon 2 et membre de l'équipe de recherche Coactis (Conception de l'action en situation ; EA 4161; équipe de recherche en gestion des Universités de Lyon et de Saint-Étienne).

McEown, Don
Don McEown is a secretary emeritus of the Board of Governors at Carleton University. Together with H. Blair Neatby, he is the co-author of *Creating Carleton: The Shaping of a University*, published in 2002.

Meisel, John
John Meisel is the Sir Edward Peacock professor emeritus of political science at Queen's University and a former president of the Royal Society of Canada.

Michalowski, Wojtek
Wojtek Michalowski is a professor at the Telfer School of Management, University of Ottawa, and a university research chair in health informatics and decision support. He is studying how to provide comprehensive decision support to clinicians at the point of care. In free time, Wojtek loves reading and talking about the books.

Miller, Riel
Riel Miller is the founder of XperidoX: Futures Consulting (in Paris, France), and a specialist in long-run strategic thinking and the design of advanced foresight processes. His extensive publications address a range of issues, and for over twenty-five years he has assisted senior decision makers to assess and direct the potential for socioeconomic transformation in both the private and the public sectors.

Mitchell, James R.
James Mitchell is the head of the Ottawa policy-consulting firm Sussex Circle. A former university lecturer, diplomat, and central agency official, he holds a PhD in philosophy from the University of Colorado. He has a particular interest in the theory and practice of Westminster government.

Navarre, Christian
Christian Navarre est agrégé de l'Université (France) et docteur d'état en Sciences de gestion (Lille, France). Depuis 1984, il enseigne l'École Telfer de l'Université d'Ottawa. Ses travaux de recherche l'ont conduit à décrire et à projeter la dynamique de la chaîne de valeur de l'industrie automobile mondiale. Christian Navarre est régulièrement invité par les médias à commenter l'évolution de l'industrie automobile.

Neatby, H. Blair
H. Blair Neatby is a professor emeritus of history at Carleton University. Together with Don McEown, he is the co-author of *Creating Carleton: The Shaping of a University*, published in 2002.

Roy, Jeffrey
Jeffrey Roy is an associate professor in the School of Public Administration at Dalhousie University, specializing in multi-stakeholder governance, service transformation, and electronic government. He is also an associate editor of the *International Journal of E-Government Research*, a featured columnist in *CIO Government Review*, and the author of two recent books.

Skolnik, Michael L.
Michael Skolnik is a professor emeritus in the Ontario Institute for Studies in Education of the University of Toronto. He has conducted research on post-secondary education in Ontario and Canada since 1968, focusing on the design and governance of post-secondary systems. He held the William G. Davis chair in community college leadership from its establishment in 1999 until 2007.

Leroy O. Stone
Leroy Stone is the author of several books dealing with the population of Canada, the most recent being *New Frontiers of Research on Retirement*. He is an associate director general in the National Accounts and Analytical Studies, Statistics Canada, and an adjunct professor of demography at the University of Montréal. He is a past president of the Canadian Population Society and a member of the Board of Directors of the Population Association of America.

Wallot, Jean-Pierre
Historien de formation, Jean-Pierre Wallot est chercheur associé au Département d'histoire de l'Université d'Ottawa. Il est l'auteur d'une quinzaine d'ouvrages et plus de 150 articles savants. Il a été Archivist National du Canada (1985–1997) et ancien Prèsident de la Société Royale du Canada. Il a assuré la direction du Centre de recherche en civilisation canadienne-française (CRCCF) à l'Université d'Ottawa.

Wilson, Chris
Chris Wilson is a management consultant and the principal of Christopher Wilson & Associates, which specializes in issues of organizational development, collaboration, governance, and stewardship. Since 1997, he has been a research fellow at the University of Ottawa and a part-time lecturer in the Telfer School of Management, University of Ottawa.

Wolfe, David A.
David A. Wolfe is a professor of political science at the University of Toronto, Mississauga, and a co-director of the Program on Globalization and Regional Innovation Systems (PROGRIS) at the Munk Centre for International Studies. He is also the national coordinator of the Innovation Systems Research Network and is currently the principal investigator on its SSHRCC-funded Major Collaborative Research Initiative on the Social Dynamics of Economic Performance: Innovation and Creativity in City Regions, which runs from 2006 to 2010.

Zussman, David
David Zussman is the Jarislowsky chair in public sector management in the Graduate School of Public and International Affairs and the Telfer School of Management, University of Ottawa. He is also the president of the Canadian Association of Programs in Public and International Affairs (CAPPA). He has been Gilles Paquet's colleague since 1984, when they first worked together in the former Faculty of Administration at the University of Ottawa.

23. Michael Small 2009
    The Forgotten Peace – Mediation at Niagara Falls, 1914

22. Gilles Paquet 2009
    Crippling Epistemologies and Governance Failures – A Plea for Experimentalism

21. O. P. Dwivedi, Timothy Mau, and Byron Sheldrick 2009
    The Evolving Physiology of Government – Canadian Public Administration in Transition

20. Caroline Andrews, Ruth Hubbard, and Jeffrey Roy (eds) 2009
    Gilles Paquet – Homo Hereticus

19. Luc Juillet and Ken Rasmussen 2008
    Defending a Contested Ideal – Merit and the Public Service Commission: 1908–2008

18. Luc Juillet et Ken Rasmussen 2008
    À la défense d'un idéal contesté – le principe de mérite et la CFP, 1908–2008

17. Gilles Paquet 2008
    Deep Cultural Diversity – A Governance Challenge

16. Paul Schafer 2008
    Revolution or Renaissance – Making the Transition from an Economic Age to a Cultural Age

15. Gilles Paquet 2008
    Tableau d'avancement – petite ethnographie interprétative d'un certain Canada français

14. Tom Brzustowski 2008
    The Way Ahead – Meeting Canada's Productivity Challenge

13. Jeffrey Roy 2007
    Business and Government in Canada

12. N. Brown and L. Cardinal (eds) 2007
    Managing Diversity – Practices of Citizenship

11. Ruth Hubbard and Gilles Paquet 2007
    Gomery's Blinders and Canadian Federalism

10. Emmanuel Brunet-Jailly (ed.) 2007
    Borderlands – Comparing Border Security in North America and Europe

9. Christian Rouillard, E. Montpetit, I. Fortier, and A.G. Gagnon 2006
   Reengineering the State – Toward an Impoverishment of Quebec Governance

8. Jeffrey Roy 2006
   E-Government in Canada

7. Gilles Paquet 2005
   The New Geo-Governance – A Baroque Approach

6. C. Andrew, M. Gattinger, M.S. Jeannotte, and W. Straw (eds) 2005
   Accounting for Culture – Thinking Through Cultural Citizenship

5. P. Boyer, L. Cardinal, and D. Headon (eds) 2004
   From Subjects to Citizens – A Hundred Years of Citizenship in Australia and Canada

4. Linda Cardinal and D. Headon (eds.) 2002
   Shaping Nations – Constitutionalism and Society in Australia and Canada

3. Linda Cardinal et Caroline Andrew (dir.) 2001
   La démocratie à l'épreuve de la gouvernance

2. Gilles Paquet 1999
   Governance Through Social Learning

1. David McInnes 1999, 2005
   Taking It to the Hill – The Complete Guide to Appearing Before Parliamentary Committees

Composed by Brad Horning in Adobe Garamond Pro 10 on 13

The paper used in this publication is Roland Opaque Natural 60lb

Printed and bound in Canada